Contemporary Chinese Civil and Commercial Law

Tianqi Gu

Chinese SOE Reforms and Global FDI

Legal and Policy Analysis with an Australian Perspective

Springer

Tianqi Gu
The Global Intellectual Property Institute & The School of Law
Nanjing University
Nanjing, China

ISSN 2524-6194 ISSN 2524-6208 (electronic)
Contemporary Chinese Civil and Commercial Law
ISBN 978-981-92-3180-5 ISBN 978-981-92-3181-2 (eBook)
https://doi.org/10.1007/978-981-92-3181-2

This Springer imprint is published by the registered company Springer Nature Singapore Pte Ltd.
The registered company address is: 152 Beach Road, #21-01/04 Gateway East, Singapore 189721, Singapore

Acknowledgements This book is the outcome of my Ph.D. research at the University of Sydney. The past three and a half years have been an extraordinary journey, marked by challenges, uncertainties, and invaluable growth. I am profoundly grateful to my supervisors, Professor Vivienne Bath and Professor Luke Nottage. This work could not have been completed without their constant guidance, encouragement, and extraordinary patience throughout the entire process.

I also wish to extend my sincere appreciation to Professor Simon Bronitt, Professor Yane Svetiev, Professor Emeritus Terry Carney, Professor Bing Ling, Professor Simon Butt, Associate Professor Jeanne Huang, and Dr Fady Aoun at the Sydney Law School for their invaluable support and guidance during my doctoral studies.

I acknowledge that Chaps. 2, 7, and 8 of this book include updated materials from previous publications. In particular, some early materials were published as Tianqi Gu (2024) The Latest Round of China's State-owned Enterprise Reforms: The State Advances, the Private Sector Retreats?. Cogent Social Sciences 10(1): 1–17; Tianqi Gu (2025) Restrictions on Chinese SOE Investments for Data Security Reasons: The Case of Australia. Chinese Journal of Transnational Law 2(1): 14–38; Tianqi Gu (2023) Evolution of China's SOE Reforms: Grasping the Large and Releasing the Small?. European Chinese Law Research Hub; Tianqi Gu (2023) The SOE Chapter of the CPTPP: An Effective Way to Regulate Chinese SOEs' Foreign Direct Investments?. ANZSIL Perspective Edition 33. I acknowledge the kind permission of the publishers to reuse some of the contents published therein.

Last but not least, I dedicate this work to myself and to my family, in particular, to my grandmother, Mrs Huiqun Ni, in heaven:

Your memory continues to guide and inspire me, and I dedicate this achievement to honouring your hopes and expectations.

Competing Interests The author has no competing interests to declare that are relevant to the content of this book.

About the Book

Over the past few decades, the world has witnessed China's remarkable economic growth, which has resulted in the global proliferation of Chinese foreign direct investment (FDI). Notwithstanding China's transition to a market economy, the country still has a massive number of State-owned enterprises (SOEs). These SOEs have played an important role in the expansion of Chinese FDI. In the context of the last decade's escalating geopolitical tensions, the proliferation of Chinese SOE FDI has raised concerns among host States, especially developed host States. The concerns stem mainly from the presumed ties of Chinese SOEs with the Chinese government and the Chinese Communist Party (CCP). The concern has contributed to the trend towards increased legal barriers to Chinese SOEs' ability to invest in developed countries. Australia, for example, has significantly tightened its legislative framework for its foreign investment review regime in 2021, including tightening reviews for investment from foreign government investors.

China's attempts to reform SOEs have been ongoing since 1978 as an integral part of the Chinese economic reform. Chinese SOE operational activities have been profoundly affected by the four decades of SOE reforms. In 2012, the Xi Jinping administration launched the fourth round of SOE reforms. The latest round of SOE reforms is unprecedented in its complexity and duration, encompassing State economy restructuring reform, mixed ownership reform, SOE governance system reform, and State-owned assets management system reform. Previous legal studies have contributed to comprehending the Chinese State economy and SOEs, with some of them recognising the implications of China's SOE reforms. However, no comprehensive study has yet been conducted to examine how China's latest round of SOE reforms may affect Chinese SOE investments and their interactions with foreign investment legal regimes in developed host States.

Given this background, this book provides an in-depth investigation of the impact of China's latest round of SOE reforms on the political ties of Chinese SOEs as commercial operators and their FDI in developed countries. This research takes Australia as an example, examining the efficacy of Australia's existing legislative frameworks in regulating Chinese SOE FDI under both domestic and international laws, and provides recommendations on legal measures for Australia to better manage the potential risks associated with Chinese SOE FDI in Australia.

Through a comprehensive analysis of the design and implementation of each sub-reform within China's latest round of SOE reforms, this research finds that China's latest round of SOE reforms has significantly enhanced SOEs' connections with the government and the CCP. These connections are strengthened through a variety of means, including the enhancement of inter-SOE consolidations, the expansion of SOE equity networks into private sectors, the resurgence of CCP control over the SOE governance system, and the assignment of policy tasks to specific types of SOEs. On this basis, this book investigates the mechanisms by which the Chinese government and the CCP exert influence over SOE FDI activities and argues that the ongoing round of SOE reforms has resulted in an overall escalation of political influence and oversight over Chinese SOE FDI and their overseas subsidiaries. The enhanced political control is intended to ensure that Chinese SOE investments are consistent with government policies and national strategies.

This book then presents a longitudinal examination of China's foreign investment policies, concluding that, in the context of the latest round of SOE reforms, protecting the broadly defined concept of 'national security' has emerged as a significant policy objective motivating Chinese SOE outbound FDI. This, however, is concerning for host States regarding the potential harm to their national interest or national security. Based on the findings regarding China's latest round of SOE reforms and their implications for Chinese SOE FDI, this research assesses the effectiveness of Australia's domestic foreign investment framework and the current international investment agreements between Australia and China in regulating Chinese SOE investments, and concludes that, in the context of China's ongoing round of SOE reforms, Australia's current legal regimes do not adequately address the potential adverse effects of Chinese SOE investments on Australian interests. As a result, this research offers recommendations for Australia on how to improve the legal regimes that are specifically tailored to modern Chinese SOEs. This research aims to lay the groundwork for policymakers in Australia and other developed countries to strike a balance between maximising the benefits of Chinese SOE investments and protecting national interests, with the ultimate goal of contributing to the maintenance and improvement of China's international investment relationships with developed countries, primarily through its SOEs.

Contents

List of Abbreviations

AA	Articles of Association
AHKIA	Australia–Hong Kong Investment Agreement
AML	Anti-Monopoly Law of the PRC
ASX	Australian Securities Exchange
AUD	Australian Dollar
BG	Business Group
BIT	Bilateral Investment Treaty
BOC	The People's Bank of China
BRI	Belt and Road Initiative
CABIT	Australia–China Bilateral Investment Treaty
CCCC	China Communications Construction Company
CCDI	CCP Central Commission for Disciplinary Inspection
CCP	Chinese Communist Party
CDB	China Development Bank
CETC	China Electronics Technology Group Corporation
CEXIM	Export-Import Bank of China
CGN	China General Nuclear Power Group
ChAFTA	China–Australia Free Trade Agreement
CIC	China Investment Corporation
CNNC	China National Nuclear Corporation
CNOOC	China National Offshore Oil Corporation
CNPC	China National Petroleum Corporation
CNY	Chinese Yuan/Renminbi
COFCO	China Oil and Foodstuffs Corporation
COSCO	China Ocean Shipping Company
CPTPP	Comprehensive and Progressive Agreement for Trans-Pacific Partnership
CREC	China Railway Group Limited
DFAT	Australian Government Department of Foreign Affairs and Trade
EU	European Union
FATA	Foreign Acquisitions and Takeovers Act 1975 (Cth)

FATR	Foreign Acquisitions and Takeovers Regulation 2015 (Cth)
FET	Fair and Equitable Treatment
FTA	Free Trade Agreement
GAC	General Administration of Customs of the PRC
GATS	General Agreement on Trade in Services
GATT	General Agreement on Tariffs and Trade
GVC	Global Value Chain
ICSID	International Centre for Settlement of Investment Disputes
IIA	International Investment Agreement
ISDS	Investor-State Dispute Settlement
LNG	Liquefied Natural Gas
M&A	Merger and Acquisition
MFA	Ministry of Foreign Affairs of the PRC
MFN	Most Favoured Nation Treatment
MIC 2025	Made in China 2025 Development Initiative
MOE	Mixed Ownership Enterprise
MOF	Ministry of Finance of the PRC
MOFCOM	Ministry of Commerce of the PRC
MOR	Mixed Ownership Reform
NBS	National Bureau of Statistics of the PRC
NCA	Non-commercial Assistance
NCM	Non-conforming Measure
NDRC	National Development and Reform Commission of the PRC
NPC	National People's Congress
NSL	National Security Law of the PRC
NT	National Treatment
OECD	Organisation for Economic Co-operation and Development
PLA	The People's Liberation Army
POE	Privately Owned Enterprise
PRC	People's Republic of China
R&D	Research and Development
RCEP	Regional Comprehensive Economic Partnership
RMB	Renminbi
SAFE	State Administration of Foreign Exchange of the PRC
SAMR	State Administration for Market Regulation of the PRC
SASAC	State-owned Assets Supervision and Administration Commission
SCIC	State-owned Capital Investment Company
SCIO	State-owned Capital Investment and Operation Company
SCOC	State-owned Capital Operation Company
SDIC	State Development and Investment Corporation
SEHK	Stock Exchange of Hong Kong
SOCI Act	Security of Critical Infrastructure Act 2018 (Cth)
SOE	State-owned enterprise
SPC	Supreme People's Court of the PRC
STA	State Administration of Taxation of the PRC

SWF	Sovereign Wealth Fund
UK	United Kingdom
UN	United Nations
UNCTAD	United Nations Conference on Trade and Development
US	United States
USD	United States Dollar
WSOE	Wholly State-owned Enterprise
WTO	World Trade Organisation

Chapter 1
Introduction

Abstract China's State-owned enterprises (SOEs) have emerged as major players in global investment flows, particularly following decades of reform and the launch of the 'Go Global' strategy. As Chinese SOEs expand their presence in developed economies, concerns over their ties to the Chinese Party-State have intensified, prompting legal and policy responses from host countries. This introductory chapter frames the book's central inquiry: how the latest round of SOE reforms since 2013, led by the Xi Jinping administration, has reshaped the governance of SOE outbound investment, and how developed host States can respond to the associated risks through legal means without undermining investment openness. Using Australia as a case study, the book situates its analysis at the intersection of Chinese political economy, foreign investment law, and international treaty regimes. The chapter defines key concepts, outlines the book's structure, and identifies three overarching research questions that guide the analysis: the evolving relationship between SOEs and the Party-State; the implications for SOE-led FDI; and the adequacy of host State legal frameworks. Framing Chinese SOEs as both commercial actors and instruments of national strategy, the chapter provides essential context for understanding the legal complexities of China's outward investment in an era of strategic rivalry.

1.1 Research Background

Since the turn of the century, the world has witnessed China's remarkable economic growth and, as a result, the global spread of Chinese foreign direct investment (FDI), particularly since the launch of the 'Go Global' policy in 2000.[1] According to the United Nations Conference on Trade and Development's (UNCTAD) annual World Investment Reports, China has been ranked among the world's top five

[1] 1 Chaisse (2018), pp 544–545.

T. Gu, *Chinese SOE Reforms and Global FDI*, Contemporary Chinese Civil and Commercial Law, https://doi.org/10.1007/978-981-92-3181-2_1

largest sources of foreign direct investment since 2013 and briefly surpassed the United States (US) as the world's largest source of FDI in 2020.[2]

A massive State presence characterises the Chinese economy. Notwithstanding China's transition to a market economy, which commenced in 1992 and accelerated significantly after it acceded to the World Trade Organisation (WTO) in 2000,[3] the country still maintains over 300,000 State-owned enterprises (SOEs) at the central and regional levels as of December 2022.[4] These SOEs continue to play a significant role in China's national economy. According to the Ministry of Finance of the People's Republic of China (MOF), China's national fiscal revenue in 2021 was US Dollar (USD) 3.19 trillion, with SOEs contributing more than a quarter.[5]

Chinese SOEs have played a significant role in the expansion of Chinese FDI. According to the 2021 Statistical Bulletin of China's Outward Foreign Direct Investment released by the Chinese government, at the end of 2021, SOEs accounted for 51.6 percent of China's stock of non-financial FDI.[6]

Countries needing foreign capital to stimulate economic growth generally welcome substantial investment from Chinese SOEs.[7] Nevertheless, in the context of China's assertive foreign policy, launched amid the escalating geopolitical tensions of the last decade,[8] the proliferation and target areas of Chinese SOE FDI have raised concerns among host States, especially developed host States, regarding potential implications for their national interest or security. The concerns stem mainly from the presumed ties of Chinese SOEs with the Chinese government and the Chinese Communist Party (CCP), leading to scepticism regarding the political motivations of Chinese SOEs in investing abroad. The concern has already resulted in an escalation of legal barriers to the ability of Chinese SOEs to invest in developed countries.

By the end of 2023, over half of the 39 'advanced economies' identified by the International Monetary Fund have enacted legislative frameworks for foreign investment screening,[9] allowing them to scrutinise proposed foreign investment to

---

[2] This does not include Chinese FDI from or through the Hong Kong Special Administrative Region (Hong Kong SAR). UNCTAD (2023) World Investment Report 2023. Annual Report No UNCTAD/WIR/2023, p 17.

[3] Ding (2009), pp. 235–236; Bohnet (1997), pp. 242–250.

[4] By the end of 2022, there were 361,996 SOEs operating in China. National Bureau of Statistics of China (NBS) (2020) National Data. https://data.stats.gov.cn/easyquery.htm?cn=C01. Accessed 2 Aug 2025.

[5] 《2021年财政收支情况》 [Fiscal Revenue and Expenditure of 2021] (People's Republic of China) MOF, 29 January 2022.

[6] MOFCOM, NBS and State Administration of Foreign Exchange (SAFE) (2022) 2021 Statistical Bulletin of China's Outward Foreign Direct Investment. China Commerce and Trade Press, p 30.

[7] Former Australian Treasurer Joe Hockey stated at a foreign investment roundtable in 2014 that the Australian government welcomes Chinese investment, including SOE investments. Hockey (2014).

[8] Tsai (2019), pp. 223–245. For China's current foreign policy, see generally Jinping (2014).

[9] By the end of 2022, 22 out of 37 countries that have introduced foreign investment screening mechanisms are developed countries. UNCTAD (2023) Investment Policy Monitor: The Evolution

manage risks against national interests or security.[10] Many developed countries have converged in tightening their foreign investment policy over the past five years,[11] including through enhancing screening procedures, particularly in the case of FDI made by foreign SOEs or foreign government-affiliated investors. As a result, Chinese SOE investments have become increasingly susceptible to screening mechanisms implemented by host States at the point of admission or during operations.

In addition, a growing number of modern international investment agreements (IIAs) have included SOE rules to regulate trade and investment activities by SOEs from the Parties.[12] Though China has not concluded any IIAs containing SOE-specific provisions, countries concerned about the potential harm of Chinese SOE investments may seek to include SOE rules in future IIAs with China to manage the risks associated with Chinese SOEs. Notably, China's potential accession to the *Comprehensive and Progressive Agreement for Trans-Pacific Partnership* (CPTPP),[13] a free trade agreement (FTA) among 12 Parties now including six developed countries (Australia, Canada, Japan, New Zealand, Singapore and the United Kingdom (UK)) would result in Chinese SOEs being subject to the CPTPP's standalone chapter on SOEs (Chapter 17).[14]

China, as a socialist emerging power, keeps reforming its SOEs and State economy as an integral part of the Chinese economic reform known as 'Reform and Opening Up' that commenced at the Third Plenary Session of the 11th Central Committee of the CCP held in December 1978.[15] The prolonged SOE reforms have proceeded in four rounds initiated under different leaders to serve distinct priorities with substantial policy adjustments. Figure 1.1 depicts the chronological progression of China's SOE reforms. A concise summary of the primary goals and accomplishments of each round of the reforms is as follows.

China's first round of SOE reforms (1978–1992) aimed primarily at increasing operational autonomy, financial independence and individual responsibility of

of FDI screening mechanisms: key trends and features. p 4. https://unctad.org/system/files/official-document/diaepcbinf2023d2_en.pdf. Accessed 2 Aug 2025.

[10] Organisation for Economic Co-operation and Development (OECD) (2023) Investment policy developments in 61 economies between 16 October 2021 and 15 March 2023. p 10. https://www.oecd.org/daf/inv/investment-policy/Investment-policy-monitoring-April-2023.pdf. Accessed 2 Aug 2025.

[11] UNCTAD (2023a), pp 5–7.

[12] Nawawi (2021), pp 144–148.

[13] Ministry of Foreign Affairs (2023) 《中国有意愿有能力加入CPTPP》 [China Willing, Capable of Joining CPTPP]. https://www.mfa.gov.cn/web/wjdt_674879/zwbd_674895/202308/t20230821_11129519.shtml. Accessed 2 Aug 2025.

[14] *Comprehensive and Progressive Agreement for Trans-Pacific Partnership*. signed 8 March 2018. [2018] ATS 23 (entered into force 30 December 2018), incorporating *Trans-Pacific Partnership Agreement*. signed 4 February 2016. [2016] ATNIF 2 (not in force).

[15] Xinhua (2021) Resolution of the Central Committee of the Communist Party of China on the Major Achievements and Historical Experience of the Party over the Past Century. State Council. https://english.www.gov.cn/policies/latestreleases/202111/16/content_WS6193a935c6d0df57f98e50b0.html. Accessed 2 Aug 2025.

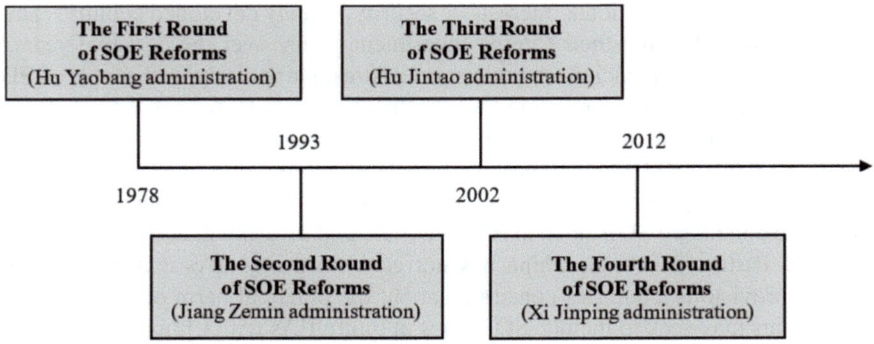

Fig. 1.1 The Timeline of China's SOE Reforms

State-owned factories (the predecessors of SOEs in China). The second round of SOE reforms (1993–2002) was initiated amid the Chinese State economy's overall desperation caused by the intensifying competition among enterprises with various forms of ownership in the Chinese market, with the primary goal of corporatising State-owned factories and revitalising the State economy. The third round of SOE reforms (2003–2011) focused on the government administration system for SOE and State-owned assets. Significantly, the reforms resulted in the establishment of the State-owned Assets Supervision and Administration Commissions (SASACs) at all levels, serving in the multiple capacities of owners of State-owned assets and shareholders and regulators of SOEs.[16]

The 18th National Congress of the CCP in November 2012 marked the commencement of the fourth round of China's SOE reforms.[17] Led by the Xi Jinping administration, the latest round of SOE reforms is unprecedented in its complexity and duration. The stated goal of the latest round of SOE reforms is to address the seemingly intractable issues besetting Chinese SOEs, such as low operational efficiency, week competitiveness, poor corporate governance practices and lax government oversight of State-owned assets, leading to loss and damage.[18]

In 2018, China repealed the presidential term limit.[19] At the 14th National People's Congress held in March 2023, President Xi Jinping formally announced the

[16] For more details regarding the preceding rounds of China's SOE reforms, see generally 国企改革历程编写组 [SOE Reform Process Writing Group] (2019) 《国企改革历程 1978-2018》 [The Course of Chinese State-Owned Enterprise Reform 1978-2018]. 中国经济出版社 [Economic Press China], pp 3–47.

[17] Ibid 48.

[18] 《中共中央关于全面深化改革若干重大问题的决定》 [Decision of the Central Committee of the CCP on Some Major Issues Concerning Comprehensively Deepening the Reform]. (People's Republic of China) The CCP Central Committee. 12 November 2013.

[19] The Economist (2018) Xi Jinping decides to abolish presidential term limits. https://www.economist.com/china/2018/03/01/xi-jinping-decides-to-abolish-presidential-term-limits. Accessed 2 Aug 2025.

continuation of reform policies issued since 2013,[20] implying the extension of the latest round of SOE reforms under continuing presidency.

Chinese SOE operational activities, including outbound FDI activities, have been significantly influenced by China's over four decades of SOE reforms and are still being reshaped in the latest round of SOE reforms. Given this background, this research provides a comprehensive examination of the implications of China's latest round of SOE reforms on Chinese SOE investments in developed countries. This research then takes Australia as an example, examining the efficacy of Australia's existing legislative frameworks in regulating Chinese SOE FDI under both domestic and international laws.

There are two main reasons for choosing Australia as the example. First, the substantial expansion of Chinese SOEs in Australia is a paradigmatic case. According to the Australian Department of Foreign Affairs and Trade (DFAT), China has become a top 10 source of FDI to Australia in the last decade.[21] The Klynveld Peat Marwick Goerdeler (KPMG) and University of Sydney (USYD)'s 2024 Report on Chinese Investment in Australia reveals that 59 percent of the total volume of Chinese investment in Australia in 2023 came from SOEs.[22] By July 2022, nearly half of Chinese SOEs owned by the central government (through the SASAC of the State Council) had invested in Australia.[23] Secondly, Australia stands out for the extent to which it has adopted policy measures under domestic and international laws to manage risks associated with inbound FDI. Specifically, Australia established a legislative framework for foreign investment screening in 1975.[24] In 2021, the framework was comprehensively tightened in response to national security concerns.[25] The framework explicitly targets foreign SOE investments, requiring all investments proposed by a 'foreign government investor' to be subject to a national interest test.[26] At the level of international law, Australia's IIAs with a number of countries, such as the US and Japan, include SOE rules.[27] Australia is also a signatory to the CPTPP and thus committed to the SOE chapter. Despite the absence

[20] 习近平 [Xi Jinping] (2023) 《在第十四届全国人民代表大会第一次会议上的讲话》 [Speech at the 1st Session of the 14th National People's Congress]. Speech. 14th National People's Congress.

[21] DFAT (2025) Statistics on who invests in Australia. https://www.dfat.gov.au/trade/trade-and-investment-data-information-and-publications/foreign-investment-statistics/statistics-on-who-invests-in-australia. Accessed 2 Aug 2025.

[22] KPMG and USYD (2024) Demystifying Chinese investment in Australia 2024. Report. p 4.

[23] The author had collected the data from the official announcements posted on the websites of China's central SOEs. The list of China's 100 central SOEs can be accessed at: http://wap.sasac.gov.cn/n2588045/n27271785/n27271792/c14159097/content.html. Accessed 2 Aug 2025.

[24] See, e.g., Carlos Esplugues (2018) Australia: The 'National Interest' Test. In: Carlos Esplugues (ed) Foreign Investment, Strategic Assets and National Security. Intersentia, p 355.

[25] Josh Frydenberg (2020) Major reforms to Australia's foreign investment framework pass the parliament. Media Release.

[26] *Foreign Acquisitions and Takeovers Regulation 2015* (Cth) s. 17.

[27] *Australia-United States Free Trade Agreement*. signed 18 May 2004. [2005] ATS 1 (entered into force 1 January 2005) art. 14.4, 14.8, 14.12; *Agreement between Australia and Japan for an*

of SOE-specific rules in existing IIAs between Australia and China, Australia's demonstrated awareness of the need to regulate foreign SOE investments points to the possibility of including SOE rules in future IIAs with China, as evidenced by its refusal to raise the zero-dollar screening threshold for Chinese SOEs in the *China-Australia Free Trade Agreement* (ChAFTA) negotiations.[28]

This study aims to lay the groundwork for policymakers in developed countries to balance maximising the benefits of Chinese SOE investments and protecting national interests. Ultimately, this research aims to contribute to the maintenance and improvement of China's international investment relationships with developed countries, mainly through its SOEs.

1.2 Research Questions

This research seeks to answer three overarching questions, each of which is further broken down into several specific sub-questions:

1. How does China's latest round of SOE reforms affect the relationship between Chinese SOEs as commercial operators and the Chinese government and the CCP?

   To investigate this question, this research focuses on the reform policy and progress of China's latest round of SOE reforms, and it addresses the following sub-questions:

   a. What are the major policy and objective of each sub-reform in the latest round of SOE reforms?
   b. How is each sub-reform progressing in practice?
   c. With the synergistic implementation of the sub-reforms, what is the true objective of the latest round of SOE reforms?
   d. How have the reforms affected, and how will they affect, the connections between Chinese SOEs, the government and the CCP?

2. How does China's latest round of SOE reforms affect Chinese SOEs' FDI in developed countries?

   To investigate this question, this research addresses the following sub-questions:

   a. How do the Chinese government and the CCP exert political influence or control over Chinese SOEs' outbound FDI activities? How does the latest round of SOE reforms impact the controlling mechanism(s)?

Economic Partnership. signed 8 July 2014. [2015] ATS 2 (entered into force on 15 January 2015) art. 15.4.

[28] DFAT (2018) Factsheet: Investment and Investor-State Dispute Settlement (ISDS). https://www.dfat.gov.au/sites/default/files/chafta-fact-sheet-investor-state-dispute-settlement.pdf. Accessed 2 Aug 2025.

   b. What impact does the latest round of SOE reforms have on the political control over the overseas subsidiaries of SOEs?
   c. In the latest round of SOE reforms, what policy objectives may Chinese SOEs' FDI in developed countries pursue?
   d. If the answer to these questions is that Chinese SOEs' approach to FDI is more, rather than less, policy-driven, what potential threats does this present to developed host States?

3. What legal measures should Australia take to manage the potential risks associated with Chinese SOE FDI in Australia?

   This research question shifts to a problem-solving perspective. To answer this question, this research explores the following sub-questions:
   a. How effective is Australia's current foreign investment framework under domestic law in mitigating the threats associated with FDI from Chinese SOEs undergoing the latest round of SOE reforms?
   b. What enhancements could be made to Australia's foreign investment framework to mitigate the potential threats associated with investments from contemporary Chinese SOEs?
   c. How effective are Australia-China IIAs in balancing Australia's interests with those of Chinese SOE investors?
   d. How should Australia improve future IIAs with China to better balance national interests and the protection of investments by contemporary Chinese SOEs?

1.3 Methodology

This research employs documentary analysis as its primary methodology, with different types of data being analysed at different stages of the research process in accordance with different research objects.

Specifically, in the stage of exploring the essence of the latest round of SOE reforms, this research presents an analysis based on the following data: (1) a comprehensive collection of latest Chinese laws, regulations, policies and other administrative documents, including CCP rules, concerning the latest round of SOE reforms; (2) factual evidence relating to the practical implementation of the reform policies gleaned from credible sources, such as press releases from the State media and announcements on the official websites of specific SOEs; and (3) the existing scholarship concerning China's SOE reforms.

Notably, the genuine objectives and progress of China's SOE reforms cannot be simply ascertained from public statements in a general framework document of the reforms; instead, they must be discovered through the reform policy mix and their actual implementation. The primary data sources regarding the latest round of SOE reforms are not legislation or legal texts but policies and administrative documents issued by the Chinese government at various levels. In addition, speeches given by high-level government or the CCP officials and outputs from State-backed media provide rich clues concerning the government's intent, political dynamics and contextual reality, ultimately revealing the facts about the latest round of SOE reforms.

In China, however, administrative documents, official press releases and speeches are typically obscure due to bureaucratic language and lack of foreign language translations. Typically, enormous volumes of material are issued by different parts and levels of the bureaucracy, they have rapid update rates and an intricate hierarchy of sources, and they can be tricky to access, particularly for researchers outside China. In addition, the pervasive political influence in China's one-party system may cast doubt on the credibility of documents originating in China, especially government-funded scholarship and media outputs. Therefore, when analysing these types of documents, it is necessary to pay close attention to the context in which they were produced, especially the purpose for which they were written and the intended audience.

Recognising these issues concerning Chinese data sources, the author has collected, selected and interpreted the latest data based on an in-depth understanding of the Chinese language and the Chinese political context, including hierarchy, authority, and socioeconomic environment. To maximise the comprehensiveness and timeliness of the research, the author has captured the latest political dynamics of China's state economy as the research progressed. This contributes to the originality and distinctiveness of this research.

In investigating FDI activities of Chinese SOEs or SOE-affiliated investors, this research primarily uses data released by credible sources, such as the governments of China or relevant countries and world-leading consulting firms such as KPMG and McKinsey & Company, and the China Global Investment Tracker jointly launched by the American Enterprise Institute and the Heritage Foundation (2022), which is the only publicly accessible dataset compiling Chinese outbound investments valued over USD 100 million from 2005.[29] When conducting case studies of typical Chinese SOE investments, this research accesses transaction details from additional sources, such as transaction announcements made by the relevant parties, shareholder structures of the relevant Parties, and host States' published government decisions regarding the transactions.

In examining Australia's legal frameworks concerning foreign investment, this research presents doctrinal analyses of relevant legislation, treaties and ISDS arbitration cases. In addition, this research uses law commentaries, legal scholarship and publicly available data from the Australian government as supplementary sources to investigate the practical application of the relevant law or treaty.

It is worth noting that, given China's ongoing lack of transparency and complexity in policy implementation and law enforcement, empirical studies can shed light on practical issues concerning Chinese SOEs and their FDI activities, such as interviews with SOE executives and their professional advisors to investigate how the

[29] The American Enterprise Institute and the Heritage Foundation (2025) China Global Investment Tracker. AEI. https://www.aei.org/china-global-investment-tracker/. Accessed 2 Aug 2025.

enterprises have implemented relevant reform policies, as well as how policy considerations and their dual roles as both CCP officials and corporate executives shape their stances on the enterprises' engagement in specific FDI transactions. However, ongoing Sino-Western geopolitical tensions and increased political control over Chinese SOEs as a result of the latest round of SOE reforms (as demonstrated in Chap. 5) render it impractical for the author, a researcher from a foreign university, to conduct fieldwork with insiders from those State-owned giants. In light of this, the author hopes that future empirical studies can use this research as a springboard to verify and expand upon its findings.

1.4 Research Originality in Relation to Existing Literature

Previous studies have contributed significantly to comprehending the Chinese State economy and SOEs.[30] Some scholarly works provide snapshots of parts of China's ongoing SOE reforms.[31] These prior works serve as important foundations for this research. However, no in-depth legal study currently examines how China's SOE reforms may impact Chinese SOE investments in developed countries. This research gap distinguishes this study as original.

Although there is an absence of scholarly literature examining the impacts of China's SOE reforms on Chinese SOE FDI, legal studies have provided insights into the potential implications of China's latest round of SOE reforms on the international trade activities of SOEs and the resulting implications for international trade law. For example, Zhou, Gao and Bai in 2019 investigated whether the existing WTO rules adequately address China's State capitalism, which is undergoing changes in SOE reforms, and reached a positive conclusion.[32] Gao and Zhou then updated their findings on the SOE reforms in their 2022 book on Chinese SOEs and international trade and argued that China's latest round of SOE reforms 'is likely to reverse the promised market-oriented transformation'.[33] Both works present a comprehensive overview of China's latest round of SOE reforms, which are concise in comparison to the intricate nature of the reform framework.

Some legal studies have looked into Chinese SOEs' political ties. Lin and Milhaupt, for example, examined the political ties of over a hundred of China's largest SOEs in their analysis of China's State capitalism and argued that Chinese SOEs are embedded in a State-controlled network that is ultimately linked to the government and the CCP.[34] Lin's 2017 article further elucidated the intricate links between

---

[30] See, e.g., Barry Naughton (2006) Top-Down Control: SASAC and the Persistence of State Ownership in China. Paper presented at the China and the World Economy conference. 23 June 2006; Lin (2015), pp. 81–127; Kovacic (2017), pp. 693–711; Wu (2016), pp. 261–324.

[31] See, e.g., Naughton (2017), pp. 282–298; Doyon et al. (2016).

[32] Zhou et al. (2019), pp. 977–1022.

[33] Gao and Zhou (2022).

[34] Lin and Milhaupt (2013), pp. 697–759.

Chinese SOEs and the State. This, she argued, could explain the perplexing behaviour of individual Chinese SOEs, even though the work did not address specific FDI practices.[35]

China's policy on outbound FDI has also been the subject of many legal studies. Huang and Wilkes, for example, provided a historical overview of China's foreign investment policy, but only up to 2011.[36] Bath examined the relationship between China's regulatory regimes for inbound and outbound FDI and China's foreign investment policy at the international level.[37] Chaisse, in his comprehensive study of China's IIA treaty-making practices, presented a brief yet comprehensive overview of China's applicable laws, regulations and policies for outbound FDI up to 2017. However, the work does not examine the policies themselves in any detail.[38] All of these works were published before the initiation of China's latest round of SOE reforms and did not address the potential impact of the policy on Chinese SOE FDI.

Several empirical studies have examined the policy factors that motivate Chinese SOE FDI. For example, using a comprehensive firm-level data set on Chinese FDI from 2000 to 2013, Stone, Wang and Yu demonstrated the high degree of conformity between Chinese SOE FDI and State policies, concluding that China uses SOE FDI to advance its foreign policy objectives.[39] However, no scholarly investigation has been conducted into China's current legislation and political documentary instruments outlining the mechanisms by which the government and the CCP exert political interference in SOEs' outbound FDI activities.

Considerable scholarly investigation has been undertaken concerning Chinese investment in Australia's legal system. For example, Mendelsohn and Fels in 2014 analysed the operations of Australian foreign investment screening for Chinese investments and provided recommendations on how Australia's screening regime could better serve Australia's broader policy interests while reducing Chinese investors' perception of uncertainty about the review.[40] In a 2018 article, Jiang explored the operations of Australia's foreign investment screening regime for Chinese investments through fieldwork interviews with legal experts involved in the Australian review process and case studies of prominent Chinese investments.[41] These studies shed light on the significant concerns that Chinese investment has triggered from the Australian government. These studies, however, were conducted before the 2021 reform of Australia's foreign investment framework. Voon and Merriman in 2022 assessed the compliance of Australia's reformed foreign investment framework with Australia's obligations under IIAs, identifying the potential claims that foreign investors could bring against Australia's foreign investment

[35] Lin (2017), pp. 583–600.

[36] Huang and Wilkes (2011), p. 5.

[37] Bath (2011).

[38] Chaisse (2018).

[39] Stone et al. (2022), pp. 229–250.

[40] Mendelsohn and Fels (2014), pp. 59–83.

[41] Jiang (2018), pp. 14–35.

policy under applicable IIAs.[42] In another 2022 article, they broadened their focus to the general relationship between the foreign investment screening regime and international investment law.[43] These previous studies, however, did not pay special attention to Chinese SOE investments. At the level of international investment law, Voon and Sheargold in 2017 presented an overview of the concurrent multiple IIAs between Australia and China, focusing on the interpretation and application issues involved in the co-existence of successive treaties under public international law.[44] However, there is a lack of studies in the existing literature that examine Chinese SOE investments within the Australia-China IIA framework in the context of China's latest round of SOE reforms.

Given the research gap, this research aims to present a comprehensive legal study into the implications of China's latest round of SOE reforms on Chinese SOE investments to work out how a developed host State should balance safeguarding national security and retaining its attractiveness to future Chinese SOE investors.

1.5 Book Structure

This Book contains seven substantive chapters, excluding this introduction (Chap. 1) and conclusion (Chap. 9). As mentioned briefly in the preceding sections, the seven chapters are divided into three parts. Chapters 2, 3 and 4 investigate the essence and progress of China's latest round of SOE reforms. Chapters 5 and 6 explore the implications of the latest round of SOE reforms on the political control over Chinese SOE investments in developed countries. Chapters 7 and 8 examine the effectiveness of Australia's regulatory coping strategies under domestic and international law in mitigating the potential threats associated with FDI from contemporary Chinese SOEs. Table 1.1 below sets out the structure of the Book, including chapter titles.

1.6 Explanations of Key Terminology

The following are some of the most important terms used throughout this Book and their abbreviations. Their meanings must be clarified to avoid any misunderstandings.

In this Book, an 'SOE' refers to a non-financial enterprise incorporated within China or elsewhere in which the Chinese government, government-affiliated agencies or other SOEs hold a controlling stake. This term is based on ownership and

42 Voon and Merriman (2022b), pp. 62–113.

43 Voon and Merriman (2022a), pp. 75–114.

44 Voon and Sheargold (2017), pp 227–233.

Table 1.1 Book Structure and Chapter Titles

Chapter 1:	Introduction
Chapter 2:	China's State Economy Restructuring Reform: Grasping the Large and Releasing the Small?
Chapter 3:	China's Mixed Ownership Reform: An Expanding State-owned Enterprises Equity Network
Chapter 4:	China's State-owned Assets Management and SOE Governance Reform: CCP Control is Looming Again
Chapter 5:	The Mountains are High, but the Emperor is not Far Away: The Escalation in Political Control over Chinese SOE Outbound Investments
Chapter 6:	Protecting National Security: An Increasingly Important Dimension of Chinese SOE Investments in Developed Countries
Chapter 7:	A 'Great Wall' with Cracks: The Implications of China's SOE Reforms for Australia's Foreign Investment Framework
Chapter 8:	Chinese SOE Investments Under the Australia-China International Investment Agreements: Wild Grass with Hidden Thorns
Chapter 9:	Conclusion

thus broadly encompasses the various types of SOE in China's market entity registration system, such as collective enterprises, joint enterprises and companies limited by shares.[45]

This research exclusively focuses on Chinese non-financial SOEs because, in the international investment arena, the number of Chinese non-financial SOEs is significantly greater than that of financial SOEs, such as State banks and China Investment Corporation, China's only sovereign wealth fund. In addition, Chinese financial and non-financial SOEs are governed by distinct legislative regimes and administrative supervision systems and are undergoing different SOE reform policies.[46] In the context of China's SOE reforms, the confusion surrounding the true identities of Chinese non-financial SOEs has heightened compared to financial SOEs, as financial SOEs are additionally subject to the Chinese government's centralised control over the domestic financial sector.

This Book uses the term 'national business group' (BG) to refer to Chinese State-owned business groups directly supervised by the central SASAC and its local branches, i.e. local SASACs. In 1986, the Chinese government determined to

[45] 《中华人民共和国市场主体登记管理条例实施细则》 [Implementing Rule for the Administrative Regulation of the People's Republic of China on the Registration of Market Entities]. (People's Republic of China) State Administration for Market Regulation (SAMR). 1 March 2022.

[46] As an example, Chinese financial SOEs are subject to centralised supervision by Central Huijin Investment Ltd, which acts as the controlling shareholder for all Chinese financial SOEs. Chinese non-financial SOEs are under the supervision by SASACs at various levels. For more details on the differences and relationship between Chinese financial and non-financial SOEs, see generally Wu (2016), p 273; Lin (2015), pp 597–598.

organise SOEs in the formation of a BG, a vertically integrated, multi-layered structure based on ownership relationships, to facilitate centralised control over SOEs.[47] In this sense, the term SOE in this Book typically refers to a BG or an enterprise that belongs to a BG, either as the BG's core company (the group's parent company) or as a subsidiary. The relationships between the BG, SOE, core company and subsidiary are shown in Fig. 1.2. Accordingly, 'central BG' and 'local BG' refer to Chinese national business groups directly supervised by the central SASAC and local SASACs, respectively.

The term 'State economy' in this Book, which may also be known as 'public economy', refers to the domain of the Chinese national economy consisting of enterprises, public institutions and other entities directly and indirectly invested by the Chinese government at various levels using State-owned assets and State-owned assets at the disposal of the entities.

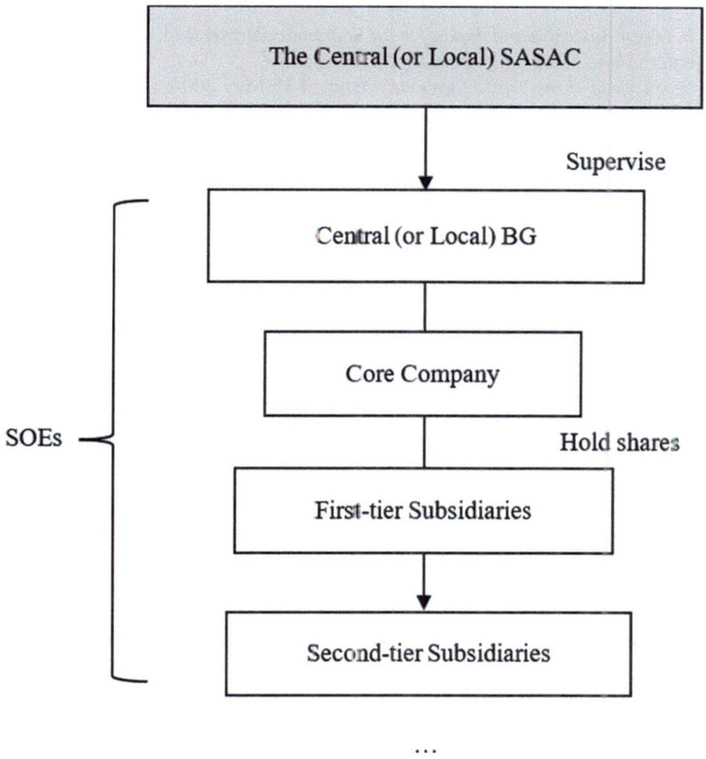

Fig. 1.2 The Relationships Between the Terms BG, SOE, Core Company and Subsidiary Used in This Book

47 《关于进一步推动横向经济联合若干问题的规定》 [Provisions on Several Issues Concerning Further Promoting Horizontal Economic Association]. (People's Republic of China) The State Council. 23 March 1986.

The term 'critical industries' in this Book is an abbreviation of 'critical industries and key fields relevant to the lifeblood of the national economy and national security' frequently used in China's legislation.[48] The central SASAC explained this term as referring to essential industries of social, economic or political strategic importance to China, such as energy, telecommunications, transportation and defence.[49]

Due to the close relationship between the government and the CCP in China's one-party system, the term 'Party-State' is used to collectively refer to the Chinese government and the CCP when there is no particular need to differentiate between them.

References

Agreement between Australia and Japan for an Economic Partnership. signed 8 July 2014. [2015] ATS 2 (entered into force on 15 January 2015) art. 15.4

Australia-United States Free Trade Agreement. signed 18 May 2004. [2005] ATS 1 (entered into force 1 January 2005) art. 14.4, 14.8, 14.12

Bath V (2011) The quandary for Chinese regulators: controlling the flow of investment into and out of China. In: Bath V, Nottage L (eds) Foreign investment and dispute resolution law and practice in Asia. Routledge

Bohnet A (1997) The 'socialist' market economy in a communist system: taking stock of china's economic reforms. Inter Econ 32(5):242–250

Chaisse J (2018) China's international investment policy: formation, evolution, and transformation(s). In: Chaisse J, Nottage L (eds) International investment treaties and arbitration across Asia. Brill, pp 544–545

Comprehensive and Progressive Agreement for Trans-Pacific Partnership. signed 8 March 2018. [2018] ATS 23 (entered into force 30 December 2018), incorporating Trans-Pacific Partnership Agreement. signed 4 February 2016. [2016] ATNIF 2 (not in force)

DFAT (2018) Factsheet: Investment and Investor-State Dispute Settlement (ISDS). https://www.dfat.gov.au/sites/default/files/chafta-fact-sheet-investor-state-dispute-settlement.pdf. Accessed 2 Aug 2025

DFAT (2025) Statistics on who invests in Australia. https://www.dfat.gov.au/trade/trade-and-investment-data-information-and-publications/foreign-investment-statistics/statistics-on-who-invests-in-australia. Accessed 2 Aug 2025

Ding X (2009) The socialist market economy: China and the world. Sci Soc 73(2):235–236

Doyon J, Godement F, Leutert W (2016) Big is beautiful? State-owned enterprise mergers under Xi Jinping. European Council on Foreign Relations. https://ecfr.eu/publication/china_state_owned_enterprise_mergers_under_xi_jinping7196/. Accessed 2 Aug 2025

---

[48] See, e.g., 《中华人民共和国国家安全法》 [National Security Law of People's Republic of China 2015]. (People's Republic of China) Adopted at the 12th National People's Congress Standing Committee. 1 July 2015. art 19; 《中华人民共和国企业国有资产法》 [Law of the People's Republic of China on State-Owned Assets of Enterprises]. (People's Republic of China) Adopted at the 11th National People's Congress Standing Committee. 1 May 2009. art 7.

[49] 《关于推进国有资本调整和国有企业重组的指导意见》 [Guiding Opinions on Promoting the Adjustment of State-Owned Capital and the Reorganization of State-Owned Enterprises]. (People's Republic of China) The Central SASAC. 5 December 2006.

Esplugues C (2018) Australia: the 'National Interest' test. In: Esplugues C (ed) Foreign investment, strategic assets and national security. Intersentia, p 355
Foreign Acquisitions and Takeovers Regulation 2015 (Cth) s. 17
Frydenberg J (2020) Major reforms to Australia's foreign investment framework pass the parliament. Media Release
Gao H, Zhou W (2022) Between market economy and state capitalism: China's state-owned enterprises and the world trading system. Cambridge University Press
Hockey J (2014) Keynote address to the foreign investment roundtable. Speech, Foreign Investment Roundtable, Sydney
Huang W, Wilkes A (2011) Analysis of China's overseas investment policies. Working Paper 79. Center for International Forestry Research, p 5
Jiang H (2018) Beaming light on Australia's national interest test: an empirical study of Chinese investments under it. Asia Pac Law Rev 26(1):14–35
Jinping X (2014) The Chinese dream of the great rejuvenation of the Chinese nation. Foreign Languages Press
Kovacic WE (2017) Competition policy and state-owned enterprises in China. World Trade Rev 16(4):693–711
KPMG and USYD (2024) Demystifying Chinese investment in Australia 2024. Report. p 4
Lin L-W (2015) China's national champions: governance change through globalization? Univ Pa Asian Law Rev 11(1):81–127
Lin L-W (2017) A network anatomy of Chinese state-owned enterprises. World Trade Rev 16(4):583–600
Lin L-W, Milhaupt CJ (2013) We Are the (National) champions: understanding the mechanisms of state capitalism in China. Stanf Law Rev 65(4):697–759
Mendelsohn R, Fels A (2014) Australia's foreign investment review board and the regulation of Chinese investment. China Econ J 7(1):59–83
Ministry of Foreign Affairs (2023) 《中国有意愿有能力加入CPTPP》 [China Willing, Capable of Joining CPTPP]. https://www.mfa.gov.cn/web/wjdt_674879/zwbd_674895/202308/t20230821_11129519.shtml. Accessed 2 Aug 2025
MOFCOM, NBS and SAFE (2022) 2021 Statistical bulletin of China's outward foreign direct investment. China Commerce and Trade Press, p 30
National Bureau of Statistics of China (NBS) (2020) National Data. https://data.stats.gov.cn/easyquery.htm?cn=C01. Accessed 2 Aug 2025
Naughton B (2006) Top-Down Control: SASAC and the Persistence of State Ownership in China. Paper presented at the China and the World Economy conference. 23 June 2006
Naughton B (2017) The current wave of state enterprise reform in China: a preliminary appraisal. Asian Econ Policy Rev 12(2):282–298
Nawawi WK (2021) New Rules for State-Owned Enterprises in the CPTPP. In: Cassey L, Bhattacharya P (eds) The Comprehensive and Progressive Agreement for Trans-Pacific Partnership. ISEAS - Yusof Ishak Institute, pp 144–148
OECD (2023) Investment policy developments in 61 economies between 16 October 2021 and 15 March 2023. p 10. https://www.oecd.org/daf/inv/investment-policy/Investment-policy-monitoring-April-2023.pdf. Accessed 2 Aug 2025
Stone RW, Wang Y, Shu Y (2022) Chinese power and the state-owned enterprise. Int Org 76(1):229–250
The American Enterprise Institute and the Heritage Foundation (2023) China Global Investment Tracker. AEI. https://www.aei.org/china-global-investment-tracker/. Accessed 2 Aug 2025
The Economist (2018) Xi Jinping decides to abolish presidential term limits. https://www.economist.com/china/2018/03/01/xi-jinping-decides-to-abolish-presidential-term-limits. Accessed 2 Aug 2025
Tsai MH-J (2019) The Chinese dream: Chinese capitalism and identity politics. Asian Surv 59(2):223–245

UNCTAD (2023a) Investment Policy Monitor: The Evolution of FDI screening mechanisms: key trends and features. p 4. https://unctad.org/system/files/official-document/diaepcbinf2023d2_en.pdf. Accessed 2 Aug 2025

UNCTAD (2023b) World Investment Report 2023. Annual Report No UNCTAD/WIR/2023, p 17

Voon T, Merriman D (2022a) Incoming: how international investment law constrains foreign investment screening. J World Invest Trade 24(1):75–114

Voon T, Merriman D (2022b) Is Australia's foreign investment screening policy consistent with international investment law? Melbourne J Int Law 23(1):62–113

Voon T, Sheargold E (2017) Australia, China, and the Co-Existence of Successive International Investment Agreements. In: Picker C, Wang H, Zhou W (eds) The China Australia Free Trade Agreement: a 21st century model. Hart Publishing, pp 227–233

Wu M (2016) The "China, Inc." challenge to global trade governance. Harv Int Law J 57(2):261–324

Xinhua (2021) Resolution of the Central Committee of the Communist Party of China on the Major Achievements and Historical Experience of the Party over the Past Century. State Council. https://english.www.gov.cn/policies/latestreleases/202111/16/content_WS6193a935c6d0df57f98e50b0.html. Accessed 2 Aug 2025

Zhou W, Gao H, Bai X (2019) Building a market economy through WTO-inspired reform of state-owned enterprises in China. Int Comp Law Quart 68(4):977–1022

Xi Jinping [习近平] (2023) 《在第十四届全国人民代表大会第一次会议上的讲话》 [Speech at the 1st Session of the 14th National People's Congress]. Speech. 14th National People's Congress

Additional Sources

《中共中央关于全面深化改革若干重大问题的决定》 [Decision of the Central Committee of the CCP on Some Major Issues Concerning Comprehensively Deepening the Reform]. (People' s Republic of China) The CCP Central Committee. 12 November 2013

《2021年财政收支情况》 [Fiscal Revenue and Expenditure of 2021] (People' s Republic of China) MOF, 29 January 2022

《关于推进国有资本调整和国有企业重组的指导意见》 [Guiding Opinions on Promoting the Adjustment of State-Owned Capital and the Reorganization of State-Owned Enterprises]. (People' s Republic of China) The Central SASAC. 5 December 2006

《中华人民共和国市场主体登记管理条例实施细则》 [Implementing Rule for the Administrative Regulation of the People' s Republic of China on the Registration of Market Entities]. (People' s Republic of China) State Administration for Market Regulation (SAMR). 1 March 2022

《中华人民共和国企业国有资产法》 [Law of the People' s Republic of China on State-Owned Assets of Enterprises]. (People' s Republic of China) Adopted at the 11th National People's Congress Standing Committee. 1 May 2009. art 7

《中华人民共和国国家安全法》 [National Security Law of People' s Republic of China 2015]. (People' s Republic of China) Adopted at the 12th National People's Congress Standing Committee. 1 July 2015. art 19

《关于进一步推动横向经济联合若干问题的规定》 [Provisions on Several Issues Concerning Further Promoting Horizontal Economic Association]. (People' s Republic of China) The State Council. 23 March 1986

国企改革历程编写组 [SOE Reform Process Writing Group] (2019) 《国企改革历程1978-2018》 [The Course of Chinese State-Owned Enterprise Reform 1978-2018]. 中国经济出版社 [Economic Press China], pp 3 - 47

Chapter 2
China's State Economy Restructuring Reform: Grasping the Large and Releasing the Small?

Abstract Amid China's transition to a market economy, the persistence and consolidation of a massive State sector remain a defining feature of its political-economic model. This chapter asks whether the latest round of State economy reforms, framed as 'Grasp the Large and Release the Small', signals a retreat from State ownership or a strategic recalibration of it. It investigates how these reforms restructure the distribution of SOEs across critical and non-critical sectors, and how this evolving configuration shapes Chinese SOEs' role in outbound investment. The analysis shows that China has not pursued genuine privatisation at any stage of SOE reforms. Instead, it has advanced a dual-track strategy: reinforcing SOE monopolies in industries tied to national security, while withdrawing State ownership from peripheral sectors through managed competition, asset consolidation, and internal reorganisation. This approach strengthens centralised control and enhances the global competitiveness of a select group of national champions. By clarifying the ideological, institutional, and policy foundations of China's State economy, the chapter reveals how these reforms recalibrate the structure and motivation of SOE-led outbound investment. It provides a critical basis for understanding why host States view such investments as both commercially significant and strategically sensitive in international legal governance.

China has achieved remarkable economic growth and made significant progress in its transition to a market economy since the launch of the 'Open Door' Policy in 1978.[1] Despite this, this emerging socialist power maintains a chronically massive State economy. According to the National Bureau of Statistics of China (NBS), China still has 361,996 SOEs at the central and regional levels as of December 2022.[2]

---

[1] 1 The World Bank and Development Research Centre of the State Council (2013), p. 4 https://www.worldbank.org/content/dam/Worldbank/document/China-2030-complete.pdf Accessed 11 Aug 2025.

[2] NBS (2025) National Data. https://data.stats.gov.cn/easyquery.htm?cn=C01. Accessed 11 Aug 2025.

T. Gu, *Chinese SOE Reforms and Global FDI*, Contemporary Chinese Civil and Commercial Law, https://doi.org/10.1007/978-981-92-3181-2_2

Chinese SOEs play an important role not only in the Chinese economy, but also in China's integration with the global economy.[3] The conventional analysis assumed that China would adopt a progressive privatisation strategy.[4] Boycko, Shleifer and Vishny, for example, argued in the 1990s that the massive privatisation practiced in Eastern Europe would be practically infeasible in China, as it would result in the loss of State-owned assets to the insiders of the government, the CCP and SOEs, as well as their associates.[5] Gallagher noted in 2015 that the market-oriented and State-dominated nature of China's socialist market economy makes a massive privatisation that would transfer State-owned assets to the general public politically infeasible.[6]

In fact, China keeps reforming its State economy as an integral part of its SOE reforms that commenced in 1978. In the second round of SOE reforms launched in 1993,[7] the Jiang Zemin administration promoted a State economy restructuring program under the name 'Grasp the Large and Release the Small' (discussed in Sect. 2.2). This seeming privatisation program nearly halved the number of Chinese SOEs at the time.[8] China's latest round launched in 2012 also puts forth State economy reform in the form of multiple concurrent programs, such as 'Resolve the Overcapacity' and 'Compress and Reduce' programs (discussed in Sect. 2.3). The persistence of the massive State economy in China and the intricate design of China's ongoing State economy reform prompt the following fundamental questions:

What is the reform objective of the Chinese government concerning restructuring China's State economy in the latest round of SOE reforms? In essence, does China want to strengthen or weaken its State economy? How may China's State economy reform in the latest round of SOE reforms impact Chinese SOEs' outbound FDI activities?

This chapter aims to answer these questions, which are crucial for the rest of the world to gain a clear outlook on China's State economy and lays the groundwork for gaining specific insights into Chinese SOEs' increasing engagement in international investment activities. This chapter demonstrates that, throughout the history of SOE reforms in China, the country has never undertaken genuine privatisation to weaken its SOEs. Instead, beginning in the mid-1990s and continuing in the ongoing round of SOE reforms, China has followed the guiding strategy of 'Grasp the Large and Release the Small' in restructuring its State economy. This chapter argues that the policy continuity underlying China's State economy restructuring reforms speaks to a goal that successive Chinese leaders have sought to achieve, maintaining SOE monopolies in critical industries and bolstering the overall strength of its State

---

[3] OECD (2011), p. 14. https://www.oecd.org/china/2011-03-ChinaBrochureEN.pdf. Accessed 11 Aug 2025.

[4] Milhaupt and Zheng (2015), pp. 665–722.

[5] Boycko et al. (1994), pp. 249–266. p. 254.

[6] Gallagher (2015).

[7] 江泽民 [Jiang Zemin] (2002) 《中国共产党第十六次全国代表大会上的报告》 [Report of the 16th National Congress of the CCP]. Speech. 16th National Congress of the CCP.

[8] Gallagher (2015).

economy. This overarching goal stems from the importance of SOEs in China's national economy, which has been firmly established in the country's socialist ideology, Constitution and national value system. In addition, the ongoing State economy restructuring reform will have substantive impact on Chinese SOEs' outbound FDI activities.

This chapter is organised as follows. Section 2.1 begins with demonstrating SOEs and the State economy's importance in China's political-economic system, which has been well established ideologically, statutorily and practically. If the CCP continues in power, it is unrealistic to expect China to attempt weakening of its State economy. Section 2.2 provides an overview of the 'Grasp the Large and Release the Small' program in the second round of SOE reforms. This section argues that the privatisation program was intended to revitalise the State economy rather than shrink it. Section 2.3 examines how the current government is reforming the Chinese State economy in the latest round of SOE reforms, including an analysis of the geopolitical implications of the reform. It argues that in this round of SOE reforms, the current Chinese government continues to 'Grasp the Large and Release the Small' as the guiding strategy in restructuring the State economy to forge a more powerful State economy. Section 2.4 concludes with remarks on the potential implications of China's State economy restructuring reform on Chinese SOE outbound FDI activities.

2.1 The Ideological and Practical Primacy of SOEs in China

Forty years after Deng Xiaoping initiated the 1978 'Open Door' Policy, the current Chinese leadership continues to insist on the primacy of the State economy in the national economy, stating that this primacy 'must be consolidated and developed'.[9] This long-held stance has been enshrined in the Constitution of China since 1999, reading 'the State shall uphold a fundamental economic system under which public ownership is the mainstay' and 'the State economy shall be the *leading force* in the national economy. The State shall ensure the consolidation and growth of the State economy' (emphases added).[10] Consistent with this constitutionally mandated priority, the CCP leadership pledged at the 16th National People's Congress in 2002 to 'unwaveringly consolidate and develop the State economy and encourage, support and guide the development of the non-State economy'.[11]

---

[9] 《中国共产党第十九届中央委员会第六次全体会议公报》 [Communique of the Sixth Plenary Session of the 19th Central Committee of the CCP]. (People's Republic of China) CCP Central Committee. 11 November 2021.

[10] 《中华人民共和国宪法》 [Constitution of the People's Republic of China]. (People's Republic of China) Adopted at the 1st Session of the 13th National People's Congress. 11 March 2018. Art 6, 7.

[11] 江泽民 [Jiang Zemin] (2002) 《中国共产党第十六次全国代表大会上的报告》 [Report of the 16th CCP National Congress]. Speech. 16th CCP National Congress.

Since acceding the World Trade Organization (WTO) in 2001, China has achieved a tremendous economic rise and made significant progress in transitioning to a market economy. However, in the eyes of the current CCP leadership and Chinese government, the State economy's primacy remains. Therefore, in 2020, Xi Jinping publicly reiterated the overriding role of SOEs as an 'important material foundation', the 'political foundation' and the 'economic pillar' of China's socialist political regime, as well as the 'important backbone for the CCP to govern and rejuvenate the country'.[12]

Despite undergoing three previous rounds of SOE reforms, as noted earlier, China still maintains hundreds of thousands of SOEs. These SOEs contribute significantly to national revenue. According to MOF, China's national fiscal revenue in 2021 was USD 3.19 trillion, of which more than a quarter was contributed by SOEs.[13] Chinese SOEs' significant role in supporting the national economy stems from their long-standing dominance over China's critical industries, such as the energy, telecommunications, transportation and military industries. These industries are the most profitable, which explains the enormous wealth of Chinese SOEs.

The Chinese government has maintained the dominance of SOEs on purpose since the launch of the SOE reforms in 1978 due to the industries' close connection to vital national interests and security. Parallel to operating businesses pursuing economic maximisation, SOEs in these critical industries must be prepared for government orders to adjust their production and operation plans to meet the requirements necessary for social stability. For example, in October 2021, when China was experiencing a severe power shortage that resulted in widespread power outages in the northeast of the country, the government ordered central BGs in energy industries to improve the power supply at any cost to ensure a stable energy supply to meet domestic demand.[14]

In China's unique socio-political system, the SOEs in critical industries and the entire group of SOEs serve as the primary implementers of national directives, policies and strategies—which the Chinese government and Chinese State media have consistently propagated. For example, during the COVID-19 pandemic, a media blitz by government-controlled State media focused on SOEs serving the government's command in rescuing the collapsing society 'regardless of the cost' (including the personnel safety of their employees) by, for instance, spearheading the provision of emergency supplies, providing medical support and stabilising the industrial and supply chain.[15] In addition, Chinese SOEs also contribute

---

[12] 习近平 [Xi Jinping] (2002) 《在中央全面深化改革委员会第十四次会议上的讲话》 [Speech at the 14th Meeting of the Central Committee for Comprehensively Deepening Reform]. Speech. 14th Meeting of the Central Committee for Comprehensively Deepening Reform.

[13] 《2021年财政收支情况》 [Fiscal Revenue and Expenditure of 2021]. (People's Republic of China) MOF. 29 January 2022.

[14] 杜燕飞 [Du Yanfei] (2021) 《国资委要求央企加大能源保供力度》 [The Central SASAC requires central enterprises to strengthen energy supply]. People. http://finance.people.com.cn/n1/2021/1004/c1004-32245570.html. Accessed 11 Aug 2025.

[15] The State Council (2020) 《国有企业分类有序复工复产》 [SOEs resume work and production in an orderly and categorised manner]. https://www.gov.cn/xinwen/2020-02/16/con-

significantly to the Innovation-driven Development Strategy, China's primary development strategy that seeks to break the monopoly of Western countries in cutting-edge technologies. Chinese SOEs in the high-tech sector have arguably endeavoured to live up to the government's expectation that they will spearhead technological advancement. They have mastered several high-profile technologies, including the third-generation technique of advanced high-strength steel production owned by the China Baosteel Group, the microelectronics technology owned by the China Resources Group and the C919 airliner manufacturing technology owned by the China General Aviation Corporation.[16]

The Chinese Party-State admits that SOEs implement national strategies and initiatives at their behest, proclaiming that this benefits China's socialist market economy.[17] This indicates that the Chinese Party-State has and will continue to view the primacy of SOEs and the State economy in the national economy as part of the country's existential core and the pillar of China's future prosperity. Therefore, it is implausible that China pursued or pursues genuine privatisation of its State economy as part of the SOE reforms to accelerate the transition to a market economy. Privatisation aimed at weakening Chinese SOEs did not occur in the second round of SOE reforms and is not happening in the latest round of the reforms.

2.2 An Overview of the 'Grasp the Large and Release the Small' Program

Although SOEs play essential roles in maintaining and promoting Chinese national development, China's former Prime Minister Zhu Rongji initiated a 'Grasp the Large and Release the Small' State economy restructuring reform in the second round of SOE reforms in 1997, which nearly halved the number of Chinese SOEs at that time. The program, therefore, made many believe that China was determined to shrink the size and power of the State economy.[18] Nonetheless, based on the preceding analysis, we can see that the Chinese Party-State's consistent firm adherence to the basic socialist economic system suggests a different story.

The 'Grasp the Large and Release the Small' program was launched in the context of the overall desperation of the Chinese State economy following the unprecedented decision of the government to allow non-State enterprises to coexist and compete with SOEs in many sectors of the Chinese economy in the late

tent_5479683.htm. Accessed 11 Aug 2025.

[16] The Central SASAC (2018) 《国有企业作用不可替代》 [The Role of State-Owned Enterprises is Irreplaceable]. http://www.sasac.gov.cn/n2588025/n2588139/c9875479/content.html. Accessed 11 Aug 2025.

[17] Ibid.

[18] Milhaupt and Zheng (2015), p. 694.

1980s.[19] The catastrophic performance of SOEs in competition caused a severe economic downturn and threatened social stability, necessitating government intervention.[20]

At the outset of the program, the CCP Central Committee proclaimed that SOE dominance must be maintained in China's critical industries; it also made it clear that the layout of the State economy could be adjusted strategically in non-critical industries.[21] Accordingly, the essence of the program can be summarised as to partially marketise China's economic sectors—preserving the so-called 'critical' industries for continued monopolisation by SOEs, while in non-critical industries, allowing multiple ownership forms to compete and promoting the privatisation of SOEs that lost grounds to non-State competitors. Here the term 'critical industries' is an abbreviation of 'critical industries and key fields relevant to the lifeblood of the national economy and national security' in China's Constitution, which is the fixed phrase that Chinese authorities usually use to refer to the essential industries of social, economic or political strategic importance to China, such as energy, telecommunications, transportation and defence.[22]

The continued SOE monopoly was mainly achieved via market-entry barriers erected by the Chinese government, mainly through extensive requirements for regulatory approvals, combined with *de facto* discrimination in administering the industrial entry-related regulations and policies.[23] In practice, China's critical industries were shielded from competition and monopolised by a few central BGs.[24] To foster the efficiency of the State-owned monopolies in critical industries, the government orchestrated limited competition on a closed playing field by breaking up the central BGs into smaller successor entities or establishing rival BGs, which came under the meaning of 'Grasp the Large'. For instance, China's telecommunications industry used to be monopolised by China Telecommunications Corporation (China Telecom). The government orchestrated the gradual dismantling of the industrial monopoly by first establishing China United Network Communications Group (China Unicom) in 1994 and then in 1999 splitting China Telecom on a business basis into two telecom carriers, including the China Telecom that is known today and China Mobile Communications Group (China Mobile).[25] The same year,

---

19 国企改革历程编写组 [SOE Reform Process Writing Group] (2019) 《国企改革历程 1978-2018》 [The Course of Chinese State-Owned Enterprise Reform 1978-2018]. 中国经济出版社 [Economic Press China], pp. 21–24 ('*SOE Reforms 1978-2018*').

20 Naughton (2017), pp. 282–298.

21 江泽民 [Jiang Zemin] (1997) 《中国共产党第十五次全国代表大会上的报告》 [Report of the 15th National Congress of the CCP]. Speech. 15th CCP National Congress.

22 《关于推进国有资本调整和国有企业重组的指导意见》 [Guiding Opinions on Promoting the Adjustment of State-Owned Capital and the Reorganization of State-Owned Enterprises] (People's Republic of China) The Central SASAC. 5 December 2006.

23 Kovacic (2017), pp. 693–711, p. 695; Wu (2016), pp. 261–324, p 272.

24 Naughton (2017).

25 《国务院关于同意组建中国联合通信有限公司的批复》 [Reply of the State Council on Approval of the Establishment of China United Communications Co, LTD]. (People's Republic of

three other telecom central BGs were set up to intensify further industrial competition.[26]

In contrast to the critical industries, China's non-critical industries, such as manufacturing, hospitality and entertainment, generally became competitive, allowing head-to-head competition between SOEs and non-SOEs. Chinese SOEs at local levels, including provincial, municipal and township SOEs or BGs, are primarily clustered in these non-critical industries. Unsurprisingly, local SOEs lacking sufficient support from their government owners quickly lost ground to emerging privately-owned enterprises (POEs) and advanced foreign enterprises.[27] The fierce market competition provided chances for the re-distribution of public wealth in China, including the rapid accumulation of private wealth. To 'strategically adjust' the State economy in non-critical industries, China resorted to two privatisation strategies: the 'Grasp the Large' and 'Release the Small' programs, which targeted different types of SOEs.

The 'Grasp the Large' strategy targeted SOEs showing competitiveness in the market. The government consolidated these SOEs in the same or complementary industries into larger SOEs and had their subsidiaries go public (mainly on the stock exchanges in Shenzhen and Shanghai).[28] It was assumed that introducing non-State shareholders in the stock markets would enhance SOEs' corporate governance practice, improving their operational scale and efficiency.[29] Haier, one of China's most prominent home appliance producers, is an example of the 'large' so-created.[30] The 'Release the Small' strategy generally targeted the rest of SOEs: Those with a chance of survival could be saved through selling stakes to private interests (or, in some cases, through a debt-for-equity swap arrangement with a State-owned bank in which the bank agreed to acquire the SOE's non-performing assets and become a shareholder in the SOE) while the local government owners still retained a significant stake. Those with little chance of survival were shut down or wholly sold to private hands.[31]

Section 2.3 demonstrates that in the latest round of SOE reforms, the Xi Jinping administration continues to follow 'Grasp the Large and Release the Small' as the guiding strategy in restructuring the State economy, with the goal shifting from revitalisation to forging a more robust State economy. From 1994 to 2008, the 'Grasp the Large and Release the Small' State economy restructuring program led to a reduction of two-thirds in the number of Chinese SOEs, which were mainly at a local level, at the cost of a wave of over 40 million lay-offs of employees in the

China) The State Council. 14 December 1993.

[26] *SOE Reforms 1978-2018* (n 19) p. 311.

[27] Milhaupt and Zheng (2015), p. 697.

[28] *SOE Reforms 1978-2018* (n 19) pp. 130–131.

[29] Yifu Lin (2021), pp. 106–111.

[30] *SOE Reforms 1978-2018* (n 19) p. 348.

[31] 《国务院关于在若干城市试行国有企业破产有关问题的通知》 [Notice of the State Council on Issues Relating to the Trial Bankruptcy of State-Owned Enterprises in Certain Cities]. (People's Republic of China) The State Council. 15 November 2010.

late 1990s.[32] Nonetheless, as the above explanation demonstrates, China's State economy restructuring programme in its second round of SOE reforms was not a privatisation move. Instead, it was a State-orchestrated effort to revitalise the State economy rather than shrink it, which was substantively distinct from the privatisation programmes implemented in Europe, Latin America, Asia and Africa at the time—hence a pseudo-privatisation. The program generally achieved the revitalisation goal and, in addition, promoted Chinese SOEs to concentrate on critical industries, establishing the foundation for future State economy restructuring.

2.3 'Grasp the Large and Release the Small' in the Present

Upon assuming the presidency in 2012, Xi Jinping declared that China would continue and enhance its reliance on the State economy to advance national development. Since China acceded to the WTO in 2001, the country has entered a fast lane of development.[33] The analysis in this section demonstrates that the Xi Jinping administration's government has continued the core thinking of 'Grasp the Large and Release the Small' in restructuring China's State economy in the latest round of SOE reforms, albeit with a varied policy tailored to the altered foreign and domestic situations. The ongoing restructuring program in the latest round of SOE reforms distinguishes central and local SOEs due to their industrial concentration, scale, market power and strategic mission disparities.

2.3.1 Central Level: A New Version of 'Grasp the Large and Release the Small'

The State Council has officially enumerated the objectives of the latest round of SOE reforms targeting central BGs as follows:

> To improve central BGs' capacity to support fields related to national security and to control the significant infrastructure and critical industries associated with the lifeblood of the national economy, and improve their influence and leading position in strategic emerging industries, such as biomedicine, high-end manufacturing, energy conservation, environmental protection, new materials, new energy, aerospace, etc.[34]

---

[32] *SOE Reforms 1978-2018* (n 19) p. 306.

[33] 习近平 [Xi Jinping] (2021) 《中华民族伟大复兴进入了不可逆转的历史进程》 [The Great Rejuvenation of the Chinese Nation Has Entered an Irreversible Historical Process]. Xinhua News Agency. http://www.xinhuanet.com/politics/2021-10/09/c_1127939783.htm. Accessed 11 Aug 2025.

[34] 《关于推动中央企业结构调整与重组的指导意见》 [Guiding Opinions on Promoting Structural Adjustment and Reorganization of Central Enterprises]. (People's Republic of China) The General Office of the State Council. 26 July 2016.

The Xi Jinping administration put forward two restructuring policies to achieve these objectives. Briefly, an inter-BG merger tactic comes under the scope of 'Grasp the Large', and a series of slimmed down-oriented programs come under the scope of 'Release the Small'.

2.3.1.1 Grasp the Large: Create World Champions in Critical Industries

The latest round of SOE reforms brought a merger wave to central BGs with the aspirational goal of strategically consolidating those national champions already dominating critical industries to create world champions. China has displayed persistent interest in making its SOEs 'world-class' since the 1990s.[35] In particular, in the 18th National Congress of the CCP held in 2012, which marked the commencement of the latest round of SOE reforms, the top leadership committed to making central BGs 'stronger, better, and larger and to become world-class enterprises'.[36] This objective is so thoroughly established that the Chinese Party-State has constantly reaffirmed it.[37]

To fulfil this aspirational goal, the Chinese Party-State has relied on initiating massive government-orchestrated mergers between central BGs to create corporate behemoths, wishing to catapult them into world champions in critical industries. The strategy has proved fruitful. By August of 2023, the State Council has orchestrated 20 high-profile mergers among central BGs in the latest round of SOE reforms.[38] This move has created behemoths in China's critical industries and even global industrial dominant players overnight—in 2020, China became the country hosting the most Fortune Global 500 companies, with 133 companies in total (including 7 Hong Kong enterprises and 9 from Taiwan), followed by the US hosting 121 enterprises in total.[39] Table 2.1 provides a compilation of the 20 mega mergers, including information about the merged BGs, the resulting BGs, their industries and the ranking of the resulting BGs in the Global Fortune 500 in 2023.

Both push and pull factors are responsible for the massive merger wave promoted in the latest round of SOE reforms. The primary pull factors largely stemmed from China's determination to stand out in the intensifying global competition. Since 2012, China's growth in the international order system has been accompanied by increasing competition with existing great powers, particularly the

[35] 《关于确定第一批技术创新试点城市的通知》 [Notice on Selecting the First Batch of Pilot Cities and Enterprises for Technological Innovation]. (People's Republic of China) The State Economic and Trade Commission. 25 April 1997.

[36] *SOE Reforms 1978-2018* (n 19) p. 351.

[37] 《关于推动中央企业结构调整与重组的指导意见》 [Guiding Opinions on Promoting Structural Adjustment and Reorganization of Central Enterprises]. (People's Republic of China) General Office of the State Council. 26 July 2016.

[38] The Central SASAC (2021) 《央企变更》 [Ownership Changes of Central Enterprises]. http://www.sasac.gov.cn/n2588045/n27271785/n27271802/index.html. Accessed 11 Aug 2025.

[39] Fortune (2020) Global 500. https://fortune.com/global500/2020/search/. Accessed 11 Aug 2025.

Table 2.1 The Major Planned Mergers among Central BGs in the Latest Round of SOE Reforms

Date	Industry	Merged BGs	Resulting BGs	2023 Global 500
March 2013	Audio & video press	China Hualu Group, China Record Group	China Hualu Group	N/A
July 2013	Heavy equipment manufacturing	China Sinomach Group, China Erzhong Group	China Sinomach Group	279st
March 2015	Rolling Stock manufacturing	China CSR Group, China CNR Group	China CRRC Group	434st
June 2015	Nuclear power	China Power Investment Corporation, State Nuclear Power Technology Corporation	China Power Investment Corporation	262nd
December 2015	Metals and mineral trading	China Minmetals Group, China Metallurgical Group	China Minmetals Group	65th
December 2015	Logistics and marine transportation	China Merchants Group, Sinotrans & CSC Holdings	China Merchants Group	175th
February 2016	Marine transportation	China COSCO Group, China Shipping Group	China COSCO Shipping Group	115st
July 2016	Tourism	The China National Travel Service (HK) Group, China International Travel Service Limited	China Tourism Group	N/A
July 2016	Cotton trading	China Oil and Foodstuffs Corporation, Chinatex Corporation	China Oil and Foodstuffs Corporation	87th
August 2016	Building materials	China National Building Material Corporation, China Sinoma Group	China National Building Material Corporation	247th
September 2016	Iron & steel	China Baosteel Group, Wuhan Iron and Steel Group	China Baowu Steel Group	44th
July 2017	Textile equipment	China Sinomach Group, China Hi-Tech Group	China Sinomach Group	279st
August 2017	Crafts and arts	China Poly Group, China Light Industrial Corporation, China National Arts & Crafts Group Corporation	China Poly Group	174th

(Continued)

Table 2.1 (Continued)

Date	Industry	Merged BGs	Resulting BGs	2023 Global 500
August 2017	Mining and energy	China Guodian Corporation, China Shenhua Group	China Energy Investment Group	76th
January 2018	Nuclear power	China General Nuclear Power Group, China Nuclear Engineering & Construction Group	China General Nuclear Power Group	381st
July 2019	Textile	China Poly Group, China Silk Group	China Poly Group	191st
October 2019	Shipbuilding	China State Shipbuilding Corporation, China Shipbuilding Industry Group	China State Shipbuilding Corporation	272ed
March 2021	Chemical	China National Chemical Corporation, SinoChem Group	SinoChem Group	38th
June 2021	Telecommunications equipment	China Electronics Technology Group, Potevio Group	China Electronics Technology Group	252th
January 2022	Rare earths	Aluminum Corporation of China, China Minmetals Corporation, Ganzhou Rare Earth Group, China Iron & Steel Research Institute Group, Grinm Group Corporation	China Rare Earth Group	N/A

US. Unsurprisingly, China focused on SOEs to cope with the global rivalry and further national prosperity. By orchestrating mergers among central BGs, the Chinese Party-State hopes to create a national corporate armada to compete with international rivals and seize industrial dominance in the world, or, in the government's words, serve as national 'crack troops' or 'vanguards' in the global market.[40] Regarding push forces, China has relied on inter-BG mergers to eliminate industrial overcapacity and minimise irrational competition among central BGs. China is

[40] 经济日报 [Economic Daily] (2013) 《充分发挥国企排头兵作用》 [Give Full Play to the Vanguard Role of State-Owned Enterprises]. http://paper.ce.cn/jjrb/html/2013-02/22/content_145319.htm. Accessed 11 Aug 2025.

suffering severe production overcapacity in numerous heavy industries, including iron and steel, coal and electrolytic aluminium. Some companies in these industries attempted to absorb extra production by dumping products on the global market; these efforts sparked international pressure on China for violating the WTO norms.[41] In this context, China regarded multiple BGs operating in the same industries and their irrational competition as significant causes of the overproduction. Therefore, many central BGs in the same industries were merged to eliminate excessive competition and facilitate centralised production control. The planned mergers between China's two mining giants, China Minmetals and China Metallurgical Group, in 2015 and China's two major steel producers, Baosteel Group and Wusteel Group, in 2016 were typical examples.

Here an apparent volte face in reform policy may be perceived: as noted above, the 'Grasp the Large and Release the Small' program of the 1990s featured the break-up of most national monopolies in critical industries into smaller successor entities. However, many successor entities were recombined into national monopolies in the latest round of SOE reforms. For example, China CNR Group and China CSR Group were recombined. They became the CRRC Group. China Nuclear Engineering & Construction Corporation was merged into the China National Nuclear Corporation. This does not mean that China's SOE reform roadmap has been torn apart with the transition of Chinese leadership.

On the contrary, international and domestic conditions have drastically changed in the past few decades which has driven China to restructure its State economy in different directions. It must be emphasised, however, that both the dismantling of monopolies in the past and the creation of monopolies in the present are founded in the unshakeable primacy of SOEs in China's national economy, firmly established since 1949. As the senior official in the central SASAC explained in 2016:

> Now, facing increasingly fierce global competition, China has no other option but to build up 'aircraft carrier-level enterprises' with international competitiveness through mergers among central BGs to cope with the competition with foreign giant multinational enterprises.[42]

Is there an alternative to the gigantic mergers of central BGs capable of preserving China's place in a troubled global economy? The likely answer is no. As William Kovacic pointed out, no advanced economy in the world has achieved global competitiveness, sustained economic growth and high-income status by relying on State ownership.[43] Possibly, China could depend on the limitless vitality of its private sector. However, China's basic socialist financial system ideology will not tolerate

---

[41] Holly Ellyatt and Karen Tso (2016) China has conducted a 'War'—not trade—with steel, experts say. CNBC. https://www.cnbc.com/2016/05/20/china-steel-overcapacity-war.html. Accessed 11 Aug 2025.

[42] 经济日报 [Economic Daily] (2016) 《专家学者畅谈新一轮国企改革 央企重组如何实现"1+1>2"》 [Experts and scholars talk about how to realise '1+1 > 2' in the new round of SOE reform and central enterprises reorganization]. People. http://ccnews.people.com.cn/n1/2016/0822/c141677-28653916.html. Accessed 11 Aug 2025.

[43] Kovacic (2017), p. 705.

other options until China's top leadership makes a significant socialist theoretical breakthrough, which is highly improbable in the near future.

2.3.1.2 Release the Small: Reduce the Size of Central National Business Groups

In tandem with the 'Grasp the Large' merger strategy, the restructuring program targeting central BGs in the latest round of SOE reforms also 'Releases the Small'. Here 'Release the Small' does not mean privatising central BGs. Instead, it refers to trimming undesired subsidiaries of central BGs, thereby improving the national champions' overall operational efficiency.

Chinese central BGs' chronic problem of redundant subsidiaries is derived from their organisation form. Since the outset of the SOE reforms in 1978, China has determined to organise SOEs into alliances to facilitate centralised control. After a failed try with a contract-based alliance form in 1986, the Chinese government finally nailed down the formation of the BG, a vertically integrated, multi-layered structure based on ownership relationships, for central SOEs.[44] Every BG must include a core company and at least five holding subsidiaries, while other affiliates and contractual members are optional.[45]

Along with China's tremendous economic rise, Chinese central BGs have also expanded their businesses significantly. As a result, a central BG may have a business pyramid with more than 10 tiers and more than 500 subsidiaries spreading over various industries. An excessively long chain of subsidiaries makes for governance inefficiency, as it can be practically difficult for the core company to exercise effective oversight and control along the sprawling chain. Consequently, unprofitable subsidiaries and subsidiaries whose businesses are unrelated to BG's principal businesses have substantially undermined the central BGs' overall operational efficiency.

To get rid of the undesired subsidiaries of central BGs, the Chinese Party-State has launched several specialised programs in the latest round of the SOE reforms, including the 'Dispose of Zombie Enterprises and Enterprises in Difficulties' program ('处僵治困'), 'Reduce the Leverage Ratio' program ('去杠杆'), 'Resolve the Overcapacity' program ('化解产能过剩'), 'Principal Business Management' program ('主业管理') and 'Compress and Reduce' program ('压减'). Each program targets a specific type of undesired subsidiaries of central BGs. However, the interrelationships between the programs are more intertwined in practice. Figure 2.1 depicts the objectives and interrelationships of the programs promoted

---

44 《关于进一步推动横向经济联合若干问题的规定》 [Provisions on Several Issues Concerning Further Promoting Horizontal Economic Association]. (People's Republic of China) The State Council. 23 March 1986.

45 《企业集团登记管理暂行规定》 [Interim Provisions on the Administration of Business Group Registration]. (People's Republic of China) State Administration for Industry and Commerce. 6 April 1998.

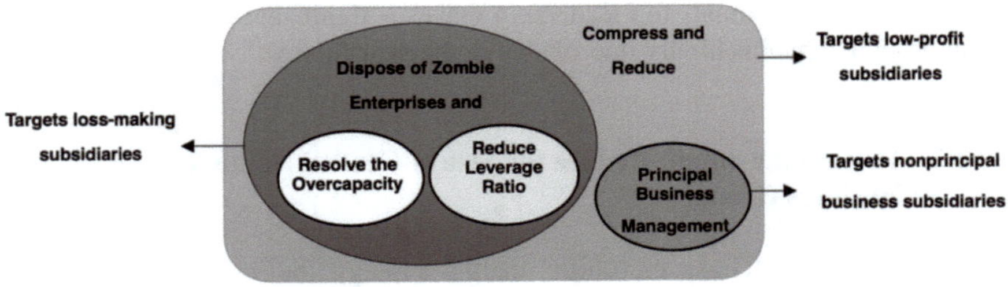

Fig. 2.1 The Incarnation of the 'Release the Small' Thinking at the Central Level in the Latest Round of SOE Reforms.

under the 'Release the Small' thinking in the central level's latest round of SOE reforms.

a. *'Dispose of Zombie Enterprises and Enterprises in Difficulties', 'Reduce the Leverage Ratio' and 'Resolve the Overcapacity' program*

In 2016, the Chinese Party-State launched the 'Dispose of Zombie Enterprises and Enterprises in Difficulties' program. Generally, the program required central BGs to revive or dispose of chronically unprofitable subsidiaries (which 'zombie enterprises and enterprises in difficulties' refers to) in three years. Under the guidance of the central SASAC, the specific disposal methods included reorganising and merging subsidiaries with growth potential, enhancing the managerial practice of those subsidiaries whose management was abysmal, and shutting down those with limited development prospects.[46]

This program was carried out in close coordination with the 'Reduce the Leverage Ratio' and the 'Resolve the Overcapacity' programs launched in the same year. The 'Reduce the Leverage Ratio' program required central BGs to reduce their debt ratios by two percentage points in three years to improve their risk-management capacity.[47] Reviving or eliminating their unprofitable subsidiaries thus became an effective means to fulfil the central mandate. Moreover, many central BGs' chronically unprofitable subsidiaries are clustered in industries with severe overcapacity. Therefore, in addition to the inter-BG merger tactic, the Chinese Party-State also launched the 'Resolve the Overcapacity' program, which requires central BGs in the relevant industries to cut their production capacity.[48] Furthermore, in the 2017 and 2018 Central Economic Work Conference, the Chinese central government explicitly required central BGs to fulfil the 'Resolve the Overcapacity' program by

[46] 《关于深化国有企业改革的指导意见》 [The Guiding Opinions on Deepening the Reform of State-Owned Enterprises]. (People's Republic of China) The CCP Central Committee and the State Council. 24 August 2015.

[47] 《关于进一步做好"僵尸企业"及去产能企业债务处置工作的通知》 [Disposing Losing-Making Zombie and Difficult Enterprises can also Help Reduce State-Owned Enterprises' Debts]. (People's Republic of China) National Development and Reform Commission. 23 November 2018.

[48] *SOE Reforms 1978-2018* (n 19) p. 330.

implementing the 'Dispose Zombie Enterprises and Enterprise in Difficulties' program.[49]

The three programs have come to an end with satisfactory results. By the end of the 'Dispose of Zombie Enterprises and Enterprises in Difficulties' program in 2019, 1954 subsidiaries of central BGs had been disposed of. In 2020, the central SASAC pronounced that central BGs cut off 16.44 million tons of steel and 119 million tons of coal production capacity in the 'Resolve the Overcapacity' program.[50] As the result of the 'Reduce the Leverage Ratio' program, the central SASAC announced in 2021 that central BGs had reduced their overall leverage ratio by more than two percentage points in 2020.[51]

b. *'Principal Business Management' Program*

In addition to the programs levelled at unprofitable subsidiaries of central BGs, the Chinese Party-State also put forward a 'Principal Business Management' program to specifically target central BGs' subsidiaries engaged in business activities that had little relevance to the principal businesses of the groups.[52] As required by Xi Jinping, 'it is the duty of an enterprise to devote itself to principal businesses'.[53] every central BG has a few specific principal businesses designated by the central SASAC, usually in critical industries.[54] However, central BGs tend to engage in lucrative businesses in non-critical industries, notably real estate. These sprawling business scopes exacerbated central BGs' operational inefficiency and made for SOEs' entrenchment in China's non-critical industries. Therefore, the 'Principal Business Management' program mandates central BGs to concentrate more on their principal businesses and divest subsidiaries engaged in non-principal businesses. Central BGs have two approaches for implementing the mandate: business

[49] Xinhua News Agency (2017) 《中央经济工作会议在北京举行》 [Central Economic Work Conference was Held in Beijing]. The State Council. http://www.gov.cn/xinwen/2017-12/20/content_5248899.htm. Accessed 11 Aug 2025; Xinhua News Agency (2018) 《中央经济工作会议举行，习近平李克强作重要讲话》 [Xi Jinping and Li Keqiang Make Important Speeches at Central Economic Work Conference]. The State Council. https://www.gov.cn/xinwen/2018-12/21/content_5350934.htm. Accessed 11 Aug 2025.

[50] 李婕 [Li Jie] (2021) 《去产能任务提前完成》 [Central Enterprises Completed the Task of Cutting Overcapacity Ahead of Schedule]. People. http://ccnews.people.com.cn/n1/2021/0104/c141677-31987782.html. Accessed 11 Aug 2025.

[51] The State Council. (2021) 《2020年末央企平均资产负债率为64.5% 降杠杆目标如期完成》 [At the End of 2020, the Average Asset-Liability Ratio of Central Enterprises is 64.5%, and the Target of Reducing Leverage has been Met on Time]. https://www.gov.cn/xinwen/2021-01/19/content_5581045.htm. Accessed 11 Aug 2025.

[52] *SOE Reforms 1978-2018* (n 19) p. 326.

[53] Xinhua News Agency. (2019) 《习近平:做实体经济要实实在在、心无旁骛做主业》 [Xi Jinping: It is the Duty of an Enterprise to Devote Itself to One Principal Business]. http://www.xinhuanet.com/politics/2019-03/10/c_1124215846.htm. Accessed 11 Aug 2025.

[54] Principal businesses of Central BGs as designated by the central SASAC are updated at: The Central SASAC (2018) 《央企主业》 [Principal Businesses of Central Enterprises]. http://www.sasac.gov.cn/n2588035/n2641579/n2641665/index.html. Accessed 11 Aug 2025.

integration and business transfer.[55] Both approaches are subject to the central SASAC's substantial involvement.

By doing so, the Chinese government can promote central BGs to concentrate on their principal businesses and, in addition, avoid 'unnecessary' competition between central BGs. In the case where several central BGs operate overlapping non-principal businesses, the central SASAC would adopt the business integration strategy of stripping the overlapping businesses from each of them and consolidating the stripped business assets into a single company which then usually becomes the standard service or good provider to the central BGs. For example, in 2014, the central SASAC stripped China Mobile, China Unicom and China Telecom of their overlapping communication tower construction businesses outside their common principal business—telecommunication services. The stripped assets were then integrated into China Tower Company, a newly formed company. As a result, all three telecom giants hold significant stakes in China Tower Company and share the communication tower-related services it provides.[56]

Business transfer means that at the central SASAC's behest, a central BG transfers its non-principal business to another central BG specialising in the specific business, with or without compensation. Under the government's directive, in 2016, China's State-owned aerospace corporation Aviation Industry Corporation of China, sold its nearly 100 real estate subsidiaries to China Poly Group, a central BG principally engaging in real estate.[57] In 2017, China Poly Group also transferred its Poly Energy Company and its 25 subsidiaries in the energy sector to China Coal Group. The transferred assets were worth USD 4.1 billion.[58]

Chinese central BGs may also dispose of their non-principal business subsidiaries through privatisation. For example, in 2017, China Oil and Foodstuffs Corporation sold the controlling stakes of its 63 subsidiaries operating packaging and meat business to POEs, thereby considerably enhancing its concentration on its principal business.[59] However, privatisation is not an officially favoured approach in the 'Principal Business Management' program, unlike business integration and transfer. This may be due to the potential risk of loss of State-owned assets that

[55] *SOE Reforms 1978-2018* (n 19) p. 338.

[56] Xinhua News Agency. (2015) 《中国铁塔公司收购三大运营商存量铁塔资产》 [China Tower Corporation Acquires Existing Iron Tower Assets of Three Major Operators]. http://www.xinhuanet.com/politics/2015-10/15/c_128319016.htm. Accessed 11 Aug 2025.

[57] China Poly Group Corporation (2016) 《中航工业地产业务全部划入保利集团》 [AVIC Real Estate Business is All Transferred to Poly Group]. https://www.poly.com.cn/s/1965-6728-22030.html. Accessed 11 Aug 2025.

[58] China Poly Group Corporation (2017) 《致保利能源公司全体人员的公开信》 [An Open Letter to All Personnel of Poly Energy]. https://www.poly.com.cn/s/2001-6779-20759.html. Accessed 11 Aug 2025.

[59] *SOE Reforms 1978-2018* (n 19) p. 327.

privatisation may entail and the potential agitation among the employees of privatised subsidiaries who would be deprived of 'cradle-to-grave' careers in SOEs.[60]

c. *'Compress and Reduce' Program*

Both the 'Dispose of Zombie Enterprises and Enterprises in Difficulties' program, as well as its synergic programs discussed above, and the 'Principal Business Management' program were implemented by central BGs as ways to fulfil another grander three-year special task assigned by the Chinese Party-State in 2016—the 'Compress and Reduce' program. As a catch-all program in the latest round of SOE reforms, it was levelled at the issue of central BGs' overstretched multilayer ownership structures. In general, it required central BGs to compress their ownership pyramids and reduce the number of their subsidiaries.

While central BGs' unprofitable subsidiaries and subsidiaries operating non-principal businesses had been addressed by specialised reform programs, central BGs' low-profit subsidiaries were captured by the 'Compress and Reduce' program. To implement this program, the China Merchants Group disposed of 110 low-profit enterprises whose total profit was less than CNY 1 million. The China Railway Engineering Group reduced the number of its subsidiaries by promoting mergers among its comprehensive engineering subsidiaries that failed to meet certain annual profit thresholds (different thresholds applied to different types of subsidiaries). The China State Construction Engineering Group used the net profit rate and net return on assets to identify low-profit subsidiaries and dispose of them through restructuring or privatisation.[61] As of May 2019, when the 'Compress the Reduce' program ended, central BGs had reduced the number of their subsidiaries by 25.9 percent, 14,023 in total. 95 percent of central BGs had managed to compress their ownership pyramid to fewer than 10 layers.[62]

By the end of 2021, all the slim-down-oriented reform programs discussed above, except the 'Principal Business Management' program, will have ended. According to the official statistics released by the NBS, the overall size of China's State economy at the central level has been significantly reduced, and there was a noticeable improvement in the financial performance of central BGs from 2012 to 2021. Specifically, the number of central BGs decreased from 116 in 2012 to 96 in 2021,[63] the total revenue of central BGs increased from USD 3.55 trillion in 2012 to USD 5.72 trillion in 2021, the total net profits increased from USD 205.1 billion in

---

[60] China Economic Review (2014) Chinese Graduates Prefer to Work for SOEs and that Could be Bad for the Economy. https://chinaeconomicreview.com/chinese-graudates-prefer-working-soes-bad-for-economy/. Accessed 11 Aug 2025.

[61] *SOE Reforms 1978-2018* (n 19) p. 326.

[62] 杜雨萌 [Du Yumeng] (2019) 《央企提前超额完成三年压减20%任务》 [Central Enterprises Overfulfilled the Target of 20% Reduction in Three Years]. People. http://ccnews.people.com.cn/n1/2019/0705/c141677-31215561.html. Accessed 11 Aug 2025.

[63] In 2025, the number of central BGs increased to 100. The list of central BGs can be accessed at http://wap.sasac.gov.cn/n2588045/n27271785/n27271792/c14159097/content.html. Accessed 11 Aug 2025.

2012 to USD 283.9 billion in 2021. The average rate of profit successively rose from 3.4 percent in 2012 to 6.8 percent in 2021.[64] Therefore, it is fair to say that a more robust Chinese State economy is indeed being forged in the latest round of SOE reforms.

2.3.2 Local Level: 'Release the Small' in Non-critical Industries

The *SOE Reforms 2020–2022 Three-Year Action Plan* issued by the central SASAC did not indicate that the government intended to cultivate national champions at the local level in the same interventionist manner as it did at the central level, as the merger wave has not spread to local SOEs.[65] The reason may be that after decades of SOE reforms, central BGs have expanded their dominance in critical industries and become extremely powerful and profitable. In addition, due to the inherent proximity to the central government, central BGs had an advantage over their local competitors regarding preferential treatment, corporate size and market power. Hence, developing central SOEs, as opposed to local SOEs, into a national elite force appears to be the most effective method for China to defend and advance the national economy and security against global competition.

As discussed, since the launch of the 'Open Door' Policy in 1978, the Chinese Party-State has insisted on the dichotomous landscape of the State economy, preserving critical industries for State-sanctioned SOE monopolies while seeking to foster robust and equitable competition among all forms of ownership in its non-critical industries where most Chinese local SOEs cluster. Consistent with this stance, in the latest round of SOE reforms, the Chinese government has clarified that SOEs, primarily local SOEs, should progressively withdraw from non-critical industries.[66]

However, China's SOE reforms are promoted from the top down, which inevitably leads to a lack of motivation for reform at lower levels or from the bottom up. This is evident from the dilatory implementation of the reform policies by local governments and the resistance of local SOE incumbents to reform.[67] This explains the continued presence, but not necessarily dominance, of SOEs in almost all non-

[64] NBS (2020) National Data. https://data.stats.gov.cn/easyquery.htm?cn=C01. Accessed 11 Aug 2025.

[65] The Central SASAC (2020) 《国企改革三年行动》 [SOE Reform 2020-2022 Three-Year Action Plan]. http://www.sasac.gov.cn/n4470048/n13461446/n15390485/index.html. Accessed 11 Aug 2025.

[66] 余晖, 周耀东 [Yu Hui, Zhou Yaodong] (2016) 《国有垄断企业问题研究: 文献回顾及政策建议》 [Research on State-Owned Monopolies: Literature Review and Policy Recommendations]. Brookings. pp. 32–35. https://www.brookings.edu/wp-content/uploads/2016/06/Chinese-State-Owned-Enterprises.pdf. Accessed 11 Aug 2025.

[67] Zhao and Zhang (2015), pp. 143–157, p. 144.

critical industries in China, even after decades of SOE reforms. According to the NBS, as of 2022, SOEs were still present in virtually all industrial sectors in China.[68] This continued entrenchment of local SOEs can also be ascribed to the regional protectionism exercised by local governments under the pressure of boosting local economic growth. After three rounds of SOE reforms, the presence of SOEs in China's non-critical industries has, however, decreased significantly. For example, in 1997, SOEs held 69.4 percent of companies in the food industry on an assets value basis, but only 13.3 percent in 2017. Similar trends can be observed in the rubber and plastic industry and the textile industry.[69] Currently, Chinese POEs exhibit extraordinary innovation capacity and growth potential. In addition, Chinese local governments have begun fostering POEs in the region to promote the regional economy. As a result, the gradual withdrawal of State ownership from non-critical industries will likely accelerate.

2.4 Concluding Remarks: The Potential Implications on Chinese SOEs' Outbound FDI

Through an examination of the reform designs and implementation of China's State economy restructuring programs promoted in the latest round of SOE reforms, as well as a historical analysis of the 'Grasp the Large and Release the Small' program in the second round of SOE reforms, this chapter answers the research questions as follows:

First, the objective of the Xi Jinping administration concerning China's State economy is to foster a group of national champions with global competitiveness in critical industries while encouraging State ownership to withdraw gradually from non-critical industries through free competition with non-State firms. Second, the State economy restructuring programs are consistent with the preceding launched in the second round of SOE reforms restructuring program in the mid-1990s in terms of the general reform thinking, namely 'Grasp the Large and Release the Small', despite the significantly different strategies shaped by the specific circumstances of the different times. Third, in both the past and present State economy restructuring programs, the Chinese Part-State has insisted on the partial marketisation of the State economy, preserving critical industries for SOEs monopolies while deregulating market competition in non-critical industries. Last but not least, even featuring a controversially extensive State economy, China has never initiated genuine privatisation to weaken its SOEs, neither in the 1990s nor in the present when China has achieved a remarkable rise. This firm stance stems from the primacy of SOEs in China's national economy, firmly established in China's socialist ideology,

---

[68] NBS (2015) Statistical Yearbook 2022. China Statistics Press.

[69] NBS (2020) National Data. https://data.stats.gov.cn/easyquery.htm?cn=C01. Accessed 11 Aug 2025.

Constitution and national value system. The importance has also been corroborated by the valuable role played by SOEs as the significant implementers of government directives and national policies in support of China's social stability and strategic development.

Based on the analyses of this chapter, it is reasonable to expect that the State-economy restructuring reforms would have a significant effect on Chinese SOEs' outbound FDI activities. Despite the worsening geopolitical tensions and the global economic fallout associated with the COVID-19 pandemic outbreak at the end of 2019, China's efforts to reform its State economy following the 'Grasp the Large and Release the Small' through multiple programs promoted in tandem towards central and local SOEs not only improve the overall efficiency of China's State economy but also significantly facilitate Beijing's centralised support, monitoring and control over a handful of central BG monopolies in critical industries. Globally, the newly created State-owned behemoths could considerably benefit from their advantages of scale and, more importantly, State support in their international investment activities, despite political constraints.

Early in 2014, Nolan correctly pointed out that China was attempting to create State-owned national champions in key strategic sectors and fostering them to become globally competitive through State support, technocratic management and external competition.[70] Milhaupt and Zheng also pointed out that all large Chinese SOEs had close ties to State power and benefited from receiving state-generated rents.[71] China's ongoing State economy restructuring efforts undoubtedly highlight the likelihood that its government-backed SOE's engagement in international business expansions could distort global market competition. In addition, as the Xi Jinping administration has launched a series of assertive foreign policies, such as the *Belt-and-Road Initiative* and *Made in China 2025*,[72] there may be rising scepticism that Chinese major SOEs' outbound FDI activities serve purely commercial goals as opposed to policy objectives. The resulting mistrust concerning Chinese SOEs among the rest of the world, particularly in developed economies, may hinder the legitimate overseas expansion of Chinese SOEs through, for instance, the enhanced FDI screening mechanisms that most developed countries have adopted.[73]

[70] Nolan (2014), pp. 747–764.

[71] Milhaupt and Zheng (2015).

[72] Geoff Wade (2016) China's 'One Belt, One Road' Initiative. Parliament of Australia. https://www.aph.gov.au/about_parliament/parliamentary_departments/parliamentary_library/pubs/briefingbook45p/chinasroad. Accessed 11 Aug 2025; 《中国制造2025》 [Made in China 2025]. (People's Republic of China) The State Council. 19 May 2015.

[73] OECD (2023) Investment Policy Developments in 61 Economies between 16 October 2021 and 15 March 2023. https://www.oecd.org/daf/inv/investment-policy/Investment-policy-monitoring-April-2023.pdf. Accessed 11 Aug 2025.

References

Boycko M, Shleifer A, Vishny RW (1994) Voucher privatization. J Financ Econ 35(2) 249–266. p 254

China Economic Review (2014) Chinese graduates prefer to work for SOEs and that could be bad for the economy. https://chinaeconomicreview.com/chinese-graudates-prefer-working-soes-bad-for-economy/. Accessed 11 Aug 2025

China Poly Group Corporation (2016) 《中航工业地产业务全部划入保利集团》 [AVIC Real Estate Business is All Transferred to Poly Group]. https://www.poly.com.cn/s/1965-5728-22030.html. Accessed 11 Aug 2025

Du Yanfei [杜燕飞] (2021) 《国资委要求央企加大能源保供力度》 [The Central SASAC requires central enterprises to strengthen energy supply]. People. http://finance.people.com.cn/n1/2021/1004/c1004-32245570.html. Accessed 11 Aug 2025

Du Yumeng [杜雨萌] (2019) 《央企提前超额完成三年压减20%任务》 [Central Enterprises Overfulfilled the Target of 20% Reduction in Three Years]. People. http://ccnews.people.com.cn/n1/2019/0705/c141677-31215561.html. Accessed 11 Aug 2025

Economic Daily [经济日报] (2013) 《充分发挥国企排头兵作用》 [Give Full Play to the Vanguard Role of State-Owned Enterprises]. http://paper.ce.cn/jjrb/html/2013-02/22/content_145319.htm. Accessed 11 Aug 2025

Economic Daily [经济日报] (2016) 《专家学者畅谈新一轮国企改革 央企重组如何实现"1+1>2"》 [Experts and scholars talk about how to realise '1+1 > 2' in the new round of SOE reform and central enterprises reorganization]. People. http://ccnews.people.com.cn/n1/2016/0822/c141677-28653916.html. Accessed 11 Aug 2025

Ellyatt H, Tso K (2016) China has conducted a 'War'—not trade—with steel, experts say. CNBC. https://www.cnbc.com/2016/05/20/china-steel-overcapacity-war.html. Accessed 11 Aug 2025; http://wap.sasac.gov.cn/n2588045/n27271785/n27271792/c14159097/content.html. Accessed 11 Aug 2025

Fortune (2020) Global 500. https://fortune.com/global500/2020/search/. Accessed 11 Aug 2025

Gallagher ME (2015) The Social Relations of Chinese State Capitalism. In: Liebman BL, Milhaupt CJ (eds) Regulating the visible hand? The institutional implications of Chinese state capitalism. Oxford University Press

Geoff Wade (2016) China's 'One Belt, One Road' Initiative. Parliament of Australia. https://www.aph.gov.au/about_parliament/parliamentary_departments/parliamentary_library/pubs/briefingbook45p/chinasroad. Accessed 11 Aug 2025; 《中国制造2025》 [Made in China 2025]. (People's Republic of China) The State Council. 19 May 2015

Jiang Zemin 江泽民 (1997) 《中国共产党第十五次全国代表大会上的报告》 [Report of the 15th National Congress of the CCP]. Speech. 15th CCP National Congress

Jiang Zemin 江泽民 (2002) 《中国共产党第十六次全国代表大会上的报告》 [Report of the 16th National Congress of the CCP]. Speech. 16th National Congress of the CCP

Kovacic WE (2017) Competition policy and state-owned enterprises in China. World Trade Rev 16(4) 693–711, p 695

Li Jie [李婕] (2021) 《去产能任务提前完成》 [Central Enterprises Completed the Task of Cutting Overcapacity Ahead of Schedule]. People. http://ccnews.people.com.cn/n1/2021/0104/c141677-31987782.html. Accessed 11 Aug 2025

Lin JY (2021) State-Owned enterprise reform in China: the new structural economics perspective. Struct Change Econ Dyn 58:106–111

Milhaupt CJ, Zheng W (2015) Beyond ownership: state capitalism and the Chinese firm. Georgetown Law J 103(3):665–722

Naughton B (2017) The current wave of state enterprise reform in China: a preliminary appraisal. Asian Econ Policy Rev 12(2):282–298

NBS (2015) Statistical Yearbook 2022. China Statistics Press

NBS (2020) National Data. https://data.stats.gov.cn/easyquery.htm?cn=C01. Accessed 11 Aug 2025

Nolan P (2014) Globalisation and industrial policy: the case of China. World Econ 37(6):747–764
OECD (2011) China's Emergence as a Market Economy: Achievements and Challenges. p 14. https://www.oecd.org/china/2011-03-ChinaBrochureEN.pdf. Accessed 11 Aug 2025
OECD (2023) Investment Policy Developments in 61 Economies between 16 October 2021 and 15 March 2023. https://www.oecd.org/daf/inv/investment-policy/Investment-policy-monitoring-April-2023.pdf. Accessed 11 Aug 2025
The Central SASAC (2018a) 《央企主业》 [Principal Businesses of Central Enterprises]. http://www.sasac.gov.cn/n2588035/n2641579/n2641665/index.html. Accessed 11 Aug 2025
The Central SASAC (2018b) 《国有企业作用不可替代》 [The Role of State-Owned Enterprises is Irreplaceable]. The Central SASAC. http://www.sasac.gov.cn/n2588025/n2588139/c9875479/content.html. Accessed 11 Aug 2025
The Central SASAC (2020) 《国企改革三年行动》 [SOE Reform 2020-2022 Three-Year Action Plan]. http://www.sasac.gov.cn/n4470048/n13461446/n15390485/index.html. Accessed 11 Aug 2025
The Central SASAC (2021) 《央企变更》 [Ownership Changes of Central Enterprises]. http://www.sasac.gov.cn/n2588045/n27271785/n27271802/index.html. Accessed 11 Aug 2025
The State Council (2020) 《国有企业分类有序复工复产》 [SOEs resume work and production in an orderly and categorised manner]. The State Council. https://www.gov.cn/xinwen/2020-02/16/content_5479683.htm. Accessed 11 Aug 2025
The World Bank and Development Research Centre of the State Council (2013) China 2030: building a modern, harmonious, and creative society. World Bank, p 4. https://www.worldbank.org/content/dam/Worldbank/document/China-2030-complete.pdf. Accessed 11 Aug 2025
Wu M (2016) The "China, Inc." challenge to global trade governance. Harv Int Law J 57(2) 261–324, p 272
Xi Jinping [习近平] (2002) 《在中央全面深化改革委员会第十四次会议上的讲话》 [Speech at the 14th Meeting of the Central Committee for Comprehensively Deepening Reform]. Speech. 14th Meeting of the Central Committee for Comprehensively Deepening Reform
Xi Jinping [习近平] (2021) 《中华民族伟大复兴进入了不可逆转的历史进程》 [The Great Rejuvenation of the Chinese Nation Has Entered an Irreversible Historical Process]. Xinhua News Agency. http://www.xinhuanet.com/politics/2021-10/09/c_1127939783.htm. Accessed 11 Aug 2025
Xinhua News Agency (2017) 《中央经济工作会议在北京举行》 [Central Economic Work Conference was Held in Beijing]. The State Council. http://www.gov.cn/xinwen/2017-12/20/content_5248899.htm. Accessed 11 Aug 2025
Xinhua News Agency (2018) 《中央经济工作会议举行，习近平李克强作重要讲话》 [Xi Jinping and Li Keqiang Make Important Speeches at Central Economic Work Conference]. The State Council. <https://www.gov.cn/xinwen/2018-12/21/content_5350934.htm. Accessed 11 Aug 2025
Yu Hui, Zhou Yaodong [余晖, 周耀东] (2016) 《国有垄断企业问题研究: 文献回顾及政策建议》 [Research on State-Owned Monopolies: Literature Review and Policy Recommendations]. Brookings. pp 32–35. https://www.brookings.edu/wp-content/uploads/2016/06/Chinese-State-Owned-Enterprises.pdf. Accessed 11 Aug 2025
Zhao C, Zhang Y (2015) Several major issues on deepening state-owned enterprises reform. China Econ J 8(2):143–157. 144

Additional Sources

《中国共产党第十九届中央委员会第六次全体会议公报》 [Communique of the Sixth Plenary Session of the 19th Central Committee of the CCP]. (People’s Republic of China) CCP Central Committee. 11 November 2021

《中华人民共和国宪法》 [Constitution of the People’s Republic of China]. (People’s Republic of China) Adopted at the 1st Session of the 13th National People’s Congress. 11 March 2018. Art 6, 7

《关于进一步做好“僵尸企业”及去产能企业债务处置工作的通知》 [Disposing Losing-Making Zombie and Difficult Enterprises can also Help Reduce State-Owned Enterprises’ Debts]. (People’s Republic of China) National Development and Reform Commission. 23 November 2018

《2021年财政收支情况》 [Fiscal Revenue and Expenditure of 2021]. (People’s Republic of China) MOF. 29 January 2022

《关于推动中央企业结构调整与重组的指导意见》 [Guiding Opinions on Promoting Structural Adjustment and Reorganization of Central Enterprises]. (People’s Republic of China) The General Office of the State Council. 26 July 2016

《关于推进国有资本调整和国有企业重组的指导意见》 [Guiding Opinions on Promoting the Adjustment of State-Owned Capital and the Reorganization of State-Owned Enterprises] (People’s Republic of China) The Central SASAC. 5 December 2006

《企业集团登记管理暂行规定》 [Interim Provisions on the Administration of Business Group Registration]. (People’s Republic of China) State Administration for Industry and Commerce. 6 April 1998

《关于确定第一批技术创新试点城市的通知》 [Notice on Selecting the First Batch of Pilot Cities and Enterprises for Technological Innovation]. (People’s Republic of China) The State Economic and Trade Commission. 25 April 1997

《国务院关于在若干城市试行国有企业破产有关问题的通知》 [Notice of the State Council on Issues Relating to the Trial Bankruptcy of State-Owned Enterprises in Certain Cities]. (People’s Republic of China) The State Council. 15 November 2010

《关于进一步推动横向经济联合若干问题的规定》 [Provisions on Several Issues Concerning Further Promoting Horizontal Economic Association]. (People’s Republic of China) The State Council. 23 March 1986

《国务院关于同意组建中国联合通信有限公司的批复》 [Reply of the State Council on Approval of the Establishment of China United Communications Co, LTD]. (People’s Republic of China) The State Council. 14 December 1993

国企改革历程编写组 [SOE Reform Process Writing Group] (2019) 《国企改革历程 1978-2018》 [The Course of Chinese State-Owned Enterprise Reform 1978-2018]. 中国经济出版社 [Economic Press China]. p 21 - 24

《关于深化国有企业改革的指导意见》 [The Guiding Opinions on Deepening the Reform of State-Owned Enterprises]. (People’s Republic of China) The CCP Central Committee and the State Council. 24 August 2015

Chapter 3
China's Mixed Ownership Reform: An Expanding SOE Equity Network

Abstract China's latest round of SOE reforms introduced a mixed ownership reform (MOR) agenda aimed at improving efficiency, enhancing governance, and leveraging market capital without relinquishing Party-State control. This chapter examines how MOR has been implemented within the group-based structure of central SOEs, asking how equity diversification interacts with hierarchical governance in shaping the legal identity and accountability of outbound investment entities. The chapter distinguishes between two MOR pathways: 'flow-in' reform, where private capital is introduced into existing SOEs, and 'flow-out' reform, where SOEs invest in new mixed-ownership entities. It finds that both pathways have led to capital diversification at the subsidiary level while preserving centralised control through intra-group governance rules, capital layering, and Party leadership mechanisms. The reforms reconfigure formal ownership without displacing the parent company's strategic authority or the institutional role of the Party-State. These findings challenge assumptions that MOR signals privatisation or diminished State control. By analysing how capital reform is structurally embedded within vertically integrated SOE groups, the chapter reveals the functional coherence of China's State capital governance model. This insight is critical for evaluating control attribution, beneficial ownership, and regulatory responses to Chinese SOE investment in host jurisdictions.

China's latest round of SOE reforms brings a mixed ownership reform (MOR) concurrently with the State economy restructuring reform. Officially recognised by the Chinese government and the CCP as the 'breakthrough point' of the latest round of SOE reforms in 2016,[1] the MOR centres around promoting the mixture of State and private ownership in enterprises. The reform may, therefore, give rise to the plausible assumption that China is fostering a mixed-ownership economy that is less subject to Party-State control.

[1] 1 People's Daily (2016) 《更好发挥改革牵引作用》 [Give Better Play to the Leading Role of the Reform]. The Stat Council. https://www.gov.cn/xinwen/2016-12/20/content_5150293.htm. Accessed 13 Aug 2025.

T. Gu, *Chinese SOE Reforms and Global FDI*, Contemporary Chinese Civil and Commercial Law, https://doi.org/10.1007/978-981-92-3181-2_3

A mixed ownership economy had emerged in the country since the 1990s when China implemented the 'Grasp the Large and Release the Small' State economy restructuring program as part of the second round of SOE reforms.[2] Intending to revive China's State economy at the time, the programme resulted in many Chinese SOEs being partially privatised into mixed-ownership enterprises (MOEs). Haier, TCL and Lenovo are representative MOEs created in the program.[3]

In the latest round of SOE reforms, the primary goal of the MOR has been settled as to 'improve the vitality, controlling force, influence and anti-risk capacity of State economy', according to the *Opinions of the State Council on the Development of Mixed Ownership Economy by State-owned Enterprises* (*MOR Opinions*), the framework document issued by the Chinese government in 2015.[4] Despite its vagueness, the goal aligns well with the State economy restructuring reform identified in Chap. 2, which is to enhance the overall strength of the Chinese State economy. Notably, the *MOR Opinions* explicitly state that the implementation of the MOR is based on government directives, as opposed to being autonomously carried out by SOEs or relevant enterprises.[5] These statements suggest that the objective of the MOR is not simply to reduce State ownership in Chinese SOEs to enhance their market orientation and lower political interference.

Experience from other economies demonstrates that mixed ownership does not inherently diminish State control. In Singapore, for example, Temasek Holdings retains controlling stakes in major listed firms, combining commercial discipline with strategic State objectives.[6] Similarly, post-socialist economies in Central and Eastern Europe that pursued partial privatisation in the 1990s often preserved 'golden shares' or special rights, enabling governments to retain decisive influence despite private capital participation.[7] Without strong legal protections for minority shareholders and clear limits on State intervention, mixed-ownership arrangements can consolidate rather than dilute political control—mobilising private resources to serve State industrial policy. These precedents suggest that China's MOR, as presently structured, faces inherent governance risks and is predisposed toward policy-driven rather than market-driven outcomes.

So, what are the specific objectives of the MOR in China's latest round of SOE reforms, if not the liberalisation of SOEs? How does the MOR accomplish those objectives? What are the implications of the reform for China's private sectors? To answer the questions, this chapter is organised as follows: Section 3.1 provides a comprehensive analysis of the policy mix of the MOR. It examines the practical

[2] 国企改革历程编写组 [SOE Reform Process Writing Group] (2019) 《国企改革历程 1978-2018》 [The Course of Chinese State-Owned Enterprise Reform 1978-2018]. 中国经济出版社 [Economic Press China], p 374 ('*SOE Reforms 1978-2018*').

[3] Ibid 348.

[4] 《关于国有企业发展混合所有制经济的意见》 [Opinions on the Development of Mixed Ownership Economy by State-Owned Enterprises]. (People's Republic of China) The State Council. 24 September 2015 ('*MOR Opinions*').

[5] 'Being guided by government' was settled as one of the general principles of MOR. Ibid.

[6] See generally, Chen (2016), pp. 303–370, p 368.

[7] Kikeri et al. (1992), pp. 49–52.

implementation of the MOR, specifically highlighting the significant challenges that have arisen during its rollout regarding the classification of SOEs. Section 3.2 demonstrates that the MOR is not about mixing the State and private sectors to foster a hybrid economy that is more free-market oriented. Quite to the contrary, the primary objective of the reform is to integrate Chinese POEs with significant competitive advantages into SOE equity networks, thereby enabling Chinese SOEs to access desired firm resources from the private sectors to bolster the overall competitiveness of the Chinese State economy. Section 3.3 concludes with remarks on the potential implications of MOR on Chinese SOE outbound FDI activities.

3.1 Classification of SOEs in the Mixed Ownership Reform

As a significant component of the latest round of SOE reforms, the MOR entails the reduction of State ownership in certain SOEs. The State ownership reduction is being implemented based on a nationwide classification of Chinese SOEs. The category of an SOE determines the level to which its State ownership could be reduced. The classification of SOEs can indicate the true nature of a Chinese SOE, indicating the extent to which it is subject to political influence and its specific role in supporting the national economy. Nevertheless, as the essential foundation for the MOR, SOE classifications in China have encountered practical challenges that may impede the MOR's implementation.

3.1.1 Drawing a Dividing Line Between Policy-Driven and Market-Oriented SOEs?

In 2015, the central SASAC settled a two-step classification for SOEs as the basis for the MOR in the framework document for an SOE classification, namely the *Guiding Opinions on the Definition and Classification of Functions of State-owned Enterprises* (*Classification Guiding Opinions*).[8] Figure 3.1 depicts the classification rules. Notably, the rules directly apply to central SOEs under the supervision of the central SASAC while serving as a guide for local SASACs to develop their own classification rules.

As shown in Fig. 3.1, Chinese SOEs are, as the first step, classified into 'Public Welfare SOEs' or 'Commercial SOEs' depending on their roles in the State's economic growth and social development.[9] Briefly, 'Public Welfare' SOEs cover those whose primary purpose is to provide public utilities to guarantee public welfare and

[8] 《关于国有企业功能界定与分类的指导意见》 [Guiding Opinions on the Definition and Classification of Functions of State-Owned Enterprises]. (People's Republic of China) The State Council. 29 December 2015 ('*Classification Guiding Opinions*').

[9] Ibid.

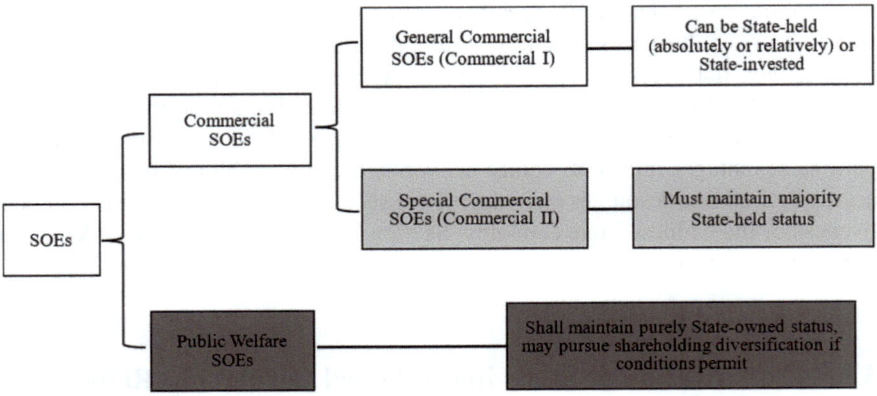

Fig. 3.1 SOE Classifications in the Mixed Ownership Reform

ensure the stability of society. Assuming such significant policy responsibilities, SOEs falling under this category shall maintain pure State-ownership but may introduce non-state shareholders' if conditions permit' (the term usually means it only happens when specially approved by the Chinese government). Then, as the second step, 'Commercial' SOEs are sub-categorised as 'General Commercial' and 'Special Commercial' (also known as 'Commercial I' and 'Commercial II'). The former covers those SOEs whose principal businesses are in critical industries or undertake major particular tasks.[10] The latter covers those SOEs whose principal businesses are in non-critical industries. According to the *Classification Guiding Opinions*, SOEs classified as 'Special Commercial' shall maintain a majority State-holding status while being encouraged to introduce non-State investors as minority shareholders. 'General Commercial' SOEs are allowed to reduce the proportion of State ownership to a minority level.

The *Classification Guiding Opinions* stated that SOEs classified as 'Commercial' should 'engage in commercial operations in accordance with market requirements, and independently carry out production and business activities according to the law.'[11] Nevertheless, the official criteria for annual performance evaluations by the SASACs for different categories of SOEs outlined in the document imply an apparent distinction between 'Special Commercial' and 'General Commercial' SOEs.

In China, the SASACs evaluate the performance of SOEs under their supervision annually. The evaluation outcome is related to the amount of State-owned capital allocated to the SOE for its next-year operations and affects the political careers of

[10] The phrase 'enterprises mainly responsible for major special tasks' was interpreted by a research group of Chinese Academy of Social Sciences (CASS) as SOEs with the functions of improving people's standard of living and ensuring urban security. 中国社会科学院工业经济研究所课题组 [Research Group of Institute of Industrial Economics of CASS] (2014), p. 24.

[11] *Classification Guiding Opinions* (n 8).

the SOE's executives.[12] According to the *Classification Guiding Opinions*, a 'General Commercial' SOE's performance will be evaluated against general business indicators, including profitability and market competitiveness. 'Special Commercial' SOEs, on the other hand, are to be evaluated on how well they carry out a wide variety of policy tasks, such as safeguarding national security, maintaining the stability of the national economy and promoting the development of China's 'forward-looking strategic industries' (typically, high-tech sectors).[13] In particular, the document emphasises the priority of these policy tasks over business indicators in SASAC evaluations.[14] Assigning a wide variety of policy missions to 'Special Commercial' SOEs, which are primarily SOEs in critical industries, is consistent with the objective of the State economy restructuring reform in the latest round of SOE reforms, which is to consolidate political control over SOE-dominated critical industries.

Therefore, it is reasonable to conclude that SOEs classified as 'Public Welfare' or 'Special Commercial' in the MOR are government instruments whose primary purpose is to serve policy objectives rather than generate profits, irrespective of how much they reduce their State ownership in the reforms. Theoretically, only 'General Commercial' SOEs could be expected to evolve into independent market players behaving in a manner primarily based on commercial considerations.

As the reform advances, the classification of SOEs in the MOR may make distinguishing between future market-oriented SOEs and policy-driven SOEs in China easier. However, the classification has encountered practical challenges that may prevent a clear dividing line from appearing.

3.1.2 SOE Classifications in Practice: Incompleteness and Opaqueness

Despite the ostensibly clear SOE classification rules established by the central SASAC, local implementation of SOE classification may encounter practical difficulties. Some scholars have argued that the inconsistent region-specific classification rules developed by Chinese local SASACs would lead to fragmented classifications in practice.[15] The following analysis demonstrates, however, that the Chinese SOE classification chaos in practice is not due to the inconsistency of classification rules at the local level. Instead, it finds that the local rules exhibit inherent

---

[12] 《中央国有资本经营预算支出管理暂行办法》 [Interim Measures for the Administration of Central State-Owned Capital Operating Budget Expenditure]. (People's Republic of China) MOF. 13 March 2017.

[13] *Classification Guiding Opinions* (n 8).

[14] Ibid.

[15] See, e.g., Zhou et al. (2019), p. 985.

consistency. The incomplete classification observed in practice can be attributed to the limited applicability scope of the rules.

China has historically promoted SOE reforms through an approach whereby the central government (in most cases, the central SASAC) formulates a framework reform policy for central SOEs, which also serves as a guide for local governments to develop policies applicable to SOEs in the regions.[16] Chinese local government authorities rarely innovate local policies that significantly depart from the central government's framework policy unless they receive special approval from the central government.[17] Hence, the *Classification Guiding Opinions* provide definitive principles for local SASACs to formulate their own classification rules, allowing them limited discretion to make modifications in accordance with the specific circumstances of their respective regions.

Table 3.1 complies the categories of SOEs in the classification rules developed by 32 local SASACs of first-level administrative regions (23 provinces, 5 autonomous regions and 4 municipalities directly under the Chinese central government). As shown in Table 3.1, none of the local SASACs substantially deviate from the *Classification Guiding Opinions* issued by the central SASAC, except for slight adaptations made according to region-specific circumstances. For instance, the municipal SASAC of Shanghai and the provincial SASACs of Heilongjiang, Shanxi and Jiangsu replicated the classification categories in the *Classification Guiding Opinions*. However, they omitted the 'Public Welfare SOEs' category because there are no such SOEs in these regions. Interestingly, most local SASACs altered the category names provided in the *Classification Guiding Opinions* while retaining the market-driven and policy-driven division consistent with the central framework document. For example, from 'General Commercial SOEs' to 'Competitive SOEs,' from 'Special Commercial SOEs' to 'Functional SOEs' or 'quasi-Public SOEs,' and from 'Public Welfare SOEs' to 'Special Functional SOEs' or 'Public Service SOEs.' In terms of classifying criteria, though not identical, local SASACs have generally resorted to a combination of qualitative and quantitative methods.

Despite their consistency, local classification rules only apply to the core companies of local BGs directly under the supervision of local SASACs, except for a few that may extend to the first-tier subsidiaries of the groups.[18] Even the scope of the *Classification Guiding Opinions* is limited to core companies and first-tier subsidiaries of central BGs.[19] According to the National Bureau of Statistics of China

---

[16] 习近平 [Xi Jinping] (2014) 《在中央全面深改革领导小组第七次会议上的讲话》 [Speech at the 7th Meeting of the Central Leading Group for Comprehensively Deepening Reform]. Speech. The 7th Meeting of the Central Leading Group for Comprehensively Deepening Reform; *SOE Reforms 1978-2018* (n 2) p 99.

[17] Zhao and Zhang (2015), p. 144.

[18] See, e.g., 《关于省属企业功能界定与分类的实施方案》 [Implementation Plan on Function Definition and Classification of Provincial Enterprises]. (People's Republic of China) SASAC of the People's Government of Hainan Province. 11 August 2016.

[19] *Classification Guiding Opinions* (n 8).

Table 3.1 List of SOE Classification Categories Developed by Local SASACs of First-Level Administrative Regions in the Mixed Ownership Reform

<table>
<tr><th>Central SASAC</th><th colspan="2">General Commercial</th><th colspan="2">Special Commercial</th><th colspan="2">Public Welfare</th></tr>
<tr><td>Local SASAC</td><td colspan="6">Trichotomy of SOEs</td></tr>
<tr><td>Beijing</td><td colspan="2">Competitive</td><td colspan="2">Special Functional</td><td colspan="2">Urban Public Service</td></tr>
<tr><td>Tianjin</td><td colspan="2">Competitive</td><td colspan="2">Functional</td><td colspan="2">Public Service</td></tr>
<tr><td>Shanghai</td><td colspan="2">Competitive</td><td colspan="2">Functional</td><td colspan="2">Public Service</td></tr>
<tr><td>Shanxi</td><td colspan="2">Competitive</td><td colspan="2">Functional</td><td colspan="2">Public Service</td></tr>
<tr><td>Guizhou</td><td colspan="2">Competitive</td><td colspan="2">Functional</td><td colspan="2">Public Service</td></tr>
<tr><td>Jilin</td><td colspan="2">Competitive</td><td colspan="2">Functional</td><td colspan="2">Public Welfare</td></tr>
<tr><td>Liaoning</td><td colspan="2">Competitive</td><td colspan="2">Functional</td><td colspan="2">Public Welfare</td></tr>
<tr><td>Anhui</td><td colspan="2">Commercial I</td><td colspan="2">Commercial II</td><td colspan="2">Public Welfare</td></tr>
<tr><td>Chongqing</td><td colspan="2">Commercial I</td><td colspan="2">Commercial II</td><td colspan="2">Public Welfare</td></tr>
<tr><td>Shandong</td><td colspan="2">Commercial I</td><td colspan="2">Commercial II</td><td colspan="2">Public Welfare</td></tr>
<tr><td>Fujian</td><td colspan="2">Commercial I</td><td colspan="2">Commercial II</td><td colspan="2">Public Welfare</td></tr>
<tr><td>Yunnan</td><td colspan="2">Commercial I</td><td colspan="2">Commercial II</td><td colspan="2">Public Welfare</td></tr>
<tr><td>Xinjiang</td><td colspan="2">Commercial I</td><td colspan="2">Commercial II</td><td colspan="2">Public Welfare</td></tr>
<tr><td>Heilongjiang</td><td colspan="2">Commercial I</td><td colspan="2">Commercial II</td><td colspan="2">Public Welfare</td></tr>
<tr><td>Henan</td><td colspan="2">Commercial I</td><td colspan="2">Commercial II</td><td colspan="2">Public Welfare</td></tr>
<tr><td>Hubei</td><td colspan="2">Commercial I</td><td colspan="2">Commercial II</td><td colspan="2">Special Functional</td></tr>
<tr><td>Qinghai</td><td colspan="2">Commercial Competitive</td><td colspan="2">Commercial Functional</td><td colspan="2">Public Welfare</td></tr>
<tr><td>Ningxia</td><td colspan="2">Profit-seeking</td><td colspan="2">Functional</td><td colspan="2">Public Welfare</td></tr>
<tr><td></td><td colspan="6">Dichotomy of SOEs</td></tr>
<tr><td>Hebei</td><td colspan="4">Commercial</td><td colspan="2">Public Welfare</td></tr>
<tr><td>Hainan</td><td colspan="4">Commercial</td><td colspan="2">Public Welfare</td></tr>
<tr><td>Shanxi</td><td colspan="4">Commercial</td><td colspan="2">Public Welfare</td></tr>
<tr><td>Gansu</td><td colspan="4">Commercial</td><td colspan="2">Public Welfare</td></tr>
<tr><td>Guangdong</td><td colspan="4">Competitive</td><td colspan="2">Quasi-Public</td></tr>
<tr><td>Jiangsu</td><td colspan="2">Commercial I</td><td colspan="2">Commercial II</td><td colspan="2"></td></tr>
<tr><td>Jiangxi</td><td colspan="2">Commercial I</td><td colspan="2">Commercial II</td><td colspan="2"></td></tr>
<tr><td>Zhejiang</td><td colspan="2">Competitive</td><td colspan="2">Functional</td><td colspan="2"></td></tr>
<tr><td>Inner Mongolia</td><td colspan="2">Commercial Competitive</td><td colspan="2">Specific Functional</td><td colspan="2"></td></tr>
<tr><td></td><td colspan="6">Multi-classification of SOEs</td></tr>
<tr><td>Sichuan</td><td>Competitive I</td><td>Competitive II</td><td>Functional I</td><td>Functional II</td><td colspan="2"></td></tr>
<tr><td>Hunan</td><td>Competitive II</td><td>Competitive II</td><td>Functional I</td><td>Functional II</td><td colspan="2"></td></tr>
<tr><td>Guangxi</td><td>Commercial I</td><td>Commercial II</td><td colspan="2">Commercial III</td><td>Public Welfare I</td><td>Public Welfare II</td></tr>
</table>

Source: The categories are hand-collected by the author from SOE classification rules that China's SASACs of 31 first-level administrative regions issued and publicised on their official websites. Tibet's autonomous region and special administrative region are not included herein

(NBS), by the end of 2022, China has 361,996 SOEs in total.[20] As noted in Chap. 2, Chinese SOEs are organised in the form of BGs, which typically include hundreds of SOEs linked by top-down ownership chains. As a result, there are only 736 local BGs of the first-level administrative regions. Each of China's 293 municipalities has an average of 23 BGs.[21] This means that the vast majority of Chinese SOEs, namely lower-tier subsidiaries of BGs, are not covered by the classification rules issued by the SASACs in the MOR.

The SASACs have delegated to the core companies of BGs the duty to classify lower-tier subsidiaries based on the classification rules. Some local SASACs, such as the SASAC of Zhejiang province, require core companies of local BGs to file their classification results.[22] Delegating classification authority will likely lead to an opaque and disorganised classification process. By the end of 2021, most of China's local SASACs had announced that they had finished classifying the SOEs under their supervision.[23] Interestingly, their classification results are never made public systematically, contrary to what they have declared and what the classification rules require, which may indicate their disorganised classification practices. Based on the media releases from the relevant SOEs' official websites or State media, the major central SOEs that fall under the three categories are listed in Table 3.2 below.

Despite limited data, Table 3.2 demonstrates how Chinese SOEs are classified in the MOR. It can be seen that 'Special Commercial' and 'General Commercial' SOEs are those large SOEs active on the global market and expanding their

Table 3.2 Major SOEs in Each Category Under the MOR SOE Classification

Public Welfare	China Grain Reserves Corporation Group Ltd., China National Cotton Information Center Ltd. Company
Special Commercial	China National Petroleum Corporation (CNPC), China Petroleum & Chemical Corporation (SINOPEC), China Mobile Communications Corporation (China Mobile), China United Network Communications Group Company (China Unicom)
General Commercial	China National Cereals, Oils and Foodstuffs Import and Export Corporation (COFCO) China Minmetals Corporation

[20] NBS (2020) National Data. https://data.stats.gov.cn/easyquery.htm?cn=C01. Accessed 13 Aug 2025.

[21] The author gathered the data through scouring the publicly available information on the official websites of SASACs at all levels.

[22] 《关于明确省属企业功能定位实施分类监管的意见》 [Opinions on Defining the Functional Orientation of Provincial Enterprises and Implementing Supervision Based on Classification]. (People's Republic of China) SASAC of the People's Government of Zhejiang Province. 5 April 2016.

[23] See, e.g., SASAC of the People's Government of Jiangsu Province (2016) 《江苏国资委完成省属企业功能界定与分类》 [Jiangsu SASAC Completed the Function Demarcation and Classification of Provincial Enterprises].

presence in developed countries. Therefore, their classifications in the ongoing SOE reforms reveal their nature.

It is unclear whether the opaqueness of SOE classification results from the Chinese government's deliberate decision to keep the results secret to prevent the exposure of the nature of SOEs or from the incomplete implementation of classifications in practice. There is no denying that the enormous number of Chinese SOEs makes it challenging to categorise them all. Since SOE classification is a prerequisite for Chinese SOEs to reduce State ownership in the MOR, an unfinished classification may impede the progress of the reform.

To date, however, incomplete classification practices have not impeded reform progress, as the Chinese government has authorised the SASACs at various levels to directly designate SOEs to carry out the MOR instead of advancing the reform solely on the basis of classification.[24] It is unclear whether the current government designation-based approach is a pilot approach for the early stage of the reform or whether it results from the Chinese government's awareness that classifying the entirety of SOEs is an arduous task in practice that may delay the progress of the MOR. However, if the practical challenges of SOE classification are not resolved, the massive SOE classification is likely to become a meaningless bureaucratic exercise.

3.2 Fostering SOEs' Competitiveness via Mixed Ownership Reform

In the latest round of SOE reforms, the MOR is concerned with integrating State and private ownership in individual enterprises.[25] In order to implement the MOR, an SOE may transform into an MOE by issuing shares or selling registered capital to non-State investors (i.e. private or foreign enterprises), adopting an employee stock ownership plan or listing on a stock exchange.[26] In addition, SOEs may implement the MOR by acquiring a stake in a POE. In this chapter, the former implementation strategy is referred to as 'flow-in MOR', while the latter is referred to as 'flow-out MOR.'

This two-way reform aims to integrate State and non-State ownership at the enterprise level, creating what is known as a mixed ownership economy. The Chinese government and the CCP advocate for mixed ownership as the optimal economic model because it permits different types of ownership to collaborate to

[24] The State Council (2019) 《第四批混改试点数量、领域均大幅增长》 [The Number and Areas of the Fourth Batch of Mixed Reform Pilot Projects Increased Significantly]. http://www.gov.cn/xinwen/2019-11/16/content_5452621.htm. Accessed 13 Aug 2025.

[25] *SOE Reforms 1978-2018* (n 2) p 369.

[26] Ibid 156.

benefit society.[27] However, the subsequent policy analyses and case studies reveal a different story.

3.2.1 Flow-In MOR: The Ownership Diversification of SOEs

Flow-in MOR may easily give rise to the illusion that the Xi administration is promoting a privatisation of Chinese SOEs, thereby shrinking China's State economy. However, the *MOR Opinions* have made it abundantly clear that the objective of the MOR is to 'strengthen the vitality, control power and influence of the State economy' to 'cope with the increasingly fierce international competition and challenges,'[28] which is in contrast to the illusion and consistent with the objective of the State economy restructuring reforms discussed in Chap. 2.

In essence, flow-in MOR is bringing diverse investors and capital into SOEs based on the SOEs' firm-specific demands for competitiveness and sustainable development.[29] When an SOE seeks to diversify its shareholder structure in flow-in MOR, it may select non-State shareholder candidates based on its development needs.[30] For example, an SOE trapped in financial difficulties or suffering capital shortage to expand its business may turn to financial investors for external support.[31] In addition, compared to POEs and foreign companies operating in the same sectors, Chinese SOEs are typically deficient in certain strategic assets, such as technology, research and development (R&D) capacity, brands, managerial know-how and human capital. Therefore, flow-in MOR provides opportunities for SOEs to form equity-based cooperative partnerships with their competitive peers, which may contribute to the growth of SOEs. Theoretically, SOEs with poor corporate governance practices may mainly introduce POEs with superior governance experience, managerial teams and expertise as strategic investors, as the participation of

---

27 《中共中央国务院深化国有企业改革的指导意见》 [The Guiding Opinions of the CCP Central Committee and the State Council on Deepening the Reform of State-Owned Enterprises]. (People's Republic of China) CCP Central Committee and the State Council. 24 August 2015 ('*Guiding Opinions*').

28 *MOR Opinions* (n 4).

29 施能自, 吴芙蓉 [Shi Nengzi and Wu Furong] (2017) 《新一轮国企改革的思考与操作实务》 [Thoughts and Operational Practices of the Latest Round of SOE Reforms]. 中国经济出版社 [Economic Press China], p 24; People's Daily (2020) 《中国化学工程集团释放最高股权比例推进混改》 [The China National Chemical Engineering Corporation has Released the Highest Proportion of Its Shareholding to Promote the Mixed Ownership Reform]. The Central SASAC. http://www.sasac.gov.cn/n2588025/n2588139/c14884977/content.html. Accessed 13 Aug 2025.

30 施能自, 吴芙蓉 [Shi Nengzi and Wu Furong] (2017), p. 25.

31 国务院国资委改革办 [Reform Office of the Central SASAC] (2018), p. 299 ('*150 Cases*'); Cui and Jiang (2010), p. 763.

these strategic investors in the corporate decision-making process may aid in improving the SOEs' governance practice and operational efficiency.[32]

Implementing flow-in MOR has proven to be instrumental in facilitating the successful business expansions of many SOEs in China. For example, China's State-owned pharmaceutical giant China Resources Pharmaceutical Company (CR Pharma) introduced Reckitt and Fuji Film, two foreign enterprises, as minority shareholders in 2020.[33] The foreign shareholders reportedly brought the SOE new drug R&D projects with significant potential to generate technological advancements essential for CR Pharma's international expansion efforts. Eastern Airline Logistics (EAL), a holding subsidiary of China's central BG, China East Airline Group, obtained a non-State capital injection of CNY 2.255 billion through flow-in MOR, significantly reducing its outstanding debt.[34] More importantly, through flow-in MOR, EAL established equity-based alignments with leading players in the logistics sector, such as Chinese privately owned logistic supplier Deppon Logistic Company and Singapore-based logistic provider Global Logistic Properties (GLP) in various industries. In addition, introducing multinational enterprises as shareholders may lay the foundation for EAL's future global expansion.[35]

The Chinese government has confirmed this demand-driven reform approach. In 2019, Hao Peng, the then-director of the central SASAC, clarified that the MOR encourages SOEs to introduce POE shareholders with a high compatibility and synergy with their business development.[36] Therefore, it is readily apparent that flow-in MOR serves as a convenient solution for Chinese SOEs to compensate for their deficiencies.

3.2.1.1 The Inter-SOE Equity Mix in Critical Industries

Flow-in MOR may raise an expectation that it will grant Chinese POEs and foreign investors access to the critical industries of China, from which they were previously barred by visible or invisible market entry barriers, by allowing them to become shareholders of Chinese SOEs. However, the reform's actual implementation has disproved these expectations.

---

[32] 《中央企业混合所有制改革操作指引》 [The Operation Guidelines on Mixed Ownership Reform of Central Enterprises]. (People's Republic of China) The Central SASAC. 31 October 2019 ('*Operation Guidelines*'); People's Daily (2020) 《以混促改'谋发展》 ['Promoting Reform via Mixing' to Pursue Development] The Central SASAC. http://www.sasac.gov.cn/n2588025/n2588139/c14884977/content.html. Accessed 13 Aug 2025.

[33] *150 Cases* (n 31) p 264.

[34] Ibid. p. 240.

[35] Ibid. p. 236.

[36] 郝鹏 [Hao Peng] (2019) 《在中央企业负责人会议上的讲话》 [Speech at the Meeting of Heads of Central Enterprises 2019]. Speech. 中央企业负责人会议 [Meeting of Heads of Central Enterprises 2019], p 25.

Many BGs whose principal businesses are in critical industries have indeed engaged in flow-in MOR involving POEs and foreign investors. However, the companies in which they introduced non-State shareholders are BG subsidiaries in non-critical industries, not their core companies or key business divisions operating in critical industries. For example, in 2016, China's biggest State-owned food producer, China Oil and Foodstuffs Corporation (COFCO), introduced ORG Packaging Limited, a Chinese privately owned package company listed on the Shenzhen Stock Exchange, into its subsidiary in the consumer goods packing industry, CPMC Holdings Limited, holding a 27 percent stake.[37] In 2017, China Baowu Steel Group, China's top iron and steel BG, introduced several strategic investors to its e-commerce platform subsidiary, Ouyeel E-Commerce.[38] The investors notably included two foreign enterprises, namely Singapore-based GLP and Japanese trading company Mitsui & Co, along with four SOE strategic investors, including Benxi Steel Group, Shagang Group, Shougang Fund and China Construction Bank Trust.[39]

In both the examples above, the sales of SOE stakes were followed by substantial cooperation between SOEs and non-SOE shareholders. 2018 ORG Packaging Limited and CPMC Holding Limited signed a partnership cooperation agreement.[40] In 2021, Ouyeel E-Commerce signed a contract with its Japanese shareholder Mitsui & Co. to import 3000 tonnes of steel scrap from Japan.[41] These post-reform actions provide factual evidence bolstering the objective of flow-in MOR, as identified earlier, enabling SOEs to form equity-based partnerships with POEs that can contribute to their development.

In contrast, when it came to the core companies or key subsidiaries engaged in the group's principal businesses in critical industries, their flow-in MOR transformation seldom involved non-State investors—only State shareholders, such as other SOEs, government agencies and public institutions can be introduced.

There have been a limited number of cases in which BG core companies carried out flow-in MOR. This first pilot case occurred in 2019, when China National Pharmaceutical Group Corporation, China's central pharmaceutical BG, introduced strategic investors into its core company. However, the investors it introduced were two central BGs: State Development and Investment Corporation (SDIC) and China Reform Holdings Corporation.[42] In the same year, China's local pharmaceutical

---

[37] *150 Cases* (n 31) p. 251.

[38] Wataru Kodaka (2017) China Baowu Steel Divests Portion of E-commerce Subsidiary. Nikkei Asia. https://asia.nikkei.com/Business/China-Baowu-Steel-divests-portion-of-e-commerce-subsidiary. Accessed 13 Aug 2025.

[39] *150 Cases* (n 31) p 219.

[40] ORG Technology (2018) The Era of 2.0 of Strategic Cooperation between O.R.G. and CPMC Holdings Limited. https://www.orgtech.cn/en/index.php?m=content&c=index&a=show&catid=73&id=10. Accessed 13 Aug 2025.

[41] Reuters (2021) China Baowu Steel unit opens 2.8 mln tonnes/year steel scrap plant. https://www.reuters.com/article/china-baowu-scrap-idINL4N2JG0RL. Accessed 13 Aug 2025.

[42] SDICFUND (2019) 《国投参与国药股权多元化改革试点》 [SDIC Successfully Participates in Sinopharm's Equity Diversification Reform Pilot Programme]. https://sdicfund.com/gtcx/gszx/gsxw/webinfo/2020/11/1606378077763607589.htm. Accessed 13 Aug 2025.

BG, Jiangzhong Pharmaceutical Company, sold a controlling stake in its core company to the central pharmaceutical BG, CR Pharma.[43] The Chinese government acknowledged this transaction as the second case of MOR involving a BG's core company.[44] Interestingly, the transaction can also be viewed as an inter-SOE merger under the State economy restructuring reform, since it involved only SOEs.

Flow-in MOR of BG key subsidiaries in critical industries rarely involves POEs. For example, in 2019, China's major electricity generation BG, State Power Investment Corporation, sold 35 percent stakes in its first-tier subsidiary, Huanghe Hydropower Development Company, to eight strategic investors. Given that the subsidiary is engaged in energy generation, which falls under critical industries, it is unsurprising that all the investors introduced were SOEs.[45] Nonetheless, in 2017, there was an exception. China's telecommunications giant China Unicom Group sold 35.2 percent of its stake in its key subsidiary, China United Network Communications Limited, to fourteen strategic investors, including preeminent technological POEs like Baidu, Inc., Alibaba Group, Tencent Holdings and JD. Com (collectively referred to as BATJ), while the subsidiary retains State-controlled status.[46] This transaction aimed to rejuvenate China Unicom Group by acquiring external technological assistance from strategic investors such as BATJ. [47] It was jointly approved by NDRC, the central SASAC and the China Securities Regulatory Commission,[48] indicating its expectational significance.

In 2019, the central SASAC required that all MOR plans of central BGs' subsidiaries who were categorised as 'Special Commercial' must be approved by the central SASAC or the State Council.[49] One year later, it announced that the MOR of SOEs in critical industries would not involve non-SOE investors in the foreseeable

[43] China Daily (2022) 《江中药业成功入选"科改示范企业"》 [Jiangzhong Pharmaceutical was Successfully Selected as 'Science and Technology Reform Demonstration Enterprise']. https://jx.chinadaily.com.cn/a/202203/30/WS6243b108a3101c3ee7ace037.html. Accessed 13 Aug 2025.

[44] The Central SASAC (2022) 《华润集团国企改革三年行动取得积极成效》 [China Resources Group's Three-Year Action on SOE Reforms Produces Positive Results]. http://www.sasac.gov.cn/n4470048/n13461446/n15390485/n15769618/c24856155/content.html. Accessed 13 Aug 2025.

[45] The strategic investors included two State banks and the China Life Insurance Company, the SDIC+, the China Reform Holdings Corporation, the Zhejiang Energy Group Company, the Yunnan Energy Investment Company, and CITIC Securities. People (2019) 《国家电投黄河项目引入8家战略投资者增资242亿元》 [China Power Investment Corporation's Yellow River Project Introduces 8 Strategic Investors to Increase Capital by 24.2 Billion Yuan]. http://energy.people.com.cn/n1/2019/1218/c71661-31511396.html. Accessed 13 Aug 2025.

[46] 王春晖 [Wang Chunhui] (2017) 《剖析中国联通混改的战略意义》 [Analyzing the Strategic Significance of China Unicom's Mixed Ownership Reform: Three Highlights]. People. http://ccnews.people.com.cn/n1/2017/0821/c141677-29483853.html. Accessed 13 Aug 2025.

[47] China Unicom (2017) 《中国联通混改三个没想到》 [The Mixed Ownership Reform of China Unicom: 'Three Unexpected']. http://www.chinaunicom.com.cn/news/201708/1503301913304050446.html. Accessed 13 Aug 2025.

[48] Xinhua News Agency (2017) 《联通混改方案获国资委放行》 [Unicom's Mixed Ownership Reform Plan has been Approved by the Central SASAC]. http://m.news.cn/tech/2017-09/18/c_1121678597.htm. Accessed 13 Aug 2025.

[49] *Operation Guidelines* (n 32).

future,[50] thereby blocking access for POEs and foreign investors to China's critical industries via MOR.

Notably, inter-SOE consolidation, as discussed in Chap. 2, is also a key means of implementing the flow-in MOR in critical industries. However, such consolidation may give rise to anti-trust issues, which will be examined in Sect. 3.3. The application of the flow-in MOR underscores the Xi administration's commitment to strengthening SOE dominance in China's critical sectors, consistent with the objectives of State economy restructuring reform outlined in Chap. 2.

3.2.1.2 The Autonomy of Private Investors in SOEs: The Absence of a Minority Shareholder Protection Mechanism

China's flow-in MOR, which also appeared in the "Release the Small" programme during the second round of SOE reforms discussed in Chap. 2, has long been the subject of debate over whether, and to what extent, it enables non-State investors to exercise genuine autonomy within SOEs free from state influence. Since mixed ownership emerged in the 1990s as an alternative to pure public ownership, many Chinese POEs have been reluctant to invest in SOEs, fearing the loss of influence in decision-making and the erosion of their legitimate interests.

An early case from the pilot phase of MOR underscores the validity of these concerns. In 2006, Shanxi Shenmu Chemical Industry Company (Shenmu), a State-owned methanol producer, introduced five POEs as minority shareholders. In 2010, however, Shenmu's controlling shareholders, two provincial SOEs, transferred their shares in Shenmu to a third party without notifying the POE minority shareholders, without affording them the opportunity to object, and without respecting their statutory pre-emptive rights under the *Company Law.*[51] In 2018, the Shanxi Provincial High Court ruled in favour of the POEs on claims of shareholder oppression, and in 2019 the Supreme People's Court dismissed the respondents' appeal.[52] This case illustrates the inherent vulnerability of private investors in MOR.

Assessing whether this issue persists in the ongoing flow-in MOR necessarily begins with a threshold question: are private investors permitted to hold a majority shareholding in SOEs, or only a minority stake? Although the *Classification Guiding*

---

[50] The Central SASAC (2021) 《2020 央企经济运行情况新闻发布会实录》 [Record of Press Conference on Economic Operation of Central Enterprises 2020]. http://www.sasac.gov.cn/n2588035/n2588330/n2588360/c16563166/content.html. Accessed 13 Aug 2025.

[51] 《中华人民共和国公司法》 [Company Law of the People's Republic of China] (People's Republic of China) adopted at the 8th National People's Congress Standing Committee, 29 December 1993, amended 25 December 1999, 28 August 2004, 28 December 2013 and 26 October 2018, art 71 ('*Company Law*').

[52] 《中国神华煤制油化工有限公司、上海福辉化工有限公司损害公司利益责任纠纷二审民事裁定书》 [Civil Decision on Liability Dispute for Injuring the Company's Interests in the Second Instance between China Shenhua Coal-to-Oil Chemical Industry Co, Ltd and Shanghai Fuhui Chemical Industry Co]. Supreme People's Court of the PRC. 最高法民辖终481号 [Economic Appeal No 481]. 19 December 2019.

Opinions allows SOEs falling under the 'General Commercial' category to pursue a reduction of State ownership to a minority stake, the implementation of the MOR demonstrates that most 'General Commercial' SOEs still retain a State-holding status in the latest round of SOE reforms, introducing non-SOE investors as minority shareholders, unless the SOE is mired in a debt quagmire or development bottleneck and therefore desperate for external emergency assistance. For instance, in 2014, TenCent Holding, a prominent privately-owned technology company in China, acquired the second-largest stake (a 11.28 percent of stake) in Navinfo, a State-owned provider of navigation software in China.[53] The deal was intended to alleviate Navinfo's development constraints, which was accomplished through subsequent extensive collaboration between Tencent and Navinfo.[54]

Under such an arrangement, the minority shareholder status of private investors makes their autonomy within SOEs fundamentally a question of minority shareholder protection. The *Company Law* grants shareholders a range of rights comparable to those found in many Western jurisdictions, including voting rights, inspection rights, the right to claim dividends, and the right to bring legal action for wrongful acts.[55] The 2018 and 2023 amendments to the *Company Law* significantly enhanced these protections by introducing cumulative voting, expanding shareholders' rights to information, crystallising the right of rescission, and granting the right to challenge unlawful board decisions and to petition for corporate dissolution in cases of severe financial distress.[56]

In practice, however, these legal safeguards are constrained by the governance realities of Chinese SOEs. Their executives often hold dual roles, as enterprise leaders and as CCP cadres, and are subject to considerable political pressure. As discussed in Chap. 4, the primacy of political control in SOE governance has been reinforced in the latest round of reforms, notably through the institutionalisation of the CCP 'Party Committee' as the supreme decision-making body within SOEs and the deepening of political–personnel integration. These features of SOE governance underscore the persistent vulnerability of private minority shareholders' autonomy to oppression by controlling shareholders, who are most often government entities or SOEs with entrenched political influence.

The absence of robust minority shareholder protection mechanisms remains a significant disincentive for private investors to participate in flow-in MOR, given the substantial risk of losing autonomy once invested. In this context, the Chinese government's call for SOEs to pursue 'self-improvement' through MOR has prompted a small number of enterprises to experiment with governance

[53] China Daily (2014) Tencent to Buy Stake in Digital Map Provider Navinfo. https://www.chinadaily.com.cn/bizchina/tech/2014-05/06/content_17487186.htm. Accessed 13 Aug 2025.

[54] See, e.g., Reuters (2016) NavInfo, Tencent, GIC Buy 10 pct Stake in Mapping Firm HERE. https://www.reuters.com/article/here-equity/navinfo-tencent-gic-buy-10-pct-stake-in-mapping-firm-here-idUKL5N1EM0BA. Accessed 13 Aug 2025.

[55] *Company Law* (n 51) art. 20, 21, 22, 33, 71, 72; For shareholder rights in western countries, see, e.g., Kim et al. (2007), pp. 859–880.

[56] *Company Law* (n 51) art. 22, 33, 75, 105, 182.

arrangements that circumvent the limitations of the *Company Law*.[57] These initiatives, however, reveal both the potential and the limits of institutional innovation under a system in which political control remains paramount.

China United Network Communications Limited, a key subsidiary of China Unicom Group, illustrates this dynamic. When introducing BATJ as minority strategic investors in 2017, the company adopted a director over-appointment mechanism enabling each POE shareholder to appoint one director, thereby securing a collective majority for POE representatives on the board.[58] It also instituted a formal review process for Party Committee decisions, creating a procedural check on the CCP-led body's capacity to silence minority voices.[59] While these measures may offer a degree of substantive influence, they remain dependent on the willingness of the controlling SOE to sustain such arrangements and do not fundamentally displace the Party Committee's supremacy.

At the local level, similar experiments have emerged. For instance, in 2017 the Shandong Provincial SASAC encouraged local SOEs to introduce POE shareholders and, in cases of minority holdings, to grant each the right to nominate a director regardless of ownership proportion or to appoint directors collectively under a special shareholders' agreement. Such policies, however, are discretionary, lack statutory force, and are vulnerable to reversal if political or commercial priorities shift.[60]

Although certain SOEs and local SASACs have experimented with minority shareholder protection mechanisms, and these innovations have been formally endorsed by the State Council as potential models for future MOR implementation,[61] they remain discretionary and isolated. As of August 2025, neither the central SASAC nor the State Council has promulgated a uniform, mandatory framework to safeguard the rights of non-SOE minority shareholders in flow-in MOR transactions. The absence of such a binding mechanism exposes the structural imbalance of power within SOEs and signals that minority shareholder protection is not a central policy priority.

This institutional gap undermines the credibility of official assurances that MOR respects private investor autonomy. Although China has ostensibly moved away

---

[57] See, e.g., *Operation Guidelines* (n 32).

[58] The State Council (2017) 《从中国联通试点方案看国企混改新动向》 [See the New Trend of Mixed Ownership Reform of SOEs Through the China Unicom Reform Pilot Programme]. https://www.gov.cn/xinwen/2017-08/22/content_5219638.htm. Accessed 13 Aug 2025.

[59] Ibid.

[60] 《关于省属国有企业混合所有制改革发挥中小股东作用的指导意见》 [Guiding opinions on Promoting the Role of Small and Medium Shareholders in the Mixed Ownership Reform of Provincial State-Owned Enterprises]. (People's Republic of China) SASAC of the People's Government of Shandong Province. 3 February 2017.

[61] The State Council (2017) 《山东:国企混改允许中小股东董事提名表决权合并计算》 [Shandong: Mixed Ownership Reform of SOEs Allows Small and Medium-sized Shareholders to Nominate Directors based on Combined Voting Rights]. https://www.gov.cn/xinwen/2017-02/09/content_5166777.htm. Accessed 13 Aug 2025; The State Council (2017) 《深入推进国企混改》 [Deepening the Mixed Ownership Reform of SOEs]. https://www.gov.cn/xinwen/2017-12/19/content_5248342.htm. Accessed 13 Aug 2025.

from the coercive treatment of private enterprises characteristic of the command economy era, recent events cast doubt on this shift. The State's abrupt takeover of Dawu Agricultural and Animal Husbandry Group in 2020, following the arrest of its executives, demonstrates the persistence of State authority to unilaterally expropriate private assets.[62] This episode directly contradicts the commitment, set out in the State Council and CCP Central Committee's *Guiding Opinions*, to prohibit coercion of POEs into MOR participation, rendering such policy promises unreliable.[63]

From a broader perspective, the structural realities of China's political economy further explain why POEs and foreign investors may still be drawn into flow-in MOR despite its weak autonomy safeguards. China remains one of the world's least economically free jurisdictions, ranking among the "most unfree" economies in the Heritage Foundation's 2021 *Index of Economic Freedom*.[64] The State economy remains extensive, government intervention pervasive, and legal protections for private property underdeveloped.[65] POEs, in particular, face systematic disadvantages in access to critical resources, most notably finance, market opportunities, and regulatory approvals, relative to SOEs.[66]

In this environment, aligning with SOEs through flow-in MOR offers non-State investors strategic benefits unrelated to corporate governance rights.[67] MOR can provide an avenue to cultivate political ties with State owners of SOEs, securing a form of political patronage that may shield against arbitrary State interference and open access to preferential treatment,[68] including fiscal subsidies, business licences, tax benefits, and financing opportunities—what Milhaupt and Zheng term 'government-generated rents'.[69] Moreover, association with an SOE can bolster a POE's or foreign enterprise's credibility in China's commercial landscape, strengthening its long-term viability in a system where political and economic capital are deeply intertwined.

Seen in this light, flow-in MOR operates less as a mechanism to empower private investors within SOEs and more as a policy instrument to consolidate State control while co-opting private capital to advance State industrial and political objectives. The absence of enforceable protections for minority shareholders is not an oversight but a structural feature of a system designed to maintain the primacy of State ownership and political oversight in strategic sectors.

---

[62] Emily Feng (2021) The Latest Target in China's Crackdown on Entrepreneurs is an Outspoken Billionaire. NPR. https://www.npr.org/2021/05/15/996241784/the-latest-target-in-chinas-crackdown-on-entrepreneurs-is-an-outspoken-billionai. Accessed 13 Aug 2025.

[63] *Guiding Opinions* (n 27).

[64] The Heritage Foundation (2023) 2023 Index of Economic Freedom. https://www.heritage.org/index/. Accessed 13 Aug 2025.

[65] Xu (2011), pp. 1076–1151.

[66] Wang and Peng (2014), pp. 83–95.

[67] Tao et al. (2013).

[68] Faccio (2006), pp. 369–386.

[69] Milhaupt and Zheng (2015), p. 688.

3.2.2 *Flow-Out MOR: State Ownership's 'Invasion' of the Private Sector*

Flow-in MOR transforms SOEs into MOEs, generally by bringing in POE or foreign enterprise shareholders, except for the inter-SOE MOR in critical industries. Flow-out MOR runs in the opposite direction, transforming POEs into MOEs by having SOEs acquire a stake in them, essentially a form of partial nationalisation.

Unlike flow-in MOR, which is promoted across all industries, the Chinese government especially encourages flow-out MOR in 'strategic emerging industries'. According to the NBS, this concept encompasses the vast majority of high-tech industries necessary for modern national competitiveness, such as biomedicine, advanced manufacturing, energy conservation, environmental protection and aerospace.[70] In addition, the Chinese government has primarily restricted the scope of SOEs that can implement flow-out MOR to core companies or first- and second-tier subsidiaries of central BGs.[71]

Unlike flow-in MOR, which specifies various State ownership proportion requirements, flow-out MOR does not specify a minimum or maximum stake size that SOEs can acquire in POEs. As of December 2023, there have only been a handful of flow-out MOR cases. Nevertheless, central SOEs tend to acquire a controlling stake in targeted POEs when implementing flow-out MOR. This can lead to extensive SOE acquisitions in China's emerging strategic industries, resulting in a State-sanctioned invasion of the State economy into private sectors, substantial State intervention in the Chinese high-tech market and political control over SOE-invested POEs.

3.2.2.1 The Limited Scope of Flow-out MOR

As noted above, flow-out MOR has been promoted primarily in 'strategic emerging industries'. Its limited industrial scope can be attributed to three considerations closely aligned with the State's strategic and policy objectives.

The first reason is China's pressing need to advance its technological industries. The rising geopolitical tensions between China and most parts of the developed world in the view of the Chinese government, amid a period of rapid technological advancement, highlight the urgent need for China to promote technological innovation, especially in cutting-edge fields related to national strength and sustainable development. Parallel to the launch of the latest round of SOE reforms at the 18th National Congress of the CCP in 2012, the CCP launched the ambitious Innovation-Driven Development Strategy (the Strategy), establishing

---

[70] 《战略性新兴产业分类 (2018)》 [Classification of Strategic Emerging Industries (2018)]. (People's Republic of China) NBS. 7 November 2018.

[71] *SOE Reforms 1978-2018* (n 2) p 387.

technological innovation as the basis of China's national development.[72] China's 13th and 14th Five-Year Plans, the supreme national development plans for 2016 to 2025, both include a strategy focusing on enhancing China's science and technology capacity.[73] In addition, the Xi Jinping administration has put forward initiatives focusing on advanced technological development, such as the *Made in China 2025 Development Initiative*.[74] The intensive policy moves indicate China's urgent need to accelerate innovation development in the global race for technological supremacy.[75]

Secondly, China intends to expand the influence of central SOEs in critical industries-related strategic high-tech sectors. Unlike the critical industries that have been deliberately preserved for SOEs, particularly central SOEs, since the launch of the 'Open Door' Policy in 1978, China's technological industries that emerged in the modern digital era are dominated by POEs, such as BATJ or large foreign tech companies that invest in China, such as South Korea-based Samsung Electronics Company and the US-based electronic vehicle manufacturer Tesla, Inc. In contrast, Chinese SOEs are less competitive in these industries as they have exhibited a general weakness in innovation capacity, business foresight and incentives to explore or participate in novel businesses.[76]

The Chinese government has made it abundantly clear that one of the goals of the MOR is to increase the influence of central SOEs in critical industries-related technological sectors, such as information and communications, biomedicine and marine engineering, and particularly requires that central SOEs have a leadership position in designed technological industries, such as new energy, new materials aerospace and intelligent manufacturing.[77] This policy stance indicates that the government intends to ensure that the central SOEs that are more closely affiliated with the central government maintain dominance over critical industries and emerging high-tech sectors that have recently become essential to the nation's development.

Thirdly, flow-in MOR is of inherent sensitivity. In flow-out MOR, central SOEs or their subsidiaries are encouraged to acquire a stake in POEs in 'strategic

---

[72] Jintao Hu (2012) Firmly March on the Path of Socialism with Chinese Characteristics and Strive to Complete the Building of a Moderately Prosperous Society in All Respects. 18th CCP National Congress. Report.

[73] The 13th Five-Year Plan for Economic and Social Development of the People's Republic of China (2016-2020). (People's Republic of China) The CCP Central Committee. May 2021, pt. II ch 6. https://en.ndrc.gov.cn/policies/202105/P020210527785800103339.pdf. Accessed 13 Aug 2025; The State Council (2021) Major Targets in the 14th Five-Year Plan (2021-2025). http://english.www.gov.cn/w/14thfiveyearplan/. Accessed 13 Aug 2025.

[74] 《中国制造 2025》 [Made in China 2025]. (People's Republic of China) The State Council. 8 May 2015.

[75] See generally Zhong (2021).

[76] Milhaupt and Zheng (2015), p. 699.

[77] 《关于推动中央企业结构调整与重组的指导意见》 [Guiding Opinions on Promoting Structural Adjustment and Reorganization of Central Enterprises]. (People's Republic of China) General Office of the State Council. 17 July 2016.

emerging industries' to establish equity-based cooperative partnerships with POEs that possess advanced technologies and superior innovation capacity.[78] This suggests that flow-out MOR shares with flow-in MOR the objective of pursuing inter-firm resource integration and strategic cooperation between SOEs and select POEs in an effort to strengthen the State economy.

Implementing the reform has already led to a significant instance of SOE incursion. CGN Nuclear Technology, the first-tier subsidiary of China's central BG specialising in nuclear energy generation, China General Nuclear Power Group (CGN), acquired controlling stakes in nine leading POEs that dominated China's nuclear technology industry in 2017. These massive acquisitions enabled CGN Nuclear Technology to attain absolute dominance in the industry virtually overnight.[79] The Chairman of CGN Nuclear Technology justified the massive acquisitions by stating, 'it is not the SOE devouring the private enterprises; it is long-term cooperation between the SOE and the private sector in a mixed economy.'[80]

Like flow-in MOR cases analysed earlier, flow-out MOR instances have typically resulted in substantial technological cooperation between the SOEs and their acquired (or invested) POEs. The POEs acquired by CGN Nuclear Technology have aided CGN in undertaking government-funded major technological projects in collaboration with other State-owned institutes, such as the Chinese Academy of Sciences.[81] Notably, CGN is a central BG directly owned by the State Council and has ties to the People's Liberation Army (PLA).[82] This case demonstrated how flow-out MOR incorporates high-tech POEs into SOE equity networks that ultimately connect to the government.

Despite the relatively limited scope of implementation, flow-out MOR has encountered challenges in practice that might hinder it from achieving its goal of enhancing the innovation capacity of SOEs. However, it does not seem that the challenges will hamper the MOR's integration of POEs into SOE networks in high-tech industries.

---

[78] People (2017) 《国资委:鼓励国有资本以多种方式入股非国有企业》 [SASAC: Encourage State-Owned Capital to Join Non-SOEs in Various Ways]. http://ccnews.people.com.cn/n1/2017/1213/c141677-29703045.html. Accessed 13 Aug 2025.

[79] National Energy Administration (2019) 《中广核四项改革试点齐发动 争创"世界一流"》 [CGN Launches Four Pilot Reforms in an Attempt to Achieve 'World-Class']. http://www.nea.gov.cn/2019-01/17/c_137751944.htm. Accessed 13 Aug 2025.

[80] 欧阳凯 [Ouyang Kai] (2017) 《张剑锋:混改是核技术产业化的下一个突破口》 [Interview with Zhang Jianfeng, Chairman of CGN Nuclear Technology: Mixed Ownership Reform is the Next Breakthrough of Nuclear Technology Industrialization]. National Business Daily. http://www.nbd.com.cn/articles/2017-07-16/1128407.html. Accessed 13 Aug 2025.

[81] CGN Power (2018) 2017 Annual Report. Report.

[82] CGN was identified by the US Department of Defence as Chinese Military Companies in 2021. US Department of Defense (2021) Entities Identified as Chinese Military Companies Operating in the United States. https://media.defense.gov/2021/Jun/03/2002734519/-1/-1/0/ENTITIES-IDENTIFIED-AS-CHINESE-MILITARY-COMPANIES-OPERATING-IN-THE-US.PDF. Accessed 13 Aug 2025.

3.2.2.2 Policy-Driven Risks in SOE–POE Equity Integration

Although the Chinese government may continue to exercise a degree of coercion toward POEs, many POEs still have strong incentives to seek equity integration with SOEs. Such connections can offer protection in an environment where sustainable development often depends on political ties. For example, Shenzhou High-speed Railway Technology Company (CSHR), a leading high-speed rail supplier, acknowledged that becoming a subsidiary of the central SOE SDIC Gaoxin Industrial Investment Corporation allowed it to qualify for government-funded projects for which it had previously been ineligible.[83]

The policy rationale for flow-out MOR is to channel SOE capital into technologically advanced POEs to compensate for SOEs' innovation deficit. In principle, this requires preserving the acquired POEs' innovation capacity post-acquisition. While SOEs can provide financial resources and political backing, substantial equity stakes enable them to intervene in corporate management. In practice, acquisitions are often accompanied by the appointment of SOE executives or the establishment of Party Committees, embedding SOE influence deep into corporate decision-making. Such arrangements risk displacing market-oriented governance with policy-driven oversight, potentially eroding the entrepreneurial dynamism and efficiency of the acquired enterprise.

Even within official discourse,[84] the dangers of excessive SOE intervention have been recognised. In 2017, Li Yang, Director of the Chinese Academy of Social Sciences' Institute of Finance, advised at a central SASAC forum that SOEs involved in MOR should act strictly as financial investors, refraining from sending in executives or intervening in daily operations.[85] A number of SOEs have attempted to follow this guidance. For example, China National Agricultural Development Group and China Iron & Steel Research Institute Group's subsidiary, Advanced Technology & Materials Company, have allowed the original management of acquired POEs to remain in place.[86] SDIC Gaoxin, established in 2015 as a wholly owned subsidiary of SDIC to implement flow-out MOR in strategic emerging industries, initially

[83] 丁怡婷 [Ding Yiting] (2021) 《国投集团——服务国计民生 发展新兴产业(国企改革三年行动)》 [SDIC—Serving the National Economy and the People's Livelihood and Developing Emerging Industries (Three-year Action Plan for the SOE Reforms)]. People. http://cpc.people.com.cn/n1/2021/0527/c64387-32114629.html. Accessed 13 Aug 2025.

[84] The State Council (2021) 《国家发展改革委介绍支持民营企业改革发展情况》 [NDRC Introduces the Support for POE Reform and Development]. https://www.gov.cn/xinwen/2021-10/22/content_5644185.htm. Accessed 13 Aug 2025; NDRC (2021) 《混合所有制改革如何"混"怎么"改"?》 [Mixed Ownership Reform: How to 'Mix' and How to 'Reform'?]. https://www.ndrc.gov.cn/wsdwhfz/202112/t20211231_1311180.html. Accessed 13 Aug 2025.

[85] The Central SASAC (2017) 《专家为国企改革提高效能建言献策》 [Experts Offer Advice on the SOE Reform to Improve Effectiveness]. http://www.sasac.gov.cn/n2588025/n2588134/c4542476/content.html. Accessed 13 Aug 2025.

[86] *150 Cases* (n 31) p 322.

committed to non-interference in daily operations when acquiring controlling stakes in high-tech firms such as CSHR and Hefei Bolin Advanced Materials Company.[87]

However, such pledges are structurally fragile. In 2019, SDIC Gaoxin required all its controlling companies to establish Party Committees with supreme decision-making authority,[88] in line with the SOE governance system reform of the latest round of SOE reforms (discussed in Chap. 4). Other central SOEs undertaking flow-out MOR in technology sectors have adopted similar measures, on the basis that nationalised POEs are technically SOEs and thus subject to the same governance reforms. These systemic requirements override any individual SOE's earlier commitment to managerial autonomy, reaffirming the primacy of political control over market autonomy.

This tension exposes the central risk for POEs integrated into SOE equity networks: the erosion of decision-making independence in favour of policy-driven objectives. While central SOEs may have pragmatic reasons to preserve innovation capacity—particularly where technological cooperation and transfer are involved—the institutional environment ensures that POEs become embedded in SOE-controlled technological and industrial networks, potentially extending to State and military projects. Once incorporated into these networks, the strategic direction of the enterprise is shaped as much by state industrial and political priorities as by market logic.

In sum, flow-out MOR in the latest round of SOE reforms functions less as a mechanism to empower private enterprises and more as a strategic tool for SOEs to absorb critical resources, most notably technological know-how and innovation capacity, from high-performing POEs. While SOE investors may, in some instances, preserve the original management structure to safeguard operational efficiency, such arrangements operate within an institutional framework that embeds acquired firms into SOE-controlled technological and industrial networks. These networks, which can extend to State agencies and even the PLA, inevitably subordinate corporate decision-making to state industrial and political priorities. As a result, the integration of POEs into SOE equity structures carries an inherent risk that market-oriented strategies will be displaced by policy-driven objectives.

[87] 杜燕飞 [Du Yanfei] (2021) 《以改革创新激发高质量发展动力 开启新国投建设新征程》 [Reforming and Innovating to Promote Growth, Embarking on the Construction of a New SDIC]. People. http://finance.people.com.cn/n1/2021/0407/c1004-32071951.html. Accessed 13 Aug 2025.

[88] SDIC Gaoxin (2020) 《国投高新着力提升相对控股混合所有制企业党建工作水平》 [SDIC Gaoxin is Committed to Bolstering MOEs' Party-Building Efforts]. https://www.gaoxin-china.com.cn/gtgx/djyqywh/dqjs/webinfo/2020/01/1580510268314622.htm. Accessed 13 Aug 2025.

3.3 Anti-trust Regulation and Enforcement in MOR

In the latest round of SOE reforms, MOR essentially refers to the State economy's integration with the private sector, aimed at enhancing the dominance of central SOEs in critical industries and expanding their influence over 'strategic emerging industries'. However, antitrust concerns can arise when inter-SOE MOR or consolidations occur in critical industries, or when a single SOE acquires multiple high-tech POEs in the same field to gain market dominance, as in the case of CGN Nuclear Technology's flow-out MOR.

China's anti-trust legal framework is primarily based on the *Anti-Unfair Competition Law of the PRC*, enacted in 1993, and the *Anti-Monopoly Law of the PRC* (AML), enacted in 2007.[89] The *Anti-Unfair Competition Law* does not address issues relating to industrial dominance positions.[90] The AML regulates monopolistic conducts in China, specifically, including monopoly agreements, abuse of dominant market position, and concentrations of undertakings that have or may have the effect of eliminating or restricting competition.[91] Inter-SOE consolidation under flow-in MOR and SOE acquisitions of controlling stakes in high-tech POEs under flow-out MOR may arguably constitute a 'concentration of undertakings' under the AML, which encompasses the merger of undertakings and the acquisition by one undertaking of control over, or the ability to exert decisive influence on, another undertaking through equity acquisition, contractual arrangements, or other means.[92]

It is noteworthy that the AML permits concentrations of undertakings, recognising their commercial rationale in facilitating business expansion and enhancing competitiveness, provided they are achieved through fair competition, arise from voluntary arrangements, and comply with the law.[93] A concentration of undertakings that meets the reporting thresholds set by the State Council must be filed in advance with the State Administration for Market Regulation (SAMR) for an anti-trust review and may not be implemented without approval.[94] The thresholds were set in 2024 as a combined global turnover of all undertakings involved of at least RMB 12 billion (around USD 1.65 billion) or a combined domestic turnover of at least RMB 4 billion (around USD 550 million) in the previous fiscal year, with at least two undertakings each recording domestic turnover above RMB 800 million

---

[89] 《中华人民共和国反垄断法》 [Anti-Monopoly Law of the PRC]. (People's Republic of China) Adopted at the 10th National People's Congress Standing Committee. 30 August 2007, amended 24 June 2022 ('*AML*').

[90] Monopoly practices are not covered by the law's anti-unfair competition practices. 《中华人民共和国反不正当竞争法》 [Anti-Unfair Competition Law of the PRC]. (People's Republic of China) Adopted at the 8th National People's Congress Standing Committee. 2 September 1993, amended 4 November 2017, 23 April 2019, art. 6-12.

[91] *AML* (n 89) art. 3.

[92] Ibid. art. 20.

[93] Ibid. art. 5.

[94] *AML* (n 89) art. 21.

(around USD 110 million) in that year.[95] These thresholds are readily met by most central SOEs engaged in MOR, making it highly likely that inter-SOE consolidations or SOE acquisitions of high-tech POEs will trigger mandatory anti-trust review. The critical question, therefore, is whether the MOR in China's latest round of SOE reforms operates within a grey area under the AML.

The threshold question in assessing the legality of inter-SOE consolidation under the AML is its applicability to SOEs, a matter that has been the subject of long-standing debate.[96] While the AML does not expressly exclude SOEs from its scope, Article 7 has been contested as potentially creating a carve-out for SOEs operating in critical industries. This clause stipulates:

> In industries that are related to the lifeline of the national economy and national security in which the State-owned economy holds a controlling position…the State shall protect the lawful business activities of the undertakings therein.
>
> The undertakings in the industries specified in the preceding paragraph shall operate in accordance with the law, act in good faith, exercise strict self-discipline, accept supervision from the public, and shall not use their controlling position…to harm consumers' interests.[97]

Interestingly, while the AML seeks to regulate and prevent monopolistic conduct, Article 7 underscores the State's protective role toward SOEs dominating critical industries. Notably, it prohibits such SOEs only from abusing their controlling positions to the detriment of consumer interests, without reference to the other objectives set out in Article 1, including safeguarding fair market competition, enhancing economic efficiency, protecting the public interest, and promoting the socialist market economy.[98] This formulation can reasonably be interpreted as signalling an implicit tolerance of monopoly in these industries, subject only to the minimal constraint of avoiding harm to consumers.[99] This tolerance likely stems from the State's deliberate establishment of SOE dominance in critical industries during the 'Grasp the Large and Release the Small' reforms in the second round of SOE reforms and reinforced in the latest round.[100] As discussed in Chap. 2, such dominance was designed to secure national economic efficiency and safeguard the public interest. This context helps explain why the sole restriction on such intentional State monopolies is not to harm consumer interests.

However, from its wording, Article 7 cannot reasonably be interpreted as a carve-out for SOEs from the application of the AML. For the purposes of this section, it

[95] 《国务院关于经营者集中申报标准的规定》 [Provisions of the State Council on the Notification Thresholds for Concentrations of Undertakings]. (People's Republic of China) The State Council. 26 January 2024. art. 3.

[96] See, e.g., Wang (2014), pp. 65–70; Owen et al. (2008), pp. 231–265.

[97] *AML* (n 89) art. 7.

[98] Ibid. art. 1

[99] As of June 2025, Chinese legislation interpretative authorities (the Standing Committee of the National People's Congress of China or Supreme People's Court) have not issued an official interpretation of Article 7, clarifying whether it is intended to exempt SOEs in critical industries.

[100] Ng et al. (2020), pp. 297–311.

remains relevant to the anti-trust review of concentrations of undertakings. This view is corroborated by the fact that, since 2019, the SAMR has been publishing the *China Annual Anti-trust Enforcement Reports*, which disclose the number of anti-trust reviews of concentrations of undertakings decided each year, confirming that SOEs do fall within the scope of the AML. For example, in 2024, the SAMR unconditionally approved 623 out of 643 concentration of undertakings filings, over half of which involved SOEs (335 filings).[101] This indicates that SOEs are the primary actors in mega concentrations of undertakings in China (i.e. the concentrations that meet the prescribed thresholds), consistent with the 'Grasp the Large' policy underpinning the State economy restructuring sub reform in the latest round of SOE reforms. The consistently high approval rate, as shown in successive annual reports,[102] further suggests that the Chinese government maintains a notably permissive stance toward such concentrations.

However, what warrants further investigation is whether all mega inter-SOE consolidations in critical industries are subject to anti-trust review under the AML. AML Article 22 exempts concentrations involving undertakings all of which are controlled through an absolute majority of voting rights or assets by the same undertaking, irrespective of that undertaking's participation in the concentration.[103] This exemption raises significant interpretive questions in the context of inter-SOE consolidations. At least at the first tier of business groups, all Chinese SOEs are owned by SASACs at various levels and, ultimately, by the State.[104] This institutional structure gives rise to three possible interpretations of Article 22. First, if the State is treated as a single 'undertaking' under the AML, then Article 22 would exempt all consolidations of SOEs whose absolute majority of voting rights or assets is held by the State from anti-trust review. Second, if SASACs are regarded as the relevant 'undertakings', the exemption would apply only to consolidations of SOEs directly under the same SASAC. Third, if neither the State nor SASACs qualify as 'undertakings' under the AML, Article 22 would not apply to inter-SOE consolidations at all. The AML defines 'undertaking' as a person or organisation engaged in the production, operation, or provision of goods or services.[105] From this definition, it is unclear whether 'organisation' can include the State or SASACs, which indeed perform functions of operating SOEs. However, despite the legislation interpretative authorities' silence on the anti-trust implications of inter-SOE consolidations, enforcement practice under the AML indicates that the second interpretation is the one most likely to prevail.

---

101 《中国反垄断执法年度报告(2024)》 [China Annual Antitrust Enforcement Report (2024)] SAMR. Report, p 17, 18

102 SAMR's unconditional approval rate for antitrust reviews of concentrations of operators was 96% in 2024, 98% in 2023, and 99% in 2022. Ibid; 《中国反垄断执法年度报告(2023)》 [China Annual Antitrust Enforcement Report (2023)] SAMR. Report, p 8; 《中国反垄断执法年度报告(2022)》 [China Annual Antitrust Enforcement Report (2022)] SAMR. Report, p 15.

103 *AML* (n 89) art. 22.

104 For a detailed discussion of the ownership structure of Chinese SOEs, see Chap. 4, Sect. 4.1.2.

105 *AML* (n 89) art. 12.

Notably, there have been instances in which inter-SOE consolidations that failed to submit the required filing for anti-trust review have resulted in administrative penalties. A prominent example is the December 2017 consolidation of Dalian Port Group and Yingkou Port Group.[106] At that time, the Dalian Municipal SASAC and the Yingkou Municipal SASAC, both within Liaoning Province, entered into separate agreements with Liaoning Port and Shipping, an SOE wholly owned by the Liaoning Provincial SASAC, to transfer gratuitously their respective 100 percent equity holdings in the two port groups. The stated objective was to integrate the province's port resources. Although the turnover of each acquired company exceeded the notification threshold, the transaction was not submitted for anti-trust review. SAMR subsequently determined that it constituted a reviewable concentration of undertakings and imposed a fine of RMB 350,000 on Liaoning Port Group.[107] This case demonstrates that consolidations involving SOEs held by different SASACs do not fall within the exemption for concentrations under Article 22 of the AML, nor are they shielded by Article 7, which, at most, might be read as lowering the substantive criteria applied in anti-trust reviews of inter-SOE consolidations, rather than eliminating such reviews altogether.

In contrast, the requirement for anti-trust review is far less certain in the context of central SOE consolidations. The central SASAC's published factors for considering mergers between central SOEs make no explicit reference to anti-trust concerns or the potential restrictive effects on market competition.[108] Instead, the considerations emphasise industrial policy objectives, notably including accelerating the optimisation of the State economy's structure, enhancing the efficiency of resource allocation, safeguarding the stability of supply chains, and fostering globally competitive enterprises.[109] This suggests that, for central SOE consolidations, policy priorities may take precedence over AML enforcement, potentially signalling a more permissive or discretionary approach compared with the stricter treatment applied to local SOE consolidations.

This observation is consistent with the fact that announcements of central SOE mergers have never referred to SAMR's approval for anti-trust review. The absence of such references, however, cannot be taken as evidence that inter-central SOE mergers were exempt from anti-trust review under the AML, as the law only requires SAMR to publish decisions that impose restrictions or prohibitions on

106 《市场监管总局发布对辽宁港口集团取得大连港集团和营口港务集团股权未依法申报案的行政处罚决定书》 [The State Administration for Market Regulation issued an administrative penalty decision concerning Liaoning Port Group's failure to file for review in its acquisition of equity in Dalian Port Group and Yingkou Port Group]. (People's Republic of China) SAMR. 9 December 2019.

107 Ibid. p 2, 3.

108 Central SASAC (2021)《国资委对中央企业的合并重组有哪些考虑?》 [What factors does the SASAC consider in the merger and restructuring of central SOEs?]. http://www.sasac.gov.cn/n2588040/n2590387/n9854157/c19805098/content.html. Accessed 13 Aug 2025.

109 Ibid.

concentrations of undertakings.[110] Therefore, it remains possible that such transactions were reviewed and approved.

The AML specifies a range of factors that SAMR typically considers when reviewing concentrations of undertakings, with decisive weight placed on whether the transaction would exclude or restrict competition in the relevant market.[111] In practice, this decisive criterion is generally unfavourable to mergers between central SOEs, which typically occur in critical industries dominated by SOEs, where consolidation would further increase market concentration and restrict market access. However, Article 28 of the AML provides an important exception, allowing SAMR to approve a concentration if the undertakings can demonstrate that it serves the public interest, even when the concentration has restrictive effects on competition. The statement of Peng Jianguo, Deputy Director of the Research Centre of the Central SASAC, in an interview with State-run media, reflect the Chinese government's favourable disposition toward SOE monopolies in critical industries. Peng stated:

> To judge whether there is a monopoly and whether the monopoly is good or not… we should consider whether the monopoly is conducive to improving the international competitiveness of Chinese enterprises, to safeguarding national industrial security, to protecting the fundamental interests of the people, and to preserving the long-term ecological environment for the survival and development of small and medium-sized enterprises.[112]

This statement reveals that, from the perspective of Chinese policymakers, a monopoly aligned with national development strategies and policy objectives constitutes a 'good' monopoly—one to be supported rather than dismantled. Consequently, it appears unlikely that the Chinese government would prohibit inter-SOE consolidations in critical industries through anti-trust review under the AML, as any resulting restriction of market competition would be an intentional and desirable policy outcome rather than an adverse effect to be remedied.

From an imperative perspective, it remains possible that the AML affords the enforcement authority, SAMR,[113] considerable discretion to conduct anti-trust reviews of inter-SOE consolidations.[114] In the case of central SOEs, their core business operations and restructuring plans are subject to close oversight and, in many

---

[110] *AML* (n 89) art. 30.

[111] Ibid.

[112] 经济日报 [Economic Daily] (2016) 《专家学者畅谈新一轮国企改革 央企重组如何实现"1+1>2"》 [Experts and scholars talk about how to realise '1+1 > 2' in the new round of SOE reform and central enterprises reorganization]. People. http://ccnews.people.com.cn/n1/2016/0822/c141677-28653916.html. Accessed 13 Aug 2025.

[113] 《国务院机构改革方案》 [The State Council Institutional Restructuring Plan]. (People's Republic of China) National People's Congress Standing Committee. 17 March 2018. The enforcement responsibility was shared by MOFCOM, NDRC and the State Administration for Industry and Commerce before 2018. Kovacic (2017), pp. 696–697.

[114] Scholars have observed that China's AML enforcement agencies may have incentives to apply the law selectively, aligning enforcement decisions with broader government policies and strategic interests. Ibid. pp. 696–697; Ng et al. (2020), pp. 297–311.

instances, direct orchestration by the central SASAC.[115] As both the central SASAC and SAMR operate at the same administrative level directly under the State Council, it is less likely that SAMR would block concentrations of SOE undertakings initiated by the central SASAC. By contrast, in the context of local SOE consolidations, SAMR may be more inclined to intervene through AML anti-trust review as a means of safeguarding State-owned assets and preventing their potential loss.

When SOEs acquire controlling stakes in high-tech POEs through flow-out MOR, transactions that meet the turnover thresholds for a reviewable concentration of undertakings clearly fall within the scope of mandatory anti-trust review by SAMR under the AML. However, given China's generally permissive approach to concentrations of undertakings, evident from the consistently high approval rates reported in the annual *China Anti-trust Enforcement Reports*, such review is unlikely to pose a substantial obstacle to SOE–POE acquisitions. As of August 2025, there has been no published SAMR decision imposing restrictions or prohibitions on a flow-out MOR transaction. This absence of adverse decisions may reflect the fact that undertakings involved in flow-out MOR are typically pre-selected or vetted by the relevant SASACs and are aligned with national reform policies. As a result, SAMR would be inclined to intervene only in exceptional circumstances, such as where transactions occur at the local level and present a high risk of loss of State-owned assets.

3.4 Concluding Remarks: The Potential Implications on SOEs' Outbound FDI Activities

In the latest round of SOE reforms, the MOR is expanding China's mixed-ownership economy, characterised by the equity integration of State and non-State ownership. This chapter demonstrates that the MOR is not meant to privatise SOEs and weaken the State economy but rather to strengthen it by establishing equity ties with POEs or foreign enterprises with strategic competitiveness that can make up for the deficit of SOEs.

The MOR is implemented in two distinct approaches: flow-in and flow-out. Despite differences in implementation scope and specific policies, the two approaches incorporate Chinese POEs or foreign enterprises that participate in the reform into SOE equity networks that are becoming increasingly intertwined in the State economy restructuring reform, another sub-reform of the latest round of SOE reforms. In addition, the classification of SOEs, which is a prerequisite for the implementation of flow-in MOR, can help differentiate between Chinese SOEs that may evolve into policy-driven SOEs and those that may evolve into market-oriented SOEs in the latest round of SOEs.

[115] For a detailed discussion of the State-orchestrated nature of inter-SOE consolidations, see Chap. 2, Sect. 2.3.1.

Several practical challenges are highlighted in this chapter that might impede the MOR's progress, primarily including the incomplete classification of SOEs, the lack of non-SOE minority shareholder protection mechanism with respect to flow-in MOR, and the absence of a mechanism to preserve the original innovation capacity and efficiency of targeted POEs with respect to flow-out MOR. Therefore, how significantly the MOR can strengthen the Chinese State economy remains to be seen. Regardless of how the MOR will be carried out, the reform is extending the reach of China's SOEs into the private sector through the expansion of equity networks. However, the MOR will not alter the *status quo*, in which POEs and foreign investors are barred from China's critical industries, which are dominated by SOEs.

Given the formation and expansion of Chinese SOE-POE ties in the MOR, the reform may have the following implications for Chinese FDI.

Firstly, the presence of POE shareholders or foreign shareholders in Chinese SOEs may contribute to the commercial rationale for SOE FDI decisions, provided that the non-SOE shareholders are not completely marginalised in SOE governance practices. Whether they are marginalised depends on the percentages of stake they are permitted to acquire and whether non-SOE minority shareholder protection mechanisms are in place to ensure their participation in the SOE's decision-making process.

Secondly, FDI from Chinese SOEs whose shareholders include not only the government or government-affiliated entities, such as other SOEs, but also POEs and foreign companies, may reduce the sensitivity of the investments in the eyes of host States and local communities. This is because non-State shareholders could promote the perception that Chinese SOE investors are politically independent. This is especially important when the FDI is subject to national security-based government scrutiny at entry or during operations in the host States.

Thirdly, Chinese high-tech POEs acquired or invested in by SOEs in flow-out MOR may become FDI instruments for their SOE shareholders, specialising in making FDI in developed countries with technological superiority in fields related to China's 'strategic emerging industries'.

In the context of the global race for technological breakthroughs and the growing Sino-Western geopolitical tensions, developed countries are becoming increasingly vigilant against Chinese technology acquisitions, especially from Chinese SOEs. This makes it difficult for Chinese SOE investments in high-tech sectors to pass the foreign investment screening mechanisms in the host States. FDI from Chinese POEs may cause fewer concerns than SOE investments.

The implications of the MOR on Chinese investments pivot around the SOE-POE equity ties and, as a result, the increasingly intensified intra-firm resource integration and transfer connections. Suppose host States acknowledge the expanding SOE equity networks in the MOR. In that case, they may pay special attention to Chinese POE investments in technological sectors due to the possibility of technology transfer back to their SOE shareholders.

References

Central SASAC (2021) 《国资委对中央企业的合并重组有哪些考虑?》 [What factors does the SASAC consider in the merger and restructuring of central SOEs?]. http://www.sasac.gov.cn/n2588040/n2590387/n9854157/c19805098/content.html. Accessed 13 Aug 2025

CGN Power (2018) 2017 Annual Report. Report

Chen C (2016) Solving the Puzzle of Corporate Governance of State-Owned Enterprises: the path of the Temasek model in Singapore and lessons for China. Northwestern J Int Law Bus 36(2):303–370, 368

China Daily (2014) Tencent to Buy Stake in Digital Map Provider Navinfo. https://www.chinadaily.com.cn/bizchina/tech/2014-05/06/content_17487186.htm. Accessed 13 Aug 2025

China Daily (2022) 《江中药业成功入选"科改示范企业"》 [Jiangzhong Pharmaceutical was Successfully Selected as 'Science and Technology Reform Demonstration Enterprise']. https://jx.chinadaily.com.cn/a/202203/30/WS6243b108a3101c3ee7ace037.html. Accessed 13 Aug 2025

China Unicom (2017) 《中国联通混改三个没想到》 [The Mixed Ownership Reform of China Unicom: 'Three Unexpected']. http://www.chinaunicom.com.cn/news/201708/1503301913304050446.html. Accessed 13 Aug 2025

Cui L, Jiang F (2010) Behind ownership decision of Chinese outward FDI: resources and Institutions. Asia Pac J Manage 27(4):751–774. 763

Ding Yiting [丁怡婷] (2021) 《国投集团——服务国计民生 发展新兴产业(国企改革三年行动)》 [SDIC—Serving the National Economy and the People's Livelihood and Developing Emerging Industries (Three-year Action Plan for the SOE Reforms)]. People. http://cpc.people.com.cn/n1/2021/0527/c64387-32114629.html. Accessed 13 Aug 2025

Du Yanfei [杜燕飞] (2021) 《以改革创新激发高质量发展动力 开启新国投建设新征程》 [Reforming and Innovating to Promote Growth, Embarking on the Construction of a New SDIC]. People. http://finance.people.com.cn/n1/2021/0407/c1004-32071951.html. Accessed 13 Aug 2025

Economic Daily [经济日报] (2016) 《专家学者畅谈新一轮国企改革 央企重组如何实现"1+1>2"》 [Experts and scholars talk about how to realise '1+1 > 2' in the new round of SOE reform and central enterprises reorganization]. People. http://ccnews.people.com.cn/n1/2016/0822/c141677-28653916.html. Accessed 13 Aug 2025

Emily Feng (2021) The Latest Target in China's Crackdown on Entrepreneurs is an Outspoken Billionaire. NPR. https://www.npr.org/2021/05/15/996241784/the-latest-target-in-chinas-crackdown-on-entrepreneurs-is-an-outspoken-billionai. Accessed 13 Aug 2025

Faccio M (2006) Politically connected firms. Am Econ Rev 96(1):369–386

Hao Peng [郝鹏] (2019) 《在中央企业负责人会议上的讲话》 [Speech at the Meeting of Heads of Central Enterprises 2019]. Speech. 中央企业负责人会议 [Meeting of Heads of Central Enterprises 2019], p 25

Hu J (2012) Firmly March on the Path of Socialism with Chinese Characteristics and Strive to Complete the Building of a Moderately Prosperous Society in All Respects. 18th CCP National Congress. Report

Kikeri S, Nellis J, Shirley M (1992) Privatization: the lessons of experience. The World Bank, pp 49–52

Kim KA, Kitsabunnarat-Chatjuthamard P, Nofsinger JR (2007) Large shareholders, board independence, and minority shareholder rights: evidence from Europe. J Corp Finance 13(5):859–880

Kovacic WE (2017) Competition policy and state-owned enterprises in China. World Trade Rev 16(4):693–711, 696–697

Milhaupt CJ, Zheng W (2015) Beyond ownership: state capitalism and the Chinese Firm. Georgetown Law J 103(3):665–722. 688

National Energy Administration (2019) 《中广核四项改革试点齐发动 争创"世界一流"》 [CGN Launches Four Pilot Reforms in an Attempt to Achieve 'World-Class']. http //www.nea.gov.cn/2019-01/17/c_137751944.htm. Accessed 13 Aug 2025
NBS (2020) National Data. https://data.stats.gov.cn/easyquery.htm?cn=C01. Accessed 13 Aug 2025
NDRC (2021) 《混合所有制改革如何"混"怎么"改"?》 [Mixed Ownership Reform: How to 'Mix' and How to 'Reform'?]. https://www.ndrc.gov.cn/wsdwhfz/202112/t20211231_1311180.html. Accessed 13 Aug 2025
Ng W et al (2020) State interest and the state-centered approach to competition law in China. Antitrust Bull 65(2):297–311
ORG Technology (2018) The Era of 2.0 of Strategic Cooperation between O.R.G. and CPMC Holdings Limited. https://www.orgtech.cn/en/index.php?m=content&c=index&a=show&catid=73&id=10. Accessed 13 Aug 2025
Ouyang Kai [欧阳凯] (2017) 《张剑锋:混改是核技术产业化的下一个突破口》 [Interview with Zhang Jianfeng, Chairman of CGN Nuclear Technology: Mixed Ownership Reform is the Next Breakthrough of Nuclear Technology Industrialization]. National Business Daily. http //www.nbd.com.cn/articles/2017-07-16/1128407.html. Accessed 13 Aug 2025
Owen BM, Sun S, Zheng W (2008) China's competition policy reforms: the anti-monopoly law and beyond. Antitrust Law J 75(1):231–265
People (2017) 《国资委:鼓励国有资本以多种方式入股非国有企业》 [SASAC: Encourage State-Owned Capital to Join Non-SOEs in Various Ways]. http://ccnews.people.com.cn/n1/2017/1213/c141677-29703045.html. Accessed 13 Aug 2025
People (2019) 《国家电投黄河项目引入8家战略投资者增资242亿元》 [China Power Investment Corporation's Yellow River Project Introduces 8 Strategic Investors to Increase Capital by 24.2 Billion Yuan]. http://energy.people.com.cn/n1/2019/1218/c71661-31511396.html. Accessed 13 Aug 2025
People's Daily (2016) 《更好发挥改革牵引作用》 [Give Better Play to the Leading Role of the Reform]. The Stat Council. https://www.gov.cn/xinwen/2016-12/20/content_5150293.htm. Accessed 13 Aug 2025
People's Daily (2020a) 《中国化学工程集团释放最高股权比例推进混改》 [The China National Chemical Engineering Corporation has Released the Highest Proportion of Its Shareholding to Promote the Mixed Ownership Reform]. The Central SASAC http://www.sasac.gov.cn/n2588025/n2588139/c14884977/content.html. Accessed 13 Aug 2025
People's Daily (2020b) 《以混促改'谋发展》 ['Promoting Reform via Mixing' to Pursue Development]. The Central SASAC. http://www.sasac.gov.cn/n2588025/n2588139/c14884977/content.html. Accessed 13 Aug 2025
Reuters (2016) NavInfo, Tencent, GIC Buy 10 pct Stake in Mapping Firm HERE. https://www.reuters.com/article/here-equity/navinfo-tencent-gic-buy-10-pct-stake-in-mapping-firm-here-idUKL5N1EM0BA. Accessed 13 Aug 2025
Reuters (2021) China Baowu Steel unit opens 2.3 mln tonnes/year steel scrap plant. https://www.reuters.com/article/china-baowu-scrap-idINL4N2JG0RL. Accessed 13 Aug 2025
SASAC of the People's Government of Jiangsu Province (2016) 《江苏国资委完成省属企业功能界定与分类》 [Jiangsu SASAC Completed the Function Demarcation and Classification of Provincial Enterprises]
SDIC Gaoxin (2020) 《国投高新着力提升相对控股混合所有制企业党建工作水平》 [SDIC Gaoxin is Committed to Bolstering MOEs' Party-Building Efforts]. https://www.gaoxin-china.com.cn/gtgx/djyqywh/dqjs/webinfo/2020/01/1580510268314622.htm. Accessed 13 Aug 2025
SDICFUND (2019) 《国投参与国药股权多元化改革试点》 [SDIC Successfully Participates in Sinopharm's Equity Diversification Reform Pilot Programme]. https://sdicfund.com/gtcx/gszx/gsxw/webinfo/2020/11/160637807763607589.htm. Accessed 13 Aug 2025

Shi Nengzi and Wu Furong [施能自, 吴芙蓉] (2017) 《新一轮国企改革的思考与操作实务》 [Thoughts and Operational Practices of the Latest Round of SOE Reforms]. 中国经济出版社 [Economic Press China], p 24
SOE Reform Process Writing Group [国企改革历程编写组] (2019) 《国企改革历程 1978-2018》 [The Course of Chinese State-Owned Enterprise Reform 1978-2018]. 中国经济出版社 [Economic Press China], p 374
Tao R, Lin JY, Liu M (2013) Deregulation, decentralization, and China's growth in transition. In: Kennedy D, Stiglitz JE (eds) Law and economics with Chinese characteristics: institutions for promoting development in the twenty-first century. Oxford University Press
The 13th Five-Year Plan for Economic and Social Development of the People's Republic of China (2016-2020). (People's Republic of China) The CCP Central Committee. May 2021, pt. II ch. 6. https://en.ndrc.gov.cn/policies/202105/P020210527785800103339.pdf. Accessed 13 Aug 2025
The CCP Central Committee (2021) The 13th Five-Year Plan for Economic and Social Development of the People's Republic of China (2016-2020). pt. II ch. 6. NDRC. https://en.ndrc.gov.cn/policies/202105/P020210527785800103339.pdf. Accessed 13 Aug 2025
The Central SASAC (2017) 《专家为国企改革提高效能建言献策》 [Experts Offer Advice on the SOE Reform to Improve Effectiveness]. http://www.sasac.gov.cn/n2588025/n2588134/c4542476/content.html. Accessed 13 Aug 2025.
The Central SASAC (2021) 《2020 央企经济运行情况新闻发布会实录》 [Record of Press Conference on Economic Operation of Central Enterprises 2020]. http://www.sasac.gov.cn/n2588035/n2588330/n2588360/c16563166/content.html. Accessed 13 Aug 2025
The Central SASAC (2022) 《华润集团国企改革三年行动取得积极成效》 [China Resources Group's Three-Year Action on SOE Reforms Produces Positive Results]. http://www.sasac.gov.cn/n4470048/n13461446/n15390485/n15769618/c24856155/content.html. Accessed 13 Aug 2025
The Heritage Foundation (2023) 2023 Index of Economic Freedom. https://www.heritage.org/index/. Accessed 13 Aug 2025
The State Council (2017a) 《从中国联通试点方案看国企混改新动向》 [See the New Trend of Mixed Ownership Reform of SOEs Through the China Unicom Reform Pilot Programme]. https://www.gov.cn/xinwen/2017-08/22/content_5219638.htm. Accessed 13 Aug 2025
The State Council (2017b) 《山东:国企混改允许中小股东董事提名表决权合并计算》 [Shandong: Mixed Ownership Reform of SOEs Allows Small and Medium-sized Shareholders to Nominate Directors based on Combined Voting Rights]. https://www.gov.cn/xinwen/2017-02/09/content_5166777.htm. Accessed 13 Aug 2025
The State Council (2017c) 《深入推进国企混改》 [Deepening the Mixed Ownership Reform of SOEs]. https://www.gov.cn/xinwen/2017-12/19/content_5248342.htm. Accessed 13 Aug 2025
The State Council (2019) 《第四批混改试点数量、领域均大幅增长》 [The Number and Areas of the Fourth Batch of Mixed Reform Pilot Projects Increased Significantly]. http://www.gov.cn/xinwen/2019-11/16/content_5452621.htm. Accessed 13 Aug 2025
The State Council (2021a) 《国家发展改革委介绍支持民营企业改革发展情况》 [NDRC Introduces the Support for POE Reform and Development]. https://www.gov.cn/xinwen/2021-10/22/content_5644185.htm. Accessed 13 Aug 2025
The State Council (2021b) Major Targets in the 14th Five-Year Plan (2021-2025). http://english.www.gov.cn/w/14thfiveyearplan/. Accessed 13 Aug 2025
US Department of Defense (2021) Entities Identified as Chinese Military Companies Operating in the United States. https://media.defense.gov/2021/Jun/03/2002734519/-1/-1/0/ENTITIES-IDENTIFIED-AS-CHINESE-MILITARY-COMPANIES-OPERATING-IN-THE-US.PDF. Accessed 13 Aug 2025
Wang Chunhui [王春晖] (2017) 《剖析中国联通混改的战略意义》 [Analyzing the Strategic Significance of China Unicom's Mixed Ownership Reform: Three Highlights]. People. http://ccnews.people.com.cn/n1/2017/0821/c141677-29483853.html. Accessed 13 Aug 2025
Wang W, Peng P (2014) 《政治关系，经营环境，与民营上市公司银行贷款及其经济后果》 [Political Connection, Operating Environment and Private Listed Companies' Access to Bank Loans and Their Economic Consequences]. J Shanxi Finance Econ Univ 12:83–95

Wang X (2014) The evolution of China's anti-monopoly law: competition law in China. Edward Elgar, pp 65–70

Wataru Kodaka (2017) China Baowu Steel Divests Portion of E-commerce Subsidiary. Nikkei Asia. https://asia.nikkei.com/Business/China-Baowu-Steel-divests-portion-of-e-commerce-subsidiary. Accessed 13 Aug 2025

Xi Jinping [习近平] (2014) 《在中央全面深改革领导小组第七次会议上的讲话》 [Speech at the 7th Meeting of the Central Leading Group for Comprehensively Deepening Reform]. Speech. The 7th Meeting of the Central Leading Group for Comprehensively Deepening Reform

Xinhua News Agency (2017) 《联通混改方案获国资委放行》 [Unicom's Mixed Ownership Reform Plan has been Approved by the Central SASAC]. http://m.news.cn/tech/2017-09/18/c_1121678597.htm. Accessed 13 Aug 2025

Xu C (2011) The fundamental institutions of China's reforms and development. J Econ Liter 49(4):1076–1151

Zhao C, Zhang Y (2015) Several major issues on deepening state-owned enterprises reform. China Econ J 8(2):143–157. 144

Zhong C (2021) The innovation-driven development and nation-building strategy. In: He D, Zhixiong D, Xia J (eds) Chinese finance policy for a new era. Palgrave Macmillan

Zhou W, Gao H, Bai X (2019) Buidling a market economy through WTO-inspired reform of state-owned enterprises in China Int Comp Law Quart 68(4): 977–1022, p 985

Additional Sources

《中共中央国务院深化国有企业改革的指导意见》 [The Guiding Opinions of the CCP Central Committee and the State Council on Deepening the Reform of State-Owned Enterprises]. (People's Republic of China) CCP Central Committee and the State Council. 24 August 2015

《中华人民共和国公司法》[Company Law of the People's Republic of China] (People's Republic of China) adopted at the 8th National People's Congress Standing Committee, 29 December 1993, amended 25 December 1999, 28 August 2004, 28 December 2013 and 26 October 2018, art 71

《中华人民共和国反不正当竞争法》 [Anti-Unfair Competition Law of the PRC]. (People's Republic of China) Adopted at the 8th National People's Congress Standing Committee. 2 September 1993, amended 4 November 2017, 23 April 2019, art. 6-12

《中华人民共和国反垄断法》 [Anti-Monopoly Law of the PRC]. (People's Republic of China) Adopted at the 10th National People's Congress Standing Committee. 30 August 2007, amended 24 June 2022

《中国制造 2025》 [Made in China 2025]. (People's Republic of China) The State Council. 8 May 2015

《中国反垄断执法年度报告(2022)》 [China Annual Antitrust Enforcement Report (2022)] SAMR. Report, p 15

《中国反垄断执法年度报告(2024)》 [China Annual Antitrust Enforcement Report (2024)] SAMR. Report, p 17, 18

《中央企业混合所有制改革操作指引》 [The Operation Guidelines on Mixed Ownership Reform of Central Enterprises]. (People's Republic of China) The Central SASAC. 31 October 2019

《中央国有资本经营预算支出管理暂行办法》 [Interim Measures for the Administration of Central State-Owned Capital Operating Budget Expenditure]. (People's Republic of China) MOF. 13 March 2017

《关于国有企业功能界定与分类的指导意见》 [Guiding Opinions on the Definition and Classification of Functions of State-Owned Enterprises]. (People's Republic of China) The State Council. 29 December 2015

《关于明确省属企业功能定位实施分类监管的意见》 [Opinions on Defining the Functional Orientation of Provincial Enterprises and Implementing Supervision Based on Classification]. (People' s Republic of China) SASAC of the People' s Government of Zhejiang Province. 5 April 2016
《关于省属国有企业混合所有制改革发挥中小股东作用的指导意见》 [Guiding opinions of SASAC of Shandong Province on Promoting the Role of Small and Medium Shareholders in the Mixed Ownership Reform of Provincial State-Owned Enterprises]. (People' s Republic of China) SASAC of the People' s Government of Shandong Province. 3 February 2017
《国务院关于国有企业发展混合所有制经济的意见》 [Opinions of the State Council on the Development of Mixed Ownership Economy by State-Owned Enterprises]. (People' s Republic of China) The State Council. 24 September 2015
《国务院关于经营者集中申报标准的规定》 [Provisions of the State Council on the Notification Thresholds for Concentrations of Undertakings]. (People' s Republic of China) The State Council. 26 January 2024. art. 3
《国务院办公厅关于推动中央企业结构调整与重组的指导意见》 [Guiding Opinions on Promoting Structural Adjustment and Reorganization of Central Enterprises by the General Office of the State Council]. (People' s Republic of China) General Office of the State Council. 17 July 2016
《国务院机构改革方案》 [The State Council Institutional Restructuring Plan]. (People' s Republic of China) National People' s Congress Standing Committee. 17 March 2018
《市场监管总局发布对辽宁港口集团取得大连港集团和营口港务集团股权未依法申报案的行政处罚决定书》 [The State Administration for Market Regulation issued an administrative penalty decision concerning Liaoning Port Group' s failure to file for review in its acquisition of equity in Dalian Port Group and Yingkou Port Group]. (People' s Republic of China) SAMR. 9 December 2019
《战略性新兴产业分类 (2018)》 [Classification of Strategic Emerging Industries (2018)]. (People' s Republic of China) NBS. 7 November 2018
《江苏国资委完成省属企业功能界定与分类》 [Jiangsu SASAC Completed the Function Demarcation and Classification of Provincial Enterprises]. (People' s Republic of China) SASAC of the People' s Government of Jiangsu Province. 8 December 2016
《中国反垄断执法年度报告(2023)》 [China Annual Antitrust Enforcement Report (2023)] SAMR. Report, p 8
中国社会科学院工业经济研究所课题组 [Research Group of Institute of Industrial Economics of CASS] (2014) 《论新时期全面深化国有企业改革重大任务》 [Analysis of the Major Tasks for Comprehensively Deepening the Reform of State-Owned Economy in the New Era].中国工业经济 [China Industrial Economics] 318: 5-24, p 24
《中国神华煤制油化工有限公司、上海福辉化工有限公司损害公司利益责任纠纷二审民事裁定书》[Civil Decision on Liability Dispute for Injuring the Company' s Interests in the Second Instance between China Shenhua Coal-to-Oil Chemical Industry Co, Ltd and Shanghai Fuhui Chemical Industry Co]. 中华人民共和国最高人民法院 [Supreme People' s Court of the PRC]. 最高法民辖终481号 [Economic Appeal No 481]. 19 December 2019
《关于省属企业功能界定与分类的实施方案》 [Implementation Plan on Function Definition and Classification of Provincial Enterprises]. (People' s Republic of China) SASAC of the People' s Government of Hainan Province. 11 August 2016
国务院国资委改革办 [Reform Office of the Central SASAC] (2018) 《国企改革探索与实践—中央企业子企业150例(上)》 [Exploration and Practice of State-Owned Enterprise Reform—150 Cases of Subsidiary Enterprises of Central Enterprises (Part I)]. 中国经济出版社 [Economic Press China], p 299

Chapter 4
State-owned Assets Management and SOE Governance Reform: CCP Control Is Looming Again

Abstract The significant number of Chinese SOEs and their growing international presence have raised concerns about the extent of political control over modern SOEs. This chapter offers a comprehensive analysis of the evolving governance framework of Chinese SOEs, with a particular focus on the increasing integration of political oversight into the legal structure governing SOEs. By examining recent reforms and legislative developments, this chapter highlights how China's governance model diverges from internationally recognized corporate governance standards by embedding Chinese Communist Party (CCP) authority within SOE governance frameworks. It provides a detailed analysis of the intersection between political authority and corporate governance, emphasizing the role of CCP leadership as enshrined in the amended Company Law and related reforms. The study reveals a strategic shift in the Chinese government's approach to SOE oversight, moving from centralised control to a governance model characterised by decentralized supervision and the introduction of conceptually ambiguous institutional entities such as State-owned Capital Investment and Operation Companies. The findings offer critical insights into the institutional mechanisms shaping SOE decision-making and international expansion, underscoring the global significance of Chinese SOE reforms and their role in shaping international economic governance.

In the latest round of SOE reforms, the State economy restructuring reform aims to bolster the overall strength of the State economy through inter-SOE consolidations in critical industries and the elimination of low-performing SOEs. The mixed ownership reform is expanding SOE-POE equity networks with the intention of facilitating centralised control and intra-network firm resource mobilisation. In the meantime, the Chinese government is pushing for transformation of the SOEs' internal controlling regimes by reforming the SOE governance system and the State-owned assets management system.

The Organization for Economic Co-operation and Development (OECD), in its guidelines on corporate governance of SOEs, highlights passive ownership (which refers to the shareholder not being actively involved in the management and

T. Gu, *Chinese SOE Reforms and Global FDI*, Contemporary Chinese Civil and Commercial Law, https://doi.org/10.1007/978-981-92-3181-2_4

operations of the business) on the one hand and excessive State intervention on the other as the most pressing problems concerning SOE governance.[1] Both challenges are exceptionally significant for Chinese SOEs due to China's persistently large number of SOEs and its socialist market economy system, characterised by the coexistence of market competition and government intervention.[2]

China has made progress in prior rounds of SOE reforms in regulating the exercise of State ownership functions to ensure SOEs operate efficiently and accountably, particularly by enhancing SOE governance practices and centralising government oversight over State-owned assets to combat loss of the assets in SOE operations or corporatisation. During the second round of SOE reforms in the early 1990s, the CCP Central Committee mandated that Chinese SOEs adopt a global-standard corporate governance system consisting of a board of directors, board of supervisors and senior management team.[3] In the third round of SOE reforms launched in 2002, the Hu Jintao administration established a centralised State-owned assets management system primarily administered by the SASACs at all levels.[4] In the latest round of SOE reforms, the Xi Jinping administration has continued the reforms of the State-owned assets management system and SOE governance system,[5] but with significant innovations in institutional design.

The lengthy course of reform and the complexity of the policy mix have given rise to the question whether the ongoing reforms of China's State-owned assets management system and SOE governance system have lessened or strengthened government and the CCP control over SOEs. The answer to this question is crucial for foreign countries where Chinese SOEs are expanding their presence, as suspicions that Chinese SOEs are subject to political influence or direction are a common concern among foreign countries regarding Chinese SOE investments.

In order to answer this question, this chapter is organised as follows: Sections 4.1 and 4.2 examine the policies released in the State-owned assets management system

[1] OECD (2015b), p. 7.

[2] Ding (2009), pp. 235–241.

[3] 《中共中央关于建立社会主义市场经济体制若干问题的决定》 [Decision of the CCP Central Committee on Some Issues Concerning the Establishment of a Socialist Market Economic System]. (People's Republic of China) The CCP Central Committee. 14 November 1993 ('*The CCP Decision on Economic System*'); 《国务院关于2005年深化经济体制改革的意见》 [Opinions of the State Council on Deepening Economic Restructuring in 2005]. (People's Republic of China) The State Council. 4 April 2005.

[4] The Central SASAC was established in 2003 as the ad hoc agency directly under the State Council, while all provinces have set up their provincial SASACs by June 2004. By the end of 2018, China had set up 325 SASACs at municipal (prefectural) level in total, 133 among which are ad hoc agencies directly under local governments. 国企改革历程编写组 [SOE Reform Process Writing Group] (2019) 《国企改革历程 1978-2018》 [The Course of Chinese State-Owned Enterprise Reform 1978-2018]. 中国经济出版社 [Economic Press China], pp. 246–247 ('*SOE Reforms 1978-2018*').

[5] 《国务院办公厅关于进一步完善国有企业法人治理结构的指导意见》 [Guiding Opinions on Further Improving the Corporate Governance Structure of State-Owned Enterprises]. (People's Republic of China) The General Office of the State Council. 24 April 2017 ('*Guiding Opinions on SOE Governance*').

reform and SOE governance system reform in China's latest round of SOE reforms respectively. These sections look at case studies to investigate the progress of the reforms in practice and reveal their underlying policy rationale and demonstrate that the reforms are bringing about two significant changes in government administration of SOEs and SOE governance practice, namely the introduction of State-owned capital investment and operation companies (SCIOs), as supplements to the SASACs, and the resurgence of CCP leadership in the SOE governance system. Section 4.3 concludes.

This chapter argues that the Chinese Party-State is shifting its controlling mechanisms over SOEs in the latest round of SOE reforms. The shift from centralised control centred on SASACs to political control embedded in the governance system primarily relies on three mechanisms: the decentralisation of State ownership functions to core companies of BGs, the supremacy of the Party Committee in SOE governance and the intensification of political control over SOE personnel. The implementation these changes is significantly increasing political supervision and control over SOEs in China, encompassing their investments in foreign countries.

4.1 The State-owned Assets Management System Reform: Decentralisation of State Ownership Functions

As part of the third round of SOE reforms commenced in 2002, the Hu Jintao administration established the SASAC of the State Council, also known as the central SASAC, as the highest government department specialising in State-owned assets supervision and management. In the subsequent year, each of China's 32 province-level administrative divisions (including 23 provinces, four self-governing cities and five autonomous regions) established its own SASAC.[6] Since its inception, the SASAC system has played a central role in the Chinese government's supervision and management of State-owned assets, particularly SOEs. SASACs fulfil various functions, serving as administrator of the State-owned capital management system, acting as the State shareholder of SOEs, and regulating SOEs within their respective regions.

The multiple functions of SASACs result from the third round of SOE reforms' centralization of government control over SOEs and State-owned assets. However, the latest round of SOE reforms is decentralising the control and relieving SASACs of part of their functions. This does not mean, however, that control is effectively reduced.

[6] *SOE Reforms 1978-2018* (n 4) p 247.

4.1.1 The Centralised Role of SASACs at the Apex of SOEs

Prior to 2002, the responsibility of overseeing State-owned assets and SOEs in China was fragmented between various governmental agencies, including the Ministry of Finance, the Ministry of Labour and Social Security, the State Economic and Trade Commission (disbanded) and the Enterprise Working Committee of the CCP Central Committee (disbanded).[7] However, this multiple supervision system led to chaotic supervision practices and the substantial loss of State-owned assets. In this context, establishing the SASAC system in the third round of SOE reforms marked the beginning of centralised government supervision of SOEs in China.[8]

Setting up a centralised State-owned assets management regime was not a sudden reform innovation by the Hu Jintao administration upon taking office. In the farewell report to the 16th National Congress of the CCP in 2002, former Chinese president Jiang Zemin stated that establishing a centralised SOE and State-owned assets management regime was a planned objective for future SOE reforms.[9] In addition, Jiang laid down guiding principles for the future administration of State-owned assets, which have been adhered to thus far. The principles notably include separating State-owned assets management functions from government public administration functions ('政资分开') and separating SOEs' ownership from management rights ('所有权和经营权分开'),[10] which essentially mirrors the 'separation of ownership and control' principle of modern Western corporate governance.[11]

Under the two guiding principles, before the latest round of SOE reforms, SASACs held dual responsibilities in the State-owned assets administration regime: supervising and administering SOEs and State-owned assets invested in SOEs and exercising shareholder functions on behalf of the State in SOEs. The supervisory responsibility requires SASACs to oversee SOEs in all facets of their corporate operations, from financial management and investment planning to hiring and performance evaluation.[12] China's former President Jiang Zemin first proposed the State shareholder functions of SASAC in his report to the 16th National Congress of the CCP. According to the report, the functions originated in a dual-layer delegation of State ownership functions. As the ultimate owner of State-owned assets

[7] State Economic and Trade Commission, Enterprise Working Committee of the CCP Central Committee were disbanded in 2002 when its functions were completely transferred to the Central SASAC. Ibid. pp. 245–246.

[8] Wu (2016), pp. 261–324, p 282.

[9] 江泽民 [Jiang Zemin] (2002) 《中国共产党第十六次全国代表大会上的报告》 [Report of the 16th National Congress of the Chinese Communist Party]. Speech. 16th National Congress of the Chinese Communist Party.

[10] *SOE Reforms 1978-2018* (n 4) p 246.

[11] See generally Fama and Jensen (1983), pp. 301–325.

[12] 《国务院国有资产监督管理委员会主要职责内设机构和人员编制规定》 [The Regulation of The Internal Organs and Staffing of the State-Owned Assets and Administration Commission of the State Council]. (People's Republic of China) General Office of the State Council. 25 April 2003.

invested in SOEs, the Chinese State delegates the shareholder rights to the PRC governments at various levels, and the governments, in turn, delegate the rights to their subordinate SASACs.[13] The dual-layer delegation of State ownership functions was subsequently codified in the 2008 *Law on the State-Owned Assets of Enterprises* (*State-owned Assets Law*).[14]

The shareholder-regulator responsibilities allowed SASACs to intervene in virtually every aspect of the management and operations of SOEs. The CCP Central Committee described this all-encompassing authority as 'combining the management of State-owned capital, personnel and company affairs in SOEs' (管资、管人、管事相结合'), establishing it as a general principle of China's State-owned assets management system.[15] However, the latest round of SOE reform promotes a functional transformation of SASACs, partially relieving them of State shareholder functions, which the State Council describes as a 'shift from managing [State-owned] enterprises to managing [State-owned] capital' ('从管企到管资').[16]

The overburdening of SASACs with dual responsibilities necessitated this functional shift. Each SASAC is expected to serve concurrently as a shareholder and regulator for an average of over thirty BGs. It is typical for a Chinese State-owned BG to have a complex corporate structure with more than 10 tiers and hundreds of subsidiaries across various sectors. As a result, for example, the central SASAC is in charge of 100 central BGs with over 14,000 subsidiaries,[17] despite the trimming-off programmes implemented as part of the State economy restructuring reform (discussed in Chap. 2). Given the sheer number of SOEs, SASACs have demonstrated that they lack the proficiency, personnel and resources required to effectively track down the ownership pyramids of BGs and fulfil their responsibilities as a shareholder in the firm-specific decision-making process in an accountable manner.[18]

The factual overburdening of SASACs in fulfilling the State ownership functions has exacerbated the problem of passive State ownership in SOE governance. This could boost the likelihood of self-serving behaviour by corporate insiders, as the factual absence of the shareholder diminishes the incentives for SOE executives to act in the best interests of the enterprise and the State (i.e. the general public) as the

---

13 江泽民 [Jiang Zemin] (2002).

14 《中华人民共和国企业国有资产法》 [Law of the People's Republic of China on State-Owned Assets in Enterprises]. (People's Republic of China) Adopted at the 11th National People's Congress Standing Committee. 28 October 2008, art. 11 ('*State-Owned Assets Law*').

15 *SOE Reforms 1978-2018* (n 4) p 246.

16 《国务院国资委以管资本为主推进职能转变的方案》 [The Plan for Promoting the Functional Transition of State-Owned Assets Supervision and Administration Commission of the State Council to Focus on the Management of Capital]. (People's Republic of China) General Office of the State Council. 27 April 2017.

17 The list of China's 100 central SOEs can be accessed at: http://wap.sasac.gov.cn/n2588045/n27271785/n27271792/c14159097/content.html. Accessed 15 Aug 2025.

18 Milhaupt and Zheng (2015), pp. 665–722, p. 678; Ding (2020), pp. 637–663, p. 649.

ultimate owner.[19] In addition, there is an inherent conflict in the dual roles of SOE shareholders and regulators, leaving SASACs to act as both a player and referee in matters regarding SOE governance. This raised the incentives for SASAC officials to engage in self-serving behaviour when regulating or managing SOEs.

Since the Xi Jinping administration launched the anti-corruption campaign concerning the government and SOEs at the 18th CCP National Congress,[20] there have been numerous reports that the heads of significant SOEs and SASACs at various levels have been investigated or penalised for corruption-related violations of laws and CCP discipline. These include the former director of the central SASAC and heads of national champions that dominate critical industries, such as State Grid Corporation of China in the electric power industry, China National Offshore Oil Corporation in oil and gas industry and the China Shipbuilding Industry Corporation in the shipbuilding industry.[21]

4.1.2 The 'Retreat' of SASACs in the Latest Round of SOE Reforms

Given the overburdening of SASACs in the centralised State-owned assets management system, the latest round of SOE reforms has focused on creating a 'System of Authorised Operation of State-owned Capital' (the 'System') under which State-owned capital investment companies and State-owned capital operation companies (SCICs and SCOCs, collectively referred to as SCIOs) relieve SASACs of some of their supervisory and shareholder functions.

4.1.2.1 The System of Authorised Operation of State-owned Capital

The latest round of SOE reforms launched the System as a replacement for the dual-layer delegation of State ownership functions that Jiang announced at the 16th National Congress of the CCP.[22] Figure 4.1 compares the System's institutional

---

[19] Milhaupt and Zheng (2015), pp. 677–678. OECD (2015b), p. 12; Zhang and Freestone (2013), pp. 77–99.

[20] See generally Piao and Jung (2021), pp. 711–741.

[21] See, eg, 王子铭 [Wang Ziming] (2023) 《坚决打赢反腐败斗争攻坚战持久战》 [Unwaveringly Prevailing in the Arduous Fight Against Corruption]. The State Council. https://www.gov.cn/xinwen/2023-01/05/content_5735650.htm. Accessed 15 Aug 2025; Central Commission for Disciplinary Inspection of the Communist Party of China (2015) 《国务院国资委主任蒋洁敏涉嫌严重违纪正接受组织调查》 [Jiang Jiemin, Director of the Central SASAC, is under Investigation for Serious Violations of Discipline]. http://www.ccdi.gov.cn/scdc/zggb/zjsc/201511/t20151120_115801.html. Accessed 15 Aug 2025.

[22] 《改革国有资本授权经营体制方案》 [The Plan for Reforming the System of Authorised Operation of State-Owned Capital]. (People's Republic of China) The State Council. 28 April 2019.

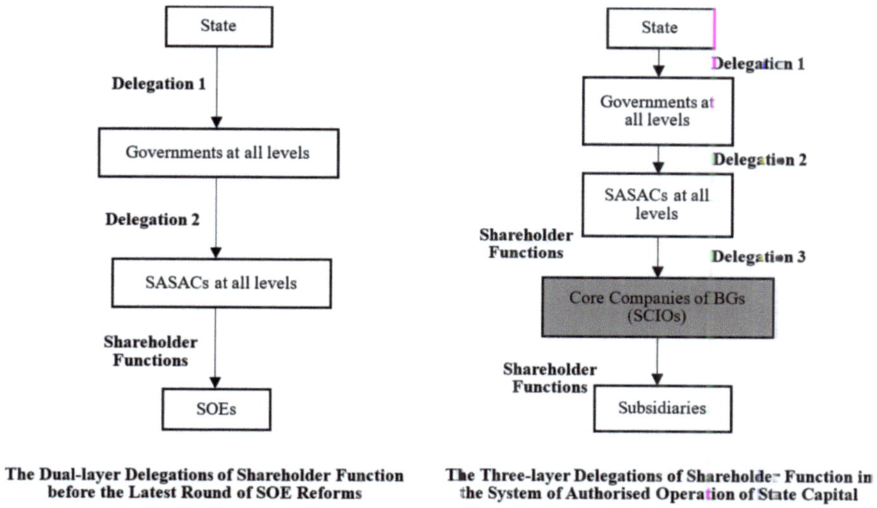

Fig. 4.1 The Institution Designs of the Authorised Operation of State-owned Capital System in the Latest Round of SOE Reforms

structure introduced in the latest round of SOE reforms to the dual-layer delegation of State ownership functions established in the third round. As depicted in the figure, the System is essentially a three-layer delegation system of State shareholder functions in SOEs, with an additional layer of delegation between the State and SOEs, namely core companies of BGs that are directly supervised by SASACs.[23]

Specifically, under the newly implemented System, SASACs are only required to perform shareholder functions for the core companies of BGs under their direct supervision. SASACs then delegate elements of shareholder functions to the core companies of BGs for their subsidiaries on a case-by-case basis.[24] As Fig. 4.1 demonstrates, the authorised core companies act as intermediaries between the SASACs and their subsidiaries while remaining accountable to the corresponding SASACs. In the meantime, they are encouraged to delegate the shareholder functions to their subsidiaries layer by layer.[25] The System is designed to facilitate SASACs to fulfil their State ownership functions more efficiently. As the System decentralises State ownership functions, it could potentially solve the contradictory roles of SASACs as SOE shareholders and regulators.

23 Ibid.

24 《国务院国资委授权放权清单(2019年版)》 [List of Shareholder functions Authorised by State-Owned Assets Supervision and Administration Commission of the State Council (2019 edition)]. (People's Republic of China) The State Council. 3 June 2019.

25 Ibid.

4.1.2.2 State-owned Capital Investment Company vs State-owned Capital Operation Company

Under the System of a three-layer delegation of State ownership functions, some core companies of BGs are additionally designated as SCICs or SCIOs to serve as professional platforms for the operation of State-owned capital.[26] As innovations put forth raised at the Third Plenum of the 18th National Congress of the CCP in 2013, the State Council defined SCIOs in 2018 as:

> [T]he solely State-owned professional platforms for the market-oriented operation of State-owned capital who perform the functions of State shareholder, bear the national missions to serve national strategies, optimise State economy industrial layout and improve the operational efficiency of State-owned capital.[27]

Additionally, the State Council specified that the State-owned capital that SCIOs are authorised to operate is (a portion of) the equity of existing SOEs that will be transferred to them.[28] The SOEs whose State owners transfer their equity to SCIOs subsequently become members of the BGs led by those SCIOs as core companies.

Despite the ambiguity, the official definition of SCIOs suggests that SCIOs are charged with substantial policy responsibilities regarding State-owned capital operations. Since 2014, the Chinese government has designated nineteen central BGs' core companies as pilot SCICs (four of these BGs later merged in the State economy restructuring reform) and two central BGs' core companies as pilot SCOCs.[29] Five pilot SCICs have officially become SCICs in 2022.[30] The pilot experience provides a wealth of empirical evidence that sheds light on the cloudy official definition of the specific functions of SCIOs and the distinctions between SCICs and SCOCs.

Based on publicly available information released by the Chinese government by 2023, Table 4.1 outlines the primary characteristics of SCICs and SCOCs, including their stated policy objectives, specific policy tasks and lists of SOEs designated as pilots or officials. The table shows that the designated SCIOs are predominantly national champions and active investors in developed countries.[31] Hence, it becomes essential for foreign nations noticing the expansion of these prominent Chinese SOEs to understand the implications associated with the SCIO identity.

---

26 《中共中央关于国有企业改革和发展若干重大问题的决定》 [Decision of the CCP Central Committee on Major Issues concerning the Reform and Development of State-Owned Enterprises]. (People's Republic of China) The CCP Central Committee. 12 November 2013.

27 《国务院关于推进国有资本投资、运营公司改革试点的实施意见》 [Opinions of the State Council on the Implementation of the Pilot Reform of State-Owned Capital Investment and Operation Companies]. (People's Republic of China) The State Council. 30 July 2018 ('*Opinions on SCIOs*').

28 Ibid.

29 *SOE Reforms 1978-2018* (n 4) p 262.

30 王希 [Wang Xi] (2022) 《5家中央企业正式转为国有资本投资公司》 [Five Central Enterprises Formally Transformed into State-Owned Capital Investment Companies]. The State Council. https://www.gov.cn/xinwen/2022-06/21/content_5696886.htm. Accessed 15 Aug 2025.

31 Ibid.

Table 4.1 SCIC and SCOC Primary Characteristics Comparison

	State-owned Capital Investment Company (SCIC)	State-owned Capital Operation Company (SCOC)
Scope	Converted from China's dominant SOEs in critical industries	Specially established SOEs
Stated policy objectives	• Serve national strategies • Optimise State economy industrial structure • Enhance industrial competitiveness	• Improve the operational efficiency of State-owned capital • Preserve and increase the value of State-owned capital
Specific policy tasks	• Invest in support of national commonweal strategies • Make investments centring on their primary businesses into those industries which are being strategically developed by the Party-State	• Accept government-designated SOEs' non-performing assets or insolvent SOEs and sell on a case-by-case basis • Assist healthy SOEs in carrying out partial reforms of the new round of SOE reform • Promote the capitalization of State-owned assets
Priorities	• Corporate competitiveness in the domestic and global market • Principal businesses in the critical industries • The controlling, influencing and guiding power of State-owned capital	• The operational efficiency and commercial prospects of the SOEs they help

SOEs designated as SCICs, as shown in Table 4.1, are primarily core companies of central BGs that dominate critical industries, such as China National Cereals, Oils and Foodstuffs Import and Export Corporation (COFCO) in the food industry, Aluminium Corporation of China in the aluminium industry, and China General Nuclear Power Group (CGN) in the nuclear energy industry.[32]

These SCICs have been publicly assigned policy tasks to invest in ways that support national strategies such as the *Poverty Alleviation Policy* and *Western Development Strategy*,[33] and to promote the concentration of State-owned capital in 'forward-looking strategic emerging industries'.[34] This is a term highlighted in the

[32] 刘志强 [Liu Zhiqiang] (2021) 《19家国有资本投资公司试点企业经营业绩超出央企平均水平》 [Operating Performance of 19 Pilot State-Owned Capital Investment Companies Exceeded the Average Level of Central Enterprises]. The State Council. https://www.gov.cn/xinwen/2021-11/03/content_5648503.htm. Accessed 15 Aug 2025.

[33] 杜燕飞 [Du Yanfei] (2022) 《国有资本运营公司管资本成效凸显》 [State-Owned Capital Operation Companies Effectively Manage Capital, Yielding Exceptional Outcomes]. People. http://finance.people.com.cn/n1/2022/0326/c1004-32384815.html. Accessed 15 Aug 2025.

[34] The Central SASAC (2021) 《国有资本投资公司发挥产业引领作用,加快培育新兴产业》 [SCICs are at the Forefront of Industrial Advancement and Help Foster the Growth of Emerging Industries]. http://www.sasac.gov.cn/n2588025/n2588139/c20082475/content.html. Accessed 15 Aug 2025.

13th Five-Year Plan as broadly referring to high-tech industries that are becoming increasingly important for national strength such as artificial intelligence, new energy, new materials, biotechnology and integrated circuits.[35]

SCICs make policy-driven investments primarily in two ways. The first approach is to invest in high-tech industries related to their principal businesses, aligning their policy tasks with their inherent commercial objectives in pursuit of business expansion. This approach also implements the 'Principal Business Management' program under the State economy restructuring reform and flow-out MOR in the latest round of SOE reforms. Both sub-reforms share the overarching objective of strengthening the State economy, with the former aiming to enhance SOE dominance over China's critical industries and the latter aiming to improve SOE influence over China's technological sectors.[36] As a pilot SCIC, the Chinese State-owned energy giant CGN, for example, had its first-tier subsidiary CGN Nuclear Technology acquire controlling stakes in nine leading POE dominant players in China's nuclear technology sector in 2017. The government has recognised these intensive acquisitions as a successful illustration of the SCIC's role in facilitating the convergence of State-owned capital in China's 'forward-looking strategic emerging industries.'[37]

The second approach is to invest via industry investment funds. Some SCICs have established industry investment funds as investment vehicles specialising in fostering the development of particular industries per national development strategies. As one of the first pilot SCICs designated in 2014, the State Development and Investment Corporation (SDIC) established several funds with distinct investment target industries.[38] The funds include, for example, the National Advanced Manufacturing Industry Investment Fund, which targets rail transit equipment, industrial robots and new energy vehicles industries. The SDIC Science and Technology Achievements Conversion Venture Investment Fund, which targets biomedicine, integrated circuits and network information security industries, and the SDIC National Venture Capital Guidance Fund for Emerging Industries, which seeks to invest in privately owned start-ups with exceptional innovation capacity in high-tech industries.[39] The SCIC funds have attracted capital from multiple sources, including governments, public entities, SOEs and private capital, thereby directing

---

[35] 《十三五国家战略性新兴产业发展规划》 [National 13th Five-Year Plan for the Development of Strategic Emerging Industries]. (People's Republic of China) The State Council. 19 December 2016.

[36] For detailed discussion in this regard, see Chap. 2 Sect. 2.3 and Chap. 3 Sect. 3.2.

[37] 王璐 [Wang Lu] (2019) 《中广核四项改革试点齐发动 争创"世界一流"》 [CGN Launches Four Pilot Reforms in an Attempt to Achieve 'World-Class']. National Energy Administration. http://www.nea.gov.cn/2019-01/17/c_137751944.htm. Accessed 15 Aug 2025.

[38] 任腾飞 [Ren Tengfei] (2019) 《十项改革试点分析之中央企业国有资本投资、运营公司试点》 [Analysis of Ten Reform Pilot Projects of State-Owned Capital Investment and Operation Companies of Central Enterprises]. The Central SASAC. http://www.sasac.gov.cn/n2588025/n4423279/n4517386/n11702115/c11704709/content.html. Accessed 15 Aug 2025.

[39] 国务院国资委改革办 [Reform Office of the Central SASAC] (2018) 《国企改革探索与实践——中央企业集团15例(上)》 [Exploration and Practice of SOE Reforms—15 Cases among the Central Business Groups]. 中国经济出版社 [China Economic Publishing House], p 172.

social capital alongside State-owned capital towards investment in technological sectors in accordance with government policy and strategy.[40]

In contrast to SCICs, which are tasked with pursuing specific policy objectives, SCOCs are primarily tasked with improving the return on State-owned capital, officially referred to as 'the maintenance and appreciation of State-owned assets.'[41] Pilot cases suggest that SCOCs are expected to fulfil this task primarily by rescuing failing SOEs or assisting other SOEs in implementing the latest SOE reforms rather than directly engaging in profit-seeking endeavours as commercial entities. These tasks require a substantial departure from commercially rational considerations, which may explain why only two SOEs have thus far been designated SCOCs.

China Chengtong Development Group (Chengtong), one of the two pilot SCOCs, has rescued failing SOEs from delisting or bankruptcy on a case-by-case basis. To fulfil the rescue function, Chengtong acquires insolvent SOEs under the direction of the central SASAC and restructures their businesses, helps them dispose of non-performing assets, or integrates their assets with those of other SOEs in the same industry.[42] Additionally, in the case of bankrupt SOEs, Chengtong may assume responsibility for liquidation disposal and post-bankruptcy employee settlement.[43] According to the publicly available information, Chengtong has, for example, successfully rescued China Record Corporation, China's oldest and largest State-owned record company, by employing various strategies, including divesting its digital music division to China Hualu Group, a State-owned electronics manufacturer.[44]

Notably, it appears that SCOCs are intended to complement, not replace, China's distressed asset management companies like China Huarong Asset Management Company (Huarong) and China Cinda Asset Management Company (China Cinda), which were established in the aftermath of the 1997 Asian financial crisis.[45] In fact, these two distinct types of SOEs have labour divisions: Huarong and China Cinda are financial SOEs owned and supervised by the MOF and established to recapitalise State banks; SCOCs, on the other hand, are under the purview of the central SASAC and are primarily tasked with rescuing failing non-financial SOEs.

An SCOC is also tasked with assisting SOEs in implementing specific programmes promoted in the latest SOE reforms. Chengtong has, for instance, assisted China Resources Group, China United Network Communications Group and China Electronics Corporation in implementing flow-out MOR (which is essentially partial nationalisation of POEs in high-tech industries), investing in prominent POEs

---

[40] 施能自, 吴芙蓉 [Shi Nengzi and Wu Furong] (2017) 《新一轮国企改革的思考与操作实务》 [Thoughts and Operational Practices of the Latest Round of SOE Reforms]. 中国经济出版社 [Economic Press China], p 100.

[41] *Opinions on SCIOs* (n 27).

[42] 国务院国资委新闻中心, 《国资报告》杂志社 [News Centre of the Central SASAC and 'State-Owned Assets Report' magazine press] (2016) 《国企改革12样本》 [12 Samples of SOE Reforms]. 中国经济出版社 [China Economic Publishing House], p 191–195.

[43] Ibid. p. 194.

[44] Ibid. p. 195.

[45] Ho and Marois (2019), pp. 728–751, p. 730.

chosen as candidates for flow-out MOR to prepare for SOE substantial investments.[46] Additionally, Chengtong has assisted China's largest State-owned rail equipment manufacturer, China Railway Rolling Stock Corporation, and China's major pharmaceuticals SOE, China National Pharmaceutical Group, in going public to diversify ownership under flow-in MOR.[47]

In practice, the functional distinctions between SCIC and SCOC may not be as distinct as they appear to be in the publicised pilot cases. Nevertheless, the preceding analyses suggest that SCIOs play a significant role as State agents while continuing to operate as the core companies of globally active BGs.

4.2 The Modern SOE Governance System Reform: The Resurgence of CCP Control

In the latest round of SOE reforms, the SOE governance system reform focuses on tightening the CCP's control over SOEs' governance practices. This complements the decentralization of SASAC State shareholder functions within the State-owned assets management system reform.

As noted earlier, the previous centralised State-owned assets supervision system exacerbated the problem of passive State ownership in SOE governance and, consequently, the problem of self-serving behaviour by corporate insiders. In addition, the factual overburdening of SASACs in supervising SOEs in shareholder and regulator capacities has made some SOEs less compliant with government policies and directives. Milhaupt and Zheng refer to this as 'agency slack' between SOEs and the Chinese State as the controlling shareholder.[48] This is especially true of monopolistic SOEs in crucial industries. For instance, despite the Chinese government's mandate that central SOEs exit non-critical industries, notably real estate, in the State economy restructuring reform, the Chinese State-owned energy giant China Power Grid Corporation did not exit the industry until 2020.[49] In addition, in 2011, an NDRC 'interview' with Kweichow Moutai Company, China's prominent liquor maker in which the Guizhou provincial government holds 62 percent, did not deter the company from raising prices.[50]

Given the observed decline in compliance among SOEs, the Xi Jinping administration emphasised in 2016 that the CCP's leadership is the 'soul' of Chinese

---

[46] 国务院国资委新闻中心, 《国资报告》杂志社 [News Centre of the Central SASAC and 'State-Owned Assets Report' magazine press] (n 42) pp. 202–203.

[47] Ibid. p 203.

[48] Milhaupt and Zheng (2015), pp. 680–681.

[49] Mujiangqu et al. (2020). Accessed 15 Aug 2025.

[50] 顾一冰 [Gu Yibing] (2011) 《茅台被约谈后再涨价: 抑制涨价只能靠纪委》 [Moutai Raises Prices again after the Interview with the Government: Curbing Price Hikes can Only Be Done by the Disciplinary Committee]. China Economic. http://www.ce.cn/cysc/sp/info/201109/27/t20110927_21047166.shtml. Accessed 15 Aug 2025.

SOEs.[51] Accordingly, the latest round of SOE reforms has introduced a 'Modern SOE Governance System with Chinese Characteristics'. This SOE governance system is defined by the integration of the leadership of the CCP into the regular governance structure, thus ensuring the CCP's ultimate authority in the decision-making process regarding significant corporate matters.

4.2.1 SOE Corporate Governance System Under Chinese Law

China currently has three statutes that deal with SOE corporate governance: the *Law of Industrial Enterprises Owned by the Whole People* (*Wholly People-owned Enterprises Law*),[52] the *State-owned Assets Law,* and the *Company Law*.[53] In practice, however, Chinese SOE corporate governance system remains largely uncodified, despite the advocacy for policy mandates regarding SOE governance in the ongoing SOE reforms.

China's *Wholly People-owned Enterprises Law* was adopted in 1988 and amended in 2009. It was an important piece of legislation when it was promulgated as it addressed the corporate governance practice of non-corporatised SOEs and set out what is now an obsolete system of overall responsibility by factory managers inherited from the centrally planning era.[54] Given that Chinese SOEs had generally transformed into corporate entities by the end of 2017, the law has been *de facto* discarded in practice.[55] The *State-owned Assets Law* enacted in 2008 succinctly specifies that State-invested enterprises shall make decisions following laws, administrative regulations and Articles of Association (AAs).[56] In the case of 'significant State-owned or State-holdings' (to be designated by the government), decisions pertaining to particular major issues are required to obtain government approval.[57] These requirements, however, are too brief to have any practical significance.

---

[51] 罗文 [Luo Wen] (2016) 《守住国有企业的"根"与"魂"》 [Keep the 'Root' and 'Soul' of State-Owned Enterprises]. The State Council https://www.gov.cn/xinwen/2016-10/18/content_5121159.htm. Accessed 15 Aug 2025.

[52] 《中华人民共和国全民所有制工业企业法》 [Law of Industrial Enterprises Owned by the Whole People of the People's Republic of China]. (People's Republic of China) Adopted at the 7th National People's Congress. 13 April 1988, amended 27 August 2009 ('*Wholly People-owned Enterprises Law*').

[53] 《中华人民共和国公司法》[Company Law of the People's Republic of China]. (People's Republic of China) Adopted at the 8th National People's Congress Standing Committee. 29 December 1993, amended 25 December 1999, 28 August 2004, 28 December 2013, 26 October 2018 and 29 December 2023 ('*Company Law*').

[54] *Wholly People-owned Enterprises Law* (n 52) art. 2, 7.

[55] 《关于印发中央企业公司制改制工作实施方案的通知》 [Notice on the Issuance of the Implementation Plan for the Corporate Restructuring of Central Enterprises]. (People's Republic of China) The General Office of the State Council. 26 July 2017.

[56] *State-owned Assets Law* (n 14) art. 30.

[57] Ibid. art. 34.

China enacted the *Company Law* in 1993 at the beginning of the second round of SOE reforms in part to facilitate the SOE reforms.[58] The law has been amended in 1999, 2004, 2013, 2018 and 2023. Before the 2023 amendment, the *Company Law* only focused on the governance norms of wholly State-owned enterprises (WSOEs), dedicating a whole chapter to outlining the functions of the principal corporate organs of WSOEs.[59] Significantly, the section emphasised the government's involvement in the governance practices of WSOEs. It conferred authority upon the SASACs to approve or formulate the AAs,[60] decide on specified major affairs (such as merger, change in registered capital, issuance of bonds, distribution of profits, dissolution and bankruptcy),[61] and assign or appoint senior executives.[62]

The 2023 amended *Company Law* broadens the purview to regulate governance systems of not only WSOEs but all State-controlling enterprises, which are referred to in the law as 'State-invested enterprises'.[63] The newly amended law will go into effect on July 1, 2024, and the entire Chap. 7 is dedicated to the governance of State-invested enterprises, with six of the 10 provisions largely repeating previous provisions on WSOE governance.[64] Notably, the chapter reflects a number of SOE governance-related policies being advanced in the ongoing SOE reforms. For example, in 2003, the CCP Central Committee mandated that the CCP cell in SOEs exert political leadership within the enterprises.[65] The latest round of SOE reforms has continued this stance.[66] In accordance with this policy mandate, the 2023 amended *Company Law* specifies that the organisations of the CCP in State-invested companies shall, in accordance with the *CCP Constitution*, play a leading role in deciding major corporate affairs.[67] The provision codifies the CCP's dominant role in SOE governance, going beyond the previous provision that required Chinese companies to establish CCP organisations in accordance with the *CCP Constitution.*[68] In

[58] 邓峰 [Deng Feng] (2022) 《中国公司理论的演变和制度变革方向》 [The Evolution of Chinese Corporate Theory and the Direction of Institutional Change]. Tsinghua University Law Journal 16(2): 42–56, p 43.

[59] 《中华人民共和国公司法》[Company Law of the People's Republic of China]. (People's Republic of China) Adopted at the 8th National People's Congress Standing Committee. 29 December 1993, amended 25 December 1999, 28 August 2004, 28 December 2013, 26 October 2018, ch II, s 4 ('*2018 Company Law*').

[60] Ibid. art. 65.

[61] Ibid. art. 66.

[62] Ibid. art. 67, 68, 70.

[63] *Company Law* (n 53) art. 168.

[64] Ibid. art. 171, 172, 173, 174, 175, 176.

[65] *The CCP Decision on Economic System* (n 3).

[66] 习近平 [Xi Jinping] (2016) 《习近平在全国国有企业党的建设工作会议上的讲话》 [Xi Jinping's speech at the National Conference on Party Building in State-owned Enterprises]. Speech. National Conference on Party Building in State-owned Enterprises.

[67] *Company Law* (n 53) art. 170.

[68] *2018 Company Law* (n 59) art. 19. The provision remains unchanged in the 2023 amended *Company Law. Company Law* (n 53) art. 18.

addition, the 2023 amendment introduces a requirement that WSOEs shall establish boards with a majority of outside directors (which will be discussed in Sect. 4.2.3).[69]

However, the 2023 amendment to the *Company Law* did not end the state of perplexity concerning SOE corporate governance practices. Chapter 7 of the law lacks specific governance norms for SOEs, which have been developed over years of the latest round of SOE reforms. It only requires State-invested companies to 'establish and improve internal supervision and risk management systems, as well as strengthen internal compliance management in accordance with the law'.[70] For example, in the latest round of SOE reforms, the Chinese Party-State mandates cross-officeholding between the Party Committee and regular governance organs in the latest round of SOE reforms in an effort to strengthen the CCP's control over SOE personnel management, which will be discussed in Sect. 4.2.3. This mandate, nevertheless, was not incorporated into the 2023 amendment to the *Company Law*.

The potential motivation behind China's choice to withhold the 'Modern SOE Governance System with Chinese Characteristics' from codification in the *Company Law* is unclear. One possible explanation for the legislative omission for SOE governance is that it allows for greater flexibility in adapting governance norms as the SOE reforms progresses. Notably, the 2023 amended *Company Law* provides that the governance structure of State-invested companies is governed by Chap. 7, and in the absence of applicable provisions in Chap. 7, other provisions of the law shall apply.[71] The other parts of the law, which are generally applicable to all Chinese companies, are largely consistent with global-standard corporate governance practices, granting decision-making powers on specified corporate affairs to the shareholders' general assembly, board of directors, board of supervisors and senior management team.[72] These general provisions are compatible with the 'Modern SOE Governance System with Chinese Characteristics', which, as noted earlier, is characterised by the integration of CCP leadership into the regular corporate governance structure. In addition, the legislative omission may be partially intended to protect Chinese SOEs from accusations of being subject to political influence in international investment arbitrations and WTO disputes.[73] Irrespective of the genuine motives behind the legislative ambiguity concerning SOE governance, China's *Company Law* allows sufficient flexibility for SOEs to uphold the CCP's supreme authority in governance practices.

[69] *Company Law* (n 53) art. 173.

[70] Ibid. art. 177.

[71] Ibid. art. 168.

[72] Ibid. ch. 3 s. 2, ch. 5 s. 2, 3, 4, 5.

[73] For example, under the WTO *Agreement on Subsidies and Countervailing Measures*, anti-subsidy measures could be imposed on a Chinese SOE that meets the criteria of a 'public body'. See generally Ding (2014), pp. 167–189.

4.2.2 *Modern SOE Governance System with 'Chinese Characteristics'*

In 2016, the Chinese government introduced a modern SOE governance system with 'Chinese characteristics', which President Xi has explained as a reference to the mandate that the CCP lead SOEs and integrate CCP leadership into the SOE corporate governance system.[74] According to the *Guiding Opinions on Further Improving the Corporate Governance Structure of State-owned Enterprises* (*Guiding Opinions on SOE Governance*) issued by the State Council in 2017, China's modern SOE governance system requires the establishment of a CCP cell known as the 'Party Committee' as a distinct decision-making organ in addition to the board of directors.[75] In the same year, the *CCP Constitution* was amended to enshrine the fundamental rule that SOE Party Committees must play a leadership role in corporate governance, discussing and deciding on major corporate issues and ensuring the enterprises implement State policies.[76]

Prior to the latest round of SOE reforms, the Chinese government made efforts to reform the SOE governance system, such as the nebulous requirement in 2010 that SOEs establish a Party Committee as a separate organ responsible for 'significant decisions, significant personnel appointments and dismissals, significant project arrangements and large-scale fund management,' which was described as the 'Three Significant and One Large Matters' ('三重一大') decision-making system in China.[77] In 2019, the CCP Central Committee finally issued a *Trial Regulation on the Work at Primary-level Party Organizations of State-owned Enterprises* in 2019 (*Trial Regulation*), which specifies the set-up of party committees in SOEs, their primary duties in corporate governance, organisational composition and interrelations with other corporate organs.[78] The modern SOE governance system is depicted in Fig. 4.2 according to the *Trial Regulation* and the *Guiding Opinions on SOE Governance*. As the figure demonstrates, the modern SOE governance system was developed to place SOE governance under the CCP's overall oversight primarily through the Party Committee's precedence in significant decisions and the mandatory cross-office holding between the Party Committee and regular governance organs.

According to the *Trial Regulation*, the Party Committee has precedence over the board of directors and senior management team in the decision-making process

[74] 习近平 [Xi Jinping] (n 66).

[75] *Guiding Opinions on SOE Governance* (n 5).

[76] 《中国共产党章程》 [Constitution of the Communist Party of China]. (People's Republic of China) Adopted at the 20th CCP National Congress. 22 October 2022, art. 33.

[77] 《关于进一步推进国有企业贯彻落实"三重一大"决策制度的意见》 [Opinions on Further Promoting the Implementation of the 'Three Major and one Significant Matters' Decision-making System in State-Owned Enterprises]. (People's Republic of China) General Office of the CCP and General Office of the State Council. 15 July 2010.

[78] 《中国共产党国有企业基层组织工作条例(试行)》 [Trial Regulation on the Work at Primary-level Party Organizations of State-Owned Enterprises]. (People's Republic of China) The CCP Central Committee. 30 December 2019 ('*Trial Regulation*').

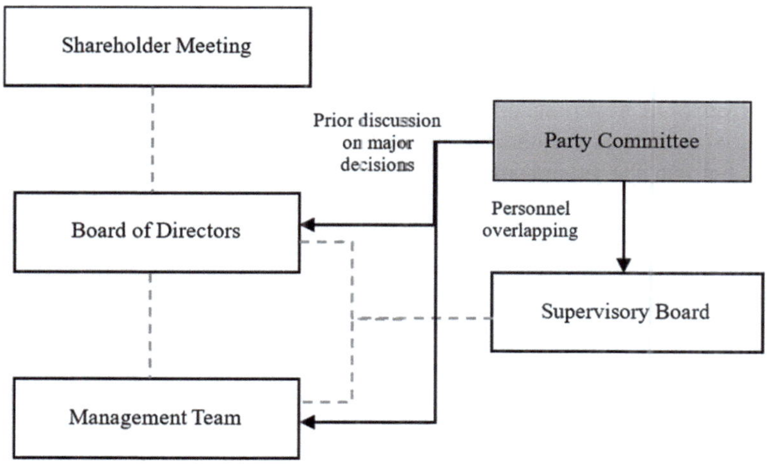

Fig. 4.2 The Modern SOE Governance System with Chinese Characteristics in the Latest Round of SOE Reforms

concerning major affairs in six areas, which are: (a) the execution of national development strategies; (b) the strategy and planning for corporate development, including reform programmes; (c) the reorganisation, transfer, operation and considerable investment of corporate assets; (d) the modification of the corporate organisational structure and significant rule formulations and adjustments; (e) major issues on production safety, stability, employee interest protection, social responsibility and others; and (f) other significant matters.[79] Issues within the specified areas must be discussed by the Party Committee before being brought to the board of directors or management teams for final decision-making.[80] In addition, the 'Three Significant and One Large' decision-making system that was brought up earlier for all Chinese public entities is mentioned in the *Trial Regulation*,[81] which implies that the Party Committee has ultimate authority over all significant business decisions, not just those in the areas specified. In practice, the Chinese government's Supervisory Commissions and the CCP's Commissions for Disciplinary Inspection (co-located agencies) undertake SOE inspections with a specific emphasis on compliance with decision-making procedures outlined in the *Trial Regulation*.[82] Given that these areas encompass the entire operation of an SOE, the Party Committee holds the utmost authority over SOE governance in the modern SOE governance system.

[79] Ibid. art. 15.

[80] Ibid.

[81] Ibid. art. 29.

[82] Central Commission for Disciplinary Inspection (2023) 《广东加强对国企领导人员权力运行监督制约》 [Guangdong Strengthens Supervision and Control over Power Exercise of State-Owned Enterprises' Leaders]. https://www.ccdi.gov.cn/yaowenn/202302/t20230210_245823.html. Accessed 15 Aug 2025.

The *Trial Regulation* also mandates personnel overlap between the Party Committee and other governance bodies (i.e. board of directors, supervisory board and management team) as the other principal means of establishing the CCP's leadership over SOE governance.[83] Specifically, it stipulates that the secretary of the Party Committee and the chair of the board of directors should be the same individual, and that the general manager and deputy secretary must also be the same individual.[84] Other members of the CCP serving on the board of directors, supervisory board or management team have to report to the Party Committee on how they carry out their responsibilities in these organs.[85]

Both the *Guiding Opinions on SOE Governance* and the *Trial Regulation* require that SOEs clarify the duties of the Party Committee in their AAs, particularly their precedence in deciding on the specified major issues.[86] Accordingly, a Chinese SOE's AA could provide insight into the CCP cell's precise role in the particular SOE's governance practices. Some SOEs have expanded the issues subject to prior Party Committee discussion beyond those specified in the *Trial Regulation*. For instance, Chengtong stipulated in its internal regulations that all issues falling under the authority of the board of directors and the chief executive officer are also subject to prior discussion by the Party Committee.[87]

4.2.3 SOE Personnel Management Modernisation: Enhanced Nomenklatura System

In the latest round of SOE reforms, Xi Jinping maintained the previous SOE governance policy introduced during the second round of the reforms,[88] which mandated the presence of 'outside directors' on SOE boards.[89] The term refers to persons who

[83] *Trial Regulation* (n 78) art. 14.

[84] Ibid. *Guiding Opinions on SOE Governance* (n 5).

[85] *Guiding Opinions on SOE Governance* (n 5).

[86] *Trial Regulation* (n 78) art. 13; Ibid. See also 《关于扎实推动国有企业党建工作要求写入公司章程的通知》 [The Notice on Solid Promotion of Writing the Party Building Work of State-Owned Enterprises into the Articles of Association]. (People's Republic of China) Organization Department of the CCP Central Committee and the Central SASAC. 15 March 2017.

[87] China Chengtong Holdings Group Ltd (2011) 《中国诚通控股集团有限公司党委议事规则》 [The Detailed Implementation Rules of the Party Committee's Study and Discussion as the Pre-Procedure for the Decision-Making on Major Issues section of the Chengtong's Rules of the Discussion Procedure of China Chengtong Holding Group' Party Committee]. http://www.cct-group.com.cn/cctgroup/djgz/djzdjs/604755/index.html. Accessed 15 Aug 2025.

[88] The outside director system was first introduced by the Central SASAC in 2004, but the document issued did not give detailed implementation rules. 《关于中央企业建立和完善国有独资公司董事会试点工作的通知》 [Notice on the Pilot Work of Establishing and Improving the Board of Directors of Wholly State Owned Companies by Central Enterprises]. (People's Republic of China) The Central SASAC. 6 June 2004.

[89] *Guiding Opinions on SOE Governance* (n 5).

serve as directors but are not otherwise employed by the SOE.[90] Specifically, authorities with State shareholder functions (i.e. SASACs or authorised core companies of BGs, including SCIOs) must assign outside directors to SOEs under their supervision, with specific requirements that in solely and wholly State-owned enterprises, the boards of directors should have a majority of outside directors, as specified in the *Guiding Opinions on Deepening the Reform of State-owned Enterprises* (*Guiding Opinions*) issued by the CCP Central Committee and the central SASAC in 2015 as the framework document for the overall latest round of SOE reforms.[91]

In addition, in the latest round of SOE reforms, the Chinese government has launched pilot programmes for the public recruitment of SOE managers and the SOE professional manager system.[92] According to the *Guiding Opinions*, SOE professional managers may be selected from the pool of current SOE managers or open talent markets.[93] SOE professional managers should be hired on a contractual basis and compensated according to market rates.[94]

The latest round of SOE reforms appears to have effectively carried out the outside director policy and the pilot programmes, resulting in a more diverse management team and SOE board compositions. In 2021, for instance, the central SASAC reported that 82 central BGs (core companies) and 78 percent of their subsidiaries had established boards on which outside directors constituted a majority.[95] China International Marine Containers Company, a Chinese State-owned transportation equipment provider, and SDIC have professional managers on their current management teams. China National Building Material Company, a Chinese SOE specialising in the supply of building materials, hired the executives of its POE shareholders as its professional managers. Beijing Automotive Group, a State-owned automobile manufacturer in China, recruited its professional managers from the open talent market.[96]

The Chinese government's efforts to modernise SOE personnel management appear to be motivated by an intention to distance SOEs from political influence.

[90] Xiaohong et al. (2004), p. 3 https://www.oecd.org/corporate/ca/corporategovernanceofstate-ownedenterprises/31603840.pdf. Accessed 15 Aug 2025.

[91] 《中共中央国务院关于深化国有企业改革的指导意见》 [The Guiding Opinions of the CCP Central Committee and the State Council on Deepening the Reform of State-Owned Enterprises]. (People's Republic of China) The CCP Central Committee and the State Council. 24 August 2015 ('*Guiding Opinions*').

[92] The State Council (2015) 《国务院国有企业改革领导小组十项试点2016年将全面展开》 [In 2016, the SOE Reform Leading Group of the State Council will Execute Ten Pilot Programmes]. https://www.gov.cn/xinwen/2015-12/11/content_5022805.htm. Accessed 15 Aug 2025.

[93] *Guiding Opinion* (n 91).

[94] Ibid.

[95] Xinhua News Agency (2021) 《央企董事会建设从"试点探索"进入"全面推进"》 [Central Enterprises from 'Pilot Exploration' to 'Comprehensive Promotion' of the Board of Directors Construction]. http://www.news.cn/fortune/2021-10/19/c_1127971133.htm. Accessed 15 Aug 2025.

[96] People (2019)《国企职业经理人制度建设加速推进》 [Accelerating the Construction of Professional Manager System in State-Owned Enterprises]. http://finance.people.com.cn/n1/2019/0301/c1004-30951497.html. Accessed 15 Aug 2025.

However, the efforts appear more like make-believe strategies to create the illusion of market-oriented characteristics in Chinese SOEs in light of the enhanced nomenklatura system of the CCP in the ongoing SOE governance system reform.

The CCP has upheld the nomenklatura system, a cadre personnel management principle imported from the Soviet Union and the Socialist Bloc, since 1938, long before the People's Republic of China was established.[97] The nomenklatura system (which was termed by the CCP as 'the Party Manages Cadres Principle' ('党管干部原则') refers to the CCP's ability to appoint to critical positions throughout the government system, as well as the CCP organisations in SOEs.[98] The nomenklatura system has been upheld throughout China's SOE reforms.[99] In the context of the ongoing round of SOE reforms, the nomenklatura system in Chinese SOEs is primarily manifested in two aspects: first, the cross-officeholding between the Party Committee and the regular governance organs in SOEs, as discussed earlier, and secondly, political authority over SOE executive appointments.

Executive appointment is a typical illustration of Chinese SOEs being exempt from the *Company Law*. According to the corporate governance system provided in the Company Law, a company's board of directors is responsible for appointing or dismissing the manager, deputy manager(s) and persons in charge of the company's financial affairs and determining their remuneration.[100] However, in Chinese SOE governance practices, the Party-State typically holds these powers.

For example, among China's 100 central BGs, 53 are identified by the State Council as 'Significant State-owned Backbone Enterprises,' considered to be of greater strategic importance than the others. For these central BGs, the Central Organisation Department of the CCP decides on the chairpersons of the board, Party Secretaries (heads of the Party Committee) and general managers of their core companies. The central SASAC can decide on the vice executive positions of the 53 central SOEs and senior executives of the other central SOEs.[101] Interestingly, this practice of appointing SOE leaders is not codified in any statute and can only be traced back to a handful of government documents issued over two decades ago.[102] The central

---

[97] This principle was first put forward in the 6th Plenary Session of the Sixth Central Committee during the Anti-Japanese War held in 1938. In November 1953, the principle was first formalised in the *Decision on Strengthening the Management of Cadres* issued by the CCP Central Committee. 《中共中央关于加强干部管理工作的决定》 [Decision of the CCP Central Committee on Strengthening the Management of Cadres]. (People's Republic of China) The CCP Central Committee. 24 November 1953.

[98] Chan (2004), pp. 703–734.

[99] 苏力 [Su Li] (2022) 《党管干部与中国宪制构建》 [The Party Supervising Cadres and the Construction of Chinese Constitutional Government]. 党内法规研究 [Research on Intraparty Rules and Regulations] 1(2): 3-20.

[100] *Company Law* (n 53) art. 46.

[101] 彭华岗 [Peng Huagang] (2017) 《国有企业改革前景及治理模式》 [Prospects for SOE Reforms and Governance Models]. 经济导刊 [Economic Herald] 1.

[102] See, e.g., 《中共中央关于成立中共中央企业工作委员会及有关问题的通知》 [Notice of the CCP Central Committee on the Establishment of the Working Committee of the CCP Central Committee for Enterprises and Related Issues]. (People's Republic of China) The CCP Central

SASAC's constant public announcements regarding the appointment (nomination) and dismissal of SOE executives indicate the continuation of this practice.[103]

Given that the Chinese Party-State continues to hold the power to decide on the heads of SOEs, it is unlikely that the implementation of the public recruitment of managers and professional manager system in SOEs can liberate the enterprises from political control—publicly recruited managers are still accountable to the board of directors and the Party Committee, which are instruments of political control. In addition, in practice, the SASACs at various levels typically lead and administer the public recruitment process for SOEs under their supervision, unlike the SOEs' independent recruitment.[104] The public recruitment rules released by SASACs indicate that the recruitment is only open to individuals with prior employment experience in the government or SOEs. Unsurprisingly, candidates are also required to uphold the CCP's leadership.[105] Therefore, the public recruitment of SOE managers is essentially only formally open to the public.

The outside director regime is also unlikely to counteract political interference in Chinese SOE governance. Policy and implementation practices imply that the selection of outside directors for SOEs is also essentially an insider's game, with limited access for outsiders. The *Guiding Opinions* explicitly states that incumbent heads of SOEs may be selected as outside directors, transforming them into full-time outside directors. Accordingly, it is customary for a former high-ranking executive of an SOE to assume the position of an outside director in the same or another SOE, typically at a comparable level. Wang Binghua, for instance, retired in 2018 as chairman of State Power Investment Corporation and served as an outside director of China Mobile Group in 2019 and China Resources Group in 2022. After retiring in 2021 as Party Committee Deputy Secretary of China Huadian Corporation, Zhang Guohou was appointed an outside director of China Rare Earth Group. He was appointed an outside director of China Baowu Group a year later.[106]

In addition, as part of the anti-corruption campaign, the Xi Jinping administration has been actively promoting personnel rotations between major SOEs, presumably to prevent insider control and empire-building within SOEs. In 2015, for instance, the CCP's Central Organisation Department announced the swap of chairmanships between China Unicom and China Mobile, two of the three SOE monopolies in China's telecommunications industry, with the then-deputy Minister of the

Committee. 1 December 1999; 《深化干部人事制度改革的纲要》 [Outline for Deepening the Cadre Personnel System Reform]. (People's Republic of China) The State Council. June 2000.

[103] The announcements can be accessed at http://www.sasac.gov.cn/n2588035/n2588325/n2588345/index.html. Accessed 15 Aug 2025.

[104] Lin (2015).

[105] See, e.g., SASAC of Shenzhen Municipal People's Government (2015) 《市场化选聘市属国有企业领导人员有关政策解读》 [Interpretation of Policies Related to Market-Based Recruitment of Leaders of Municipal State-Owned Enterprises].

[106] 曹煦 [Cao Xu] (2015) 《揭央企"一把"手退休后的五種生活》 [Five Types of Post-Retirement Lives of Central Enterprise Executives]. People. https://www.12371.cn/2015/09/15/ARTI1442316835576827.shtml. Accessed 15 Aug 2025.

Ministry of Industry and Information Technology assuming the chairmanship of China Mobile, the other telecom SOE monopoly.[107] In the same year, the Central Organisation Department of the CCP announced the appointment of the chairmen of China National Offshore Oil Corporation as the chairmen of PetroChina Company. Both the corporations are China's largest oil companies under the supervision of the central SASAC.[108]

The insider-only practices for the public recruitment and outside director mechanisms and the frequent leadership rotations for SOEs may not be in the best interest of the commercial success of Chinese SOEs, which typically require senior officers with vast talent regardless of their political backgrounds and a stable leadership committed to the enterprises' long-term growth. The preceding analysis reveals that the latest round of SOE reforms emphasises the persisting nomenklatura system more than the genuine modernisation of SOE governance practice, which is nonetheless a manifestation of the modern SOE governance system with 'Chinese characteristics.'

4.3 Concluding Remarks: The Implications for Chinese SOEs' Outbound FDI Activities

As two significant sub-reforms of the latest round of SOE reforms, the State-owned assets management system reform and the SOE governance system reform may have far-reaching implications on the overseas investment activities of Chinese SOEs. The impact is concentrated on strengthening the non-commercial motivation for Chinese SOE investments.

Specifically, the 'System of Authorised Operation of State-owned Capital' implemented as part of the State-owned assets management system reform requires the core companies of BGs to assume (at least some of) the State ownership functions formerly performed solely by the SASACs to address the issue of passive ownership in SOEs. By authorising the core companies of BGs to exercise State shareholder rights in their subsidiaries, as is a common practice for commercial corporations, the system allows a handful of companies to act as intermediaries for the government and an extensive number of SOEs at the lower tiers of BGs. In the context of the ongoing SOE reforms, the intermediaries have taken on the responsibility of implementing reform policy among their subsidiaries in parallel with their business operations. This includes but is not limited to, developing plans for

[107] China Daily (2015) 《三大电信运营商一把手大调整》 [Major Leadership Adjustments at Three Major Telecoms Operators]. http://caijing.chinadaily.com.cn/2015-08/24/content_21685702.htm. Accessed 15 Aug 2025.

[108] 赵嘉妮 [Zhao Jiani] (2015) 《"三桶油"同日宣布换帅：为何要实行轮换制？》 ['Three Barrels of Oil' Announced on the Same Day to Change the Commander in Chief: Why to Implement the Leadership Rotation Mechanism?]. People. http://theory.people.com.cn/n/2015/0505/c40531-26949339.html. Accessed 15 Aug 2025.

subsidiaries to carry out the State economy restructuring programs (as discussed in Chap. 2), classifying subsidiaries and implementing the MOR based on the classifications (as discussed in Chap. 3). In addition, core companies designated as SCIOs (especially SCICs, which are predominantly global investors) are tasked with serving national policies and development strategies in their operations. Consequently, outbound FDI activities of these Chinese SOEs and their subsidiaries will likely be significantly motivated by the newly imposed government authorities and the policy mission in the latest round of SOE reforms.

Since the Xi Jinping administration is actively promoting inter-SOE mergers to create global champions in critical industries in the State economy restructuring reform (as discussed in Chap. 2), policy-driven investments by the core companies of these behemoths could have significant influence in the host States or even the global industries, mainly when they serve the same policy objectives. For example, the Chinese State-owned giant China National Chemical Corporation (ChemChina) acquired several leading global manufacturing companies between 2014 and 2017, including the Singaporean solar power company Renewable Energy Corporation, the Italian tyre manufacturer Pirelli & C. S.p.A., the German manufacturing company KraussMaffei, the world's largest energy trading company Mercuria Energy Group based in Switzerland, and the Swiss agricultural company Syngenta.[109] These extensive acquisitions contributed significantly to China's dominant position in the global manufacturing industries. They were likely motivated by President Xi's 2012 call at the 18th National Congress of the CCP to accelerate the build-up of a world-leading manufacturing superpower and the *Made in China 2025 Development Initiative* launched in 2015.[110]

The SOE governance system reform is bringing about the resurgence of CCP leadership over Chinese SOE governance practices. This means that, in the latest round of SOE reforms, Chinese SOE governance practice is drifting away from the principles of good corporate governance outlined in the *G20/OECD Principles of Corporate Governance*, particularly the principle that 'the board should be able to exercise objective, independent judgement on corporate affairs.'[111] The reform would raise the level of the CCP's direct interference in the SOE outbound FDI decision-making process, as outbound investments typically fall within the significant affairs of an SOE (as part of the SOE's execution of national policies or development plan, or significant operations of corporate assets) specified in the *Trial Regulation* and therefore subject to prior discussion by the Party Committees. In addition, the concurrently promoted outside director and public recruitment mechanisms are subject to the enhanced nomenklatura system, emphasizing the CCP's overall control over the arrangement of SOE executive personnel. Given that

[109] The American Enterprise Institute and the Heritage Foundation (2025); Manu-Emanuele C Francia (2019).

[110] The State Council (2022) 《制造强国 步履铿锵》 [Advancing Steadily towards Prominence as the World's leading Manufacturing Superpower]. https://www.gov.cn/xinwen/2022-08/15/content_5705364.htm. Accessed 15 Aug 2025.

[111] OECD (2015a).

Chinese SOE decisions on outbound FDI are substantively influenced by the CCP, Chinese SOE investments abroad must adhere to CCP and government policies and directives.

Given the rapid international expansion of Chinese SOEs, particularly in the developed world, some Western scholars argue that exposure to advanced corporate governance practices based on sophisticated legal frameworks in host States could have a transformative effect on China's SOE governance system, transferring from overseas subsidiaries to the parent companies in China.[112] Nonetheless, the analysis provided in this chapter indicates that ongoing SOE reforms may substantially offset any transformative impact of institutional exposure. This is because SOEs in China are subject to significantly enhanced political control, which is embedded internally in the modern SOE governance system and externally in the authorised operation of State-owned capital. In conclusion, it is reasonable to assume that the increased political control is the Chinese government's proactive defence against the genuine modernization of the SOE governance system as an evolution resulting from the SOEs' accumulating experience of globalisation. This assumption is consistent with the assertiveness of the Xi Jinping administration concerning the latest round of SOE reforms.

References

Cao Xu [曹煦] (2015) 《揭央企"一把"手退休后的五種生活》 [Five Types of Post-Retirement Lives of Central Enterprise Executives]. People. https://www.12371.cn/2015/09/15/ARTI1442316835576827.shtml. Accessed 15 Aug 2025

Central Commission for Disciplinary Inspection (2023) 《广东加强对国企领导人员权力运行监督制约》 [Guangdong Strengthens Supervision and Control over Power Exercise of State-Owned Enterprises' Leaders]. Central Commission for Disciplinary Inspection https://www.ccdi.gov.cn/yaowenn/202302/t20230210_245823.html. Accessed 15 Aug 2025

Central Commission for Disciplinary Inspection of the Communist Party of China (2015) 《国务院国资委主任蒋洁敏涉嫌严重违纪正接受组织调查》 [Jiang Jiemin, Director of the Central SASAC, is under Investigation for Serious Violations of Discipline]. http://www.ccdi.gov.cn/scdc/zggb/zjsc/201511/t20151120_115801.html. Accessed 15 Aug 2025

Chan HS (2004) Cadre Personnel Management in China: the Nomenklatura System, 1990–1998. China Quart 179:703–734

China Chengtong Holdings Group Ltd (2011) 《中国诚通控股集团有限公司党委议事规则》 [The Detailed Implementation Rules of the Party Committee's Study and Discussion as the Pre-Procedure for the Decision-Making on Major Issues section of the Chengtong's Rules of the Discussion Procedure of China Chengtong Holding Group' Party Committee]. http://www.cctgroup.com.cn/cctgroup/djgz/djzdjs/604755/index.html. Accessed 15 Aug 2025

China Daily (2015) 《三大电信运营商一把手大调整》 [Major Leadership Adjustments at Three Major Telecoms Operators]. http://caijing.chinadaily.com.cn/2015-08/24/content_21685702.htm. Accessed 15 Aug 2025

[112] See, e.g., Xueli Huang (2011) Corporate Governance and Chinese FDI in Australia. East Asia Forum. https://www.eastasiaforum.org/2011/06/05/corporate-governance-and-chinese-fdi-in-australia/. Accessed 15 Aug 2025; Lin (2015), p. 583.

Deng Feng [邓峰] (2022) 《中国公司理论的演变和制度变革方向》 [The Evolution of Chinese Corporate Theory and the Direction of Institutional Change]. Tsinghua Univ Law J 16(2): 42–56., p 43

Ding R (2014) 'Public Body' or not: Chinese state-owned enterprise. J World Trade 48(1):167–189

Ding R (2020) Interface 2.0 in rules on state-owned enterprises: a comparative institutional approach'. J Int Econ Law 23(3):637–663. 649

Ding X (2009) The socialist market economy: China and the world. Sci Soc 73(2):235–241

Du Yanfei [杜燕飞] (2022) 《国有资本运营公司管资本成效凸显》 [State-Owned Capital Operation Companies Effectively Manage Capital, Yielding Exceptional Outcomes]. People. http://finance.people.com.cn/n1/2022/0326/c1004-32384815.html. Accessed 15 Aug 2025

Fama EF, Jensen MC (1983) Separation of ownership and control. J Law Econ 26(2):301–325

Manu-Emanuele C Francia (2019) China's reform process and internationalization: the case of ChemChina. China Daily. https://www.chinadaily.com.cn/a/201912/09/WS5dede3daa310cf3e3557ce56.html. Accessed 15 Aug 2025

Gu Yibing [顾一冰] (2011) 《茅台被约谈后再涨价: 抑制涨价只能靠纪委》 [Moutai Raises Prices again after the Interview with the Government: Curbing Price Hikes can Only Be Done by the Disciplinary Committee]. China Economic. http://www.ce.cn/cysc/sp/info/201109/27/t20110927_21047166.shtml. Accessed 15 Aug 2025

Ho S, Marois T (2019) China's asset management companies as state spatial–temporal strategy. China Quart 239(728-751):730

Huang X (2011) Corporate Governance and Chinese FDI in Australia. East Asia Forum. https://www.eastasiaforum.org/2011/06/05/corporate-governance-and-chinese-fdi-in-australia/. Accessed 15 Aug 2025

Jiang Zemin [江泽民] (2002) 《中国共产党第十六次全国代表大会上的报告》 [Report of the 16th National Congress of the Chinese Communist Party]. Speech. 16th National Congress of the Chinese Communist Party.

Lin L-W (2015) Balancing closure and openness: the challenge of leadership reform in China's state-owned enterprises'. In: Liebman BL, Milhaupt CJ (eds) Regulating the visible hand? The institutional implications of Chinese state capitalism. Oxford University Press

Liu Zhiqiang [刘志强] (2021) 《19家国有资本投资公司试点企业经营业绩超出央企平均水平》 [Operating Performance of 19 Pilot State-Owned Capital Investment Companies Exceeded the Average Level of Central Enterprises]. The State Council. https://www.gov.cn/xinwen/2021-11/03/content_5648503.htm. Accessed 15 Aug 2025

Luo Wen [罗文] (2016) 《守住国有企业的"根"与"魂"》 [Keep the 'Root' and 'Soul' of State-Owned Enterprises]. The State Council. https://www.gov.cn/xinwen/2016-10/18/content_5121159.htm. Accessed 15 Aug 2025

Milhaupt CJ, Zheng W (2015) Beyond ownership: state capitalism and the Chinese firm. Georgetown Law J 103(3):665–722. 678

Mujiangqu N, Xuewan C, Yutong L (2020) China's Power Grid Gets Out of Real Estate. Caixin Global. https://www.caixinglobal.com/2020-08-12/chinas-power-grid-gets-out-of-real-estate-101592031.html. Accessed 15 Aug 2025

OECD (2015a) G20/OECD principles of corporate governance. OECD Publishing

OECD (2015b) OECD guidelines on corporate governance of state-owned enterprises. OECD Publishing, p 7

Peng Huagang [彭华岗] (2017) 《国有企业改革前景及治理模式》 [Prospects for SOE Reforms and Governance Models]. 经济导刊 [Economic Herald] 1

People (2019) 《国企职业经理人制度建设加速推进》 [Accelerating the Construction of Professional Manager System in State-Owned Enterprises]. http://finance.people.com.cn/n1/2019/0301/c1004-30951497.html. Accessed 15 Aug 2025

Piao L, Jung K (2021) The effect of the Xi Jinping Administration's anticorruption campaign on the performance of state-owned enterprises. Asian Surv 61(5):711–741

Ren Tengfei [任腾飞] (2019) 《十项改革试点分析之中央企业国有资本投资、运营公司试点》 [Analysis of Ten Reform Pilot Projects of State-Owned Capital Investment and Operation

Companies of Central Enterprises]. The Central SASAC. http://www.sasac.gov.cn/n2588025/n4423279/n4517386/n11702115/c11704709/content.html. Accessed 15 Aug 2025

SASAC of Shenzhen Municipal People's Government (2015) 《市场化选聘市属国有企业领导人员有关政策解读》 [Interpretation of Policies Related to Market-Based Recruitment of Leaders of Municipal State-Owned Enterprises]

Shi Nengzi and Wu Furong [施能自, 吴芙蓉] (2017) 《新一轮国企改革的思考与操作实务》 [Thoughts and Operational Practices of the Latest Round of SOE Reforms]. 中国经济出版社 [Economic Press China], p 100

Su Li [苏力] (2022) 《党管干部与中国宪制构建》 [The Party Supervising Cadres and the Construction of Chinese Constitutional Government]. 党内法规研究 [Research on Intraparty Rules and Regulations] 1(2): 3-20

The American Enterprise Institute and the Heritage Foundation (2023) China Global Investment Tracker. AEI. https://www.aei.org/china-global-investment-tracker/. Accessed 15 Aug 2025

The Central SASAC (2021) 《国有资本投资公司发挥产业引领作用,加快培育新兴产业》 [SCICs are at the Forefront of Industrial Advancement and Help Foster the Growth of Emerging Industries]. http://www.sasac.gov.cn/n2588025/n2588139/c20082475/content.html. Accessed 15 Aug 2025

The State Council (2015) 《国务院国有企业改革领导小组十项试点2016年将全面展开》 [In 2016, the SOE Reform Leading Group of the State Council will Execute Ten Pilot Programmes]. https://www.gov.cn/xinwen/2015-12/11/content_5022805.htm. Accessed 15 Aug 2025

The State Council (2022a) 《5家中央企业正式转为国有资本投资公司》 [Five Central Enterprises Formally Transformed into State-Owned Capital Investment Companies]. https://www.gov.cn/xinwen/2022-06/21/content_5696886.htm. Accessed 15 Aug 2025

The State Council (2022b) 《制造强国 步履铿锵》 [Advancing Steadily towards Prominence as the World's leading Manufacturing Superpower]. https://www.gov.cn/xinwen/2022-08/15/content_5705364.htm. Accessed 15 Aug 2025

Wang Lu [王璐] (2019) 《中广核四项改革试点齐发动 争创"世界一流"》 [CGN Launches Four Pilot Reforms in an Attempt to Achieve 'World-Class']. National Energy Administration. http://www.nea.gov.cn/2019-01/17/c_137751944.htm. Accessed 15 Aug 2025

Wang Ziming [王子铭] (2023) 《坚决打赢反腐败斗争攻坚战持久战》 [Unwaveringly Prevailing in the Arduous Fight Against Corruption]. The State Council. https://www.gov.cn/xinwen/2023-01/05/content_5735650.htm. Accessed 15 Aug 2025

Wu M (2016) The "China, Inc." challenge to global trade governance. Harv Int Law J 57(2):261–324. 282

Xi Jinping [习近平] (2016) 《习近平在全国国有企业党的建设工作会议上的讲话》 [Xi Jinping's speech at the National Conference on Party Building in State-owned Enterprises]. Speech. National Conference on Party Building in State-owned Enterprises

Xiaohong C, Zhaoxi L, Zhengjun Z (2004) Policy dialogue on corporate Governance in China. OECD, p 3. https://www.oecd.org/corporate/ca/corporategovernanceofstate-ownedenterprises/31603840.pdf. Accessed 15 Aug 2025

Xinhua News Agency (2021) 《央企董事会建设从"试点探索"进入"全面推进"》 [Central Enterprises from 'Pilot Exploration' to 'Comprehensive Promotion' of the Board of Directors Construction]. http://www.news.cn/fortune/2021-10/19/c_1127971133.htm. Accessed 15 Aug 2025

Zhang D, Freestone O (2013) China's unfinished state-owned enterprise reforms. Econ Round-Up 2:77–99

Zhao Jiani [赵嘉妮] (2015) 《"三桶油"同日宣布换帅: 为何要实行轮换制? 》 ['Three Barrels of Oil' Announced on the Same Day to Change the Commander in Chief: Why to Implement the Leadership Rotation Mechanism?]. People. http://theory.people.com.cn/n/2015/0505/c40531-26949339.html. Accessed 15 Aug 2025

Additional Sources

《中共中央关于加强干部管理工作的决定》 [Decision of the CCP Central Committee on Strengthening the Management of Cadres]. (People's Republic of China) The CCP Central Committee. 24 November 1953

《中共中央关于国有企业改革和发展若干重大问题的决定》 [Decision of the CCP Central Committee on Major Issues concerning the Reform and Development of State-Owned Enterprises]. (People's Republic of China) The CCP Central Committee. 12 November 2013

《中共中央关于建立社会主义市场经济体制若干问题的决定》 [Decision of the CCP Central Committee on Some Issues Concerning the Establishment of a Socialist Market Economic System]. (People's Republic of China) The CCP Central Committee. 14 November 1993

《中共中央关于成立中共中央企业工作委员会及有关问题的通知》 [Notice of the CCP Central Committee on the Establishment of the Working Committee of the CCP Central Committee for Enterprises and Related Issues]. (People's Republic of China) The CCP Central Committee. 1 December 1999

《中共中央国务院关于深化国有企业改革的指导意见》 [The Guiding Opinions of the CCP Central Committee and the State Council on Deepening the Reform of State-Owned Enterprises]. (People's Republic of China) The CCP Central Committee and the State Council. 24 August 2015

《中华人民共和国企业国有资产法》 [Law of the People's Republic of China on State-Owned Assets in Enterprises]. (People's Republic of China) Adopted at the 11th National People's Congress Standing Committee. 28 October 2008, art. 11

《中华人民共和国全民所有制工业企业法》 [Law of Industrial Enterprises Owned by the Whole People of the People's Republic of China]. (People's Republic of China) Adopted at the 7th National People's Congress. 13 April 1988, amended 27 August 2009

《中华人民共和国公司法》[Company Law of the People's Republic of China]. (People's Republic of China) Adopted at the 8th National People's Congress Standing Committee. 29 December 1993, amended 25 December 1999, 28 August 2004, 28 December 2013, 26 October 2018 and 29 December 2023

《中国共产党国有企业基层组织工作条例(试行)》 [Trial Regulation on the Work at Primary-level Party Organizations of State-Owned Enterprises]. (People's Republic of China) The CCP Central Committee. 30 December 2019

《中国共产党章程》 [Constitution of the Communist Party of China]. (People's Republic of China) Adopted at the 20th CCP National Congress. 22 October 2022, art. 33

《关于中央企业建立和完善国有独资公司董事会试点工作的通知》 [Notice on the Pilot Work of Establishing and Improving the Board of Directors of Wholly State Owned Companies by Central Enterprises]. (People's Republic of China) The Central SASAC. 6 June 2004

《关于印发中央企业公司制改制工作实施方案的通知》 [Notice on the Issuance of the Implementation Plan for the Corporate Restructuring of Central Enterprises]. (People's Republic of China) The General Office of the State Council. 26 July 2017

《关于扎实推动国有企业党建工作要求写入公司章程的通知》 [The Notice on Solid Promotion of Writing the Party Building Work of State-Owned Enterprises into the Articles of Association]. (People's Republic of China) Organization Department of the CCP Central Committee and the Central SASAC. 15 March 2017

《关于进一步推进国有企业贯彻落实"三重一大"决策制度的意见》 [Opinions on Further Promoting the Implementation of the 'Three Major and one Significant Matters' Decision-making System in State-Owned Enterprises]. (People's

Republic of China) General Office of the CCP and General Office of the State Council. 15 July 2010

《十三五国家战略性新兴产业发展规划》 [National 13th Five-Year Plan for the Development of Strategic Emerging Industries]. (People's Republic of China) The State Council. 19 December 2016

《国务院关于2005年深化经济体制改革的意见》 [Opinions of the State Council on Deepening Economic Restructuring in 2005]. (People' s Republic of China) The State Council. 4 April 2005

《国务院关于推进国有资本投资、运营公司改革试点的实施意见》 [Opinions of the State Council on the Implementation of the Pilot Reform of State-Owned Capital Investment and Operation Companies]. (People' s Republic of China) The State Council. 30 July 2018

《国务院国有资产监督管理委员会主要职责内设机构和人员编制规定》 [The Regulation of The Internal Organs and Staffing of the State-Owned Assets and Administration Commission of the State Council]. (People' s Republic of China) General Office of the State Council. 25 April 2003

《国务院国资委以管资本为主推进职能转变的方案》 [The Plan for Promoting the Functional Transition of State-Owned Assets Supervision and Administration Commission of the State Council to Focus on the Management of Capital]. (People' s Republic of China) General Office of the State Council. 27 April 2017

《国务院国资委授权放权清单(2019年版)》 [List of Shareholder functions Authorised by State-Owned Assets Supervision and Administration Commission of the State Council (2019 edition)]. (People' s Republic of China) The State Council. 3 June 2019

《改革国有资本授权经营体制方案》 [The Plan for Reforming the System of Authorised Operation of State-Owned Capital]. (People' s Republic of China) The State Council. 28 April 2019

《深化干部人事制度改革的纲要》 [Outline for Deepening the Cadre Personnel System Reform]. (People' s Republic of China) The State Council. June 2000

国企改革历程编写组 [SOE Reform Process Writing Group] (2019) 《国企改革历程1978-2018》 [The Course of Chinese State-Owned Enterprise Reform 1978-2018]. 中国经济出版社 [Economic Press China], p 246 - 247

《国务院办公厅关于进一步完善国有企业法人治理结构的指导意见》 [Guiding Opinions on Further Improving the Corporate Governance Structure of State-Owned Enterprises]. (People' s Republic of China) The General Office of the State Council. 24 April 2017

国务院国资委改革办 [Reform Office of the Central SASAC] (2018) 《国企改革探索与实践——中央企业集团15例(上)》 [Exploration and Practice of SOE Reforms—15 Cases among the Central Business Groups]. 中国经济出版社 [China Economic Publishing House], p 172

国务院国资委新闻中心, 《国资报告》杂志社 [News Centre of the Central SASAC and 'State-Owned Assets Report' magazine press] (2016) 《国企改革12样本》 [12 Samples of SOE Reforms]. 中国经济出版社 [China Economic Publishing House], p 191-195

Chapter 5
The Mountains Are High But the Emperor Is Not Far Away: The Escalation in Political Control Over Chinese SOE Outbound Investments

Abstract This chapter examines the escalation of political control over Chinese SOEs and their outbound Foreign Direct Investment (FDI) in light of the latest round of SOE reforms. Despite the growing significance of private outbound FDI since China's WTO accession in 2001, SOEs continue to dominate China's outbound investment landscape. This chapter explores how the tightening political control through recent reforms has shaped SOEs' outbound investment strategies and operations. The research identifies key institutional pressures exerted on Chinese SOEs' FDI decision-making, focusing on the enhanced political control embedded in SOE governance systems, the policy tasks assigned to SOEs designated as State-owned Capital Investment and Operation Companies (SCIOs), and the multi-layered administrative approval processes for outbound investments. The chapter further highlights the role of core companies within business groups as intermediaries between the government and SOE subsidiaries, facilitating political oversight over overseas operations. This chapter shows how political influence permeates the entire FDI process, ensuring that SOE investments align with national policies and government directives. The findings underscore the growing significance of Chinese SOE FDI in the global economy and provide insights into how host countries can address the challenges posed by political influence in Chinese SOE investments.

Despite the rapid growth of private outbound FDI since China's accession to the WTO in 2001, Chinese SOEs still play a significant role in China's outbound investment since 1979, when China first permitted FDI. According to the 2021 Statistical Bulletin of China's Outward Foreign Direct Investment released by MOFCOM, NBS and the State Administration of Foreign Exchange (SAFE), at the end of 2021, SOEs accounted for 51.6 percent of China's stock of non-financial FDI.[1]

As demonstrated in the preceding chapters, China's latest round of SOE reforms is tightening the overall political control over Chinese SOEs and industries that the government considers significant for the country's sustainable development. The

[1] MOFCOM, NBS and SAFE (2022), p. 30.

T. Gu, *Chinese SOE Reforms and Global FDI*, Contemporary Chinese Civil and Commercial Law, https://doi.org/10.1007/978-981-92-3181-2_5

tightening of political control raises the question of how the latest round of SOE reforms has affected political influence over Chinese SOEs' outbound FDI activities.

In addition, the global expansion of Chinese SOEs has resulted in a growing number of overseas affiliates worldwide. According to the central SASAC, by the end of 2018, China's central BGs (97 at that time) had established 11,028 overseas affiliates across 185 countries and regions.[2] This reflects the enormous number of Chinese SOE overseas affiliates due to their massive FDI. Accordingly, several questions arise: to what extent are Chinese SOE overseas subsidiaries subject to political influence in the latest round of SOE reforms? How do the Chinese government and the CCP exert meaningful control over Chinese SOE overseas affiliates and their operations?

This chapter seeks to provide answers to these questions. Many scholarly works and governmental instruments of host States have acknowledged that Chinese SOEs engage in FDI driven by underlying policy objectives. However, the proposition is grounded primarily in empirical studies or is theoretical. For instance, Stone, Wang and Yu concluded that China uses SOE FDI to advance its foreign policy goals by demonstrating the high degree of conformity between Chinese SOE FDI and State policies, using a comprehensive firm-level data set on Chinese FDI from 2000 to 2013.[3] However, the proposition has not been grounded on China's latest legislation and political documentary instruments outlining the mechanisms through which the government and the CCP exert political interference in SOEs' outbound FDI activities. This may be a result of the continued obscurity of China's SOE reform policies.

Given the gap in the research which has been identified above, this chapter presents comprehensive analyses of the institutional mechanisms whereby the Chinese Party-State exert control over Chinese SOEs' outbound FDI activities. This chapter proves that the latest round of SOE reforms brought about an intensification of political control over Chinese SOEs' outbound investment, including both the enhancement of institutional pressures on SOEs' FDI decision-making process and an extension of political supervision over SOE overseas subsidiaries and operations through core companies of BGs.

The chapter is structured as follows: Section 5.1 outlines the institutional pressures on the Chinese SOE decision-making processes regarding FDI from multiple sources introduced or enhanced by the latest round of SOE reforms. The institutional pressures ensure that Chinese SOE FDI conforms to government directives and State policies. Section 5.2 illustrates how the core companies of BGs serve as intermediaries between the government and SOE investors, transferring political oversight to SOE overseas subsidiaries and operations. Section 5.3 identifies the practical obstacles that may impede the operation of the controlling mechanisms for Chinese SOEs' outbound FDI activities.

---

[2] The State Council (2019) 《国资委:央企境外资产总额已达7.6万亿元》 [SASAC: Central Enterprises' Overseas Assets Have Reached 7.6 Trillion Yuan]. https://www.gov.cn/xinwen/2019-10/17/content_5441316.htm. Accessed 17 Aug 2025.

[3] Stone et al. (2022), pp. 229–250.

5.1 The Multi-source Institutional Pressures on the SOE FDI Decision-making

When a Chinese SOE decides to make outbound FDI, it is subject to multiple institutional pressures. As Fig. 5.1 demonstrates, these multiple institutional pressures encompass the entire decision-making procedure. Since the Xi Jinping administration assumed leadership, the modern era has witnessed an unprecedented increase in pressure from most of these sources to ensure SOEs' outbound FDI decisions are in accordance with the State's will.

5.1.1 The Institutional Pressures Created in the Latest Round of SOE Reforms

The latest round of SOE reforms has directly impacted the political pressures surrounding Chinese SOE FDI decisions. This impact can be attributed to two sources created in the reforms: first, the heightened political control embedded in SOE governance practices as a result of the SOE governance system reform, and secondly, the policy responsibilities of SOEs that have been designated as SCIOs in the State-owned assets management system reform or classified as 'General Commercial' or 'Special Commercial' in the MOR. These newly introduced sources of pressure can contribute significantly to the conformity of SOE FDI decisions with national policies and government directives.

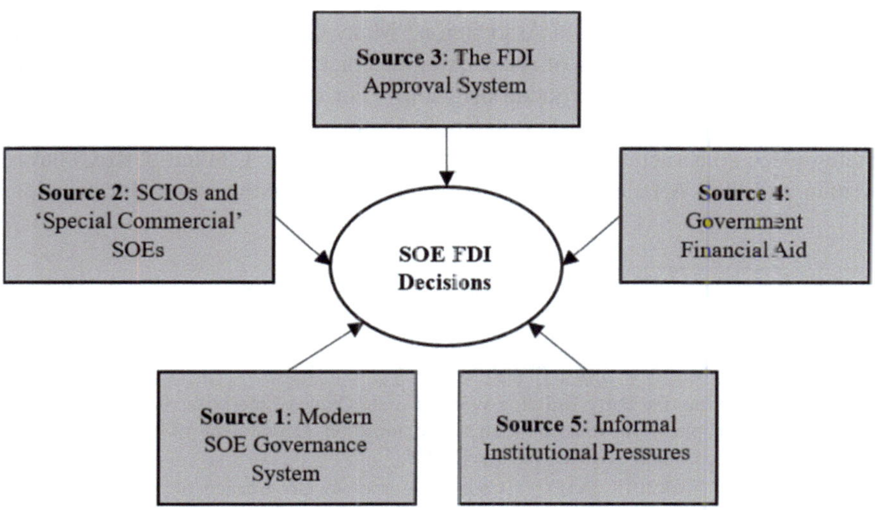

Fig. 5.1 The Multi-Source Institutional Pressures on SOEs' Outbound FDI Decision-Making Process

5.1.1.1 Political Control Embedded in SOE Corporate Governance System

The first institutional pressure comes from enhancing and embedding the CCP's leadership in Chinese SOE governance practices. As discussed in Chap. 4, in China's latest round of SOE reforms, the sub-reform targeting the SOE governance system aims to consolidate the CCP-led political control over the SOE governance system. This is accomplished primarily by introducing a distinctive 'Modern SOE Governance System with Chinese Characteristics' featuring the Party Committee's primacy in decision-making (on specified major matters) and enhanced political control over SOE senior executives.

Under the modern SOE governance system, the *Trial Regulation on the Work at Primary-level Party Organizations of State-owned Enterprises* (*Trial Regulation*) issued by the CCP central committee in 2019 stipulates that 'large investment of corporate assets' is one of the matters subject to prior discussion by the SOE's Party Committee before the board of directors can make decisions.[4] This means that a Chinese SOE's board of directors cannot pass a resolution to make a particular FDI until it has received approval from the Party Committee.

With the advancement of the SOE reforms, Chinese SOEs have promptly implemented a distinctive corporate governance system. According to the CCP Central Committee, all first- and second-tier subsidiaries of China's central BGs, totalling more than 3,000 SOEs, had stipulated the leading role of the Party Committee in corporate governance in their Articles of Association by the end of 2017.[5] China's 2018 revised *Code of Corporate Governance of Listed Companies* explicitly requires all State-holding companies listed on domestic stock exchanges (excluding the Stock Exchange of Hong Kong (SEHK)) to establish the CCP organisation (typically Party Committee) and specifies the formal role of the Party Committee in governance in their Articles of Association.[6] Many Chinese SOEs listed on SEHK have amended their Articles of Association to grant the Party Committee decisive authority over important corporate decisions.[7] For example, China's State-owned oil and gas producer, China Petroleum & Chemical Corporation (Sinopec), and State-owned construction company China Railway Group Limited (CREC) have it written into their Articles of Association that before making any major decisions,

[4] 《中国共产党国有企业基层组织工作条例(试行)》 [Trial Regulation on the Work at Primary-level Party Organizations of State-Owned Enterprises]. (People's Republic of China) The CCP Central Committee. 30 December 2019, art. 15.

[5] 《关于扎实推动国有企业党建工作要求写入公司章程的通知》 [The Notice on Solid Promotion of Writing the Party Building Work of State-Owned Enterprises into the Articles of Association]. (People's Republic of China) Organization Department of the CCP Central Committee and the Central SASAC. 15 March 2017.

[6] 《上市公司治理准则(2018 修订)》 [Code of Corporate Governance of Listed Companies (Revised in 2018)]. (People's Republic of China) China Securities Regulatory Commission. 30 September 2019, art. 5.

[7] Liu and Huyue Zhang (2019), p. 105853.

the Board of Directors must consult with the Company's Party Committees for opinions.[8] The Chinese government's Supervisory Commissions and the CCP's commissions for disciplinary inspection (co-located agencies) have inspected and penalised SOE executives who made investments without Party Committee approval.[9] The decision-making procedures required by the modern SOE governance system have been linked to the negative list-based SASAC approval system for SOE FDI, which will be discussed below.

In addition to the Party Committee's primacy in the decision-making process, the modern SOE governance system emphasises political control over the senior executive personnel of SOEs. Briefly, political control is achieved through the government and CCP's authority to appoint and remove top executives at SOEs, as well as to rotate senior executives between SOEs, and through mandatory cross-officeholding between SOEs' Party Committees and regular corporate governance organs (namely the board of directors (including outside directors), supervisory board and senior management team).[10] Personnel oversight can further compel SOE insiders to propose only FDI projects that comply with government directives and national policies. This cross-officeholding can ensure that the SOE's FDI decisions adhere to the CCP's directives.

5.1.1.2 The Policy Tasks of 'Special Commercial' SOEs and SCIOs

As discussed in Chap. 3, in the latest round of SOE reforms, Chinese SOEs have been categorised as 'Public Welfare,' 'General Commercial,' and 'Special Commercial' to implement flow-in MOR (introducing non-State shareholders into SOEs). Typically, 'Special Commercial' is the classification for SOEs primarily operating in critical industries.[11] Accordingly, many of the largest Chinese SOEs in the energy, mining and transportation sectors that are active global investors fall into this category. 'Special Commercial' SOEs are required to maintain State-holding status in the MOR and are tasked with pursuing a broad range of policy tasks in their operations, such as safeguarding national security, ensuring economic stability and promoting the development of China's high-tech sectors.[12]

[8] Ibid.

[9] See, e.g., 罗有远 [Luo Youyuan] (2023) 《专项治理国企擅自对外投资和担保问题》 [Specially Combat the Issue of Unapproved Foreign Investment and Guarantees by SOEs]. The Central Commission for Disciplinary Inspection of the CCP and the National Commission of Supervision of the PRC. <https://www.ccdi.gov.cn/yaowenn/202302/t20230210_245823.html. Accessed 17 Aug 2025.

[10] For detailed discussion in this regard, see Chap. 4 Sect. 4.2.

[11] 《关于国有企业功能界定与分类的指导意见》 [Guiding Opinions on the Definition and Classification of Functions of State-Owned Enterprises]. (People's Republic of China) The State Council. 29 December 2015.

[12] Ibid.

In addition, as discussed in Chap. 4, in the ongoing reform of the State-owned assets management system as a part of the latest round of SOE reforms, a growing number of SOEs which are dominant in China's critical industries and active in the global investment landscape have been designated as SCICs. SCICs serve as professional platforms for managing State-owned capital and are charged with the policy missions of investing in both domestic and international markets in ways that support government policy, national strategy and macro-control objectives.[13]

In practice, Chinese SOEs designated as SCICs or classified as 'Special Commercial' SOEs (which can occur simultaneously) have generally engaged in FDI strictly following State policies. For example, Sinopec (ranked 6th on the Global Fortune 500 in 2023) is a 'Special Commercial' SOE. It holds stakes in Australian Pacific liquefied natural gas (LNG) project and Qatar's North Field LNG project.[14] In addition, China Baowu Steel Group (Baowu) (ranked 44th on the Global Fortune 500 in 2023) and China Communications Construction Company (CCCC) (ranked 63rd on the Global Fortune 500 in 2023) have been designated as SCICs. Baowu recently agreed to form a joint venture with the Australian mining company Rio Tinto to develop Australia's Western Range iron ore project (2022).[15] These investments exhibited a high degree of conformity with the Xi Jinping administration's policies regarding securing critical mineral and energy supplies.[16]

Notably, as Chaps. 3 and 4 demonstrated, the Chinese government has mandated that SASACs evaluate the performance of SCICs and 'Special Commercial' SOEs and their executives under their supervision, primarily based on how well the SOEs have fulfilled their policy tasks. The evaluation results are tied to the amount of State funding that the SOE can receive the following year, known as 'SOE Capital Injection' (which will be discussed in detail below), as well as the career prospects of the SOE executives.[17] Consequently, for Chinese SOEs that have been or will be designated as SCICs or classified as 'Special Commercial' in the ongoing SOE reforms, it is reasonable to expect that their outbound FDI decisions are substantially, if not entirely, shaped by State policies and government directives.

---

[13] For discussion regarding the functions of SCICs, see Chap. 4 Sect. 4.1.2.2.

[14] El Dahan and Mills (2023).

[15] Manekar and Menon (2022).

[16] Jinping (2014). For more details regarding China's foreign investment policy, see Chap. 6 Sect. 6.1.

[17] The central SASAC revised its regulation for evaluating the performance of top executives of central SOEs, stipulating that the weight of general business indicators of 'Special Commercial' SOEs and SCIOs would be reduced in evaluations. 《中央企业负责人经营业绩考核办法》 [Measures for Business Performance Assessment of the Persons in Charge of Central Enterprises]. (People's Republic of China) The Central SASAC. 8 December 2016, art. 13, 15, 39.

5.1.2 *The Administrative Approval Systems for Outbound FDI*

The administrative approval system for outbound investments in China is a significant mechanism for the government to intervene directly in the FDI decisions of SOEs, as certain outbound investments require government approvals before implementation. As a socialist country transitioning to a market economy, China has historically implemented a complex administrative approval system for outbound investment, which has been extensively discussed in the academic literature.[18] Chinese SOEs' FDI proposals must undergo both the SOE-specific approval processes and the administrative approval system applicable to all Chinese companies. Figure 5.2 depicts the current administrative approval system applicable to SOE FDI proposals, which is comprised of four approval processes administered by distinct authorities. In conjunction with the 'Go Global' policy, China has reformed its outbound investment administrative regime over the past two decades, notably by adopting a negative list approach in the SOE-specific and general FDI approval systems. Nonetheless, in the context of the latest round of SOE reforms, China's administrative framework for SOEs' outbound FDI has been intensified despite the relaxation of the general outbound FDI approval system.

5.1.2.1 The Enhanced SOE-specific Outbound FDI Approval System in China

Despite its commitment when acceding to the WTO that the Chinese government would not directly or indirectly influence the commercial decisions of SOEs or State-invested enterprises,[19] China persists in maintaining a stringent pre-investment administrative framework for SOE FDI proposals. Notably, the framework has been

[18] See, e.g., Chaisse (2018); Bath (2011).

[19] Guoqiang (2015), p. 5, 19.

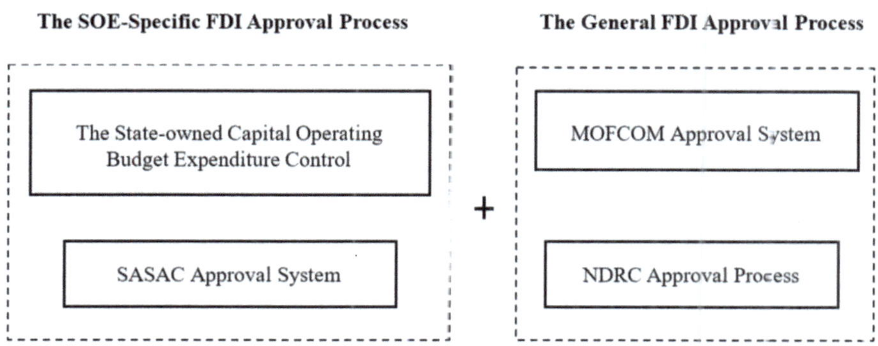

Fig. 5.2 The Four-Layer Administrative Approval Process for Chinese SOE FDI

considerably tightened in the latest round of SOE reforms with a particular emphasis on the conformity of proposed transactions with State policies and government directives. As shown in Fig. 5.2, in addition to the general outbound investment approval processes administered by MOFCOM and NDRC, SOEs' FDI proposals are subject to two specialised approval processes, namely the supervision system for 'State-owned Capital Operating Budget Expenditure' ('国有资本经营预算支出') and the SASAC-led outbound FDI approval system.

The former system is essentially a State-owned capital gains handover system, which was first introduced in China in 1993 (with only a limited pilot in a few cities[20]) and implemented nationwide in 2007.[21] The system is administered by MOF. Under the system, SOEs must return a certain proportion of their after-tax profit to their government owners (through the core companies of their respective BGs) each year according to various formulae.[22] In the latest round of SOE reforms, the Chinese government has significantly increased the proportion of handover. For example, the proportion of central SOEs has been raised from 14 percent on average in 2015 to 30 percent in 2020.[23] The governments then reinvest a portion of the handover profit in the BGs, known as a 'SOE Capital Injection' ('国有企业资本金注入') to fund the enterprises' business operations, including outbound FDI activities, in the subsequent fiscal year. The proportion of reinvestment is contingent upon the specific regulations issued by governments of different regions. It is presumed to be higher for SOEs designated as SCIOs, owing to their policy responsibilities.[24]

The SOE Capital Injection is intended to fund only the activities of SOEs that implement government and the CCP policies and directives.[25] Therefore, a BG (core company) must submit a detailed State-owned capital operating budget expenditure plan to obtain the SOE Capital Injection. The plan should include the group's

[20] The cities included Beijing, Shanghai, Shenzhen and Wuhan. 《关于实行分税制财政管理体制的决定》 [Decision on the Implementation of the Tax-Sharing Fiscal Management System]. (People's Republic of China) The State Council. 15 December 1993.

[21] 《关于试行国有资本经营预算的意见》 [Opinions on the Trial Implementation of State-Owned Capital Operating Budget System]. (People's Republic of China) The State Council. 8 September 2007.

[22] In brief, for wholly State-owned enterprises, the handovers proportion ranges from 15 to 25 percent, for other SOEs, the proportion depends on the Sate shareholding. Cui (2015), p. 115.

[23] 《关于深化国有企业改革的指导意见》 [The Guiding Opinions on Deepening the Reform of State-Owned Enterprises]. (People's Republic of China) The CCP Central Committee and the State Council. 24 August 2015.

[24] The State Council (2017) 《国企资本金注入采取三种方式》 [Capital Injections into SOEs Take Three Forms]. <https://www.gov.cn/xinwen/2017-03/30/content_5181931.htm. Accessed 17 Aug 2025.

[25] Regulations on State-owned capital operating budget expenditure control system were issued at both the central and local levels, with the central regulation serving as a framework document that was essentially followed by the local regulations. 《中央国有资本经营预算支出管理暂行办法》 [Interim Measures for the Management of Expenditure of the Central State-Owned Capital Operating Budget Expenditure]. (People's Republic of China) MOF. 13 March 2017, art. 11.3.

development strategy and investment planning and be reviewed for approval by the corresponding financial department.[26] The review is based on the national major development strategies, macro-control objectives and the outcomes of the BG's performance evaluation in prior years.[27]

In addition to the annual investment plans of BGs being subject to review under the State-owned capital operating budget expenditure control system, each SOE's individual FDI proposals must undergo reviews by the SASAC at the corresponding level. In 2008, the Chinese government established a SASAC supervision system for SOE outbound FDI.[28] Under the system, only when an SOE proposed an FDI project which was unrelated to its principal business did it require special review and approval from the supervising SASAC.[29] In 2017, during the latest round of SOE reforms, however, this relatively liberal approval requirement was replaced by a negative list-based SASAC review system, which creates restricted and prohibited lists for foreign investment and only requires FDI to go through the approval process for investments on the negative list.[30] The effect of the negative-list approval system, however, is to broaden the scope of projects which require approval beyond non-principal business FDI, and focuses on the conformity of SOE investments with State and national policies and strategies.

According to the *Measures for Supervision and Administration of Overseas Investment by Central Enterprises* (*Central SOE FDI Measures*) issued by the central SASAC in 2017 (which serves as the framework document for local SASACs when formulating their review regulations), a two-layer negative list approach applies to SOE FDI proposals:[31] The SASACs issue their negative lists for FDI proposed by core companies of BGs under their direct supervision. The core companies then use these lists as a starting point for compiling their own negative lists for their subsidiaries, taking into account the primary businesses of the BGs, and report the list to the SASACs.[32] The negative lists specify 'prohibited' and 'specially supervised' investment projects. According to the latest negative list issued by the central

---

[26] Ibid. art. 15, 16.

[27] Ibid. art. 17.

[28] 《关于进一步加强中央企业投资管理的通知》 [Notice on Further Strengthening the Investment Management of Central Enterprises]. (People's Republic of China) The Central SASAC. 19 August 2008.

[29] 《中央企业境外投资监督管理暂行办法》 [Interim Measures for Supervision and Administration of Overseas Investment by Central Enterprises]. (People's Republic of China) The Central SASAC. 18 March 2012, repealed 7 January 2017, art. 10.

[30] 《关于加强中央企业境外投资管理的有关事项的通知》[Notice on Strengthening the Administration of Overseas Investment by Central Enterprises]. (People's Republic of China) The Central SASAC. 31 December 2008.

[31] 《中央企业境外投资监督管理办法》 [Measures for Supervision and Administration of Overseas Investment by Central Enterprises]. (People's Republic of China) The Central SASAC. 7 January 2017, art. 4, 9 ('*Central SOE FDI Measures*').

[32] 《中央企业境外投资项目负面清单(2017 年版)》 [Negative List of Overseas Investment Projects of Central SOEs (2017 Edition)]. (People's Republic of China) The Central SASAC. 19 January 2017 ('*2017 Central Negative List*').

SASAC in 2017,[33] which applies to central SOEs and serves as a template for local SASACs to formulate their lists,[34] investments that central SOEs are prohibited from making include, first, those that do not conform with the development strategy and plan that SASACs formulate for each BG under their supervision according to State policies and, secondly, those that are not decided on internally by an SOE by following the decision-making procedures required by the modern SOE governance system. This heightens the primacy of the Party Committee in decisions on major affairs, including FDI, and other investments with discernible risks of incurring financial losses.[35] The 'specially supervised' FDI refers to projects with investment exceeding USD 2 billion, which require approval from the SASAC.[36] In addition, FDI proposals unrelated to SOEs' principal businesses are still subject to SASAC approval on a case-by-case basis.[37]

The State-owned capital operating budget expenditure control system and the SASAC approval system have been substantially enhanced in the latest round of SOE reforms, indicating the incumbent government's clear intent to intensify political interference in SOEs' outbound investment, thereby ensuring that they are pursuing policy goals. In addition to the SOE-specific approval processes, the FDI proposals of Chinese SOEs are also subject to the general FDI approval system applicable to all Chinese FDI, which could further ensure the political conformity of SOE investments as discussed below.

5.1.2.2 The General Outbound FDI Regulatory System in China

Chinese SOE outbound investments are also subject to China's outbound investment approval system for all companies. Although China has significantly streamlined the general approval system as it increasingly embraced international economic diplomacy over the past few decades,[38] the system can further influence the direction of FDI outflows by SOEs.

China maintained a case-by-case approval requirement for all outbound investments until relaxation of the system in 2014.[39] The Xi Jinping administration switched to adopt a negative list-based recordation (approval) system administered by MOFCOM and NDRC separately. Under the system, both MOFCOM and NDRC

---

33 Ibid.

34 The negative lists issued by local SASACs mostly mirror the central SASAC's list. See, e.g., 《四川省属国有企业境外投资项目负面清单(2017年版)》 [Negative List of Overseas Investment Projects of Sichuan SOEs (2017 Edition)]. (People's Republic of China) SASAC of Chengdu Municipal Government. 14 November 2017.

35 *2017 Central Negative List* (n 32).

36 Ibid; *Central SOE FDI Measures* (n 31) art. 9.

37 *Central SOE FDI Measures* (n 31) art. 14.

38 For discussion regarding China's foreign investment review system before 2015, see generally Bath (2015).

39 Bath (2017), p. 52.

require only investment projects falling within the negative lists to be approved ('核准') by NDRC or MOFCOM (or provincial commerce departments), while recordation ('备案') requirements apply to others.[40]

Unlike the negative lists under the SASAC approval system discussed above, the current negative lists formulated by MOFCOM and NDRC are rather concise and consistent, concentrating on investments involving 'sensitive industries and countries (regions)', subject to different definitions of terms. MOFCOM defines 'sensitive industries' as industries that export products and technologies subject to export restrictions imposed by the Chinese government and industries that are essential to national or regional interests.[41] In contrast, 'sensitive industries' defined by NDRC include the weapon development, production and maintenance industry, cross-border water resources exploitation and use and news media.[42] Both authorities define 'sensitive countries (regions)' primarily as countries without diplomatic relations with China, although NDRC's definition extends to countries and regions experiencing domestic unrest, and MOFCOM's definition includes countries subject to United Nations sanctions.[43] When evaluating FDI projects on the negative lists, authorities examine legal compliance and conformity with national interests and security.[44] Additionally, NDRC would assess whether a proposed investment project is consistent with national macroeconomic policies and strategic development plans.[45] It would take twenty to thirty working days for NDRC to review and from eighteen to twenty-three days for MOFCOM.[46]

The negative list-based recordation (approval) system signifies an easing of government control regarding the FDI outflow. MOFCOM revealed in January 2018 that 99.5 percent of outbound investments are only required to be recorded under its system (though the timeframe and criteria employed to calculate this remain unknown).[47] However, in 2018, the MOFOCM, together with six other central government departments, issued a document on the establishment of a reporting system

[40] 《境外投资管理办法》 [Measures for the Administration of Overseas Investment]. (People's Republic of China) MOFCOM. 6 September 2014, art. 6 ('*MOFCOM Approval Measures (2014)*'); 《企业境外投资管理办法》 [Measures for the Administration of Overseas Investment of Enterprises]. (People's Republic of China) NDRC. 26 December 2017, art. 13, 14 ('*NDRC Approval Measures (2017)*').

[41] *MOFCOM Approval Measures* (2014) (n 40) art. 7.

[42] *NDRC Approval Measures* (2017) (n 40) art. 13.

[43] Ibid; *MOFCOM Approval Measures* (2014) (n 40) art. 7.

[44] *NDRC Approval Measures* (2017) (n 40) art 26; *MOFCOM Approval Measures* (2014) (n 40) art. 4.

[45] *NDRC Approval Measures* (2017) (n 40) art. 26.

[46] Ibid. art. 25; *MOFCOM Approval Measures (2014)* (n 40) art. 12.

[47] MOFCOM (2018) Interpretations of the Interim Measures for the Reporting of Outbound Investments Subject to Record-filing or Approval by the Head of Outward Investment and Economic Cooperation of the Ministry of Commerce. http://english.mofcom.gov.cn/article/newsrelease/policyreleasing/201802/20180202706980.shtml. Accessed 17 Aug 2025.

to supplement its recordation (approval) system for outbound FDI.[48] The system requires domestic investors, after completing the recordation or approval process, to regularly report to competent authorities with key information about the investment projects. This includes updates on project progress, local law compliance and environmental resource protection, etcetera.[49] Additionally, it requires that investors report any unexpected safety accidents or materially adverse events.[50] As a result of this newly established reporting system, Chinese SOE outbound investment is subject to additional layers of oversight by government authorities other than the SASACs.

5.1.3 The Conditions for Governmental Financial Supports

Despite China's transition to a market economy commencing in 1978, SOEs in China continue to receive explicit and implicit fiscal or financial aid from the government, a topic that has been extensively discussed in both Western and Chinese legal and business scholarship.[51] Since 2006, China has publicly committed to providing preferential treatment in various aspects such as diplomacy, taxation, foreign exchange, credit, insurance, and more, to investment within the 'encouraged' areas outlined in its *Industrial Guiding Policy on Outbound Investment (Guiding Policy)*.[52] In 2013, the Xi Jinping administration also committed to increasing financial support for outbound investment in line with national policy.[53] It revised the *Guiding Policy* in 2017 to encourage outbound investments in advanced manufacturing, technological, energy resources mining, agriculture and service sectors and sectors related to the Belt-and-Road initiative.[54] The commitment to provide preferential

48 《对外投资备案(核准)报告暂行办法》 [Interim Measures for the Reporting of Outbound Investments Subject to Recordation or Approval]. (People's Republic of China) MOFCOM, BOC, the Central SASAC, China Banking Regulatory Commission, China Securities Regulatory Commission, China Insurance Regulatory Commission and SAFE. 18 January 2018, ch. 3 ('*FDI Reporting System Measures*').

49 Ibid. art. 3, 12, 13.

50 Ibid. art. 16. For detailed rules of the reporting system, see 《对外投资备案(核准)报告实施规程》 [Implementing Procedures the Reporting of Outbound Investments Subject to Recordation or Approval]. (People's Republic of China) The General Office of MOFCOM. 16 May 2019.

51 See, e.g., Zhang and Freestone (2013), p. 90; Herrero and Ng (2021), p. 16; Center for Macroeconomic Research of Xiamen University (2018), p. 35; 楼秋然 [Lou Qiuran] (2021), p. 78.

52 《境外投资产业指导政策》 [The Industrial Guiding Policy for Overseas Investment]. (People's Republic of China) NDRC, MOFCOM, Ministry of Foreign Affairs (MFA), MOF, General Administration of Customs, State Taxation Administration, SAFE. 5 July 2006.

53 《关于金融支持经济结构调整和转型升级的指导意见》 [Guiding Opinions on Financial Support to Economic Structure Adjustment, Transformation and Upgrading]. (People's Republic of China) General Office of the State Council. 5 July 2013.

54 《关于进一步引导和规范境外投资方向的指导意见》 [The Guiding Opinions on Further Guiding and Regulating the Direction of Overseas Investment]. (People's Republic of China) General Office of the State Council. 18 August 2017.

treatment could incentivise Chinese companies to align their FDI decisions with policy recommendations.

Given China's commitments in the *Agreement on Subsidies and Countervailing Measures* of the WTO to refrain from providing financial contributions or support to enterprises within China (Article 1 and 2), it is not surprising that a great deal of governmental financial aid is provided behind the scenes. However, the Chinese government provides explicit financial support for investment that aligns with its policies, which is not exclusively for SOEs. The support is primarily provided through government-led special project funds and policy loans from State banks.

Since 2005, the MOF and MOFCOM have been providing a special project fund for foreign trade and investment activities that advance State policies and development strategies, which is now known as the 'Special Fund for Foreign Trade and Economic Development' ('外经贸发展专项资金') (FTED Fund).[55] The application of the fund is based on a list of eligible investments updated annually by the MOF and MOFCOM.[56] The list identifies areas based on the broad sectors identified in the 2017 *Guiding Policy*, indicating the government's current preference for FDI in certain areas.[57]

Additionally, the Export-Import Bank of China (CEXIM) and the China Development Bank (CDB), two major policy State banks in China, provide below-market rate policy loans to overseas investments in accordance with their annual financing support plan for key FDI projects developed jointly with NDRC. The CEXIM and CDB began providing loans in 2003 and 2004, respectively, and offer loans for an identical list of investments, including investments in natural resources, infrastructure, R&D and mergers and acquisitions (M&As) that could increase corporate global competitiveness.[58]

[55] Before 2010, the fund was called 'Special Project Fund for Foreign Economic Cooperation'. 《对外经济合作专项资金管理暂行办法》 [Measures for the Administration of Special Project Fund for Foreign Economic Cooperation]. (People's Republic of China) MOF and MOFCOM. 9 December 2005, art. 2; 《外经贸发展专项资金管理办法》 [Measures for the Management of Special Project Fund for Foreign Trade and Economic Development]. (People's Republic of China) MOF and MOFCOM. 9 April 2014, art. 3, 6 ('*Measures for FTED Fund*').

[56] *Measures for FTED Fund* (n 55) art. 10.

[57] For example, the 2023 list sets out M&As in areas including energy, raw materials, advanced manufacturing, advanced technologies, and high-quality agricultural products, and investments in clean energy, transportation, telecommunications, among others. 《2023年中央外经贸发展专项资金(促进对外投资合作事项)申报指南》 [Application Guidelines for the Central Special Funds for the Development of Foreign Trade and Economic Cooperation (Matters of Promoting Foreign Investment and Cooperation) in 2023]. (People's Republic of China) Department of Commerce of Guangdong Province. 17 January 2023.

[58] 《关于对国家鼓励的境外投资重点项目给予信贷支持政策的通知》 [Notice on the Policy of Providing Credit Support to Key Projects of Outbound Investment Encouraged by the State]. (People's Republic of China) NDRC and the CEXIM. 27 October 2004 ('*Notice on CEXIM Credit Support*'); 《关于进一步加强对境外投资重点项目融资支持有关问题的通知》 [Notice about the Relevant Issues on Providing More Financing Support to Key Overseas-invested Projects]. (People's Republic of China) NDRC and CDB. 25 September 2005 ('*Notice on CDB Credit Support*').

Both the FTED Fund and the policy loans provided by CEXIM and CDB are contingent on the compliance of SOEs with State policies and national strategies, as the assistance is granted based on government review. Briefly, applications for the FTED Fund are reviewed centrally by MOFCOM and MOF, while NDRC or its provincial branches review the CEXIM and CDB loan applications.[59] Though these government financial aids are theoretically available to all Chinese businesses, it is evident that the allocation of financial support favours SOEs significantly. According to data on the FTED fund allocation made public by the Guangdong Provincial government in 2023, 100 of the 148 FDI projects in the province that received funding from the Fund were proposed by SOEs.[60] The FTED Fund supported SOE investments such as Hisense Home Appliances Group's acquisition of a controlling stake in Japanese automotive air-conditioning manufacturer Sanden Holdings Corporation.[61]

In addition to formal institutional pressures, Chinese companies operating in the country's State-controlled socialist economy are subject to pervasive informal institutional pressures that may significantly impact their business decisions. This is especially true for SOEs that have long benefited from the government's superior resources or would be unprofitable without them.[62] This resource dependence makes them susceptible to China's informal institutional dynamics. For instance, in 2017, the People's Daily lauded China National Chemical Corporation's USD 43 billion acquisition of Syngenta, a Swiss agriculture company, as a 'milestone' in China's 'Go Global' policy.[63] SASACs frequently host colloquia for their supervised SOEs to share their FDI success stories.[64] Such government praises can lead to a herd mentality wherein other SOEs regard engaging in similar investment projects that align with policy as a badge of distinction, modelling themselves after the success stories advocated by the government.

[59] *Notice on CEXIM Credit Support* (n 58); *Notice on CDB Credit Support* (n 58); *Measures for FTED Fund* (n 55) art. 14.

[60] 《广东省商务厅关于中央财政2023年度外经贸发展专项资金(促进对外投资合作事项)分配方案的公示》 [Announcement of the Department of Commerce of Guangdong Province on the 2023 Distribution Plan of the Special Funds for the Development of Foreign Trade and Economic Cooperation (Matters of Promoting Foreign Investment and Cooperation) of the Central Government]. (People's Republic of China) Department of Commerce of Guangdong Province. 28 August 2023.

[61] Ibid.

[62] Herrero and Ng (2021), p. 16.

[63] People (2017) 《中企最大海外收购案在欧美获批》 [The Largest Overseas Acquisition of Chinese Enterprise has been Approved in Europe and America]. http://www.chinadaily.com.cn/interface/zaker/1142842/2017-04-07/cd_28833936.html. Accessed 17 Aug 2025.

[64] See, e.g., The Central SASAC (2016) 《福建国资委召开省属企业"走出去"座谈会》 [Fujian SASAC Held a Colloquia on 'Go Global' of Provincial Enterprises]. http://www.sasac.gov.cn/n2588025/n2588129/c2755642/content.html. Accessed 17 Aug 2025.

5.2 The State Monitoring System for SOE Overseas Subsidiaries

FDI is a complex process involving making decisions, navigating regulatory approval systems (in the home State and/or the host State), and conducting overseas operations through foreign subsidiaries per the local legal regime. Through greenfield investments and acquisitions, Chinese SOEs have amassed a vast network of overseas subsidiaries over the past few decades.[65] For instance, by the end of 2017, the CRRC Group, a Chinese State-owned rolling stock manufacturer, had 83 overseas subsidiaries across 26 countries and regions.[66] According to Tomasic and Xiong, as of 2016, 66 Chinese SOEs were operating in Australia (39 central SOEs and 27 provincial SOEs) through 214 Australian subsidiaries.[67]

Subsidiaries of Chinese SOEs based in developed countries must comply with sophisticated local commercial legal frameworks and applicable foreign investment frameworks. Typically, these legislative frameworks are designed to ensure that SOEs operate on a full arm's length and commercial basis. For example, Chinese SOEs' Australian subsidiaries are subject to the *Corporations Act 2001*. The law imposes concrete corporate governance obligations on these subsidiaries, such as obligating their directors to act in the company's best interest as opposed to the Chinese parent company (with exemptions for wholly owned subsidiaries of foreign companies).[68] Chinese SOE subsidiaries listed on the Australian Securities Exchange (ASX) are subject to the ongoing disclosure obligations stipulated by the *ASX Listing Rules*.[69] However, it is uncommon for a Chinese SOE subsidiary to be listed on the ASX unless the subsidiary was already ASX-listed when it was being acquired by the SOE.[70] Additionally, the Treasurer is authorised by Australia's *Foreign Acquisitions and Takeovers Act 1975* to impose conditions on FDI either at the time of entry or after completion if national interest or security risks are perceived, and quite frequently mandates that the majority of the board of directors in the subsidiary be Australian residents.[71]

---

[65] In practice, a Chinese SOE may initiate its expansion into a foreign country by establishing a representative office abroad. These unincorporated entities serve as outposts for gathering market information without engaging in any substantive business. This chapter therefore focuses exclusively on the overseas subsidiaries of SOEs that assume direct responsibility for SOEs' overseas operations. For example, CCCC First Highway Engineering Group Company has 22 overseas representative offices spreading Africa and Asia. China First Highway Engineering Company (2025) Organisation. http://www.fheb-overseas.com/detail.aspx?newsID=12. Accessed 17 Aug 2025.

[66] CRRC (2025) CRRC group. https://www.crrcgc.cc/en. Accessed 17 Aug 2025.

[67] Tomasic and Xiong (2017), pp. 323–352, 325–327.

[68] *Corporations Act 2001* (Cth) s. 181, 182, 183, 332A.

[69] Ibid. art. 647, 674; *ASX Listing Rules* (Cth) ch. 3.

[70] Henderson (2021).

[71] For discussion regarding Australia's foreign investment framework, see Chap. 7 Sect. 7.1.

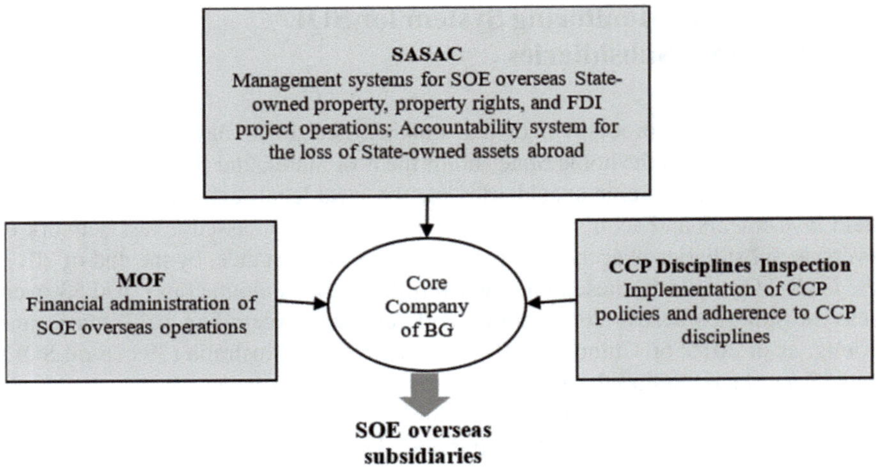

Fig. 5.3 State Monitoring System for Activities of Chinese SOE Overseas Subsidiaries

With the assumption that these legal constraints could restrict a foreign government's ability to exert a high degree of influence over its overseas SOEs, the Chinese government has significantly increased its centralised control over SOEs' overseas operations in tandem with its enhanced political control over SOEs at home in the latest round of SOE reforms. As illustrated in Fig. 5.3, the Chinese government has established a system to monitor the activities of its overseas SOE subsidiaries.

Like the multi-source institutional pressures on the FDI decisions of SOEs, State monitoring is achieved through multiple mechanisms administered by various authorities, including the SASACs, the CCP Commissions for Disciplinary Inspection, MOF and MOFCOM (and their local branches). In the latest round of SOE reforms, these multiple oversight mechanisms have been established or strengthened to varying degrees, constituting a robust mirroring framework enabling the Chinese government to control overseas SOEs and State-owned assets effectively.

Notably, as indicated in Fig. 5.3, all the State monitoring mechanisms rely on the core companies of BGs to make it possible for political influence over the subsidiaries to be exercised. Under the State monitoring system, the government holds the core companies of BGs accountable for maintaining control of the overseas subsidiaries. The direct responsible entity role of BG's core companies aligns with the 'System of Authorised Operation of State-owned Capital' promoted by the State-owned assets management system reform, which entails the decentralisation of (some of) SASACs' State ownership functions to BG's core companies for their group members.

5.2.1 SASAC-Led Supervision Framework for SOE Overseas Operations

The SASACs, as the primary regulators of State-owned assets and SOEs, bear the greatest responsibility for overseeing the overseas operations of Chinese SOEs. Since 2011, the central SASAC has developed a regulatory framework for overseas SOEs consisting primarily of four separate supervision systems, including systems for overseeing the operations of SOE overseas investment projects, overseas State-owned assets and overseas State-owned property rights, as well as accountability systems for the loss of State-owned assets. China's local SASACs have established their regulatory framework for the overseas operations of SOEs under their supervision, modelled after the central framework. The SASAC framework is intended to keep overseas SOE subsidiaries under full oversight.

The *Central SOE FDI Measures* issued by the central SASAC in 2017 mandate that the core companies of central BGs exercise comprehensive supervision throughout the post-establishment process of FDI made by group members, in addition to the pre-investment approval system described above. Specifically, core companies are responsible for dynamic tracking and staged evaluation of their groups' ongoing overseas projects and *ex-post* evaluation of completed projects thus must submit quarterly and annual reports on the progress of the FDI projects to the central SASAC.[72] Major projects are subject to random inspections by the central SASAC.[73]

In 2011, the central SASAC established a management system for overseas State-owned assets based on the *Interim Measures for the Supervision and Administration of Overseas State-owned Assets of Central Enterprises*. The system requires the core companies of central BGs to supervise their groups' overseas subsidiaries, with a particular emphasis on financial management supervision.[74] The core companies are obligated to implement a variety of control measures, such as integrating overseas subsidiaries into the group's budget management system, requiring overseas subsidiaries to report their operational and financial status regularly, limiting subsidiaries' autonomy in making major corporate affairs decisions and establishing an expatriate personnel management system for overseas subsidiaries.[75] The core companies are then responsible for reporting certain major matters to the central SASAC, such as the operational status of the subsidiaries, their use of large funds, expatriate executives management and economic responsibility audit report on the executives of overseas subsidiaries.[76] For ownership changes affecting

---

[72] *Central SOE FDI Measures* (n 31) art. 7, 17, 18, 19, 20, 22.

[73] Ibid. art. 16.

[74] 《中央企业境外国有资产监督管理暂行办法》 [Interim Measures for the Supervision and Administration of Overseas State-Owned Assets of Central Enterprises]. (People's Republic of China) The Central SASAC. 14 June 2011 ('*Measures for Overseas State-Owned Assets*').

[75] Ibid. art. 12, 13, 15, 16, 21, 29, 33, 34, 36.

[76] Ibid. art. 13, 31, 33, 34.

the State-holding status of significant overseas subsidiaries, the core companies must seek approval from the central SASAC.[77]

In the 2011 addition to the State-owned assets management system, the central SASAC launched a management system for overseas State-owned property rights based primarily on the *Interim Measures for the Administration of Overseas State-owned Property Rights of Central Enterprises*. Under the system, core companies of central BGs are responsible for monitoring the property rights of the groups' overseas State-owned assets.[78] Any changes in ownership of an overseas subsidiary of a central BG, such as a transfer, merger, division, dissolution or liquidation, is subject to approval from the core company.[79] These core companies must report significant ownership changes of their overseas subsidiaries to the central SASAC for recording or approval.[80]

The three systems above collectively constitute a SASAC supervision framework for central SOE overseas subsidiaries and operations that rely on the core companies of BGs to act as an instrument of overarching State control. The framework was consolidated in 2018 when the central SASAC revised the accountability system for the loss of State-owned assets by issuing the *Measures for the Accountability of Central Enterprises for Non-compliance with Operating and Investment Rules (for Trial Implementation)*.[81] Compared to the older 2008 system version, the 2018 system solidifies the direct responsibility of core companies for keeping the groups' overseas subsidiaries and operations under government and the CCP oversight, stipulating that the manager of central BGs' core companies would be held directly liable for any loss of State-owned assets caused by group members if they fail to exert effective control over the entire group, specifically in terms of group members' outbound FDI activities and overseas operations, as required by the three management systems discussed above.[82] In addition, if a central BG's

---

[77] Ibid. art. 30.

[78] 《中央企业境外国有产权管理暂行办法》 [The Interim Measures for the Administration of Overseas State-Owned Property Rights of Central Enterprises]. (People's Republic of China) The Central SASAC. 14 June 2011, art. 3.

[79] Ibid. art. 10, 11.

[80] Ibid.

[81] This accountability system was established in 2008 and tightened in 2018. 《中央企业资产损失责任追究暂行办法》 [Interim Measures for the Liabilities of Central Enterprises for Asset Losses]. (People's Republic of China) The Central SASAC. 18 August 2008 ('*Accountability Measures (2008)*');《中央企业违规经营投资责任追究实施办法(试行)》[Measures for the Accountability of Central Enterprises for Non-compliance with Operating and Investment Rules (for Trial Implementation)]. (People's Republic of China) The Central SASAC. 13 July 2018 ('*Accountability Trial Measures (2018)*').

[82] *Accountability Trial Measures (2018)* (n 81) art. 4 (3), 6, 7, 16, 33; The 2008 system stipulated that core companies could be held liable for major losses caused by subsidiaries but did not specify the specific circumstances that would result in core company liability. *Accountability Measures (2008)* (n 81) art. 28.

overseas subsidiary caused the loss of State-owned assets abroad, executives at all levels of the group's hierarchy would be held responsible.[83]

Most regional SASACs have developed systems modelled after central regulations after years of top-down institutional penetration.[84] As a result of the SASAC-led supervision framework, the government can monitor the activities of overseas SOEs more closely, allowing for greater centralised political influence over an extensive number of overseas SOE-affiliated businesses.

5.2.2 MOF-Led Financial Management System for SOE FDI System

In 2017, MOF issued the *Measures for Financial Management of Overseas Investment by State-owned Enterprises* (*Financial Management Measures*). Following the core company-transmission approach, the regulation sets requirements for core companies to ensure effective financial control over the group's overseas investment projects and subsidiaries.[85]

Specifically, the *Financial Management Measures* require core companies to assess the financial viability and risks of their groups' overseas projects and the competence and performance of their financial managers at their overseas affiliates.[86] Annually, the core companies must submit an evaluation of the group's FDI performance and a statement of the group's financial condition to the relevant financial departments.[87] The financial departments' assessment is linked to the supervision system for 'State-owned Capital Operating Budget Expenditure' administered by MOF, which has been discussed above, as assessment results are a major factor in determining the amount of 'SOE Capital Injection' that BGs are to receive.[88]

MOF's *Financial Management Measures* can be viewed as a supplement to the SASAC-led supervision framework for SOE overseas operations, allowing the Chinese government's financial department to play a synergistic role in enhancing the government's oversight of SOE outbound investment operations. It is unclear whether the newly issued regulation is meant to check and balance SASACs' heavy responsibility to supervise SOEs' overseas operations or reflects the improvement of interdepartmental cooperation within the Chinese government. Regardless of the

[83] *Accountability Trial Measures (2018)* (n 81) art. 4, 27.

[84] The central regulations explicitly require local SASACs to formulate their own management system according to the central system. *Measures for Overseas State-Owned Assets* (n 74) art. 39; *Accountability Trial Measures (2018)* (n 81) art. 78.

[85] 《国有企业境外投资财务管理办法》 [Measures for the Financial Management of the Overseas Investments by State-Owned Enterprises]. (People's Republic of China) MOF. 12 June 2017.

[86] Ibid. art. 6.

[87] Ibid. art. 9, 40.

[88] Ibid. art. 41.

reason, a BG core company is accountable to both the SASAC and the financial department for the group's overseas investment operations.

5.2.3 The CCP Disciplinary Inspection Mechanism

In China, the CCP plays a significant role in State governance. In addition to Chinese law, Chinese SOEs, State organs and public institutions must adhere to the CCP disciplines, which are primarily enshrined in the *Constitution of the CCP*.[89] The CCP's internal control institutions, the CCP Disciplinary Inspection Commissions, conduct routine inspections of government agencies, public entities and major SOEs to ensure their conformity with Party discipline in daily functioning or operations.[90]

From 2013 to September 2023, the CCP Central Commission for Disciplinary Inspection (CCDI) conducted 28 inspection tours, broadly covering central- and local-level State organs, public entities and all 97 central BGs that the central SASAC supervises.[91] Each inspection round consists of 15 inspections of various entities by distinct panels. Typically, the CCP inspection panels are stationed for two and a half months in the core company of each inspected BG for on-site investigations.

In 2017, the Xi Jinping administration strengthened the CCP inspection mechanism by issuing a new *Regulation on the Inspection Work of the Chinese Communist Party*.[92] According to the regulation and the inspection findings made public by the CCDI, the CCP inspection may employ various techniques, such as interviews, document analysis and questionnaires, to typically investigate how the SOE has implemented the CCP's policies and strategies, how they have fulfilled the policy tasks assigned by the Party (if any) and whether the Party Committees in the enterprises have played a dominant role in corporate governance practices.[93]

In practice, the CCP inspections have placed significant emphasis on how core companies of BGs maintain control over the group's overseas assets. This may be

---

[89] Li (2016), pp. 447–482, 447–448.

[90] 《中国共产党章程》 [Constitution of the CCP]. (People's Republic of China) adopted at the 20th CCP National Congress. 22 October 2022, art. 14.

[91] Central Commission for Disciplinary Inspection (2018) 《十九届中央第一轮巡视进驻一览表》 [List of the First Round of Inspection of the 19th Central Committee]. https://www.ccdi.gov.cn/yaowen/201802/t20180224_164650.html. Accessed 17 Aug 2025; People (2019) 《十九届中央第三轮巡视进驻一览表》 [List of the Third Round of Inspection of the 19th Central Committee]. http://fanfu.people.com.cn/n1/2019/0403/c64371-31011040.html. Accessed 17 Aug 2025.

[92] 《中国共产党巡视工作条例》[Regulations of the CCP on Inspection Work]. (People's Republic of China) The CCP Central Committee. 1 July 2017, art. 16 ('*The CCP Inspection Regulations*').

[93] Ibid. art. 2, 15, 17; See, e.g., 朱基钗 [Zhu Jichai] (2019) 《十九届中央第三轮巡视全部进驻》 [The Third Round of the 19th Central Committee's Inspections are All in Progress]. The State Council. https://www.gov.cn/xinwen/2019-04/03/content_5379207.htm. Accessed 17 Aug 2025.

partially justified by the Chinese government's increasing emphasis on managing overseas State-owned assets over the past decade, as evidenced by the recent issuance and revisions of relevant regulations discussed above. In 2015, for example, the CCDI inspected 26 central BGs in a single round of inspections and discovered several instances of wrongdoing in the management of overseas investments.[94] These included several executives of Sinopec abusing their positions to seek personal gains in overseas operations and executives of China National Machinery Industry Corporation, a BG specialising in heavy equipment production, taking bribes in overseas engineering projects.[95] In addition, the CCDI named some core BGs, criticising their core companies for lax control over the groups' overseas subsidiaries and operations. These included China's two largest telecom operators, China Mobile Group and China Telecom Group, China's largest telecom equipment manufacturer, China Electronics Corporation (CEC) and China's two largest oil and gas producers, China National Petroleum Corporation (CNPC) and China National Offshore Oil Corporation (CNOOC).[96]

Executives of SOEs found to have violated CCP discipline during a disciplinary inspection would be punished according to the CCP disciplinary rules, and if an executive is suspected of committing a crime, the case would be transferred to the People's Procuratorates for investigation and prosecution.[97] Within two months of receiving the critical feedback from the CCP discipline panels, the head of the Party Committee of the inspected SOEs is primarily responsible for addressing the issues brought up and reporting back to the CCP commissions.[98] For instance, in response to criticisms from the CCP disciplinary inspection in 2020, the inspected central BGs, including PetroChina, Sinopec, CNOOC and CEC, announced the adoption of over one hundred corrective measures.[99] The inspection results would significantly impact the career prospects of the relevant executives of the inspected enterprises.[100]

The CCP disciplinary inspection process provides an additional layer of external political oversight for the core companies of BGs, ensuring that the CCP maintains control over the groups' overseas operations. Unlike the supervision systems administered by the SASACs and financial departments, this mechanism focuses on the CCP leadership over SOEs, which is closely aligned with the Modern SOE Governance System introduced in the latest round of SOE reforms, featuring the

---

94 贾玥 [Jia Yue] (2015) 《巡视组查出多家央企境外资产监管存隐患》 [The Inspection Team Found Hidden Risks in the Supervision of Overseas Assets of Several Central Enterprises]. People. http://politics.people.com.cn/n/2015/0623/c1001-27194534.html. Accessed 17 Aug 2025.

95 Ibid.

96 Ibid.

97 *The CCP Inspection Regulations* (n 92) art. 20.

98 Ibid. art. 27.

99 姜洁 [Jiang Jie] (2020) 《十九届中央第三轮巡视公布十五家单位整改情况》 [The Third Round of Inspection of the 19th Central Committee Announced the Corrective Measures Adopted by 15 Inspected Entities]. People. http://cpc.people.com.cn/n1/2020/0321/c64094-31642317.html. Accessed 17 Aug 2025.

100 *The CCP Inspection Regulations* (n 92) art. 30.

revival of CCP leadership in SOE governance. Therefore, it is unlikely that the CCP disciplinary inspection mechanism serves as a source of direct political influence over SOEs' overseas operations. Nonetheless, it further consolidates the centralised political control over Chinese SOEs within the context of the latest round of SOE reforms.

China has established a robust State monitoring framework for SOE overseas operations, and a substantial portion of this framework has been strengthened since the beginning of the latest round of SOE reforms in 2012. It is possible that heightened State monitoring is the Chinese government's institutional response to the disorganised management of State-owned assets abroad. In 2015, Dong Dasheng, the former deputy Auditor-General of China's National Audit Office, admitted for the first time that the central BGs' overseas assets had never been thoroughly audited,[101] revealing China's lax oversight of overseas SOEs and State-owned assets. In addition, the intensification of State oversight may be an extension of the overarching goal of the ongoing SOE reforms, which is to tighten overall political control over SOEs. Regardless of the specific driving force behind it, with multiple supervision systems in place for SOE overseas operations and multiple sources of institutional pressure on SOE FDI decision-making processes, the Chinese government and the CCP can exert significant control over the entire course of the outbound investments of SOEs.

In addition to the monitoring mechanisms specifically for SOE overseas operations, it is noteworthy that Chinese SOEs' FDI activities are subject to the in-process supervision by NDRC and MOFCOM that apply generally to Chinese FDI.

Under the NDRC system, SOE investors must report to the authorities when their overseas subsidiaries invest more than USD 300 million or are involved in 'major adverse circumstances' (i.e. injuries or deaths of expatriates, major losses of assets and harm to China's diplomatic relations).[102] As has been discussed, MOCFOM has recently tightened its in-process supervision system notably by establishing a reporting system for outbound FDI. The system requiring Chinese investors to report to competent authorities specified key information about the investment projects on a regular basis and any unexpected safety accidents or materially adverse events on an individual basis.[103] The reporting system is backed up by a random inspection mechanism for overseas investment projects, allowing MOFCOM to verify the accuracy of the information reported.[104] Even with the increased MOFCOM supervision, the general in-process monitoring for all outbound FDI is still less stringent than the complex SOE-specific supervision systems. However, NDRC and MOFCOM's supervision still constitute part of the pressure on Chinese SOEs to keep their overseas subsidiaries under control.

---

[101] The State Council (2015) 《4万亿央企境外资产游离于国家审计之外》 [Four Trillion Offshore Assets Owned by Central SOEs are not Subject to State Audits]. https://www.gov.cn/xinwen/2015-03/03/content_2824205.htm. Accessed 17 Aug 2025.

[102] *NDRC Approval Measures (2017)* (n 40) art. 42, 43.

[103] *FDI Reporting System Measures* (n 48) art. 3, 12, 13.

[104] Ibid. art. 19.

5.3 Political Control Over Chinese SOE outbound FDI in Practice

As demonstrated in Sects. 5.1 and 5.2, the Chinese government and the CCP have developed a multifaceted regulatory framework to exert substantial influence or control over SOEs' outbound FDI activities, from the decision-making to the overseas operations. In particular, the latest round of SOE reforms has significantly increased CCP influence on Chinese SOEs' outbound FDI activities, which has permeated the synergistic full-process oversight mechanisms, including China's distinctive SOE governance system, which highlights the CCP's supreme power in deciding on FDI projects, the multi-layer administrative approval systems for outbound FDI that emphasise the adherence of investment proposals to the CCP policies and directives, and the CCP disciplinary inspections over SOEs' compliance with the CCP policies in operations and control over overseas assets.

Given the massive overseas expansion of Chinese SOEs, the framework's practical efficacy is being tested. For example, Chinese SOEs make substantial outbound investments in tax havens and offshore finance centres, notably Hong Kong, Cayman and the British Virgin Islands, with significant investment round-tripping back to mainland China.[105] A myriad of factors, such as superior access to foreign financing markets, financial services and tax advantages, drive this round-tripping investment practice.[106] Since these investments are not genuine FDI, they would increase the already overwhelming supervision burden on the Chinese government. However, the supervisory challenges brought about by the round-tripping FDI practice may be mitigated by the 2014 revision of MOFCOM recordation (approval) system for all outbound FDI, which requires investors to declare the ultimate investment destination when completing the recordation or approval requirements.[107]

In addition, it was historically common for Chinese SOEs to use private individuals to invest abroad on their behalf.[108] This privately held scheme was intended to circumvent host States' institutional barriers against foreign government-related investments. However, it may leave the regulatory framework with blind spots.[109] In 2020, the central SASAC prohibited central SOEs from employing such a strategy unless absolutely necessary, subject to approval and recordation requirements,[110]

---

105 Sutherland et al. (2019), pp. 337–359, 341–342.

106 Morck et al. (2008), pp. 337–350, p. 339; Cui and Jiang (2010), pp. 751–774, 764.

107 *MOFCOM Approval Measures (2014)* (n 40) art. 8.

108 张磊 [Zhang Lei] (2007) 《境外国有资产监管相关问题的思考与探讨》 [Thoughts and Discussions on Issues Related to the Supervision of Overseas State-Owned Assets]. 国际经济合作 [International Economic Cooperation] (12): 8–11.

109 A considerable portion of the privately held FDI by SOEs is not bound by entrustment agreements between the parties therefore hard to be traced by the Chinese government. Ibid.

110 《关于进一步加强中央企业境外国有产权管理有关事项的通知》 [Notice on Matters Relating to Further Strengthening the Management of Overseas State-Owned Property Rights of Central Enterprises]. (People's Republic of China) The Central SASAC. 21 January 2021.

indicating President Xi Jinping's resolve to tighten control over SOE FDI and overseas State-owned assets.

In addition to persistently problematic practices, the implementation of the framework raises two specific issues: (a) how core companies of BGs undertake accountability to the government for maintaining control over the groups' overseas subsidiaries in practice, and (b) how the ongoing MOR may affect the political influence over Chinese SOE FDI. These issues are crucial to the framework's efficacy and, therefore, warrant examination.

5.3.1 The Direct Supervision by Core Companies of BGs

In practice, the core companies of BGs have utilised various methods to keep overseas subsidiaries under monitoring. Some methods have only emerged with the latest round of SOE reforms.

Unless the host State's law or foreign investment policy requires otherwise, it has been common practice for China-based core companies to dispatch top executives to manage overseas subsidiaries and have them frequently return to China to report on their work.[111] In addition, Chinese SOEs typically apply incentive compensations and personnel evaluation mechanisms to overseas subsidiary executives. The mechanisms have a significant constraining force on executives serving abroad because they can directly link their adherence to the directives of core companies to their incomes and career prospects, especially the possibility of political advancement within the administrative hierarchy of the Chinese State economy.[112]

For example, Aluminium Corporation of China (Chinalco), China's State-owned alumina producer, sent the Vice President of its Hong Kong subsidiary, Gao Guichao, to Australia to lead Chinalco Australia as its Chairman and Managing Director. In 2021, Gao was elevated to the presidency of China Copper Industry Group, a central BG specialising in copper production.[113]

In addition to the direct executive personnel control, some major central BGs, such as Chinalco, State Power Investment Corporation Group (China's largest electricity generation company) and China FAW Group (China's largest automaker), have pioneered sending inspection teams abroad to conduct physical supervision over overseas subsidiaries, possibly as a direct response to the Xi Jinping administration's efforts to increase oversight of overseas State-owned assets over the past decade.[114] However, given the large number of overseas subsidiaries a Chinese BG

---

[111] Schüler-Zhou and Schüller (2013), pp. 321–350, 325; Warner et al. (2004), pp. 324–345, 341.

[112] Schüler-Zhou and Schüller (2013), p. 328.

[113] China Copper Industry Group (2025) 《公司领导》 [Leadership]. https://zgty.chinalco.com.cn/gywm/gsld/. Accessed 17 Aug 2025.

[114] Ministry of Justice (2018) 《中央企业加强境外机构监督》 [Central Enterprises Strengthen Supervision of Overseas Affiliates]. http://www.moj.gov.cn/pub/sfbgw/jgsz/gjjwzsfbjjz/zyzsfbjj-zzt/201809/t20180913_186138.html. Accessed 17 Aug 2025.

typically has, these on-site inspection tours organised by BGs' core companies can only cover a few significant overseas subsidiaries. China FAW Group, for instance, inspected 18 overseas subsidiaries in Eastern Europe between 2017 and 2020. However, it has subsidiaries in 48 countries across the world.[115]

5.3.2 *Can the Mixed Ownership Reform Liberate Chinese SOE FDI from Political Influence?*

Mixed ownership reform is significant to China's latest round of SOE reforms. The MOR, as described in Chap. 3, fosters the growth of a mixed ownership economy in China primarily through two approaches: introducing non-State shareholders into SOEs (referred to as 'flow-in MOR') and having SOEs to acquire stakes in selected POEs (referred to as 'flow-out MOR'). Given that the Chinese government and the CCP have increased political influence and supervision over Chinese SOEs' FDI and that the MOR is embedding POEs and foreign enterprises within the equity network of Chinese SOEs, the question naturally arises as to how the MOR may impact the political influence over Chinese SOEs' outbound investments and overseas operations.

As demonstrated by the policy analysis and empirical findings of Chap. 3, the Chinese government orchestrates the implementation of the MOR. In flow-in MOR, non-SOE shareholders are typically introduced into SOEs in non-critical industries and are only permitted to hold a minority stake unless the SOE involved is classified as 'General Commercial' (i.e. the SOE primarily operates in non-critical industries) and on the verge of insolvency or operates primarily in industries unrelated to the BG's core business and thus needs to be sold off (which is also as a part of the State economy restructuring reform). In addition, Chinese POEs and foreign investors have been generally prohibited from participating in the group-level flow-in MOR of BGs, i.e. becoming shareholders of core companies of BGs. The prohibition is absolute when the core companies have been designated as SCIOs in the State-owned assets management system reform, as these special types of SOEs are required to maintain wholly State-owned status.[116]

These constraints on participation in flow-in MOR for POEs and foreign investors suggest that the ongoing MOR is unlikely to bring non-State shareholders into an SOE with sufficient voting power to influence the enterprises' FDI decisions based on commercial considerations. In the MOR, for example, Eastern Airline Logistics (EAL), a holding subsidiary of China's central BG, China East Airline Group, introduced non-State shareholders, including Chinese privately owned logistic supplier Deppon Logistic Company (Deppon) and Singapore-based logistic provider Global Logistic Properties (GLP). However, Deppon and GLP only

[115] Ibid.

[116] For detailed discussion regarding SCIOs, see Chap. 4 Sect. 4.1.2.

acquired 5 percent and 10 percent of stakes, respectively, with China East Airline Group still holding the remaining stakes.[117] In this instance, they lack sufficient voting rights to exert significant influence over EAL's FDI decisions if they are made or agreed to by the majority of SOE shareholders.

A non-SOE investor may, however, be able to influence the FDI decisions of the SOE in which it has invested in the event it was permitted to acquire a significant stake in the SOE, or if the SOE adopts innovative approaches to ensure the meaningful participation of non-SOE minority shareholders in decision-making processes.[118] Nonetheless, even in such exceptional cases, the influence of the non-SOE investors is probably constrained by overwhelming institutional pressures from a variety of sources, such as the CCP leadership within the corporate governance system, the multi-layer approval system, the government financial assistance system and pervasive informal pressures—as a whole, these pressures push SOE FDI in a direction consistent with State policy and government mandates. For example, the Chinese State-owned automobile manufacturer Beijing Automotive Group Company (BAIC) introduced 23 POE shareholders with a collective stake of 32.04 percent in 2017.[119] However, the BAIC 2023 prospectus makes it clear that all FDI decisions are directed by the Beijing SASAC.[120]

Similarly, China's robust political oversight of SOE overseas subsidiaries and operations is unlikely to be disrupted by flow-in MOR. As noted earlier, in implementing flow-in MOR, POEs and foreign enterprises are barred from investing in the core companies of BGs. This indicates that the introduction of non-SOE shareholders into SOEs will not be permitted to disrupt the government-core company-subsidiaries monitoring chain, as the influence of non-SOE shareholders in this regard is limited to their ownership-based voting powers within the particular SOEs on matters pertaining to their overseas operations.

While flow-in MOR introducing non-SOE shareholders into Chinese SOEs is unlikely to have a direct impact on the political influence over Chinese SOEs' FDI, flow-out MOR may well result in the extension of political influence to Chinese POEs' outbound FDI activities based on the State ownership in POE investors. As a result, this may present difficulties for host States in determining whether Chinese

---

[117] 国务院国资委改革办 [Reform Office of the Central SASAC] (2018) 《国企改革探索与实践—中央企业子企业150例(上)》 [Exploration and Practice of State-Owned Enterprise Reform—150 Cases of Subsidiary Enterprises of Central Enterprises (Part I)]. 中国经济出版社 [Economic Press China], p 236.

[118] For detailed discussion regarding the minority shareholders protection mechanism, see Chap. 3 Sect. 3.2.1.2.

[119] The Central SASAC (2020) 《北汽新能源深化改革促发展》 [BAIC New Energy Improvements SOE Reforms to Promote Growth]. http://www.sasac.gov.cn/n2588025/n2588139/c15056194/content.html. Accessed 17 Aug 2025.

[120] Shanghai Stock Exchange (2023) 《2023 年面向专业投资者公开发行公司债券募集说明书》 [Prospectus for Public Issuance of Corporate Bonds to Professional Investors in 2023]. http://www.sse.com.cn/disclosure/bond/announcement/company/c/new/2023-04-07/115198_20230407_L5MJ.pdf. Accessed 17 Aug 2025.

investment is subject to political influence under their foreign investment screening regimes, which will be discussed in detail in Chap. 7.

5.4 Concluding Remarks

As demonstrated in the preceding chapters, the latest round of SOE reforms is tightening control over Chinese SOEs. Consistent with this overarching reform objective, Chinese SOE FDI activities are subject to intensified political influence throughout the investment process. Chinese SOEs are subject to institutional pressures from a variety of sources when making FDI decisions, including the CCP leadership within the corporate governance system, the FDI administrative approval systems, government financial assistance and the SCIO or 'Special Commercial' SOE identity with attached policy tasks, as well as pervasive informal institutional pressures. The cumulative effect of these various pressures is to ensure that SOEs' FDI decisions are in line with State policies and government directives.

Concurrently, over the past decade, China has strengthened its political oversight framework for overseas SOE subsidiaries. This framework consists of supervision systems independently administered by SASACs, MOF and the CCP commission for disciplinary inspections, as well as the general in-process monitoring systems administered by MOFCOM and NDRC. The systems, which were largely established or tightened in the latest round of SOE reforms, all heavily rely on core companies of BGs to assume the direct responsibility for keeping the groups' overseas subsidiaries and operations under government and the CCP oversight.

Given the tightened supervisory framework over Chinese SOEs' outbound FDI activities, it is reasonable to conclude that Chinese SOE FDI are subject to enhanced political influence over the SOEs' FDI decision-making and operations in the context of the latest round of SOE reforms. Additionally, the ongoing MOR in the latest round of SOE reforms is unlikely to disrupt the political control over Chinese SOEs' FDI by introducing non-SOE shareholders into SOEs. This highlights the significance of delving into China's current outbound FDI policy and exploring the strategies host States can employ in domestic and international law to address potential negative effects associated with Chinese SOE investments, which are addressed in the following chapters

References

Bath V (2011) The quandary for Chinese regulators: controlling the flow of investment into and out of China. In: Bath V, Nottage L (eds) Foreign investment and dispute resolution law and practice in Asia. Routledge

Bath V (2015) Chinese companies and outbound investment: the balance between domestic and international concerns. In: Toohey L, Picker CB, Greenacre J (eds) China in the international economic order: new directions and changing paradigms. Cambridge University Press

Bath V (2017) The south and alternative models of trade and investment regulation: Chinese investment and approaches to international investment agreements. In: Morosini F, Badin MRS (eds) Reconceptualizing international investment law from the global south. Cambridge University Press, p 52

Center for Macroeconomic Research of Xiamen University (2018) Policy Simulation: Effects of Changing Budget Constraints on the Non-Financial SOEs. In: Center for Macroeconomic Research of Xiamen University (ed) China's Macroeconomic Outlook. Springer Singapore, p 35

Central Commission for Disciplinary Inspection (2018) 《十九届中央第一轮巡视进驻一览表》 [List of the First Round of Inspection of the 19th Central Committee]. https://www.ccdi.gov.cn/yaowen/201802/t20180224_164650.html. Accessed 17 Aug 2025

Chaisse J (2018) China's international investment policy: formation, evolution, and transformation(s). In: Chaisse J, Nottage L (eds) International investment treaties and arbitration across Asia. Brill

China Copper Industry Group (2025) 《公司领导》 [Leadership]. https://zgty.chinalco.com.cn/gywm/gsld/. Accessed 17 Aug 2025

China First Highway Engineering Company (2025) Organisation. http://www.fheb-overseas.com/detail.aspx?newsID=12. Accessed 17 Aug 2025

CRRC (2025) CRRC group. https://www.crrcgc.cc/en. Accessed 17 Aug 2025

Cui L, Jiang F (2010) Behind ownership decision of Chinese outward FDI: resources and institutions. Asia Pac J Manage 27(4):751–774, 764

Cui W (2015) Taxation of state-owned enterprises a review of empirical evidence from China. In: Liebman BL, Milhaupt CJ (eds) Regulating the visible hand? The institutional implications of Chinese state capitalism. Oxford University Press, p 115

El Dahan M, Mills A (2023) China's Sinopec to take stake in Qatar's North Field East. Reuters. https://www.reuters.com/markets/deals/chinas-sinopec-take-5-share-qatars-north-field-east-qna-2023-04-12/. Accessed 17 Aug 2025

Guoqiang L (2015) Overview: an emerging power's new strategy of opening up to the outside: entry into the WTO: a look back over the past ten years and a look forward. In: Luolin W (ed) China's WTO accession reassessed. Routledge, p 5, 19

Henderson R (2021) Delisting Leaves Just 20 Chinese Companies on ASX. Financial Review. https://www.afr.com/markets/equity-markets/delisting-leaves-just-20-chinese-companies-on-asx-20210409-p57hv0. Accessed 17 Aug 2025

Herrero AG, Ng G (2021) China's state-owned enterprises and competitive neutrality. World Econ 22(1):1–19, 16

Jia Yue [贾玥] (2015) 《巡视组查出多家央企境外资产监管存隐患》 [The Inspection Team Found Hidden Risks in the Supervision of Overseas Assets of Several Central Enterprises]. People. http://politics.people.com.cn/n/2015/0623/c1001-27194534.html. Accessed 17 Aug 2025

Jiang Jie [姜洁] (2020) 《十九届中央第三轮巡视公布十五家单位整改情况》 [The Third Round of Inspection of the 19th Central Committee Announced the Corrective Measures Adopted by 15 Inspected Entities]. People. http://cpc.people.com.cn/n1/2020/0321/c64094-31642317.html. Accessed 17 Aug 2025.

Jinping X (2014) A holistic view of national security. QIUSHI. http://en.qstheory.cn/2020-12/04/c_607611.htm. Accessed 17 Aug 2025

Li L (2016) The rise of the discipline and inspection commission, 1927–2012: anticorruption investigation and decision-making in the Chinese communist party. Modern China 42(5):447–482, 447–448

Liu Z, Huyue Zhang A (2019) Ownership and political control: evidence from charter amendments. Int Rev Law Econ 60:105853

Lou Qiuran [楼秋然] (2021) 《国有企业公司治理改革:政治逻辑与经济逻辑的协调融合之道》 [Political and economic logics and paths of SOE's corporate governance in the context of deepened reform].华中科技大学学报(社会科学版)[J Huazhong Univ Sci Technol (Soc Sci Edn)] (2):74–83, p 78

Luo Youyuan [罗有远] (2023) 《专项治理国企擅自对外投资和担保问题》 [Specially Combat the Issue of Unapproved Foreign Investment and Guarantees by SOEs]. The Central Commission for Disciplinary Inspection of the CCP and the National Commission of Supervision of the PRC. <https://www.ccdi.gov.cn/yaowenn/202302/t20230210_245823.html Accessed 17 Aug 2025

Manekar S, Menon P (2022) Rio Tinto, China Baowu to Develop Australian Iron Ore Project for $2 Bln. Reuters. https://www.reuters.com/markets/commodities/rio-tinto-joins-china-baowu-develop-western-range-iron-ore-project-2-bln-2022-09-14/. Accessed 17 Aug 2025

Ministry of Justice (2018) 《中央企业加强境外机构监督》 [Central Enterprises Strengthen Supervision of Overseas Affiliates]. http://www.moj.gov.cn/pub/sfbgw/jgsz/gjjwzsfbjjz/zyzsfbjjzzt/201809/t20180913_186138.html. Accessed 17 Aug 2025

MOFCOM (2018) Interpretations of the Interim Measures for the Reporting of Outbound Investments Subject to Record-filing or Approval by the Head of Outward Investment and Economic Cooperation of the Ministry of Commerce. http://english.mofcom.gov.cn/article/newsrelease/policyreleasing/201802/20180202706980.shtml. Accessed 17 Aug 2025

MOFCOM, NBS and SAFE (2022) 2021 Statistical Bulletin of China's Outward Foreign Direct Investment. China Commerce and Trade Press, p 30

Morck R, Yeung B, Zhao M (2008) Perspectives on China's outward foreign direct investment. J Int Bus Stud 39(3):337–350, 339

People (2017) 《中企最大海外收购案在欧美获批》 [The Largest Overseas Acquisition of Chinese Enterprise has been Approved in Europe and America]. http://www.chinadaily.com.cn/interface/zaker/1142842/2017-04-07/cd_28833936.html. Accessed 17 Aug 2025

People (2019) 《十九届中央第三轮巡视进驻一览表》 [List of the Third Round of Inspection of the 19th Central Committee]. http://fanfu.people.com.cn/n1/2019/0403/c64371-31011040.html. Accessed 17 Aug 2025

Schüler-Zhou Y, Schüller M (2013) An empirical study of Chinese subsidiaries' decision-making autonomy in Germany. Asian Bus Manage 12(3):321–350, 325

Shanghai Stock Exchange (2023) 《2023年面向专业投资者公开发行公司债券募集说明书》 [Prospectus for Public Issuance of Corporate Bonds to Professional Investors in 2023]. http://www.sse.com.cn/disclosure/bond/announcement/company/c/new/2023-04-07/115198_20230407_L5MJ.pdf. Accessed 17 Aug 2025

Stone RW, Wang Y, Shu Y (2022) Chinese power and the State-owned enterprise. Int Org 76(1):229–250

Sutherland D, Hennart J-F, Anderson JR (2019) How does the routing of FDI to and via Tax Havens confound our understanding of Chinese MNE identity? A critical review of the empirical literature on Chinese MNEs. Asian Bus Manage 18(5):337–359, 341–342

The Central SASAC (2016) 《福建国资委召开省属企业"走出去"座谈会》 [Fujian SASAC Held a Colloquia on 'Go Global' of Provincial Enterprises]. http://www.sasac.gov.cn/n2588025/n2588129/c2755642/content.html. Accessed 17 Aug 2025

The Central SASAC (2020) 《北汽新能源深化改革促发展》 [BAIC New Energy Improvements SOE Reforms to Promote Growth]. http://www.sasac.gov.cn/n2588025/n2588139/c15056194/content.html. Accessed 17 Aug 2025

The State Council (2015) 《4万亿央企境外资产游离于国家审计之外》 [Four Trillion Offshore Assets Owned by Central SOEs are not Subject to State Audits]. https://www.gov.cn/xinwen/2015-03/03/content_2824205.htm. Accessed 17 Aug 2025.

The State Council (2017) 《国企资本金注入采取三种方式》 [Capital Injections into SOEs Take Three Forms]. <https://www.gov.cn/xinwen/2017-03/30/content_5181931.htm. Accessed 17 Aug 2025

The State Council (2019) 《国资委:央企境外资产总额已达7.6万亿元》 [SASAC: Central Enterprises' Overseas Assets Have Reached 7.6 Trillion Yuan]. The State Council. https://www.gov.cn/xinwen/2019-10/17/content_5441316.htm. Accessed 17 Aug 2025

Tomasic R, Xiong P (2017) Mapping the legal landscape: Chinese state-owned companies in Australia. Victoria Univ Wellington Law Rev 48(2):323–352, 325–327

Warner M, Hong NS, Xiaojun X (2004) Late development' experience and the evolution of transnational firms in the People's Republic of China. Asia Pacific Bus Rev 10(3–4):324–345, 341
Zhang D, Freestone O (2013) China's unfinished state-owned enterprise reforms. Econ Round-Up 2:79–102, 90
Zhang Lei [张磊] (2007) 《境外国有资产监管相关问题的思考与探讨》 [Thoughts and Discussions on Issues Related to the Supervision of Overseas State-Owned Assets]. 国际经济合作 [Int Econ Cooperat] 12:8–11
Zhu Jichai [朱基钗] (2019) 《十九届中央第三轮巡视全部进驻》 [The Third Round of the 19th Central Committee's Inspections are All in Progress]. The State Council. https://www.gov.cn/xinwen/2019-04/03/content_5379207.htm. Accessed 17 Aug 2025

Additional Sources

《2023年中央外经贸发展专项资金(促进对外投资合作事项)申报指南》 [Application Guidelines for the Central Special Funds for the Development of Foreign Trade and Economic Cooperation (Matters of Promoting Foreign Investment and Cooperation) in 2023]. (People's Republic of China) Department of Commerce of Guangdong Province. 17 January 2023
《上市公司治理准则(2018 修订)》 [Code of Corporate Governance of Listed Companies (Revised in 2018)]. (People's Republic of China) China Securities Regulatory Commission. 30 September 2019, art. 5
《中国共产党国有企业基层组织工作条例(试行)》 [Trial Regulation on the Work at Primary-level Party Organizations of State-Owned Enterprises]. (People's Republic of China) The CCP Central Committee. 30 December 2019, art. 15
《中国共产党巡视工作条例》 [Regulations of the CCP on Inspection Work]. (People's Republic of China) The CCP Central Committee. 1 July 2017, art. 16
《中国共产党章程》 [Constitution of the CCP]. (People's Republic of China) adopted at the 20th CCP National Congress. 22 October 2022, art. 14
《中央企业境外国有产权管理暂行办法》 [The Interim Measures for the Administration of Overseas State-Owned Property Rights of Central Enterprises]. (People's Republic of China) The Central SASAC. 14 June 2011, art. 3
《中央企业境外国有资产监督管理暂行办法》 [Interim Measures for the Supervision and Administration of Overseas State-Owned Assets of Central Enterprises]. (People's Republic of China) The Central SASAC. 14 June 2011
《中央企业境外投资监督管理办法》 [Measures for Supervision and Administration of Overseas Investment by Central Enterprises]. (People's Republic of China) The Central SASAC. 7 January 2017, art. 4, 9
《中央企业境外投资监督管理暂行办法》 [Interim Measures for Supervision and Administration of Overseas Investment by Central Enterprises]. (People's Republic of China) The Central SASAC. 18 March 2012, repealed 7 January 2017, art. 10
《中央企业境外投资项目负面清单(2017 年版)》 [Negative List of Overseas Investment Projects of Central SOEs (2017 Edition)]. (People's Republic of China) The Central SASAC. 19 January 2017
《中央企业负责人经营业绩考核办法》 [Measures for Business Performance Assessment of the Persons in Charge of Central Enterprises]. (People's Republic of China) The Central SASAC. 8 December 2016, art. 13, 15, 39
《中央企业资产损失责任追究暂行办法》 [Interim Measures for the Liabilities of Central Enterprises for Asset Losses]. (People's Republic of China) The Central SASAC. 18 August 2008

《中央企业违规经营投资责任追究实施办法(试行)》 [Measures for the Accountability of Central Enterprises for Non-compliance with Operating and Investment Rules (for Trial Implementation)]. (People's Republic of China) The Central SASAC. 13 July 2018
《中央国有资本经营预算支出管理暂行办法》 [Interim Measures for the Management of Expenditure of the Central State-Owned Capital Operating Budget Expenditure]. (People's Republic of China) MOF. 13 March 2017, art. 11.3
《企业境外投资管理办法》 [Measures for the Administration of Overseas Investment of Enterprises]. (People's Republic of China) NDRC. 26 December 2017, art. 13, 14
《关于加强中央企业境外投资管理的有关事项的通知》 [Notice on Strengthening the Administration of Overseas Investment by Central Enterprises]. (People's Republic of China) The Central SASAC. 31 December 2008
《关于国有企业功能界定与分类的指导意见》 [Guiding Opinions on the Definition and Classification of Functions of State-Owned Enterprises]. (People's Republic of China) The State Council. 29 December 2015
《关于实行分税制财政管理体制的决定》 [Decision on the Implementation of the Tax-Sharing Fiscal Management System]. (People's Republic of China) The State Council. 15 December 1993
《关于对国家鼓励的境外投资重点项目给予信贷支持政策的通知》 [Notice on the Policy of Providing Credit Support to Key Projects of Outbound Investment Encouraged by the State]. (People's Republic of China) NDRC and the CEXIM. 27 October 2004
《关于扎实推动国有企业党建工作要求写入公司章程的通知》 [The Notice on Solid Promotion of Writing the Party Building Work of State-Owned Enterprises into the Articles of Association]. (People's Republic of China) Organization Department of the CCP Central Committee and the Central SASAC. 15 March 2017
《关于深化国有企业改革的指导意见》 [The Guiding Opinions on Deepening the Reform of State-Owned Enterprises]. (People's Republic of China) The CCP Central Committee and the State Council. 24 August 2015
《关于试行国有资本经营预算的意见》 [Opinions on the Trial Implementation of State-Owned Capital Operating Budget System]. (People's Republic of China) The State Council. 8 September 2007
《关于进一步加强中央企业境外国有产权管理有关事项的通知》 [Notice on Matters Relating to Further Strengthening the Management of Overseas State-Owned Property Rights of Central Enterprises]. (People's Republic of China) The Central SASAC. 21 January 2021
《关于进一步加强中央企业投资管理的通知》 [Notice on Further Strengthening the Investment Management of Central Enterprises]. (People's Republic of China) The Central SASAC. 19 August 2008
《关于进一步加强对境外投资重点项目融资支持有关问题的通知》 [Notice about the Relevant Issues on Providing More Financing Support to Key Overseas-invested Projects]. (People's Republic of China) NDRC and CDB. 25 September 2005
《关于进一步引导和规范境外投资方向的指导意见》 [The Guiding Opinions on Further Guiding and Regulating the Direction of Overseas Investment]. (People's Republic of China) General Office of the State Council. 18 August 2017
《关于金融支持经济结构调整和转型升级的指导意见》 [Guiding Opinions on Financial Support to Economic Structure Adjustment, Transformation and Upgrading]. (People's Republic of China) General Office of the State Council. 5 July 2013
《四川省属国有企业境外投资项目负面清单(2017年版)》 [Negative List of Overseas Investment Projects of Sichuan SOEs (2017 Edition)]. (People's Republic of China) SASAC of Chengdu Municipal Government. 14 November 2017
《国有企业境外投资财务管理办法》 [Measures for the Financial Management of the Overseas Investments by State-Owned Enterprises]. (People's Republic of China) MOF. 12 June 2017
《境外投资产业指导政策》 [The Industrial Guiding Policy for Overseas Investment]. (People's Republic of China) NDRC, MOFCOM, Ministry of Foreign Affairs (MFA), MOF, General Administration of Customs, State Taxation Administration, SAFE. 5 July 2006

《境外投资管理办法》 [Measures for the Administration of Overseas Investment]. (People's Republic of China) MOFCOM. 6 September 2014, art. 6
《外经贸发展专项资金管理办法》 [Measures for the Management of Special Project Fund for Foreign Trade and Economic Development]. (People's Republic of China) MOF and MOFCOM. 9 April 2014, art. 3, 6
《对外投资备案(核准)报告实施规程》 [Implementing Procedures the Reporting of Outbound Investments Subject to Recordation or Approval]. (People's Republic of China) The General Office of MOFCOM. 16 May 2019
《对外投资备案(核准)报告暂行办法》 [Interim Measures for the Reporting of Outbound Investments Subject to Recordation or Approval]. (People's Republic of China) MOFCOM, BOC, the Central SASAC, China Banking Regulatory Commission, China Securities Regulatory Commission, China Insurance Regulatory Commission and SAFE. 18 January 2018, ch. 3
《对外经济合作专项资金管理暂行办法》 [Measures for the Administration of Special Project Fund for Foreign Economic Cooperation]. (People's Republic of China) MOF and MOFCOM. 9 December 2005, art. 2
《广东省商务厅关于中央财政2023年度外经贸发展专项资金(促进对外投资合作事项)分配方案的公示》 [Announcement of the Department of Commerce of Guangdong Province on the 2023 Distribution Plan of the Special Funds for the Development of Foreign Trade and Economic Cooperation (Matters of Promoting Foreign Investment and Cooperation) of the Central Government]. (People's Republic of China) Department of Commerce of Guangdong Province. 28 August 2023
Corporations Act 2001 (Cth) s. 181, 182, 183, 332A
国务院国资委改革办 [Reform Office of the Central SASAC] (2018) 《国企改革探索与实践—中央企业子企业150例(上)》 [Exploration and Practice of State-Owned Enterprise Reform—150 Cases of Subsidiary Enterprises of Central Enterprises (Part I)]. 中国经济出版社 [Economic Press China], p 236

Chapter 6
Protecting National Security: An Increasingly Important Dimension of Chinese SOE Investments

Abstract This chapter examines the increasing role of Chinese SOEs in outbound FDI, focusing on the growing emphasis on national security. Since China's emergence as a major source of global FDI, Chinese SOEs have aligned their investment strategies with national policy objectives. This chapter explores the impact of China's latest SOE reforms and geopolitical tensions on the national security-driven FDI of Chinese SOEs. The research addresses two key questions: what are the policy drivers behind Chinese SOE FDI in developed countries, and how have SOE reforms shaped their ability to pursue national security objectives? By analysing China's foreign investment policies, the chapter argues that national security has become a central driver for outbound FDI, with SOEs playing a significant role in securing strategic assets such as energy, critical minerals, and technology. The findings highlight that Chinese SOEs, in response to tightening foreign investment controls, employ tactical alliance strategies to minimise barriers in developed countries. The chapter emphasises the potential risks posed by these investments to host countries and calls for tailored legal frameworks to mitigate these challenges. It concludes by underscoring the importance of understanding the interplay between national security concerns and Chinese SOE investment strategies.

Since 1978, when China initiated the Open Door Policy, the country has achieved remarkable success in gaining a foothold in the global economy, transforming from a net capital importer to one of the world's largest sources of outbound FDI.[1] As discussed in Chap. 5, China has progressively liberalised its legal and regulatory framework for outward FDI, particularly since adopting the 'Go Global' policy in 2000 and joining the WTO with commitments to liberalise foreign investment in 2001. China's policy for outbound investment has evolved considerably over the past few decades as the country has progressed through various stages of national development and changing geopolitical dynamics.[2]

[1] OECD (2025) Foreign Direct Investment Statistics: Data, Analysis and Forecasts. https://www.oecd.org/investment/statistics.htm. Accessed 19 Aug 2025.

[2] Chaisse (2018), p. 557.

T. Gu, *Chinese SOE Reforms and Global FDI*, Contemporary Chinese Civil and Commercial Law, https://doi.org/10.1007/978-981-92-3181-2_6

As demonstrated in preceding chapters, China's latest round of SOE reforms has substantially strengthened the political control over Chinese SOEs. This has operated in conjunction with a tightening of political oversight over SOEs' outbound FDI activities. This enhanced political oversight enables the Chinese government and the CCP to exert substantial influence over SOEs' outbound FDI activities throughout the entire process, from decision-making to overseas operations. Given the heightened political ties with the Chinese government and the CCP, Chinese SOEs are naturally substantially influenced by State policy when making outward FDI.

In the context of deteriorating Sino-Western geopolitical tensions, the massive global expansion of Chinese SOEs has raised concerns among developed host States regarding their ulterior objectives. The Xi Jinping administration's assertive geostrategic, economic and military posture, displayed alongside the latest round of SOE reforms, has exacerbated these concerns.[3] Such concerns have accelerated the global trend towards a stricter foreign investment policy, particularly among advanced countries, typically on the grounds of protecting national security or interests.[4] For instance, Australia enacted a comprehensive reform to its foreign investment framework in 2021, significantly enhancing its foreign investment screening mechanism to protect the national interests and national security.[5] In 2019, the European Union (EU) adopted a legislative framework for foreign investment screening across the Union, establishing minimum standards for the national FDI screening for the Member States based on national security or public order.[6]

In this context, it is imperative to investigate the policy drivers for Chinese SOE investments in the developed world. Therefore, this chapter aims to explore the following fundamental questions: What are the latest policy drivers for Chinese SOE FDI in developed countries under the current Chinese administration? How have China's latest SOE reforms impacted Chinese SOEs' ability to pursue policy objectives through FDI?

Answering these questions is crucial for the rest of the world to gain specific insights into Chinese SOEs' substantial engagement in international investment activities. Extensive international business studies have investigated the drivers of Chinese SOE FDI, concluding that policy is a significant factor.[7] To answer these questions, this chapter provides a comprehensive review of China's current foreign investment policies, including policies launched independently or as part of national development strategies or initiatives, policies applicable to all Chinese investors and SOE-specific policies.[8] Based on the documentary analysis, this chapter argues that maintaining national security has become one of the most important drivers for

---

[3] See generally Zhao (2023), pp. 1–27.

[4] UNCTAD (2023) World Investment Report 2023. UNCTAD/WIR/2023. Annual Report.

[5] Australia's foreign investment reform will be discussed in details in Chap. 7 Sect. 7.1. See generally Frydenberg (2020).

[6] Dimitropoulos (2021), p. 529.

[7] See, e.g., Cui and Jiang (2009), pp. 751–774; Luo and Tung (2007), pp. 481–498.

[8] China's foreign investment policy continues to evolve, so this chapter draws on information about relevant laws, regulations, policies, and strategies that was made available to the public as of December 1, 2023.

Chinese SOE FDI in developed countries. This chapter further argues that Chinese SOEs employ a tactical alliance strategy when making strategic FDI based on increased SOE-government links in response to the global trend of increasingly stringent FDI control regimes. In addition, this article enumerates the potential threats that Chinese SOEs' national-security-motivated FDI pose to host States, aiming to lay the groundwork for future academic and policy research on mitigating the relevant risks.

The chapter is structured as follows: Section 6.1 provides a longitudinal overview of China's laws, regulations, development strategies and initiatives that impact outbound investment. This section reveals that China's foreign investment policy has been evolving in response to shifting domestic demands and has been woven into multiple major national development strategies since 2012. Section 6.2 examines the evolving meaning of 'national security' in Chinese law and particularly in foreign investment policy in the context of China's heightened focus on national security since 2014. This section argues that China has expanded the concept of 'national security' to include virtually all elements essential to national prosperity in its foreign investment policy and that protecting the security of energy, critical minerals and technology has become the primary policy objective for Chinese SOE outbound investments. Section 6.3 explores the specific tasks of Chinese SOEs' FDI in pursuing the policy mission of safeguarding national security. This section investigates the role of Chinese SOE investments in developed countries in achieving national security goals. Section 6.4 reveals the tactical alliance strategies that Chinese SOEs may employ to minimise institutional barriers at the point of entry when making strategic FDI in developed countries within the context of the latest round of SOE reforms. Section 6.5 concludes.

6.1 Overview of China's Outbound Investment Policies

The rise of China in the global economy as a major source of FDI is a recent phenomenon due to the country's explosive economic growth since it launched the 'Go Global' policy in 2000 and joined the WTO in 2001.[9] Since 1979, when China first officially permitted 'Enterprising Abroad,'[10] successive Chinese governments have insisted on an interventionist approach concerning the directions of outbound FDI.[11]

In contrast to the intricate legal framework for FDI approval and administration systems, the Chinese government has been relatively forthright regarding its preference for specific types of FDI. These preferences are communicated to the public through either stand-alone policies or as part of broader national development

[9] Chaisse (2018), p. 545.

[10] Chen (2018), pp. 595–618.

[11] Bath (2011), p. 73.

strategies or initiatives that impact outbound investments. They are subject to ongoing adjustments to accommodate shifting national demands and geopolitical dynamics.[12]

The list of primary government documents that embodied China's evolving foreign investment policies includes, but is not limited to:

– Opinions on Strengthening Overseas Investment Project Management (State Planning Commission 1991)
– The 10th Five-Year Plan (2001–2005) for Economic and Social Development of the PRC (The 9th National People's Congress 2001)
– Notice on the Policy of Providing Credit Support to Key Projects of Outbound Investment Encouraged by the State (National Development and Reform Commission (NDRC) and Export-Import Bank of China (CEXIM) 2004)
– Catalogue of Industries by Country for Outward Investment (I) (MOFCOM and Ministry of Foreign Affairs (MFA) 2004)
– Catalogue of Industries by Country for Outward Investment (II) (MOFCOM and MFA 2005)
– The 11th Five-Year Plan (2006–2010) for Economic and Social Development of the PRC (The 10th National People's Congress 2006)
– The Industrial Guiding Policy for Overseas Investment (NDRC, MOFCOM, MFA, MOF, General Administration of Customs (GAC), State Administration of Taxation (STA), State Administration of Foreign Exchange (SAFE) 2006)
– Catalogue of industries by Country for Outward Investment (III) (MOFCOM and MFA 2007)
– The 12th Five-Year Plan (2011–2015) for Economic and Social Development of the PRC (The 11th National People's Congress 2011)
– Guiding Opinions on Resolving Serious Contradictions in Overcapacity (State Council 2013)
– Vision and Actions on Jointly Building Silk Road Economic Belt and 21st-Century Maritime Silk Road (NDRC, MOFCOM and MFA 2015)
– Guiding Opinions on Promoting International Cooperation in Production Capacity and Equipment Manufacturing (State Council 2015)
– Made in China 2025 Development Initiative (The State Council 2015)
– Opinions on Building a New Open Economic System (The CCP Central Committee and the State Council 2015)
– The 13th Five-Year Plan (2016–2020) for Economic and Social Development of the PRC (The 12th National People's Congress 2016)
– Outline of the National Strategy for Innovation-driven Development (The CCP Central Committee and the State Council 2016)
– Guiding Opinions on Strengthening International Cooperation to Improve the Position of China's Industries in the Global Value Chain (MOFCOM, NDRC, Ministry of Science and Technology, Ministry of Industry and Information Technology, The People's Bank of China (BOC), GAC, NBS 2016)

[12] Bath (2017), p. 48.

- The Guiding Opinions on Further Guiding and Regulating the Direction of Overseas Investment (NDRC, MOFCOM, MFA and BOC 2017)
- The 14th Five-Year Plan (2021–2025) for Economic and Social Development and Long-Range Objectives Through the Year 2035 of the PRC (The 13th National People's Congress 2021)

A quick count of the items on the list indicates that China's major foreign investment policies have undergone quantitative and qualitative changes. Despite the wide variety of documents issued by various authorities, successive Chinese governments have generally followed a pattern of encouraging outbound FDI in pursuit of foreign markets, natural resources and technology-based strategic assets to meet the changing needs of a rapidly developing economy.

6.1.1 Prior to 2012: Seeking Overseas Markets and Resources

In the 1980s and the early 1990s, China permitted outbound investments to promote domestic exports to circumvent trade barriers to Chinese goods, such as quota restrictions and anti-dumping penalties.[13] In the *Opinions on Strengthening Overseas Investment Project Management* issued in 1991, the State Planning Commission (the predecessor of NDRC) acknowledged China's inability to engage in large-scale FDI at the time, but it encouraged 'qualified firms' to engage in FDI to promote the export of goods and labour services, thereby exploiting overseas markets.[14] Since the private sector was not fully permitted in China then and outbound FDI was subject to stringent approval requirements, 'qualified firms' primarily referred to State-owned trade companies.[15]

After joining the WTO in 2001, China's transition to a market-oriented economy accelerated considerably, while the country's industrialisation flourished with the rise of private sectors. Development led to a surge in demand for natural resources to make up for the lack of domestic raw materials and energy. China's 10th Five-Year Plan (FYP) (2001–2005), which enshrined the 'Go Global' policy for the first time, stated explicitly that China encouraged FDI in natural resource development and trade sectors and committed credit support for such investments.[16] This statement

[13] Chaisse (2018), p. 544; Warner et al. (2004), pp. 324–345.

[14] 《国家计划委员会关于加强海外投资项目管理的意见》 [Opinions of the State Planning Commission on Strengthening Overseas Investment Project Management]. (People's Republic of China) The State Planning Commission of the People's Republic of China. 5 March 1991.

[15] 祁春凌 [Qi Chunling] (2015) 《中国对外直接投资:基于投资动因，制度因素，以及政治经济学视角的分析》 [China's Foreign Direct Investment: an Analysis from the Perspective of Investment Motivation, Institutional Factors, and Political Economy]. 对外经济贸易大学出版社 [University of International Business and Economics Press], p. 46.

[16] 《中华人民共和国国民经济和社会发展第十个五年规划》 [The 10th Five-Year Plan (2001-2005) for Economic and Social Development of the PRC]. (People's Republic of China) The State Council. 15 March 2001.

remained in the 11th FYP (2006–2010) and 12th FYP (2011–2015).[17] The supporting documents issued by NDRC and State banks on credit support for FDI reiterated this official stance.[18]

From 2004 to 2007, MOFCOM and the MFA issued three country–specific catalogues of industries in which investment was encouraged.[19] The catalogues identified specific resources that Chinese FDI was encouraged to seek, such as iron ore, natural gas, coal mines, bauxite, oil shale, and bauxite in Australia and petroleum and natural gas in Canada.[20] In 2006, seven central government agencies issued the *Industrial Guiding Policy for Overseas Investment* (*2006 Guiding Policy*), encouraging Chinese companies to look abroad for scarce raw materials and other natural resources essential for national economic growth.[21]

With such strong official encouragement, Chinese SOEs made significant efforts to acquire foreign natural resources. For instance, from 2008 to 2013, China's three largest State-owned oil companies, China National Offshore Oil Corporation (CNOOC), China National Petroleum Corporation (CNPC) and China Petroleum & Chemical Corporation (Sinopec), spent over USD 27.67 billion on the acquisition of overseas petroleum resources.[22] CNOOC bought four Canadian energy companies—Energy Group, OPTI Canada, Northern Cross and Nexen—between 2005 and 2012 to tap into Canada's oil sands.[23]

---

17 《中华人民共和国国民经济和社会发展第十一个五年规划》 [The 11th Five-Year Plan (2006-2010) for Economic and Social Development of the PRC]. (People's Republic of China) The State Council. 14 March 2006; 《中华人民共和国国民经济和社会发展第十二个五年规划》 [The 12th Five-Year Plan (2006-2010) for Economic and Social Development of the PRC]. (People's Republic of China) The State Council. 16 March 2011.

18 《关于对国家鼓励的境外投资重点项目给予信贷支持政策的通知》 [Notice on the Policy of Providing Credit Support to Key Projects of Outbound Investment Encouraged by the State]. (People's Republic of China) NDRC. 27 October 2004.

19 《对外投资国别产业导向目录(一)》 [Catalogue of Industries by Country for Outward Investment (I)]. (People's Republic of China) MOFCOM. 21 July 2004 ('*Catalogue I*'); 《对外投资国别产业导向目录(二)》 [Catalogue of Industries by Country for Outward Investment (II)]. (People's Republic of China) MOFCOM and MFA. October 2005; 《对外投资国别产业导向目录(三)》 [Catalogue of Industries by Country for Outward Investment (III)]. (People's Republic of China) MOFCOM, MFA and NDRC. 31 January 2007.

20 *Catalogue I* (n 19).

21 《境外投资产业指导政策》 [Industrial Guiding Policy for Overseas Investment]. (People's Republic of China) NDRC, MOFCOM and MFA. 5 July 2006, art. 6 ('*2006 Guiding Policy*').

22 Xinhua News Agency (2010) 《三桶油海外收购大丰收》 [The 'Three Barrels' Scored Big with Their Foreign Acquisitions]. http://www.xinhuanet.com/energy/zt/rht/08.htm. Accessed 19 Aug 2025.

23 Dawson (2015).

6.1.2 Since 2012: Diversifying Foreign Investment Encouragement

Since 2012 when the Xi Jinping administration assumed power, China's foreign investment policy has been framed within various national strategies rather than government outbound investment guiding directives. As indicated in the list above, the Xi Jinping administration has launched several major strategies that involve foreign investment policy, primarily including the *Innovation-driven Development Strategy*, the *Made in China 2025 Development Initiative* (MIC 2025), the overcapacity resolution policy and the *Belt and Road Initiative* (BRI).

Following the development pattern of Asian early comer nations like Japan and South Korea,[24] China prioritised technological development as the key to national prosperity. The *2006 Guiding Policy* focussed on the encouragement of FDI that could bring cutting-edge technology, innovative capacity and managerial expertise.[25] In 2012, the CCP put forth the Innovation-driven Development Strategy at the 18th National Congress of the CCP, establishing the overriding importance of technological innovation in promoting national strength.[26] The strategy was subsequently solidified in the *Outline of the National Strategy for Innovation-driven Development* and enshrined in the 13th FYP (2016–2020) and 14th FYP (2021–2025),[27] which encouraged outbound FDI in pursuit of foreign advanced technologies for the purpose of developing domestic high-tech industries (which are termed as 'strategic emerging industries').[28]

In conjunction with the innovation-driven development strategy, the Chinese government launched MIC 2025 in 2015 to encourage China to ascend and dominate global value chains (GVCs) for advanced manufacturing sectors by 2025 (discussed in the following section).[29] As a supplement to MIC 2025, in 2016, seven

---

[24] Warner et al. (2004), pp. 327–329.

[25] Ibid.

[26] 胡锦涛 [Hu Jintao] (2012) 《在中国共产党第十八次全国代表大会上的报告》 [Report on the 18th National People's Congress of the CCP]. Speech. 18th National People's Congress of the CCP.

[27] 《国家创新驱动发展战略纲要》 [Outline of the National Strategy for Innovation-driven Development]. (People's Republic of China) The State Council. 19 May 2016; 《中华人民共和国国民经济和社会发展第十三个五年规划》 [The 13th Five-Year Plan (2016–2020) for Economic and Social Development of the PRC]. (People's Republic of China) The State Council. 16 March 2016; 《中华人民共和国国民经济和社会发展第十四个五年规划和2035年远景目标纲要》 [The 14th Five-Year Plan (2021-2025) for Economic and Social Development and Long-Range Objectives Through the Year 2035 of the PRC]. (People's Republic of China) The State Council. 11 March 2021 ('*The 14th FYP (2021-2025)*').

[28] The term 'strategic emerging industries' encompasses a variety of high-tech industries, such as biomedicine, advanced manufacturing, energy conservation, environmental protection, and aerospace. 《战略性新兴产业分类(2018)》 [Classification of Strategic Emerging Industries (2018)]. (People's Republic of China) NBS. 26 November 2018.

[29] 《中国制造 2025》 [Made in China 2025]. (People's Republic of China) The State Council. 8 May 2015 ('*MIC 2025*').

central government departments issued the *Guiding Opinions on Strengthening International Cooperation to Improve the Position of China's Industries in the Global Value Chain*, encouraging Chinese companies to gain access to foreign advanced technology, technological talents and other strategic assets through M&As, joint ventures with foreign technological companies and the establishment of overseas R&D centres.[30]

While the Xi Jinping administration prioritises developing advanced manufacturing, it has undertaken significant efforts to address excessive production capacity in the traditional manufacturing sector, particularly in the iron and steel, coal mining, cement, electrolytic aluminium and shipbuilding industries.[31] These efforts include the 'Resolve the Overcapacity' programme promoted in the State economy restructuring reform as part of the ongoing latest round of SOE reforms, as discussed in Chap. 2. In addition, the Chinese government has turned to outbound FDI as a solution to industrial overcapacity. Between 2013 and 2015, the State Council issued three documents to encourage domestic Chinese manufacturers to 'Go Global', thus releasing their production capacity.[32]

In addition, China proposed the BRI in September 2013 during President Xi's official visit to Kazakhstan.[33] The BRI has been regarded as a pillar of the Xi Jinping administration's foreign policy, which is also arguably an integral part of China's efforts to address overcapacity.[34] According to the BRI framework document issued by NDRC, MOFCOM and MFA in 2015, the initiative's primary goal is to promote Chinese investment in the connectivity sectors along the Silk Road, such as transportation, water, energy and telecommunications, as well as traditional manufacturing sectors.[35] The government has officially tasked Chinese SOEs to spearhead BRI infrastructure investments.[36] According to the central SASAC, central SOEs have

30 《关于加强国际合作提高我国产业全球价值链地位的指导意见》 [Guiding Opinions on Strengthening International Cooperation to Improve the Position of China's Industries in the Global Value Chain]. (People's Republic of China) MOFCOM, NDRC, Ministry of Science and Technology, Ministry of Industry and Information Technology, BOC, GAC, NBS. 6 December 2016.

31 Li et al. (2019), p. 2; Xu and Liu (2018).

32 《关于化解产能严重过剩矛盾的指导意见》 [Guiding Opinions on Resolving Serious Contradictions in Overcapacity]. (People's Republic of China) The State Council. 15 October 2013; 《关于推进国际产能和装备制造合作的指导意见》 [Guiding Opinions on Promoting International Cooperation in Production Capacity and Equipment Manufacturing]. (People's Republic of China) The State Council. 16 May 2015; 《关于构建开放型经济新体制的若干意见》 [Opinions on Building a New Open Economic System]. (People's Republic of China) The CCP Central Committee and the State Council. 5 May 2015.

33 See generally OECD (2018).

34 However, the effect of the BRI on resolving overcapacity issues in China's domestic industry is contested. See generally Carrai et al. (2020), pp. 120–138.

35 《推动共建丝绸之路经济带和21世纪海上丝绸之路的愿景与行动》 [Vision and Actions on Jointly Building Silk Road Economic Belt and 21st-Century Maritime Silk Road issued]. (People's Republic of China) NDRC, MFA and MOFCOM. 28 March 2015.

36 The Central SASAC (2019) 《国有企业推动共建一带一路走深走实》 [State-Owned Enterprises to Promote the Deepening of the Belt and Road Initiative]. https://www.sasac.gov.cn/n2588025/n2588134/c10574090/content.html. Accessed 19 Aug 2025.

undertaken over seventy percent of the BRI infrastructure projects by contract value and fifty percent by number as of 2018.[37]

Although most BRI countries are developing economies,[38] the China Global Investment Tracker records several BRI investment projects made by Chinese SOEs in the developed world. Examples include the 2016 investment by China Ocean Shipping Company in Singapore to construct berths at the Southeast Asian port and the 2017 acquisition of Singaporean logistics firm CWT Limited by a major Chinese airline company, HNA Holding Group.[39]

In 2017, NDRC, MOFCOM, MFA and BOC jointly issued the *Guiding Opinions on Further Guiding and Regulating the Direction of Overseas Investment* (*2017 Guiding Policy*).[40] The document provides an overview of China's current FDI preferences within the context of the diverse array of significant policies the Xi Jinping administration implemented over the past decade. The *2017 Guiding Policy* classifies specific FDI as 'encouraged', 'restricted' or 'prohibited' (as did the *2006 Guiding Policy*).

The 'encouraged' category includes BRI infrastructure investment (corresponding to the BRI), investments that can promote exports of manufacturing capacity and seek traditional energy resources but are subject to 'sober assessment of economic benefits' (corresponding to the overcapacity resolution policy), investments that involve cooperation with foreign advanced technological companies and establishment of R&D centres (corresponding to the innovation-driven development strategy and MIC 2025) and investments in agriculture and service sectors.[41]

'Restricted' investments, on the other hand, are those that go against China's foreign policy or macroeconomic policy, notably including investment in real estate, hotels, cinemas, entertainment industry and sports clubs and investment in politically unstable countries or regions, or those with which China has no diplomatic ties or which are subject to international treaty restrictions.[42] Restricted investments are subject to government approval.[43] 'Prohibited' investments are those which may

[37] The State Council (2018) 《央企承建"一带一路"项目3116个》 [Central Enterprises Constructed 3,116 'Belt and Road' Projects]. https://www.gov.cn/xinwen/2018-10/31/content_5336052.htm. Accessed 19 Aug 2025.

[38] The latest list of countries participating in the BRI can be accessed at https://www.yidaiyilu.gov.cn/country. Accessed 19 Aug 2025.

[39] The American Enterprise Institute and the Heritage Foundation (2023) China Global Investment Tracker. https://www.aei.org/china-global-investment-tracker/. Accessed 19 Aug 2025.

[40] 《关于进一步引导和规范境外投资方向的指导意见》 [Guiding Opinions on Further Guiding and Regulating the Direction of Overseas Investment]. (People's Republic of China) General Office of the State Council. 18 August 2018 ('*2017 Guiding Policy*').

[41] Ibid. art. 3.

[42] Other investments, such as those utilising obsolete production equipment or equity investment funds/platforms without specific industrial projects, are also included. Ibid. art. 4.

[43] For detailed discussion regarding China's current administrative approval system for outbound FDI, see Chap. 5 Sect. 5.1.2.

jeopardise China's national interests and security, such as the export of unapproved military technology and products.[44]

China's foreign investment policy reflects the government's geopolitical ambitions. Therefore, it is necessary to examine the policy from a longitudinal perspective, tracking shifts in domestic growth demands and a broader context, considering the Xi Jinping administration's resolute geopolitical stance. The latter can shed light on the deeper rationale underlying China's current foreign investment policy, thereby advancing the understanding of Chinese SOEs' FDI, subject to heightened political control in the context of ongoing SOE reforms.

6.2 National Security and Foreign Investment Policy in China

Parallel with those mentioned above major national development strategies and the massive fourth round of SOE reforms, the Xi Jinping administration has placed great emphasis on national security as the core and bottom-line of foreign policy in its pursuit of realising the 'Chinese Dream' of the great rejuvenation of the Chinese nation.[45] As a result, the past decade has seen China's intensive legislative efforts to establish a national security framework, enacting or revising a series of laws, such as the *National Security Law 2015* (NSL 2015), the *Cybersecurity Law 2016*, the *National Intelligence Law 2017*, the 2018 revised *Counter-Terrorism Law*, the *Cryptography Law 2020* and the 2023 revised *Counter-Espionage Law*.[46] In addition, the Chinese government adopted the 'Holistic View of National Security' strategic thinking initiative in 2014 and, for the first time, a National Security Strategy in 2021.

Such strenuous national security measures provide a broader justification for China's current and future foreign investment policy. In addition, the Chinese government's emphasis on national security comes into confront with the enhanced national security protections that form the basis of foreign investment screening regimes in most developed countries. Therefore, the emergence of the national security-based opposition necessitates examining the role of national security in Chinese foreign investment policy and Chinese SOEs' outbound investment activities.

---

[44] *2017 Guiding Policy* (n 40) art. 6.

[45] Jinping (2014b).

[46] 温璐, 李楠楠 [Wen Lu and Li Nannan] (2022) 《全国人大法工委介绍近十年来国家安全立法成绩单》 [The Legislative Affairs Commission of the National People's Congress Standing Committee Reports on National Security Legislation over the Last Decade]. People. http://cpc.people.com.cn/n1/2022/0425/c64387-32408102.html. Accessed 19 Aug 2025.

6.2.1 The General Legal Concept of National Security

As noted earlier, China has embarked on a succession of legislative efforts in establishing a comprehensive national security legal framework under the leadership of the Xi Jinping administration. Parallel with these efforts, the meaning of national security in the context of China's foreign investment policy has been significantly broadened.

The concept of 'national security' first appeared as a pivotal concept in Chinese law in 1993, when the Standing Committee of the 7th National People's Congress promulgated the *National Security Law* (NSL 1993). The law outlines the responsibilities of State organs and the obligations of Chinese nationals and entities to protect national security. However, NSL 1993 did not clearly define 'national security'. Instead, Article 4 of the law listed 'acts endangering national security', primarily including activities that threaten political stability and state sovereignty.[47] The provisions suggest that China's national security appeared to prioritise traditional concerns, which is understandable given the geopolitical climate when the developed world had adopted an engagement strategy towards China to incorporate this emerging power into the established global economic and political order.[48]

Chinese engagement with developed countries has declined since the mid-2010s as (and partially due to) the Xi Jinping administration has taken a more aggressive geopolitical stance to achieve 'the Great Rejuvenation of the Chinese Nation' and become a global power.[49] The 14th FYP (2021–2025) described the current global geopolitical environment as 'becoming increasingly complex, with increasing instability and uncertainty'.[50] This perception of an unfavourable international environment prompted an overhaul of China's national security framework.

In April 2014, President Xi set forth a 'Holistic View of National Security' strategic thinking initiative, calling for a comprehensive understanding of national security as the basis for China's future sustainable development.[51] In 2015, the Standing Committee of the 12th National People's Congress promulgated the new *National Security Law* (NSL 2015).[52] NSL 2015 codifies the 'Holistic View of National Security' initiative (incorporated in the *CCP Constitution* in 2022). Article 2 of the law broadly defines 'national security' as:

> [T]he relative absence of international or domestic threats to the State's power to govern, sovereignty, unity and territorial integrity, the welfare of the people, sustainable economic

[47] Such as plotting to subvert the government, dismember the State or overthrow the socialist system.

[48] Arase (2016), pp. 10–12.

[49] Jinping (2014b).

[50] *The 14th FYP (2021-2025)* (n 27).

[51] Jinping (2014a).

[52] 《中华人民共和国国家安全法》 [National Security Law of People's Republic of China 2015]. (People's Republic of China) adopted at the 12th National People's Congress Standing Committee. 1 July 2015 ('*NSL 2015*').

and social development and other major national interests and the ability to ensure a continued state of security.

This definition suggests that the concept of 'national security' expands well beyond political and sovereign security to encompass a state where China is relatively safe from immediate threats to its stability and can keep itself secure continuously. NSL 2015 specifies various tasks for protecting national security, further elucidating the breadth of the concept.[53] The tasks are listed in Table 6.1 and their associated national security components, as outlined in the 'Holistic View of National Security' initiative. As Table 6.1 shows, China's national security under NSL 2015 and the CCP initiative has been broadened to cover virtually all elements required for a country's national strength and continuous development. The various security components correspond to subsequently enacted or revised legislations focussing

Table 6.1 The all-encompassing coverage of China's national security

Traditional National Security		
Territorial Security Safeguard national territorial sovereignty and national interests.	**Military Security** Promote military revolution, modernisation and standardisation to safeguard national sovereignty and world peace.	**Political Security** Insist on the CCP ruling position and the people's democratic dictatorship.
Non-traditional National Security		
Economic Security Maintain the socialist market order and the basic economic system; Safeguard the country's vital economic interests.	**Energy and Resource Security** Ensure the supply of resources required for economic and social development.	**Technological Security** Improve innovation capacity; Accelerate the development of advanced technology in crucial fields.
Financial Security Improve macroeconomic management and financial risk mitigation systems.	**Cyber and Data Security** Establish cyber and data security protection systems; enhance digital security protection capabilities; develop key technology	**Food Security** Improve the overall food production capacity and the food reserve system.
Social Security Strengthen the mechanism for avoiding and resolving social conflicts and unforeseen occurrences that threaten social stability.	**Ethnic Security** Improve the regional ethnicity autonomy system; promote ethnic group equality, unity, interdependence and harmony.	**Religious Security** Insist on the principle of religious freedom and protect the rights of citizens to practice their religion freely.
Anti-terrorism Oppose all forms of terrorism and extremism.	**Nuclear Security** Utilise nuclear power and technology peacefully, prevent nuclear proliferation and strengthen defences against nuclear attacks.	**Cultural Security** Preserve China's rich cultural heritage, foster socialist values and bolster the overall cultural power and competitiveness.

(continued)

[53] Ibid. art. 15–34.

Table 6.1 (continued)

Ecological Environment Security Enhance the ecological environment protection system; bolster environmental protection efforts.	**Overseas Interests Security** Safeguard the overseas interests of China and the legitimate rights and interests of Chinese citizens, organisations and institutions abroad.	**Outer Space, International Seabed Areas and Polar Region Security** Explore and utilise outer space, international seabed areas and polar regions and protect China's interests.

on particular components, such as the *Cybersecurity Law* and the *Counter-Terrorism Law*. The National Security Strategy (2021–2025) that the CCP Central Committee issued in 2021 confirms the broad spectrum of national security coverage.[54]

6.2.2 National Security in Foreign Investment Policy

National security has played an increasingly significant role in Chinese foreign investment policy, with its underlying implication converging on the comprehensive scope under NSL 2015. Notably, 'national security' appears more frequently in China's inbound investment policy than outbound one. This is substantive because China has historically been an FDI importer since 1979, whereas its emergence as a significant FDI source is a relatively recent phenomenon.[55] As a result, China has developed sophisticated screening and regulatory regimes for inbound investment to safeguard national security,[56] a defensive interest that typically underpins inbound investment policy in most developed countries.[57]

6.2.2.1 National Security in Inbound Investment Policy

The concept of 'national security' first appeared in China's inbound investment policy in 1995 when the 1995 *Interim Provisions Guiding Foreign Investment Direction* explicitly prohibited investment 'endangering national security or harming the public social interest'.[58] The prohibition was retained in the 2002 *Provisions*

[54] 《国家安全战略(2021-2025年)》 [The National Security Strategy (2021-2025)]. (People's Republic of China) Politburo of the Chinese Communist Party. 18 November 2021.

[55] Molnar et al. (2021), pp. 1–50.

[56] Bath (2011), pp. 69, 70; Li and Bian (2016), pp. 149–175.

[57] OECD (2009) Recommendation of the Council on Guidelines for Recipient Country Investment Policies relating to National Security. OECD/LEGAL/0372. Report, p. 5; For discussion regarding the national security-based foreign investment policy in the US, Canada, and Australia, see Knight and Voon (2020), pp. 104–139.

[58] 《指导外商投资方向暂行规定》 [Interim Provisions Guiding Foreign Investment Direction]. (People's Republic of China) State Planning Commission, State Economic and Trade Commission,

Guiding Foreign Investment Direction and the *Foreign Investment Law of the PRC* (FIL) enacted in 2019.[59] The omnibus phrase appeared to imply that national security does not include the public social interest,[60] which was consistent with the narrow meaning of 'national security' under NSL 1993.

In 2003, China first introduced a security review mechanism for particular foreign M&As in the *Interim Provisions on Foreign Investors' Mergers and Acquisitions of Domestic Enterprises*, which authorised competent authorities to request foreign investors to file a report if their M&As posed significant threats to 'market competition or national economic security'.[61] The system was revised in 2006 and 2009, requiring M&As that impacted or could impact 'national economic security' to file mandatory reports with MOFCOM, which was authorised to take mitigating measures against the risks to national economic security or terminate the transaction.[62] The system suggests the then-Chinese government's concerns regarding inbound investment's potential adverse effects on the national economy, which should be considered part of national security.

Since China set up the national security review system for inbound investment in 2011, the concept of 'national security' has progressively risen to the centre of China's inbound investment policy. In the *2011 Notice on the Establishment of a Security Review System for Foreign Investors' Mergers and Acquisitions of Domestic Enterprises* (the *2011 Notice*),[63] the State Council required national security review for foreign M&As in defence-related sectors and sectors relating to significant agricultural products, significant energy and resources, critical infrastructure, critical transport services, key technologies and major equipment manufacturing, among others.[64] In addition, the document specified four factors to be considered during the review, including the impact of the transactions on national defence security, the

Ministry of Foreign Trade and Economic Cooperation. 20 June 1995, art. 7.

59 《指导外商投资方向规定》 [Provisions Guiding Foreign Investment Direction]. (People's Republic of China) The State Council. 21 February 2002, art. 7; 《中华人民共和国外商投资法》 [Foreign Investment Law of the PRC]. (People's Republic of China) Adopted at the 13th National People's Congress. 15 March 2019, art. 6.

60 Bath (2012), pp. 5–34.

61 《外国投资者并购境内企业暂行规定》 [Interim Provisions on Foreign Investors' Mergers and Acquisitions of Domestic Enterprises]. (People's Republic of China) Ministry of Foreign Trade and Economic Cooperation. 12 April 2003, art. 19.

62 《关于外国投资者并购境内企业的规定》 [Provisions on Foreign Investors' Mergers and Acquisitions of Domestic Enterprises]. (People's Republic of China) MOFCOM, the Central SASAC, the State Taxation Administration, State Administration for Industry and Commerce, China Securities Regulatory Commission, State Administration of Foreign Exchange. 8 August 2006, art. 12; 《关于外国投资者并购境内企业的规定》 [Provisions on Foreign Investors' Mergers and Acquisitions of Domestic Enterprises]. (People's Republic of China) MOFCOM. 22 June 2009, art. 12.

63 《关于建立外国投资者并购境内企业安全审查制度的通知》 [Notice on the Establishment of a Security Review System for on Foreign Investors' Mergers and Acquisitions of Domestic Enterprises]. (People's Republic of China) General Office of the State Council. 3 February 2011.

64 Additionally, the transaction must result in the transfer of control of domestic enterprises. Ibid. art. 1.

stability of the national economy, the basic order of social life and the R&D capability of key national security-related technologies.[65] The application scope and consideration factors suggest that the 'national security' concept has expanded beyond the traditional sphere and economic security to include elements regarding agriculture, infrastructure, resources and technology.

The legislative history of the FIL suggests that China considered a substantial broadening of the purview of the national security review system for inbound investment.[66] The draft FIL that MOFCOM published in 2015 for public comment contains a standalone chapter with 26 articles on security review (Chap. 4), which stipulated that any inbound investment that jeopardises or may jeopardise national security would be subject to the review.[67] In addition, the draft FIL enumerated ten non-exhaustive factors to be considered in the review, including the impact of the investments on China's leading position in national security-related technologies, dual-use products and technologies, critical infrastructure and associated key technologies, information and cyber security, long-term demands for energy, food and other critical resources and whether the investment is foreign government-controlled, in addition to the four factors specified in the *2011 Notice*.[68] The proposed enhancement of the National Security Review 2015 suggests a further expansion of the meaning of 'national security' to include additional elements relating to food, energy and infrastructure, among others. This expansion of the concept of 'national security' in the context of foreign investment policy aligns with the 2014-launched 'Holistic View of National Security' initiated and NSL 2015. In addition, the expansion of national security review in the draft FIL may also be motivated by China's market access negative list' regime since 2015.[69] This regime aims at liberalising inbound investment, requiring prior approval only for investments in negative list sectors while other investments receive national treatment,[70] which therefore calls for a heightened national security review for inbound investments.

Interestingly, the entire security review chapter was cut from the final FIL that the 13th National People's Congress promulgated in 2019, leaving only a brief mention that China establishes a security review mechanism for foreign investment that affects or may affect national security.[71] In 2020, NDRC and MOFCOM issued a *Measures for Security Review of Foreign Investment* (the *2020 Security Review*

---

[65] Ibid. art. 2.

[66] For detailed discussion regarding the national security review system under the draft FIL, see generally Li and Bian (2016), pp. 162–174.

[67] 《中华人民共和国外国投资法(草案征求意见稿)》 [Foreign Investment Law of the PRC (Draft for Comment)]. (People's Republic of China) MOFCOM. 19 January 2015, art. 48.

[68] Ibid. art. 57.

[69] 《关于实行市场准入负面清单制度的意见》 [The Opinions of the State Council on Implementing the Market Access Negative List System]. (People's Republic of China) The State Council. 19 October 2015.

[70] Kong (2023), pp. 114–115.

[71] 《中华人民共和国外国投资法》 [Foreign Investment Law of the PRC]. (People's Republic of China) Adopted at the 13th National People's Congress. 15 March 2019, art. 35.

Measures) as the framework document for the security review system.[72] The decision to formulate the security review system in a regulation rather than in the FIL is probably because regulations are more amenable to future revisions than laws, which can only be amended by the National People's Congress and its Standing Committee.[73]

Notably, the *2020 Security Review Measures* takes the national security review application scope back to the pre-draft FIL era. It requires foreign investors to file reports with the competent authority (a ministerial working panel jointly led by NDRC and MOFCOM) for national security review only when their investments are to acquire actual controlling power of Chinese businesses and in the sectors relating to significant cultural products and services, considerable information technology and internet products and services and significant financial services, as well as the sectors specified in the *2011 Notice*.[74] Despite the narrower purview of national security review than that provided in the draft FIL, the extended list of investment sectors that are subject to national security review indicates that the concept of 'national security' has been broadened to include China's cultural, internet, information and financial interests beyond what was implied in the draft FIL. However, review considerations are not mentioned in the *2020 Security Review Measures*. This is likely the result of the Chinese government's reverting to its typical opaque regulatory practices allowing for greater discretion over the admission of FDI.[75]

Since 1995, China's inbound investment policy has gradually expanded the conception of 'national security', moving from emphasising economic security to converging on the all-encompassing national security in NSL 2015. Despite the probable unpredictability regarding the results of the security review, the expansion is consistent with international practice regarding foreign investment policy, which is typically based on a broad understanding of national security (or national interest) to preserve the government's broad discretion in screening FDI.[76]

6.2.2.2 National Security in Outbound Investment Policy

As the concept of 'national security' has become the focal point of China's inbound investment policy, the Chinese government has also increasingly emphasised national security protection as a general objective for Chinese companies making outbound investments in recent years.

---

72 《外商投资安全审查办法》 [Measures for Security Review of Foreign Investment]. (People's Republic of China) NDRC and MOFCOM. 19 December 2020 ('*Security Review Measures*').

73 The potential downside is that the regulations' legitimacy may be challenged. 漆彤 [Qi Tong] (2015) 《外资国家安全审查立法中的若干重要问题》 [Some Important Issues Regarding the Legislation on National Security Review for Foreign Investment]. 中国法律评论 China Law Review 1:79–85.

74 *Security Review Measures* (n 72) art. 4.

75 For China's lack of transparency in regulatory practices, see generally Baruffi (2011), pp. 52–58.

76 See, e.g., Bath (2012), p. 21.

'National security' first appeared in the Chinese outbound investment policy in the *2006 Guiding Policy*, which explicitly prohibited Chinese companies from making investments 'endangering national security or harming the public social interest'.[77] The 2017 Guiding Policy continues to restrict outbound investment that 'may endanger national interest and national security', which is explained as including investments that involve the unauthorised export of military products and technologies, the use of export-prohibited technologies, techniques and products, gambling and pornography, activities prohibited by international treaties to which China is a party and others.[78] The enumeration suggests China's continued emphasis on traditional aspects of national security (interest) with heightened concerns over the loss of core technologies in agriculture, pharmaceutics, transportation, manufacturing and telecommunications, as listed in the *Catalogue of Export-Prohibited and Export-Restricted Technologies* issued and updated by MOFCOM and Ministry of Science and Technology (MOST).[79]

In 2015, the State Council and the CCP Central Committee issued the *Opinions on Building a New Open Economic System*. The document links national security with Chinese FDI for the first time, requiring the government to promote the 'Go Global' and 'Bring In' policies while protecting national security.[80] The 14th FYP (2021–2025) highlights the national development objective to uphold 'Holistic View of National Security' initiatives.[81] In particular, the supreme national strategic development plan prioritises improving energy, critical minerals and key technology security through 'global cooperation' within 2021–2025.[82] This 'global cooperation' obviously refers to international trade and investment, which suggests expanding the concept of 'national security' in accordance with the 'Holistic View of National Security' initiative within the context of outbound investment policy.

China's emphasis on the security of energy, critical minerals and technology as objectives for Chinese outbound investment should be attributed to its heavy reliance on foreign supplies to meet domestic demand for strategic assets. Specifically, due to rapid industrialisation development, China's sustainable growth depends on steady energy supplies. Therefore, as noted earlier, the *2017 Guiding Policy* encourages investment in overseas fossil fuel resources. In addition, China, like the rest of the world, is experiencing increased demand for critical metallic minerals, such as copper, lithium and rare earth elements, due to technological advances and clean

[77] *2006 Guiding Policy* (n 21) art. 7.

[78] *2017 Guiding Policy* (n 40) art. 5.

[79] 《中国禁止出口限制出口技术目录》 [Catalogue of Export-Prohibited and Export-Restricted Technologies]. (People's Republic of China) MOFCOM and MOST. 28 August 2020.

[80] 《关于构建开放型经济新体制的若干意见》 [Opinions on Building a New Open Economic System]. (People's Republic of China) The CCP Central Committee and the State Council. 5 May 2015; for discussion regarding the 'Bring in' policy, which aims to attract foreign investment to fuel China's economic development, see Chaisse (2018), pp. 550–553.

[81] *The 14th FYP (2021-2025)* (n 27) ch. 52.

[82] Ibid. ch. 4, 53.

energy development.[83] In 2017, the Chinese government designated 19 metallic minerals and 5 energy minerals as mineral resources of critical importance, for which supplies must be guaranteed in light of the rising demand and the scarcity of domestic mineral reserves.[84] In addition, China, as a latecomer in the industrialisation process, has long recognised the importance of innovation capability in accelerating its catch-up development.[85] The country relies on advanced industrialised countries for cutting-edge technologies and highly sophisticated components necessary for advanced manufacturing. For example, China has to import extreme ultraviolet lithography machines from Japan and the Netherlands in the semiconductor industry to fabricate advanced chips.[86] China's foreign investment policy that encourages outbound investment in foreign technological sectors mirrors the country's rising demand for critical minerals essential to technology development and application and cutting-edge technologies.

In China's foreign investment policy, 'national security' has expanded significantly beyond the defence and economic spheres to encompass virtually all elements necessary for national growth. In particular, the Chinese government has emphasised protecting the security of energy, critical minerals and technology as a primary policy objective for outbound investments. Given the strengthened connection between Chinese SOEs and the government and CCP in the latest round of SOE, Chinese SOEs play an important role in pursuing global national security through outbound FDI.

6.3 Chinese SOEs in Pursuit of National Security

With the escalation in political control over Chinese SOEs in the latest round of SOE reforms, Chinese SOEs undertake foreign expansion more in line with the foreign policy goals. Specifically, they play an increasingly important role in protecting national security, typically through overseas acquisitions of world-leading companies with proprietary technology or rich resource deposits.

---

[83] See generally Kalantzakos (2020), pp. 1–16.

[84] NDRC (2017) 《全国矿产资源规划 (2016-2020)》 [National Mineral Resources Plan (2016-2020)]. https://www.ndrc.gov.cn/fggz/fzzlgh/gjjzxgh/201705/t20170511_1196755.html. Accessed 19 Aug 2025. ('*Resources Plan 2016-2020*').

[85] Normile (2022).

[86] Allen et al. (2023).

6.3.1 *National Security Tasks of SOEs Under Made in China 2025*

China's enlarged national security approach highlights its need for strategic natural resources and technology. The effective way to cater for the needs is to acquire control of the related overseas resources and assets. However, the Chinese government's apprehension about national security has evolved into an aspiration for a radical fulfilment of national security embodied mainly to dominate the GVCs for sectors critical to the country's national competitive advantage in the international order.[87] The Chinese government mandates Chinese SOEs to head the aspiration, recorded in the *Modern Industrial Chain Length Action Plan* (*Chain Length Plan*).[88]

The MIC 2025 was outlined in 2015 to promote China to become a global powerhouse for advanced manufacturing by 2025.[89] Underlies the initiative is the Chinese government's belief that advanced manufacturing is decisive for China's sustainable growth into a high-income country. As discussed above, securing supplies of strategic natural resources located abroad and ensuring availability of foreign advanced technology are considered to be required by China's all-encompassing national security concerns, while energy resources, critical minerals and key technology are indispensable production inputs in upstream GVCs for advanced manufacturing.

Although China has become influential in the GVCs of several sectors as a major manufacturing and consumption hub, it is still located relatively low in some of the chains.[90] This primarily results from China's lack of competitiveness in proprietary technology and know-how due to the weak national innovation capacity.[91] As a result, China relies on advanced industrialised economies that have specialised in upstream high-value-adding activities for technology-intensive inputs. Moreover, although China has already established controlling positions in global supplies of strategic minerals through its domestic natural resources and foreign acquisitions, it still heavily relies on foreign supplies for critical minerals, such as iron ores and nickel with import-dependency ratios exceeding 80 percent.[92] The suppliers include developing countries where mines are located, such as Kazakhstan and Peru, and

---

[87] *MIC 2025* (n 29).

[88] Xinhua News Agency (2022a) 《国资委:着力提升央企固链补链强链塑链能力》 [The Central SASAC: Promote the Central SOEs to improve the Ability of Fixing Chains, Reinforcing Chains, Enhancing Chains, and Forming Chain]. The Central SASAC. http://www.sasac.gov.cn/n4470048/n22624391/n24633216/n24633236/c24718924/content.html. Accessed 19 Aug 2025.

[89] *MIC 2025* (n 29).

[90] WTO (2018) Trade in Value Added and Global Value Chains: Country Profiles Explanatory Notes. https://www.wto.org/english/res_e/statis_e/miwi_e/explanatory_notes_e.pdf. Accessed 19 Aug 2025.

[91] Deng (2009), pp. 74–84.

[92] 王静 [Wang Jing] (2023) 《我国进口结构变化新趋势与优化方向》 [Improvement of China's Import Structure: Emerging Tendencies and Future Directions]. BOC, p. 6. https://www.boc.cn/fimarkets/summarize/202305/t20230509_23169385.html. Accessed 19 Aug 2025.

developed countries where mining companies holding mines worldwide are based, such as Australia, Canada and the US.[93]

Acknowledging that China's manufacturing is subject to a high degree of foreign reliance, the MIC 2025 is targeted at reducing China's reliance on foreign core components and key base materials, aiming to increase the share of domestic inputs to 40 percent by 2020 and 70 percent by 2025. Further, the plan aims to establish complete value chains for critical manufacturing sectors, especially in ten key technology sectors related to national security, including new information technology, aerospace equipment, new materials and power equipment.[94]

It is worth noting that it is not the goal of the MIC 2025 to indigenise GVCs for advanced manufacturing simply and decouple China from the global production networks. Quite to the contrary, it aims to accelerate Chinese penetration in advanced manufacturing GVCs, especially in the upstream end, through acquiring foreign strategic resources and assets and, based on this, pursuing a higher position in related global industries by 2025.[95] This ambition is identified by the governmental commitments recorded in the MIC 2025 to support Chinese companies to 'utilise global resources' and, as a primary method, to 'Go Global' and make wide-ranging FDI.[96] More obviously, the 2016 *Guiding Opinions on Strengthening International Cooperation to Improve the Position of China's Industries in the Global Value Chain*, a MIC 2025 supporting document issued jointly by seven ministries, also mandates that Chinese companies utilise foreign innovation resources and downstream production resources, mainly through cross-border acquisitions, to collectively promote China to move up the GVCs for advanced manufacturing and deepen Chinese penetration into the GVCs.[97] This ambitious goal has also been affirmed in the 14th FYP (2021–2025), in which the Ministry of Commerce committed to 'support Chinese firms to reshape the global industrial chains and supply chains'.[98]

The MIC 2025 indicates that the Chinese government takes the view that pursuing dominance over GVCs for advanced manufacturing is an effective way to achieve national security outright. The basic logic underpinning the ambition can be boiled down to a simple question: should China dominate, or to be dominated? Although the Chinese government has reduced the propaganda relating to the MIC 2025 since 2018, it is evident that the grand blueprint remains in place. In December 2021, the Chinese government issued a *14th Five-Year Plan of Intelligent*

[93] Yao et al. (2010), pp. 313–325.

[94] *MIC 2025* (n 29).

[95] Zhou et al. (2025), pp. 257–281; Lin (2020), pp. 91–114.

[96] *The 14th FYP (2021-2025)* (n 27).

[97] 《关于加强国际合作提高我国产业全球价值链地位的指导意见》 [Guiding Opinions on Strengthening International Cooperation to Improve the Position of China's Industries in the Global Value Chain]. (People's Republic of China) MOFCOM, NDRC, Ministry of Science and Technology, Ministry of Industry and Information Technology, BOC, GAC, NBS. 6 December 2016.

[98] 《十四五商务发展规划》 [The 14th Five-Year Plan for Business Development Plan]. (People's Republic of China) MOFCOM. 30 June 2021.

Manufacturing Development which continued the goal of the MIC 2025—to make China a global powerhouse for advanced manufacturing.

Given the significance of pursuing dominance over GVCs for strategic sectors to national security, the Chinese government, in the *2022 Government Work Report* government, explicitly assigned the mission to SOEs to support the development of value and supply chains for critical industries and to secure and stabilise the chains. This SOE mission was then reinforced and crystallised by the *Chain Length Plan* released by the central SASAC. According to the plan, SOEs are required to enhance the resilience of domestic critical and high-tech industries' value and supply chains. The plan further requires SOEs to become the controllers of the chains. This reveals the government's genuine objective not only to dominate GVCs in most strategic sectors but also to have the dominant position occupied by Chinese SOEs. With such grand missions, the political pressures imposed on Chinese SOEs, driving them to make FDI pursue dominant positions in the related global production networks for national security, becomes intense.

6.3.2 *Practical Importance of SOE Investments to China's National Security*

Figure 6.1 shows the volume of acquisition transactions (only acquisitions of more than 10 percent stake are counted) made by Chinese SOEs in strategic sectors, namely energy, metal and technology, in developed countries from January 2013 to December 2021, and the comparison with the total volumes of Chinese acquisitions.

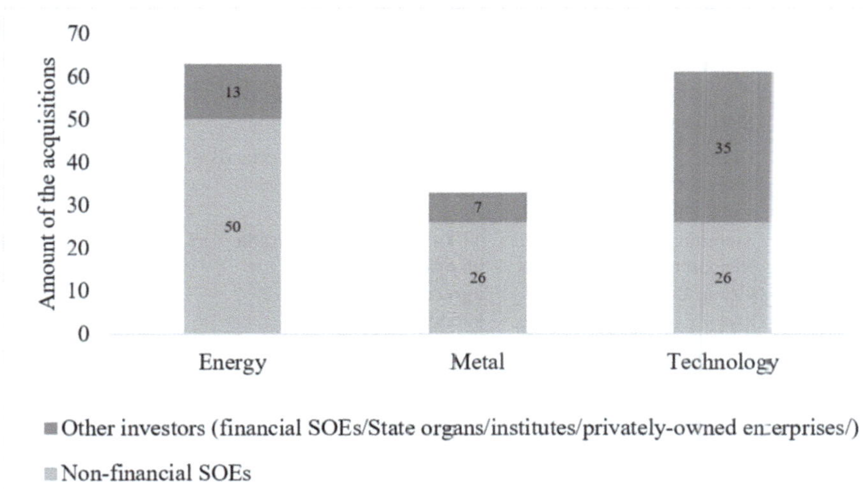

Fig. 6.1 The Comparison of the Volume of Acquisitions in Strategic Sectors of Developed Countries by Different Types of Chinese Investors from 2013 to 2021

The figure was based on the data collected from the China Global Investment Tracker jointly launched by the American Enterprise Institute and the Heritage Foundation, which is the only publicly accessible dataset compiling Chinese outbound investment valued more than USD 100 million from 2005.[99] As seen in Fig. 6.1, more than 75 percent of Chinese acquisitions in the energy and metal sectors of developed countries from 2013 to 2021 were made by SOEs. SOEs are less dominant in the technology sector (partly due to their inherent disadvantages in innovation capacity) but still account for nearly half of the total volume. This shows that Chinese SOEs significantly acquire energy resources, critical minerals and advanced technologies in developed countries.

Chinese SOEs' active FDI in strategic sectors of developed countries indicates a strong correlative relationship with national policies. Chinese SOE FDI in the mining sector can further shed light on how they fulfil national security on a global basis:

In November 2016, the Chinese government identified nine critical metallic minerals closely related to national resource security.[100] Since then, Chinese SOEs in mining sectors have been working to acquire leading foreign companies specialising in producing these metals. Table 6.2 lists the major investment transactions conducted by Chinese SOEs in developed countries from 2017 to 2021 based on the data collected from the China Global Investment Tracker dataset, the public announcements of the transaction parties and press releases from the Dow Jones Factiva database.

[99] The American Enterprise Institute and the Heritage Foundation (n 39).

[100] *Resources Plan 2016-2020* (n 84).

Table 6.2 Chinese SOEs' Major Overseas Acquisitions in Critical Mineral Sectors of Developed Countries from 2017 to 2021

Time	SOE acquirer	Target	Share size	Target location	Metal	Mine locations
December 2017	China Molybdenum Company	Louis Dreyfus	100%	Netherlands	Trading critical minerals	None
August 2017	Sinomine Resource Group Co., Ltd.	Prospect Resources Limited	11.14% (with an offtake agreement on spodumene and petalite concentrate from the Arcadia mine for seven years and the right to appoint one board member)	Australia	Lithium	Zimbabwe

(continued)

Table 6.2 (continued)

Time	SOE acquirer	Target	Share size	Target location	Metal	Mine locations
September 2017	Great Wall Motor Company Limited	Pilbara Minerals	3.5% (with an offtake agreement on spodumene concentrate from the Pilgangoora project for five years)	Australia	Lithium	Australia
September 2018	Zijin Mining Group Company	Nevsun Resources	100%	Canada	Copper, gold, zinc	Serbia, Eritrea,
January 2019	China Molybdenum Company	Freeport-McMoRan	80% of Tenke Fungurume Mine	The US	Copper, cobalt	Congo
June 2019	Sinomine Resource Group	Cabot Corporation	100%	The US	Caesium	Canada
October 2019	Sinosteel Corporation	Crosslands Resources	100%	Australia	Iron	Australia
December 2019	Zijin Mining Group Company	Ivanhoe Mines	13.88% (with the right to appoint a board member)	Canada	Copper, gold, zinc, nickel	Congo, South Africa
December 2019	Jiangxi Copper Corporation	First Quantum Minerals	18.01%	Canada	Copper	Zambia, Panama, Peru, Argentina
December 2019	Zijin Mining Group Company	Continental Gold	100%	Canada	Gold	Colombia
December 2020	Shandong Gold Group	Cardinal Resources	100%	Australia	Gold	Ghana
December 2020	China Molybdenum Company	Freeport-McMoRan	95% of Kisanfu project	The US	Copper, cobalt	Congo
December 2021	Sinomine Resource Group	Power Metals Corporation	5.72% (with an offtake agreement on all lithium, caesium and tantalum produced from the Case Lake Property)	Canada	Lithium, caesium, tantalum	Canada
January 2022	Zijin Mining Group Company	Neo Lithium	100%	Canada	Lithium	Argentina

Instead of attempting to conceal the policy objectives, many SOE acquirers listed in Table 6.2 have publicly announced that they serve the overarching mission of protecting national resource security. For example, Sinosteel Group clearly states on its official website that it assumes the strategic responsibility of fulfilling national resources security, and it aims to secure stable and reliable raw material supplies for domestic iron and steel companies.[101] In 2021, the Chairman of Zijin Mining Group Company proclaimed that it was Zijin's responsibility to reduce China's reliance on foreign countries and increase China's controlling power over global mineral resources.[102]

In general, Chinese SOEs in the energy and technology sectors have followed the same pattern in terms of FDI to ensure national security. In the energy sector, China's State-owned power generators PetroChina Company, Sinopec Corporation and China National Offshore Oil Corporation pledged at a meeting held by the National Energy Administration in 2022 that it was their responsibility to ensure domestic energy supplies to 'fortify against external uncertainties'.[103] Other energy SOEs, such as State Power Investment Corporation (SPIC) and Geo-Jade Petroleum Corporation (Geo-Jade), have also made similar commitments publicly. These SOEs have put substantial efforts into fulfilling the responsibility by making FDI. Previously, they tended to acquire leading overseas oil and gas producers. For example, Geo-Jade successively took over Kazakhstan's Maten Petroleum in 2014, KoZhan LLP and Caspian Nature Resources NV in 2015 and Canada's Bankers Petroleum in 2016.

With the policy shift towards energy transition, Chinese State-owned energy producers began to invest in world-leading clean energy companies, mainly in developed countries, accessing their advanced clean energy assets and technology to promote domestic development. For example, in 2016, SPIC purchased Pacific Hydro Australia and acquired its wind, hydro and solar assets. In 2018, Chinese SOE China Resources Power Holding Company invested in Norway's hydropower company Statkraft to access the target's offshore wind power generation technology.

Likewise, Chinese SOEs have made strides in securing national technology security through technology-seeking FDI in the high-technology sector. For example, in the semiconductor sector, which was explicitly identified in the MIC 2025 as being closely related to national security, Chinese SOEs have actively acquired world-leading semiconductor companies, including America's RDA Microelectronics,

[101] Sinosteel Group Corporation (2025) 《社会责任》 [Social Responsibilities]. https://www.sinosteel.com/shzr/index.html. Accessed 19 Aug 2025.

[102] 陈景河 [Chen Jinghe] (2021) 《紫金矿业向世界展示中国企业的文明之美》 [Zijin Mining: To Demonstrate the Splendour of Chinese Enterprise Civilization to the World]. China Mining. http://www.chinamining.org.cn/index.php?m=content&c=index&a=show&catid=129&id=35492. Accessed 19 Aug 2025.

[103] The State Council (2022) 《国家能源局组织召开2022年大力提升油气勘探开发力度工作推进会》 [National Energy Administration Held the 2022 Promotion Meeting to Promote Oil and Gas Exploration and Development] http://www.gov.cn/xinwen/2022-07/26/content_5702850.htm. Accessed 19 Aug 2025.

Japan's New H3C Technologies, which Chinese State-owned semiconductor maker Tsinghua Unigroup purchased in 2014 and 2015, and Italy's LFoundry acquired by Chinese SOE Semiconductor Manufacturing International Corporation (SMIC) in 2016.[104] Tsinghua Unigroup and SMIC have publicly proclaimed that they have taken on the national mission of assisting in developing the domestic industrial chain for advanced chips.[105]

6.4 Strategic Investment Alliances Between Chinese SOEs

Taking on the mission to pursue strategic ascendency over GVCs for national security, Chinese SOEs have been actively engaged in massive FDI in the developed world. Some host States already know the potential tactic of alliances between Chinese SOEs when making investment. As early in 2009, the former Australian Prime Minister Malcolm Turnbull stated in relation to Chinese mining SOE Chinalco's proposed investment in Australian mining company Rio Tinto that 'it is worth noting that the transaction documents would allow Chinalco to transfer its interests in the operating joint venture including the Hamersley iron ore mines to another Chinese government SOE'.[106]

As the fourth round of SOE reforms proceeds, the likelihood of an inter-SOE tactical alliances grow. This is because all Chinese SOEs are subject to greater control by the SASAC system. Aside from the encompassing political pressures from multiple institutional sources discussed above, which drive SOEs to undertake FDI in conformity with the government's directives, the reforms also considerably build up and tighten inter-SOE linkages through government-led mergers, equity participation and strategic partnerships.

In addition, the global trend towards tighter FDI screening mechanisms impedes Chinese SOEs from investing tactically to avoid rejection decisions or entry restrictions by the host States based on local national security considerations. This article categorises Chinese SOEs' cooperative synergy in overseas expansion into two modes: overseas acquisition–domestic consolidation and overseas strategic collaboration.

[104] The American Enterprise Institute and the Heritage Foundation (n 39).

[105] Xinhua News Agency (2022b) 《紫光集团完成战略重整 紫光股份进入新发展阶段》 [Tsinghua Unigroup Completes Strategic Restructuring and Enters a New Stage of Development]. People. http://finance.people.com.cn/n1/2022/0719/c1004-32479913.html. Accessed 19 Aug 2025.

[106] Economics References Committee (2009) Parliament of Australia. Foreign investment by state-owned entities. Report, p. 53.

6.4.1 Overseas Acquisition–Domestic Consolidation Approach

This approach involves SOEs' international and domestic synergic movements. In the international dimension, Chinese SOEs are trying to take over foreign strategic resources and assets for national security goals. In the domestic dimension, Chinese SOEs' dominance over domestic industries is also substantively enhanced in the ongoing SOE reforms. As a significant part of the reforms, the mixed ownership reform (MOR) calls upon SOEs to acquire equity in or acquire Chinese POEs that possess competitive advantages. The ownership ties enable SOEs to integrate the strategic assets embedded in the non-State cooperate clusters into their operations. Moreover, in the MOR and the State sector restructuring reform, another major sub-reform under the fourth round of SOE reforms, the Chinese government is vigorously promoting mergers, equity participations or strategic cooperative partnerships between SOEs in the same industry (horizontal integrations) or related industries along a same GVC (vertical integrations), realising resources integration in the State sectors and creating State-owned industrial giants.[107]

These two dimensions work in synergy to create a group of State-owned behemoths that dominate domestic critical industries and possess considerable influence over the GVCs. The basic logic can be summarised as this: Chinese SOEs make discrete efforts to undertake overseas and domestic investments in leading companies in a particular industry, accruing influence in the GVC. Then, the Chinese government orchestrates integrations between SOEs to create influential players or corporate clusters in the global industries relatively quickly.

The creation of Sinochem Holdings, the world's largest chemical conglomerate with dominance in global chemical GVC, demonstrates how the dual-dimension approach works in practice. As Fig. 6.2 shows below, Sinochem Holdings was formed by merging two of China's State-owned chemical giants, China National Chemical Corporation (ChemChina) and China National Chemicals Import & Export Corporation (Sinochem), in 2021.

Before the merger, ChemChina and Sinochem focused on different segments of chemical value chains: ChemChina specialised in industrial chemical production, while Sinochem specialised in chemical trading. To rapidly gain a significant foothold in the global chemical industry that had been dominated by large companies based in developed countries, such as Germany-based BASF SE and the UK-based INECO Group, ChemChina adopted a robust buy-in strategy. From 2006 to 2016, it acquired ten major chemical companies, mainly in developed countries, with a special focus on acquiring cutting-edge chemical processing technologies and

[107] 国企改革历程编写组 [SOE Reform Process Writing Group] (2019) 《国企改革历程 1978-2018》 [The Course of Chinese State-Owned Enterprise Reform 1978-2018]. 中国经济出版社 [Economic Press China], p. 338.

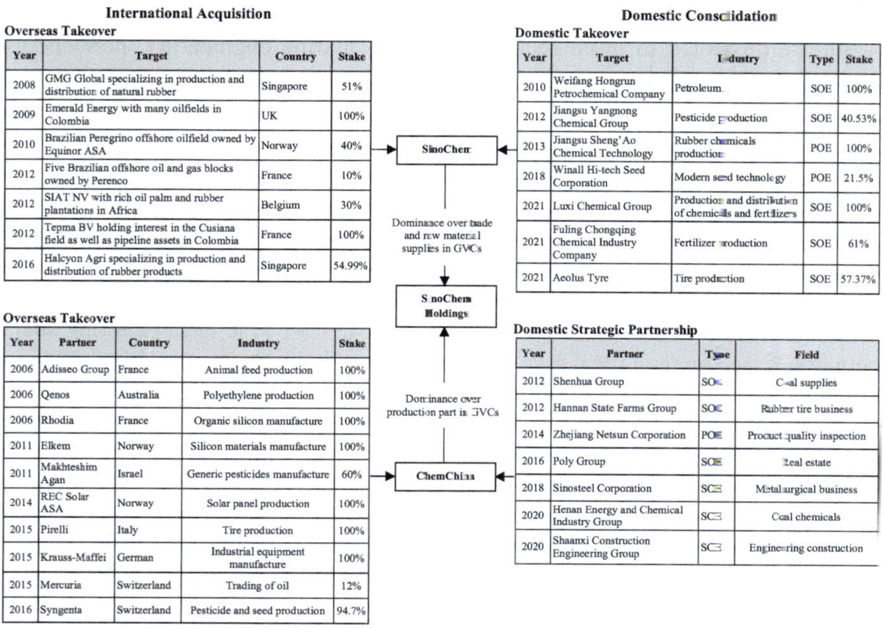

International Acquisition — Overseas Takeover

Year	Target	Country	Stake
2008	GMG Global specializing in production and distribution of natural rubber	Singapore	51%
2009	Emerald Energy with many oilfields in Colombia	UK	100%
2010	Brazilian Peregrino offshore oilfield owned by Equinor ASA	Norway	40%
2012	Five Brazilian offshore oil and gas blocks owned by Perenco	France	10%
2012	SIAT NV with rich oil palm and rubber plantations in Africa	Belgium	30%
2012	Tepma BV holding interest in the Cusiana field as well as pipeline assets in Colombia	France	100%
2016	Halcyon Agri specializing in production and distribution of rubber products	Singapore	54.99%

Overseas Takeover

Year	Partner	Country	Industry	Stake
2006	Adisseo Group	France	Animal feed production	100%
2006	Qenos	Australia	Polyethylene production	100%
2006	Rhodia	France	Organic silicon manufacture	100%
2011	Elkem	Norway	Silicon materials manufacture	100%
2011	Makhteshim Agan	Israel	Generic pesticides manufacture	60%
2014	REC Solar ASA	Norway	Solar panel production	100%
2015	Pirelli	Italy	Tire production	100%
2015	Krauss-Maffei	German	Industrial equipment manufacture	100%
2015	Mercuria	Switzerland	Trading of oil	12%
2016	Syngenta	Switzerland	Pesticide and seed production	94.7%

Domestic Consolidation — Domestic Takeover

Year	Target	Industry	Type	Stake
2010	Weifang Hongrun Petrochemical Company	Petroleum	SOE	100%
2012	Jiangsu Yangnong Chemical Group	Pesticide production	SOE	40.53%
2013	Jiangsu Sheng'Ao Chemical Technology	Rubber chemicals production	POE	100%
2018	Winall Hi-tech Seed Corporation	Modern seed technology	POE	21.5%
2021	Luxi Chemical Group	Production and distribution of chemicals and fertilizers	SOE	100%
2021	Fuling Chongqing Chemical Industry Company	Fertilizer production	SOE	61%
2021	Aeolus Tyre	Tire production	SOE	57.37%

Domestic Strategic Partnership

Year	Partner	Type	Field
2012	Shenhua Group	SOE	Coal supplies
2012	Hannan State Farms Group	SOE	Rubber tire business
2014	Zhejiang Netsun Corporation	POE	Product quality inspection
2016	Poly Group	SOE	Real estate
2018	Sinosteel Corporation	SOE	Metallurgical business
2020	Henan Energy and Chemical Industry Group	SOE	Coal chemicals
2020	Shaanxi Construction Engineering Group	SOE	Engineering construction

Fig. 6.2 The Dual-dimension Approach to Creating State-owned Dominators in GVCs—Example of Sinochem Holdings

extending its acquisitions over the whole chemical GVCs.[108] Sinochem focused more on acquiring overseas natural resources. As noted above, large energy companies based in developed countries hold many mineral deposits in resource-rich regions such as South America and Africa. Sinochem quickly established its global resources base by buying stakes in oilfields held by companies from countries like France, Norway and Belgium.[109]

After years of global acquisitions, ChemChina and Sinochem had already acquired supremacy in several global industrial and supply chains. The 2021 merger then integrated ChemChina's and Sinochem's respective competitiveness into Sinochem Holdings, creating a dominant player in the global chemical industry with businesses covering the whole GVCs and supply chains almost overnight.

The Chinese government is vigorously promoting this two-dimensional approach, which integrates the mission of Chinese SOEs to safeguard national security into the ongoing round of SOE reforms. With its experience in the chemical industry, the

[108] China Resources (2017) 《央企"并购王"的十年海外融合路》 [Ten Years' Overseas Acquisition Journey of the 'Acquisition King' of China's Central Enterprise]. https://winfo.crc.com.cn/crc_mobile/crc/magazine/224/201708/t20170816_435901.htm. Accessed 19 Aug 2025.

[109] Ibid.

central SASAC announced in 2021 that this dual-dimension cooperation mode would be promoted to more sectors, including marine engineering, new energy, digital logistics and air freight.[110]

6.4.2 *Overseas Strategic Collaboration*

Overseas strategic collaboration refers to the practice of Chinese SOEs to cluster and cooperate in overseas projects. This mode was an unspoken practice, primarily rooted in the pervasive social belief in 'guanxi' ('关系', the term denoting social networks based on reciprocal relationships between individuals or entities). Chinese SOEs tend to cooperate with peers in unfamiliar foreign markets to reduce the liability of foreignness. For instance, China's largest molybdenum producer, CMOC Group, proudly announced that it mostly collaborated with other Chinese SOEs in its overseas mining projects, from project design and construction to process equipment and research and development.[111]

In the fourth round of SOE reforms, the Chinese government overtly encourages cooperation between SOEs on a global basis.[112] In response to this tone set from the top, major SOEs have been enhancing international engagement with each other by entering into agreements on strategic cooperation in overseas expansions. For example, in 2022, two of China's State-owned construction giants, China State Construction Engineering (CSCEC) and China Communications Construction Company (CCCC), reached a strategic cooperation agreement in which they made commitments to 'share international business resources and exchange international market information' to 'jointly build international business networks and expand the international market'.[113] More typically, CMOC Group

---

[110] The Central SASAC (2023) 《千帆竞渡创一流:国企改革三年行动综述》 ['A Thousand Sails Race to the Top': An Overview of the Three-Year Campaign of the SOE Reforms]. <http://www.sasac.gov.cn/n2588020/n2877938/n2879597/n2879599/c27111973/content.html?eqid=b479ec500004831d00000006642a9620&wd=&eqid=e0e43a4200015a8e00000006646eb48a. Accessed 19 Aug 2025.

[111] CMOC Group (2021) 《洛阳钼业与多家央企达成战略合作 加速存量资源开发》 [CMOC Has Reached Strategic Cooperation with a Number of Central Enterprises to Accelerate the Development of Stock Resources]. https://www.cmoc.com/html/2021/News_1008/131.html. Accessed 19 Aug 2025.

[112] 刘志强 [Liu Zhiqiang] (2022) 《推动国有企业扛起创新大旗》 [Encourage State-Owned Enterprises to Carry the Banner of Innovation]. People. http://finance.people.com.cn/n1/2022/0406/c1004-32392041.html. Accessed 19 Aug 2025.

[113] China Communications Construction (2022) 《中国建科与中交集团签署海外业务战略合作框架协议》 [CSCEC and CCCC Signed a Strategic Cooperation Framework Agreement on Overseas Business]. https://www.ccccltd.cn/news/gsyw/202209/t20220909_198072.html. Accessed 19 Aug 2025.

reached strategic cooperation agreements with other SOEs in related industries, including China National Chemical Engineering Group and China Civil Engineering Group. As an active global investor which made many overseas acquisitions, CMOC Group made the commitments in the agreements not only to cooperate with its partners in overseas projects but also to find overseas takeover opportunities for its partners.[114]

In retrospect, the strategy of inter-SOE collaboration may have already been implemented in some previous FDI by Chinese SOEs. For instance, in 2014, China Nonferrous Metal Industry's Foreign Engineering and Construction Company (NFC), a subsidiary of China's mining SOE China Nonferrous Metal Mining Group (CNMC), signed a non-binding memorandum with Australian mining company Greenland Minerals and Energy Limited (GMEL) to cooperate in exploiting GMEL's Kvanefjeld Project in Greenland. In 2016, China's largest rare earth State-owned producer, Shenghe Resources Group (Shenghe), acquired 12.5 percent shares of GMEL and formed a 'strategic working relationship' with GMEL on the Kvanefjeld Project.[115] In 2022, Shenghe and CNMC announced that they would collaborate to pursue supremacy in the global rare earth industry—although they had already worked together in the Kvanefjeld Project.

6.5 Concluding Remarks

China has historically adopted an interventionist approach towards outbound FDI in order to ensure that it will contribute to the country's economic growth and development. Through a comprehensive examination of China's major policies affecting outbound investments, this chapter demonstrates that the Xi Jinping administration frames foreign investment policy within several major national development strategies or initiatives, primarily including overcapacity resolution policy, BRI, innovation-driven development strategy and MIC 2025. The policy indicates that the Chinese government is directing FDI to pursue cutting-edge technology and critical minerals essential for advanced manufacturing while promoting FDI that helps export excess capacity in traditional manufacturing in China.

China's extensive efforts in developing and implementing national security strategy over the past decade justify the foreign investment policy. 'National security' has been significantly expanded in the CCP ideology, law and foreign investment

[114] CMOC Group (2021) 《洛阳钼业与多家央企达成战略合作 加速存量资源开发》 [CMOC Has Reached Strategic Cooperation with a Number of Central Enterprises to Accelerate the Development of Stock Resources]. https://www.cmoc.com/html/2021/News_1008/131.html. Accessed 19 Aug 2025.

[115] Jiang et al. (2016).

policy since 2014 to include virtually all elements necessary for a country's long-term prosperity. The policy mission of protecting national security has been spelled out in the MIC 2025 and the *Chain Length Plan*, which require Chinese SOE to engage in efforts to make FDI sourcing strategic resources and assets, particularly in developed countries, thereby leading the national determination to pursue dominance over GVCs and global supplies for strategic sectors.

Given that China's latest round of SOE reforms has resulted in an all-encompassing tightening of political control over SOEs and their FDI activities, as argued in the preceding chapters, it can be expected that Chinese SOEs will play an even more significant role in ensuring global, national security than they already do. In addition, Chinese SOEs may make policy-driven FDI in a tactical alliance based on the strengthened inter-SOE and SOE-POE connections consolidated in the ongoing SOE reforms in China, which could boost the efficacy of pursuing national security protection objectives.

Chinese SOEs' FDI driven by the grand mission of fulfilling national security can be generally regarded as a response to a less favourable international environment in the eyes of the Chinese government. However, despite the plausible justification of protecting national security, the response is not just a defence but may also constitute a threat to other countries targeted. This leads to concerns that Chinese SOEs' national security-driven FDI can impose material risks on developed host States. Nowadays, many developed economies have implemented regulatory measures explicitly aimed at FDI from foreign government-affiliated investors or SOEs, primarily due to national security concerns. Given the practical risks that Chinese SOEs' nation-security-motivated FDI can pose to host States, it is imperative to tailor coping strategies in domestic and international investment legal regimes, which are addressed in Chaps. 7 and 8, respectively.

References

Allen GC, Benson E, Putnam M (2023) Japan and the Netherlands announce plans for new export controls on semiconductor equipment. CSIS. https://www.csis.org/analysis/japan-and-netherlands-announce-plans-new-export-controls-semiconductor-equipment. Accessed 19 Aug 2025

Arase D (2016) The geopolitics of Xi Jinping's Chinese Dream: problems and prospects. ISEAS–Yusof Ishak Institute, pp 10–12

Baruffi F (2011) Transparency in China: a work in progress. China Bus Rev 38(3):52–58

Bath V (2011) The Quandary for Chinese Regulators: controlling the flow of investment into and out of China. In: Bath V, Nottage L (eds) Foreign investment and dispute resolution law and practice in Asia. Routledge, p 73

Bath V (2012) Foreign investment, the national interest and national security: foreign direct investment in Australia and China. Sydney Law Rev 34(1):21

Bath V (2017) The south and alternative models of trade and investment regulation: Chinese investment and approaches to international investment agreements. In: Morosini F, Badin MRS (eds) Reconceptualizing international investment law from the Global South. Cambridge University Press, p 48

Carrai MA, Defraigne J-C, Wouters J (2020) The Belt and Road Initiative and the overcapacity connection. In: Carrai MA, Defraigne J-C, Wouters J (eds) The Belt and Road Initiative and global governance. Edward Elgar Publishing, pp 120–138
Chaisse J (2018) China's international investment policy: formation, evolution, and transformation(s). In: Chaisse J, Nottage L (eds) International investment treaties and arbitration across Asia. Brill, p 557
Chen C (2018) The liberalisation of FDI policies and the impacts of FDI on China's economic development. In: Garnaut R, Song L, Fang C (eds) China's 40 years of reform and development: 1978–2018. ANU Press, pp 595–618
China Communications Construction (2022) 《中国建科与中交集团签署海外业务战略合作框架协议》 [CSCEC and CCCC Signed a Strategic Cooperation Framework Agreement on Overseas Business]. https://www.ccccltd.cn/news/gsyw/202209/t20220909_198072.html. Accessed 19 Aug 2025
China Resources (2017) 《央企"并购王"的十年海外融合路》 [Ten Years' Overseas Acquisition Journey of the 'Acquisition King' of China's Central Enterprise]. https://winfo.crc.com.cn/crc_mobile/crc/magazine/224/201708/t20170815_435901.htm. Accessed 19 Aug 2025
CMOC Group (2021) 《洛阳钼业与多家央企达成战略合作 加速存量资源开发》 [CMOC Has Reached Strategic Cooperation with a Number of Central Enterprises to Accelerate the Development of Stock Resources]. https://www.cmoc.com/html/2021/News_1008/131.html. Accessed 19 Aug 2025
Cui L, Jiang F (2009) Behind ownership decision of Chinese Outward FDI: resources and institutions. Asia Pac J Manag 27(4):753–765
Dawson C (2015) How a Chinese Company Slipped on Canada's Oil Sands. The Wall Street Journal. https://www.wsj.com/articles/how-china-slipped-on-canadas-oil-sands-1437616832 Accessed 19 Aug 2025
Deng P (2009) Why do Chinese firms tend to acquire strategic assets in international expansion? J World Bus 44(1):75
Dimitropoulos G (2021) National security: the role of investment screening mechanisms. In: Chaisse J, Choukroune L, Jusoh S (eds) Handbook of international investment law and policy. Springer Singapore, p 529
Economics References Committee (2009) Parliament of Australia. Foreign investment by state-owned entities. Report, p 53
Frydenberg J (2020) Major reforms to Australia's foreign investment framework pass the parliament. Treasury Portfolio. Media Release
Jiang Y, Tonami A, Fejerskov AM (2016) China's overseas investment in critical infrastructure: nuclear power and telecommunications. Danish Institute for International Studies
Jinping X (2014a) A holistic view of national security. QIUSHI. http://en.qstheory.cn/2020-12/04/c_607611.htm. Accessed 19 Aug 2025
Jinping X (2014b) The Chinese Dream of the Great Rejuvenation of the Chinese Nation. Foreign Languages Press
Kalantzakos S (2020) The race for critical minerals in an era of geopolitical realignments. Int Spect 55(3):1–16
Knight L, Voon T (2020) The evolution of national security at the interface between domestic and international investment law and policy: the role of China. J World Invest Trade 2020(1):111–114
Kong Q (2023) China's foreign investment law amid evolving international investment rules. Springer Singapore, pp 114–115
Li Y, Bian C (2016) A new dimension of foreign investment law in China - evolution and impacts of the national security review system. Asia Pac Law Rev 24(2):152–154
Li P, Jiang F, Cao J (2019) Industrial overcapacity and duplicate construction in China. World Scientific, p 2
Lin Y (2020) 'Made in China 2025' and China's cross-border strategic M&As in OECD countries. J Chin Econ Bus Stud 18(2):93

Luo Y, Tung RL (2007) International expansion of emerging market enterprises: a springboard perspective. J Int Bus Stud 38(4):485–448
Molnar M, Yan T, Li Y (2021) China's outward direct investment and its impact on the domestic economy. IDEAS Working Paper Series from RePEc (1685), p 8
NDRC (2017) 《全国矿产资源规划 (2016-2020)》 [National Mineral Resources Plan (2016-2020)]. https://www.ndrc.gov.cn/fggz/fzzlgh/gjjzxgh/201705/t20170511_1196755.html. Accessed 19 Aug 2025
Normile D (2022) A Beijing Think Tank Offered a Frank Review of China's Technological Weaknesses. Then the Report Disappeared. Science. https://www.science.org/content/article/beijing-think-tank-offered-frank-review-china-s-technological-weaknesses-then-report. Accessed 19 Aug 2025
OECD (2009) Recommendation of the Council on Guidelines for Recipient Country Investment Policies relating to National Security. OECD/LEGAL/0372. Report, p 5
OECD (2018) The Belt and Road Initiative in the global trade, investment and finance landscape. In: OECD Business and Finance Outlook 2018. OECD Publishing
OECD (2025) Foreign Direct Investment Statistics: Data, Analysis and Forecasts. https://www.oecd.org/investment/statistics.htm. Accessed 19 Aug 2025
Sinosteel Group Corporation (2025) 《社会责任》 [Social Responsibilities]. https://www.sinosteel.com/shzr/index.html. Accessed 19 Aug 2025
The American Enterprise Institute and the Heritage Foundation (2023) China Global Investment Tracker. https://www.aei.org/china-global-investment-tracker/. Accessed 19 Aug 2025
The Central SASAC (2019) 《国有企业推动共建一带一路走深走实》 [State-Owned Enterprises to Promote the Deepening of the Belt and Road Initiative]. https://www.sasac.gov.cn/n2588025/n2588134/c10574090/content.html. Accessed 19 Aug 2025
The Central SASAC (2023) 《千帆竞渡创一流:国企改革三年行动综述》 ['A Thousand Sails Race to the Top': An Overview of the Three-Year Campaign of the SOE Reforms]. http://www.sasac.gov.cn/n2588020/n2877938/n2879597/n2879599/c27111973/content.html?eqid=b479ec500004831d00000006642a9620&wd=&eqid=e0e43a4200015a8e00000006646eb48a. Accessed 19 Aug 2025
The State Council (2018) 《央企承建"一带一路"项目3116个》 [Central Enterprises Constructed 3,116 'Belt and Road' Projects]. https://www.gov.cn/xinwen/2018-10/31/content_5336052.htm. Accessed 19 Aug 2025
The State Council (2022) 《国家能源局组织召开2022年大力提升油气勘探开发力度工作推进会》 [National Energy Administration Held the 2022 Promotion Meeting to Promote Oil and Gas Exploration and Development] http://www.gov.cn/xinwen/2022-07/26/content_5702850.htm. Accessed 19 Aug 2025
UNCTAD (2023) World Investment Report 2023. UNCTAD/WIR/2023. Annual Report
Warner M, Hong NS, Xiaojun X (2004) Late development' experience and the evolution of transnational firms in the People's Republic of China. Asia Pac Bus Rev 10(3–4):330–331
WTO (2018) Trade in value added and global value chains: country profiles explanatory notes. https://www.wto.org/english/res_e/statis_e/miwi_e/explanatory_notes_e.pdf. Accessed 19 Aug 2025
Xinhua News Agency (2010) 《三桶油海外收购大丰收》 [The 'Three Barrels' Scored Big with Their Foreign Acquisitions]. http://www.xinhuanet.com/energy/zt/rht/08.htm. Accessed 19 Aug 2025
Xinhua News Agency (2022a) 《国资委:着力提升央企固链补链强链塑链能力》 [The Central SASAC: Promote the Central SOEs to improve the Ability of Fixing Chains, Reinforcing Chains, Enhancing Chains, and Forming Chain]. The Central SASAC. http://www.sasac.gov.cn/n4470048/n22624391/n24633216/n24633236/c24718924/content.html. Accessed 19 Aug 2025
Xinhua News Agency (2022b) 《紫光集团完成战略重整 紫光股份进入新发展阶段》 [Tsinghua Unigroup Completes Strategic Restructuring and Enters a New Stage of Development]. People. http://finance.people.com.cn/n1/2022/0719/c1004-32479913.html. Accessed 19 Aug 2025

Xu D, Liu Y (2018) Understanding China's overcapacity. Springer
Yao S, Sutherland D, Chen J (2010) China's outward FDI and resource-seeking strategy: a case study on Chinalco and Rio Tinto. Asia-Pac J Account Econ 17(3):313–325
Zhao S (2023) Xi Jinping's Consolidation of Power at the 20th Party Congress: Implications for Chinese Foreign Policy. Issues Stud - Inst Int Relat 59(2):1–27
Zhou W, Crochet V, Wang H (2025) Demystifying China's critical minerals strategies: rethinking 'de-risking' supply chains. World Trade Rev 24(2):258

Additional Sources

《中华人民共和国国家安全法》 [National Security Law of People's Republic of China 2015]. (People's Republic of China) adopted at the 12th National People's Congress Standing Committee. 1 July 2015
《中华人民共和国国民经济和社会发展第十一个五年规划》 [The 11th Five-Year Plan (2006-2010) for Economic and Social Development of the PRC]. (People's Republic of China) The State Council. 14 March 2006
《中华人民共和国国民经济和社会发展第十三个五年规划》 [The 13th Five-Year Plan (2016–2020) for Economic and Social Development of the PRC]. (People's Republic of China) The State Council. 16 March 2016
《中华人民共和国国民经济和社会发展第十个五年规划》 [The 10th Five-Year Plan (2001-2005) for Economic and Social Development of the PRC]. (People's Republic of China) The State Council. 15 March 2001
《中华人民共和国国民经济和社会发展第一二个五年规划》 [The 12th Five-Year Plan (2006-2010) for Economic and Social Development of the PRC]. (People's Republic of China) The State Council. 16 March 2011
《中华人民共和国国民经济和社会发展第十四个五年规划和2035年远景目标纲要》 [The 14th Five-Year Plan (2021-2025) for Economic and Social Development and Long-Range Objectives Through the Year 2035 of the PRC]. (People's Republic of China) The State Council. 11 March 2021
《中华人民共和国外国投资法(草案征求意见稿)》 [Foreign Investment Law of the PRC (Draft for Comment)]. (People's Republic of China) MOFCOM. 19 January 2015, art. 48
《中华人民共和国外国投资法》 [Foreign Investment Law of the PRC]. (People's Republic of China) Adopted at the 13th National People's Congress. 15 March 2019, art. 35
《中国制造 2025》 [Made in China 2025]. (People's Republic of China) The State Council. 8 May 2015
《中国禁止出口限制出口技术目录》 [Catalogue of Export-Prohibited and Export-Restricted Technologies]. (People's Republic of China) MOFCOM and MOST. 28 August 2020
《关于加强国际合作提高我国产业全球价值链地位的指导意见》 [Guiding Opinions on Strengthening International Cooperation to Improve the Position of China's Industries in the Global Value Chain]. (People's Republic of China) MOFCOM, NDRC, Ministry of Science and Technology, Ministry of Industry and Information Technology, BOC, GAC, NBS. 6 December 2016
《关于化解产能严重过剩矛盾的指导意见》 [Guiding Opinions on Resolving Serious Contradictions in Overcapacity]. (People's Republic of China) The State Council. 15 October 2013
《关于外国投资者并购境内企业的规定》 [Provisions on Foreign Investors' Mergers and Acquisitions of Domestic Enterprises]. (People's Republic of China) MOFCOM, the Central SASAC, the State Taxation Administration, State Administration for Industry and Commerce, China Securities Regulatory Commission, State Administration of Foreign Exchange. 8 August 2006, art. 12

《关于外国投资者并购境内企业的规定》 [Provisions on Foreign Investors' Mergers and Acquisitions of Domestic Enterprises]. (People's Republic of China) MOFCOM. 22 June 2009, art. 12
《关于实行市场准入负面清单制度的意见》 [The Opinions of the State Council on Implementing the Market Access Negative List System]. (People's Republic of China) The State Council. 19 October 2015
《关于对国家鼓励的境外投资重点项目给予信贷支持政策的通知》 [Notice on the Policy of Providing Credit Support to Key Projects of Outbound Investment Encouraged by the State]. (People's Republic of China) NDRC. 27 October 2004
《关于建立外国投资者并购境内企业安全审查制度的通知》 [Notice on the Establishment of a Security Review System for on Foreign Investors' Mergers and Acquisitions of Domestic Enterprises]. (People's Republic of China) General Office of the State Council. 3 February 2011
《关于推进国际产能和装备制造合作的指导意见》 [Guiding Opinions on Promoting International Cooperation in Production Capacity and Equipment Manufacturing]. (People's Republic of China) The State Council. 16 May 2015
《关于构建开放型经济新体制的若干意见》 [Opinions on Building a New Open Economic System]. (People's Republic of China) The CCP Central Committee and the State Council. 5 May 2015
《关于进一步引导和规范境外投资方向的指导意见》 [Guiding Opinions on Further Guiding and Regulating the Direction of Overseas Investment]. (People's Republic of China) General Office of the State Council. 18 August 2018
《十四五商务发展规划》 [The 14th Five-Year Plan for Business Development Plan]. (People's Republic of China) MOFCOM. 30 June 2021
《国家创新驱动发展战略纲要》 [Outline of the National Strategy for Innovation-driven Development]. (People's Republic of China) The State Council. 19 May 2016
《国家安全战略(2021-2025年)》 [The National Security Strategy (2021-2025)]. (People's Republic of China) Politburo of the Chinese Communist Party. 18 November 2021
《国家计划委员会关于加强海外投资项目管理的意见》 [Opinions of the State Planning Commission on Strengthening Overseas Investment Project Management]. (People's Republic of China) The State Planning Commission of the People's Republic of China. 5 March 1991
《境外投资产业指导政策》 [Industrial Guiding Policy for Overseas Investment]. (People's Republic of China) NDRC, MOFCOM and MFA. 5 July 2006, art. 6
《外商投资安全审查办法》 [Measures for Security Review of Foreign Investment]. (People's Republic of China) NDRC and MOFCOM. 19 December 2020
《外国投资者并购境内企业暂行规定》 [Interim Provisions on Foreign Investors' Mergers and Acquisitions of Domestic Enterprises]. (People's Republic of China) Ministry of Foreign Trade and Economic Cooperation. 12 April 2003, art. 19
《对外投资国别产业导向目录(一)》 [Catalogue of Industries by Country for Outward Investment (I)]. (People's Republic of China) MOFCOM. 21 July 2004
《对外投资国别产业导向目录(三)》 [Catalogue of Industries by Country for Outward Investment (III)]. (People's Republic of China) MOFCOM, MFA and NDRC. 31 January 2007
《对外投资国别产业导向目录(二)》 [Catalogue of Industries by Country for Outward Investment (II)]. (People's Republic of China) MOFCOM and MFA. October 2005
《战略性新兴产业分类(2018)》 [Classification of Strategic Emerging Industries (2018)]. (People's Republic of China) NBS. 26 November 2018
《指导外商投资方向暂行规定》 [Interim Provisions Guiding Foreign Investment Direction]. (People's Republic of China) State Planning Commission, State Economic and Trade Commission, Ministry of Foreign Trade and Economic Cooperation. 20 June 1995, art. 7
《指导外商投资方向规定》 [Provisions Guiding Foreign Investment Direction]. (People's Republic of China) The State Council. 21 February 2002, art. 7
《推动共建丝绸之路经济带和21世纪海上丝绸之路的愿景与行动》 [Vision and Actions on Jointly Building Silk Road Economic Belt and 21st-Century Maritime Silk Road issued]. (People's Republic of China) NDRC, MFA and MOFCOM. 28 March 2015

刘志强 [Liu Zhiqiang] (2022) 《推动国有企业扛起创新大旗》 [Encourage State-Owned Enterprises to Carry the Banner of Innovation]. People. http://finance.people.com.cn/n1/2022/0406/c1004-32392041.html. Accessed 19 Aug 2025

国企改革历程编写组 [SOE Reform Process Writing Group] (2019) 《国企改革历程 1978-2018》 [The Course of Chinese State-Owned Enterprise Reform 1978-2018]. 中国经济出版社 [Economic Press China], p 338

温璐, 李楠楠 [Wen Lu and Li Nannan] (2022) 《全国人大法工委介绍近十年来国家安全立法成绩单》 [The Legislative Affairs Commission of the National People's Congress Standing Committee Reports on National Security Legislation over the Last Decade]. People. http://cpc.people.com.cn/n1/2022/0425/c64387-32408102.html. Accessed 19 Aug 2025

漆彤 [Qi Tong] (2015) 《外资国家安全审查立法中的若干重要问题》 [Some Important Issues Regarding the Legislation on National Security Review for Foreign Investment]. 中国法律评论 China Law Review 1:79–85

王静 [Wang Jing] (2023) 《我国进口结构变化新趋势与优化方向》 [Improvement of China's Import Structure: Emerging Tendencies and Future Directions]. BOC, p 6. https://www.boc.cn/fimarkets/summarize/202305/t20230509_23169385.html. Accessed 19 Aug 2025

祁春凌 [Qi Chunling] (2015) 《中国对外直接投资:基于投资动因，制度因素，以及政治经济学视角的分析》 [China's Foreign Direct Investment: an Analysis from the Perspective of Investment Motivation, Institutional Factors, and Political Economy]. 对外经济贸易大学出版社 [University of International Business and Economics Press], p 46

胡锦涛 [Hu Jintao] (2012) 《在中国共产党第十八次全国代表大会上的报告》 [Report on the 18th National People's Congress of the CCP]. Speech. 18th National People's Congress of the CCP

陈景河 [Chen Jinghe] (2021) 《紫金矿业向世界展示中国企业的文明之美》 [Zijin Mining: To Demonstrate the Splendour of Chinese Enterprise Civilization to the World]. China Mining. http://www.chinamining.org.cn/index.php?m=content&c=index&a=show&catid=129&id=35492. Accessed 19 Aug 2025

Chapter 7
A 'Great Wall' with Cracks: The Implications of China's SOE Reforms for Australia's Foreign Investment Framework

Abstract This chapter explores the intersection of China's latest round of SOE reforms and Australia's foreign investment framework. With China emerging as a leading investor globally, Chinese SOEs play a pivotal role in its outward foreign investment, particularly in Australia's critical sectors such as resources and infrastructure. The research investigates how the tightening of Australia's foreign investment regulations, especially the 2021 reforms, responds to the evolving structure of Chinese SOEs, which have become increasingly entangled with State policy under recent reforms. The chapter addresses the core question of whether Australia's strengthened foreign investment framework, designed to safeguard national interests, is sufficient to mitigate the risks posed by Chinese SOEs, particularly given their closer ties to the Chinese government. It argues that despite these regulatory changes, Australia's framework remains ill-equipped to fully address the emerging risks associated with these investments. The findings are significant for understanding the broader implications of foreign investment policy in the context of China's evolving SOE structure. The chapter proposes specific factors that Australia should consider when screening investments from Chinese SOEs, such as the impact of inter-SOE alliances and the political nature of these entities, contributing to a more nuanced approach to foreign investment.

China is now a major international exporter of capital. Since 2013, China has been consistently listed as one of the world's five largest investors in the World Investment Report published annually by the UNCTAD.[1] According to statistics from the Australian government's Department of Foreign Affairs and Trade (DFAT), China is now among the top 10 investors in the country.[2]

Chinese SOEs contribute significantly to overall Chinese outward investment. According to the 2021 Statistical Bulletin of China's Outward Foreign Direct Investment released by MOFCOM, NBS and SAFE, at the end of 2021, SOEs

[1] UNCTAD (2023) World Investment Report 2023. UNCTAD/WIR/2023. Annual Report.

[2] DFAT (2022) Statistics on who invests in Australia. https://www.dfat.gov.au/trade/trade-and-investment-data-information-and-publications/foreign-investment-statistics/statistics-on-who-invests-in-australia. Accessed 25 Aug 2025.

T. Gu, *Chinese SOE Reforms and Global FDI*, Contemporary Chinese Civil and Commercial Law, https://doi.org/10.1007/978-981-92-3181-2_7

accounted for 51.6 percent of China's stock of non-financial FDI,[3] despite the tremendous growth of China's private sector over the past few decades.[4] According to the KPMG and USYD's 2024 Report on Chinese Investment in Australia, 59 percent of the total volume of Chinese investment in Australia in 2023 came from SOEs.[5]

As Chap. 6 demonstrates, China has significantly broadened its concept of 'national security' in its foreign investment policy to encompass virtually any threat to the country's prosperity. The Xi Jinping administration has demonstrated a strong desire to strengthen China's position in global value chains for advanced manufacturing's high-tech industries in the context of ongoing Sino-Western geopolitical tensions.[6] This assertive official stance foreshadows that Chinese SOEs, as major policy implementors, will continue to seek to invest in Australia in pursuit of strategically significant assets such as iron ore and rare earth materials that are considered essential to China's comprehensive national security.

Australia's foreign investment framework is set out mainly in the *Foreign Acquisitions and Takeovers Act 1975* (FATA).[7] Under this framework, the Australian government can review FDI for potential threats to the national interest on a case-by-case basis. In January 2021, a comprehensive set of reforms to the regime came into effect, considerably tightening the framework in response to national security concerns.[8] Due to the inherent proximity of Chinese SOEs to their government owner and their concentration of investment in a number of Australia's strategic sectors, the reformed framework should lead to increased scrutiny of Chinese SOE investments.

Previous chapters have demonstrated that China's latest round of SOE reforms is reshaping almost every facet of Chinese SOEs, ranging from corporate governance structure to inter-SOE connections. Early in 2009, Peter Drysdale and Christopher Findley pointed out in the Australian Senate Economics References Committee's report on FDI from foreign SOEs that:

> The regime under which State-owned enterprise operates changes over time, as it clearly has changed and is changing in China. Do these changes need to inform the strategy that host countries might adopt towards FDI from this source?[9]

Chinese investments in Australia and their interaction with Australia's foreign investment framework have been the subject of considerable scholarly research. Mendelsohn and Fels in 2014 examined how Australia's foreign investment framework served Australia's broad policy interests in processing Chinese investments,[10]

---

[3] MOFCOM, NBS and SAFE (2022), p. 30.

[4] Ibid.

[5] KPMG and USYD (2024), p. 4.

[6] Zhou et al. (2025), pp. 257–281; Lin (2020), pp. 91–114.

[7] *Foreign Acquisitions and Takeovers Act 1975* (Cth) ('FATA').

[8] *Foreign Investment Reform (Protecting Australia's National Security) Act 2020* (Cth).

[9] Economic References Committee (2009) Foreign investment by state-owned entities. Report, p. 47.

[10] Mendelsohn and Fels (2014), pp. 59–83.

and Jiang in 2018 explored the actual operations of the framework for Chinese investment.[11] However, neither of these works focussed exclusively on Chinese SOE investments. In addition, most previous studies on Australia's investment screening do not address the 2021 foreign investment reforms.[12]

Given the research gap, this chapter comprehensively analyses the interaction between Chinese SOE investments and Australia's reformed foreign investment review framework in the context of China's latest round of SOE reforms. This chapter argues that Australia's reformed foreign investment framework is still insufficient to address threats associated with Chinese SOE investments. This is primarily attributable to the expansion of inter-SOE and SOE-POE equity networks in China and the strengthening of political control over Chinese SOEs and their affiliated companies as a result of the latest round of SOE reforms. Therefore, this chapter provides suggestions regarding specific factors the Australian government should consider when evaluating investments from Chinese SOEs or companies that are likely affiliated with SOEs.

The structure of this chapter is as follows: Section 7.1 outlines the screening landscape under the reformed Australian investment framework for Chinese SOE investments. Section 7.2 examines the actual operation of the framework (both before and after the reforms) concerning Chinese investments to the extent possible, based on a comprehensive compilation of the Treasury's published decisions on Chinese investment since 2008, and addresses the implications of China's latest round of SOE reforms on Chinese investments in Australia's infrastructure and resources sectors, which have been particularly sensitive sectors in investment screening. Section 7.3 provides suggestions regarding specific factors that the Australian government should consider when evaluating investments from Chinese SOE or SOE-affiliated companies to better address Chinese SOE investments in the context of the latest round of SOE reforms.

7.1 Mapping Australia's Foreign Investment Framework for Chinese SOE Investments

Australia established a case-by-case screening regime for foreign investment under the FATA. This is supplemented by the *Foreign Acquisitions and Takeovers Regulation 2015* (FATR),[13] as well as the *Foreign Investment Policy* regularly updated by the Treasury (the Policy) and the detailed guidance notes on the screening regime (Guidance Notes) issued by the Foreign Investment Review Board (FIRB), the governing body primarily responsible for implementing Australia's

[11] Jiang (2018), pp. 14–35.

[12] For example, Esplugues (2018), p. 355.

[13] *Foreign Acquisitions and Takeovers Regulation 2015* (Cth) ('FATR').

foreign investment framework.[14] The framework of Australia’s policy is that foreign investment is permitted (and indeed encouraged) unless it is considered to be contrary to Australia’s national interests. In the past decades, Australia has actively modified and tightened the framework in response to perceived risks and the changing national demands. For example, the monetary threshold for foreign investment review was temporarily lowered to zero dollars in 2020 to prevent opportunist acquisitions during the pandemic downturn.[15] On 1 January 2021, legislative amendments to Australia’s foreign investment framework entered into force to strengthen the screening mechanism, described by the then-Treasurer as ‘the most significant reforms to the FATA in nearly 50 years’.[16]

7.1.1 Overview of Australia’s Foreign Investment Screening Framework

Australia’s framework provides both *ex-ante* screening and *ex-post* monitoring of FDI. Its scope is relatively broad and encompasses both FDI and portfolio investments.[17] The 2021 reforms enhance the framework through three means: introducing a new national security test in addition to the existing national interest test to capture investments associated with national security risks that would not otherwise trigger review; enhancing the compliance and retrospective review powers to ensure continuous risk-management after the establishment of investments; and streamlining review processes for foreign investment in non-sensitive businesses.

Under the FATA, foreign acquisitions are subject to mandatory pre-notification requirements and review under the national interest test only when their deal value exceeds specified monetary thresholds (referred to as a ‘notifiable action’ in the framework).[18] Lower monetary thresholds generally apply to investments in sensitive businesses,[19] agribusinesses and mining and production tenements and land. However, a zero-dollar threshold applies to investments made by foreign

---

[14] The Treasury (2025) Australia’s Foreign Investment Policy. https://foreigninvestment.gov.au/sites/foreigninvestment.gov.au/files/2025-03/australias-foreign-investment-policy-v2.pdf. Accessed 25 Aug 2025 (‘*2025 Policy*’); See the latest Guidance Notes at FIRB (2025) Australia’s Foreign Investment Framework. https://foreigninvestment.gov.au/investing-in-australia/foreign-investment-framework. Accessed 25 Aug 2025.

[15] The change ended on 1 January 2021. FIRB (2022) Foreign Investment Review Board Annual Report 2020-21. Report.

[16] Frydenberg (2020).

[17] FATA (n 7) s. 40, 47, 54, 55, 56.

[18] Ibid. s. 47.

[19] Sensitive businesses include media, telecoms, transport, defence and military-related supply of goods, technology, equipment, security technology and communications system, nuclear facilities. *2025 Policy* (n 14).

government investors (FGIs).[20] Foreign investment that would result in substantial foreign influence over Australian businesses and their assets ('significant action' under the framework) does not require mandatory pre-notification unless it is a notifiable action, but if not notified, the Treasurer can refuse to permit, or retrospectively prohibit, the investment if it is contrary to the national interest. Under the national security amendments, the Treasurer can 'call in' the transaction for retrospective screening under the national security test within 10 years after the action has been completed if national security risks emerge.[21] Foreign investment in a 'national security business' and 'national security land' ('notifiable national security action' under the framework) is subject to pre-notification and national security tests.[22] Foreign investment which is not captured by the rules mentioned above but which may nonetheless raise national security concerns ('reviewable national security action' under the framework), is also subject to the Treasurer's 'call-in' power.[23] In addition, the amended framework also includes a 'last-resort' allowing the Treasurer, in exceptional circumstances, to unilaterally review investments that were lawfully admitted on the grounds that national security risks have since emerged.[24]

The Treasurer has the sole discretion to determine whether an investment is contrary to Australia's national interest or security, and he or she is not obliged to publicise the decisions or explain the reasons.[25] Notably, neither the FATA nor FATR defines 'national interest' or 'national security'. Although the concepts are present in some other Australian laws for which specific definitions are provided, they are tailored to the particular purposes of their respective laws. For example, the *Broadcasting Service Act 1993* provides an understanding of the notion of 'national interest' centred on the potential impact on Australia's international relations (determining whether a proposed international broadcasting service would be against Australia's national interest).[26]

Despite the lack of a definition of national security, the FATR defines 'national security business' as assets and entities covered by the *Security of Critical*

---

[20] Ibid.

[21] FATA (n 7) s. 40, 55C.

[22] Ibid. s. 55B.

[23] Ibid. s. 55D, 55E, 55F.

[24] The Treasurer may invoke the last-resort power to a lawfully admitted foreign investment made after 1 January 2021 to a retrospective national security test. The power is applicable in the circumstances where: (1) the business, structure, or organisation of the investor has materially changed; (2) the investor's activities have materially changed; (3) the investor's circumstances or the market have materially changed; or (4) the Treasurer becomes aware of a materially false or misleading statement or mistake made by the investor in the original notification, and the change or misrepresentation raises national security concerns. FATA (n 7) s. 79A, 79E.

[25] Economic References Committee (2021) Greenfields, Cash Cows and the Regulation of Foreign Investment in Australia. Report.

[26] *Broadcasting Service Act 1993* (Cth) s. 121 FD (3), (4).

Infrastructure Act 2018 (the SOCI Act) and the *Telecommunications Act 1997*,[27] and 'national security land' as defence premises governed by the *Defence Act 1903*.[28] Only the SOCI Act, of the three pieces of legislation explicitly referred to in the FATR, provides a definition of 'national security,' which broadly encompasses Australia's defence, security or international relations.[29] The Treasury's Policy provides an indicative list of general factors to be considered in the FIRB national interest review, which serves as a guide to the fundamental concepts.[30] The factors include national security implications, competition implications, impacts on other Australian government policies (including tax), consequences on the Australian economy and community, and the character of the investor and the target business,[31] reflecting the broad meaning of 'national interest' under the foreign investment framework. In addition to the general factors, the Policy also outlines special factors for investment in certain businesses (including agriculture, media, land) or investments made by FGIs.[32]

Suppose the Treasurer determines that a transaction is contrary to Australia's national security or interest. In that case, it may be prohibited outright or approved subject to conditions specially tailored to the investment (for *ex-ante* screening) or a requested change of conditions, divestment or undoing (if the investment has already been made). In general, the Treasurer's decisions under the FATA are final. The decisions are statutorily exempt from administrative review,[33] and Australian case law indicates that courts tend to uphold the Treasurer's broad discretion to decide on the admission of foreign investment under the FATA.[34] In addition, foreign investment in certain sectors or entities (such as banking, telecommunications and Telstra) may be subject to specific laws and regulations that impose restrictions on foreign ownership and other compliance obligations on investors.[35]

---

[27] FATR (n 13) s. 8AA.

[28] Ibid. s. 5.

[29] *Security of Critical Infrastructure Act* 2018 (Cth) s. 5, as amended by *Security Legislation Amendment (Critical Infrastructure Protection) Act 2022* (Cth).

[30] *2025 Policy* (n 14).

[31] Ibid.

[32] Ibid.

[33] *Administrative Decisions (Judicial Review) Act 1977* (Cth) sch. 1(h).

[34] See, e.g., *Marie Madeline Wight v The Honourable Chris Pearce, MP, Parliamentary Secretary to the Treasurer* (2007) 157 FCR 485; *Canwest Global Communications Corporation and Others v Treasurer of the Commonwealth of Australia* [1997] FCA 730; *Cathy Pacific Airways Limited v Assistant Treasurer and Minister for Competition Policy and Consumer Affairs* (2010) 186 FCR 168; *Leisure and Entertainment Pty Ltd v The Honourable Ralph Wills, Federal Treasurer of the Commonwealth of Australia* (1996) 64 FCR 205.

[35] For example, foreign ownership in any Australian international airline in limited to 49 percent. *Air Navigation Act 1920* (Cth) s. 11A and *Qantas Sale Act 1992* (Cth) s. 7; foreign ownership of designated airports is limited to 49 percent. *Airport Act 1996* (Cth) pt. 3, div. 3; Ships to be registered in Australia must be majority Australian-owned, unless the ship is designated as chartered by an Australian operator. *Shipping Requisition Act 1981* (Cth); foreign ownership of Telstra is limited to 35 percent and the stake owned by individual foreign investor is limited to 5 percent. *Telstra*

7.1.2 Regulatory Hurdles for Chinese SOEs Under the Framework

Australia's foreign investment framework requires that all proposals from FGIs to acquire a direct interest (which is an interest of no less than 10 percent, or 15 percent subject to specific conditions) in an existing business,[36] obtain an interest in Australian land or establish a new business in Australia must undergo FIRB review prior to establishment, irrespective of the deal value or industry.[37] The term FGI is defined in Section 17 of the FATR as:

1) a foreign government;
2) an individual, corporation or corporation sole that is an agency or instrumentality of a foreign country but is not part of the body politic of that foreign country (referred to as a 'separate government entity');
3) a corporation, trustee of a trust or a general partner of a limited partnership in which:
    a. A foreign government or separate government entity, alone or together with one or more associates, holds an interest of at least 20 percent; or
    b. foreign governments or separate government entities of more than one foreign country (or parts of more than one foreign country), together with any one or more associates, hold an aggregate interest of at least 40 percent.

The definition indicates that the framework aims to capture all foreign government agencies, SOEs, sovereign wealth funds (SWFs) investments and other entities with substantial ownership tied to a foreign government or foreign governments.[38] This is not limited to China, and the Australian government did not agree to raise the screening threshold for Chinese SOEs in the negotiation of ChAFTA. This was justified by Australia's Department of Foreign Affairs and Trade as 'consistent with the [Australian] Government's practice in other FTAs'.[39]

This rigorous catch-all approach does not necessarily reflect an antipathy towards FGI investments. Peter Drysdale, an Australian National University economist, believed that this approach helps maintain Australia's openness to foreign SOE investments by reassuring the public that the investments are carefully evaluated.[40] In contrast, the Business Council of Australia (BCA), an industry organisation that

Corporation Act 1991 (Cth) pt. 2A, div. 4, ss. 8BG-8BJ; foreign investment in the banking sector is additionally subject to the *Banking Act 1959* (Cth), the *Financial Sector (Shareholding) Act 1988* (Cth).

36 FATR (n 13) s. 16, which defines 'direct interest' as an interest of at least 10 percent, or 15 percent if the acquirer has entered a legal agreement relating to the target, or an interest of any percentage if the acquirer is in a position to influence or participate in the central management and control of the target or determine the policy of the target.

37 Ibid. s. 56.

38 FATR (n 13) s. 17.

39 DFAT (2018) Factsheet: Investment and Investor-State Dispute Settlement (ISDS). https://www.dfat.gov.au/sites/default/files/chafta-fact-sheet-investor-state-dispute-settlement.pdf. Accessed 25 Aug 2025.

40 Drysdale (2011), pp. 54–73.

represents Australia's top employers, in its 2014 discussion paper on Chinese investments advocated for the liberalisation of FGI screening rules, arguing that Australia would otherwise lose foreign SOEs as new sources of capital to competitor countries.[41]

7.1.2.1 A Realistic Approach Towards FGIs

Despite the catch-all approach to FGI investments, Australia has embraced a realistic approach to foreign SOE investors in foreign investment screening regarding the requirements for their political independence and commercial motivations. In 2008, the then-Treasurer Wayne Swan issued guidelines for evaluating proposals from foreign SOEs, with the first criterion emphasising SOE investor's operational independence from its government owner.[42] In 2009, Patrick Colmer, then- Executive Member of the FIRB, described this criterion as follows:

> The reality is that any government-owned entity will not be independent from the government. The questions that we look at are: What is the government of the entity, how does it operate and can we see that it is operating independently and without direct and continuing government control because any government entity will have a relationship with its government?[43]

In the 2010 Policy, the Treasury further clarified this operational independence criterion for foreign SOEs by stating that the Australian government does not have a policy prohibiting investments proposed by FGIs that 'are not operating on a fully arm's length and commercial basis'; instead, the transactions can be approved if the Treasurer determines they are not contrary to Australia's national interest.[44] This statement remains in the 2023 Policy section of special considerations for FGI investments.[45] In addition, the Policy states that 'the Australian Government also considers...if the [foreign government] investor may be pursuing political or strategic objectives that may be contrary to Australia's national interest'.[46] The wording could be interpreted as allowing the admission of FGI investments that serve non-commercial objectives, so long as those objectives do not conflict with Australia's national interests.

Concerns expressed in the Policy regarding the possible conflict between the foreign policy of FGIs' home States and Australia's national interests are

---

[41] BCA (2014) Discussion Paper on Foreign Investment and State-Owned Enterprises: Managing the Risks to Maximise the Benefits. p. 9 https://www.bca.com.au/discussion_paper_on_foreign_investment_and_state_owned_enterprises_new. Accessed 25 Aug 2025.

[42] Parliament of Australia (2008) Treasurer's 2008 guidelines for assessing proposals by SOEs. https://www.aph.gov.au/Parliamentary_Business/Committees/Senate/Economics/Completed_inquiries/2008-10/firb_09/report/e03. Accessed 25 Aug 2025.

[43] Economic References Committee (n 9), p. 68.

[44] FIRB (2010) Australia's Foreign Investment Policy. ('*2010 Policy*').

[45] *2025 Policy* (n 14).

[46] Ibid.

pertinent to what appears to be a more cautious approach adopted by the Australian government in approving Chinese SOE investments over the past decade. During the period of increasingly close economic relationship between Australia and China from 2008, of which the 2015 conclusion of ChAFTA may well have been the high point,[47] Australia generally adopted a favourable stance towards SOE investments. High-profile investments approved by the FIRB during the period include China's metal and mining enterprise Sinosteel Corporation's acquisition of Australian iron ore producers Midwest Corporation Limited and Murchison Metals Limited in 2008 and the investment by State Grid of China (State Grid) in Victoria's largest energy delivery services company SP Ausnet (now AusNet Services) in 2013.[48] In recent years, with the current Chinese government's assertive economic and military stance and the fraught diplomatic relationship with Canberra, Australia's previously favourable approach towards Chinese SOE investments appears to have been replaced by a higher level of concern, manifested in more rejections of Chinese SOE investments, which are discussed in detail in the following Sections.

7.1.2.2 Consideration Factors in the National Interest and National Security Tests

According to the Policy, in applying the national interest test, the FIRB, in conjunction with relevant government departments, typically evaluates investments against the general factors outlined above.[49] The latest Policy, released in June 2023, added to the general factor of impact on other government policies the consideration that investments must be consistent with Australian government policies for promoting critical technology.[50] This highlights Australia's growing concerns about foreign investment' impact on its technological development, including, for example, the risk of losing critical technology to other countries.[51]

The FIRB will look beyond the general considerations above for FGI investments to see if the transactions are purely commercially motivated or motivated by broader political or strategic objectives. This includes determining whether the FGI is subject to actual or potential political control through governance or funding arrangements.[52] In addition, the Policy specifies that, for FGIs not wholly owned by a foreign government, the FIRB will 'consider the size, nature and composition of

[47] Free Trade Agreement between the Government of Australia and the Government of the People's Republic of China, signed 17 June 2015, [2015] ATS 15 (entered into force 20 December 2015) ('ChAFTA').

[48] Swan (2008c); Hockey (2013).

[49] *2025 Policy* (n 14).

[50] Ibid.

[51] Productivity Commission (2020) Foreign Investment in Australia. Research Paper, p. 16.

[52] *2025 Policy* (n 14).

any non-government interests, as well as any restrictions on the exercise of their rights as interest holders'.[53]

In contrast to the national interest test, the Policy does not guide the factors to be considered in the newly introduced national security test. Instead, it only vaguely describes national security in the Policy as 'Australia's ability to protect its strategic and security interest'.[54] Despite the absence of a specific definition in the FATA or FATR, the Policy implies that the notion of 'national security' is within the implication of 'national interest' under the foreign investment framework, as national security is listed as one of the general factors to be considered in national interest test.[55] Accordingly, the national security test is narrower than the national interest test. However, the generality of 'national security' still leaves the Australian government with great space to restrict investments on national security grounds. As noted earlier, the FATR defines 'national security business' and 'national security land' with explicit references to other legislations, including the SOCI Act, the *Telecommunications Act 1997* and the *Defence Act 1903*, implying that the concept of 'national security' in Australia's foreign investment framework also picks up the usage of the national security concept of other legislations. In particular, as discussed in greater detail below, Australia has significantly amended the SOCI Act over the past two years, significantly expanding the scope of critical infrastructure assets that can raise national security risks.[56] The amendments have been summarised in the FIRB's Guidance Note 8, which provides an extensive list of assets across a wide range of industries where foreign investment may raise national security concerns.[57] The list includes not only widely recognised national security-related assets such as critical minerals, technologies and infrastructure but also those not considered particularly sensitive from a national security point of view in the past, such as financial services, food and groceries, health sector facilities, data centres and cloud providers, among others.

In the context of the official guidance on applying the national interests and security tests, some general observations should be made regarding Chinese SOE investments in Australia. First, Chinese SOEs have displayed an investment behavioural pattern in Australia (and other developed countries), pursuant to which they prefer acquisitions of existing operations over green field investments. In particular, they are keen on acquiring either large companies or companies that have established competitive advantages based on their distinctive resources or capacities to bolster their standing in domestic and international markets.[58] Therefore, it is reasonable to assume that the types of investments favoured by Chinese SOE investments would

[53] Ibid.

[54] Ibid 11.

[55] Ibid.

[56] *Security Legislation Amendment (Critical Infrastructure) Bill 2021* (Cth); *Security Legislation Amendment (Critical Infrastructure Protection) Bill 2022* (Cth).

[57] FIRB (2020) Guidance 8: National Security Test. https://foreigninvestment.gov.au/sites/firb.gov.au/files/guidance-notes/GN8-NationalSecurity-210303.pdf. Accessed 25 Aug 2025. ('*Guidance 8*').

[58] Luo et al. (2010), pp. 68–79.

raise more concerns in the FIRB review, as acquisitions have more far-reaching effects than green-field investments and raise concerns in relation to competition, the effect of foreign interference in or takeover of the existing Australian company's operations and strategic assets, potential impacts on the local community including loss of employment and vertical integration and impacts on Australian economy at large in the case where the acquisition target is a major industrial player in Australia.

Secondly, the Policy recognises that some FGIs are partially government-owned, and in such cases, the FIRB will evaluate 'the restrictions on the exercise of [non-government interests]' rights as interest holders'.[59] This is particularly relevant to China's ongoing mixed-ownership reform (MOR) as a part of the latest round of SOE reforms. The MOR aims to mix State-owned and non-State-owned capitals in enterprises through two approaches: flow-in MOR, which refers to introducing non-State-owned shareholders into SOEs, and flow-out MOR, which refers to promoting SOEs to invest in Chinese POEs.[60] The mixed-ownership enterprises (MOEs) created in the MOR will continue to be considered as FGIs under Australia's foreign investment framework if their State ownership is no less than 20 percent. For these MOE-FGI investors, in assessing the factors above, the FIRB should pay special attention to their ownership and governance structures, particularly if there are any restrictions on the non-State shareholders' participation in the investor's operations. This is because, in implementing flow-in MOR, the MOEs formed rarely have mechanisms in place to protect the interests of POE shareholders, who are typically minority shareholders, from being oppressed by majority State shareholders.[61] In addition, the CCP-led decision-making body within Chinese State-invested enterprises known as the 'Party Committee' may substantially restrict POE shareholders' participation in MOE operations.[62]

7.1.2.3 Mitigating Factors and Other Informal Factors

In addition to the factors above, the Policy specifies mitigating factors that may aid the Treasurer's determination that an FGI investment is not contrary to Australia's national interests. The mitigating factors set out in the Policy include the presence of external partners or shareholders, the level of non-associated ownership interests, the governance arrangements for the investment, ongoing arrangements to protect Australian

[59] *2025 Policy* (n 14).

[60] 《关于深化国有企业改革的指导意见》 [The Guiding Opinions on Deepening the Reform of State-Owned Enterprises]. (People's Republic of China) The CCP Central Committee and the State Council. 24 August 2015.

[61] Some Chinese SOEs have developed their own minority shareholder protection mechanisms specifically for POE shareholders introduced in the MOR. For detailed discussion in this regard, see Chap. 3 Sect. 3.2.1.2.

[62] 《中国共产党国有企业基层组织工作条例(试行)》 [Trial Regulation on the Work at Primary-level Party Organizations of State-Owned Enterprises]. (People's Republic of China) The CCP Central Committee. 30 December 2019 ('*Trial Regulation*').

interests from non-commercial dealings, the publicly listed status of the target on a recognised exchange, and the investment's size, importance and potential impact.[63]

All of these factors are arrangements that can limit the foreign investor's ability to exert control over the Australian business being acquired. In practice, the adoption of mitigating measures by investors indeed appears to contribute to the grant of FIRB approvals on Chinese SOE investments, as they are frequently included as conditions attached to the approvals. Specifically, the Treasurer typically limits the size of the acquisition by capping the stake that may be acquired to a minority or non-controlling level, for example, in the decisions on Chinese SOE investments in the resources sector. These include Aluminium Corporation China's (China's primary aluminium producer) investment in Australian mining group Rio Tinto (capped at 14.99 percent) and Chinese mining group Sinosteel Corporation's investment in Australian iron ore producer Murchison Metals (capped at 49.9 percent) in 2008.[64] It is not uncommon to find FIRB approvals for Chinese SOE investments in Australian companies with strategic assets conditioned on the targets being operated by the Australian partners or the Chinese SOE's Australian subsidiaries. Some are conditioned on the target company being listed on the Australian Stock Exchange (ASX). For example, Chinese SOE Yanzhou Coal Mining Company's acquisition of Australian coal mining and exploration company Felix Resources in 2009 was initially subject to both conditions of operating rights and commercial objectives (although these conditions were waived subsequently).[65]

It is noteworthy that, due to the broad discretion that the FATA grants the Treasurer in determining whether foreign investment is in line with Australia's national interests, in practice, the FIRB may consider factors beyond the Policy when evaluating FGI investments, such as diversity of ownership of Australian assets, market-based development of the assets, the possible need for local ownership, an acquirer's commitment to divest a portion of its shares over the medium term, Australian-resident board seats and the location of the headquarter and management team, among others.[66]

7.2 The Operations of Australia's Foreign Investment Framework for Chinese SOE Investments

Australia's foreign investment screening system has been criticised for lacking transparency, accountability and predictability,[67] and failing to fully conform to the 2009 *OECD Guidelines for Recipient Country Investment Policies Relating to*

[63] *2025 Policy* (n 14), p. 10.

[64] Swan (2008a, b).

[65] Sherry (2009).

[66] Esplugues (2018), p. 371.

[67] See, e.g., Mendelsohn and Fels (2014).

National Security and the 2016 *G20 Guiding Principles for Global Investment Policymaking*, which outline best practices for foreign investment policy.[68] The criticisms primarily stem from the wide discretion that the FATA grants the Treasurer to decide on the admission of foreign investment without imposing a corresponding transparency requirement.

Although the Treasurer and the FIRB are not required to publish or explain their decisions, some influential investment proposal decisions are published on the Treasury website, with general explanations of the specific decisions and approval conditions sometimes included. Based on publicly available decisions, this section examines how Australia has applied the foreign investment framework to investments made by Chinese SOEs or SOE-affiliated investors and how this application has impacted Chinese SOE investments in Australia's infrastructure and resource sectors, which have received a significant amount of Chinese SOE investments.

7.2.1 How Have Chinese SOE Investments Been Treated Under Australia's Foreign Investment Framework?

According to its Annual Reports, the FIRB makes decisions on over 10,000 investments every year,[69] though only a small portion of the decisions are made public. Most of the published decisions are conditional approvals or rejections, while unconditional approvals are typically not published. Therefore, the Treasury's specially published decisions can be interpreted as an indication of the government's stance on particular types of investment.

Table 7.1 compiles all the decisions on Chinese investments published by the Treasury on its website since 2008. The list contains basic information about the proposed transactions, including investors, types of investors and how the investors have been affected in the latest round of SOE reforms, targets, sectors, entry modes, decision explanations or conditions attached to the approvals. Table 7.1 uses the year 2013, the first year of China's latest round of SOE reforms, as a dividing line to facilitate the analysis of the implications of China's latest round of SOE reforms. In practice, some decisions were made publicly less formally, such as through media releases. These decisions are not included in Table 7.1 because they were not formally published by the Treasury, making them less representative of the government's stance, and they were typically reported without explanations or disclosure

[68] OECD (2009) Recommendation of the Council on Guidelines for Recipient Country Investment Policies Relating to National Security. https://legalinstruments.oecd.org/public/doc/227/227.en.pdf. Accessed 25 Aug 2025; OECD (2016) G20 Guiding Principles for Global Investment Policymaking. https://www.oecd.org/daf/inv/investment-policy/G20-Guiding-Principles-for-Global-Investment-Policymaking.pdf. Accessed 25 Aug 2025.

[69] FIRB (2018) Foreign Investment Review Board Annual Report 2016-17. Report; FIRB (2022) Foreign Investment Review Board Annual Report 2020-21. Report.

Table 7.1 Treasury-published Rejections (Formal and Preliminary) on Chinese Investments Before and After 2013

No	Date	Target	Investor	Investor type	Form of entry	Industry	Decision	Published explanation or conditions attached
1	Jul-08	Midwest Co Ltd.	Sinosteel Corporation	SOEFormer central SOE merged into the central SOE, China Baowu Steel Group Corp., Ltd. (Baowu Group), in 2020.Baowu Group was created by merger in 2016 and was designated as a pilot SCIC in 2018 formal SCIC in 2022.	Acquisition(97%)	Resources(iron ores)	Approval with conditions	Undisclosed.It is the first successful acquisition by a Chinese company of an Australian resources company.
2	Aug-08	Rio Tinto Plc	Aluminium Corporation of China Ltd.	SOESubsidiary of central SOE, Aluminium Corporation of China (Chinalco), which absorbed smaller peers. Chinalco Group was designated as a pilot SCIC in 2018.Listed in Hong Kong and in New York	Acquisition(up to 14.99%)	Resources	Approval with conditions	Restrictions on shareholding: up to 14.99%, further increase in shareholding is subject to new approvalRestrictions on board positions: No board position in Rio Tinto Plc or Rio Tinto Ltd.
3	Sep-08	Murchison Metals Ltd.	Sinosteel Corporation	See above	Acquisition(up to 49.9%)	Resources(iron ores)	Approval with conditions	Restrictions on shareholding: a shareholding of up to 49.9% in Murchison will maintain diversity of ownership within the Mid-West region.

4	Mar-09	Album Resources Private Ltd. /OZ Minerals Ltd.	China Minmetals Non-ferrous Metals Co. Ltd.	SOESubsidiary of central SOE, China Minmetals Corporation (Minmetals), which merged with China Metallurgical Group Corporation and became new Minmetals. Minmetals was designated as a pilot SCIC in 2016.	Full acquisition	Resources (Aluminium)	Resources (Aluminium)	National security grounds: The takeover proposal included Prominent Hill operations, which are situated in the Woomera Prohibited Area in South Australia.
5	Mar-09	Fortescue Metals Group	Hunan Valin Iron and Steel Group	SOEProvincial SOEsSCIC	Acquisition(up to a 17.55%)	Resources (iron ores)	Resources (iron ores)	Conditions mitigating the issue of conflicting interests:Directors nominated by Hunan Valin to Fortescue's board shall:comply with the Code of Conduct of Fortescue.notify conflict of potential interest according to Corporations Act 2001 relating to Fortescue's marketing, sales, customer profiles, price setting and cost structures for pricing and shipping;comply with the information segregation arrangements between the parties.

(continued)

Table 7.1 (continued)

No	Date	Target	Investor	Investor type	Form of entry	Industry	Decision	Published explanation or conditions attached
6	Apr-09	Album Resources Private Ltd./ OZ Minerals Ltd.	China Minmetals Non-ferrous Metals Co. Ltd.	SOESubsidiary of the central SOE, Minmetals (SCIC).(See above)	Full acquisition(Excluding the Prominent Hill mine)	Resources	Resources	Commercial objectives: Operate the acquired mines as a separate business with commercial objectives.Location and nationality requirements: Operate the mines using companies incorporated, headquartered, and managed in Australia under a predominantly Australian management team. Market-based pricing: for all off-take agreements by a sales team headquartered in AustraliaProduction and employment: Maintain or increase production and employment in certain mines; maintain and increase levels of Indigenous employment; reopen and develop certain areas (subject to economic conditions). Legality: Comply with Australian industrial relations laws and honour employee entitlements.

7	May-09	Gindalbie Metals Ltd.	Anshan Iron and Steel Group Corporation	SOECentral SOE, now Ansteel Group Corp., which absorbed Pangang Group Corp. in 2010 and BenXi Steel Group in 2021. Categorised as General Commercial SOE	Acquisition(Up to 36.28%)	Resources (iron ores)	Approval with conditions	Development undertakings: Support to develop the infrastructure (the Oakajee Port and the rail project) within the acquired assets;Future Business in China: Not alter the proposed 50:50 ownership of the pellet plant that JV participants intend to build in China without prior approval of the Australian Government.

(*continued*)

Table 7.1 (continued)

No	Date	Target	Investor	Investor type	Form of entry	Industry	Decision	Published explanation or conditions attached
8	Oct-09	Felix Resources Ltd.	Yanzhou Coal Mining Company Ltd.	SOESubsidiary of provincial SOE, Yankuang Group, which merged into Shandong Energy Group Company Ltd in 2020. Shandong Energy was designated as a SCIC in 2022.	Follow-up full acquisition	Resources (coal and iron ores)	Approval with conditions	Operating right: the Australian mines must be operated through acquirer's Australian subsidiary, Yancoal Australia,Location: Yancoal Australia is headquartered and managed in Australia,Nationality and resident requirements: Yancoal Australia uses a predominately Australian management and sales team; Yancoal Australia and its operating subsidiaries have at least two Australian resident directors, one of whom will be independent from the acquirer; Yancoal Australia's CEO and CFO are Australian residents;Board Meeting location: the majority of Yancoal Australia's board meetings holds in Australia;Listing requirement: list Yancoal Australia on the ASE before 2013 and, by that time;Ownership reduction: the acquirer reduces the ownership of Yancoal Australia to less than 70% before 2013 (condition removed in 2013);Market-based pricing: for coal produced at all Australian mines on arms-length terms

9	Jul-10	IMX Resources Ltd. and Outback Iron Pty Ltd.	Taifeng Yuanchuang International Development Co. Ltd.	POE (purely privately-owned)*Principal business: Real estateMining partner, Sichuan Geological Exploration Bureau.	Acquisition (up to a 19.9% and 49%)	Resources (critical minerals)	Approval with conditions	National security: Taifeng will provide written confirmation from the Department of Defence that a revised agreement has been concluded between the subsidiary of Outback Iron Pty Ltd and the Commonwealth regarding access to the Woomera Prohibited Area (WPA); the Department has no national security concerns over agreed access.

(continued)

Table 7.1 (continued)

No	Date	Target	Investor	Investor type	Form of entry	Industry	Decision	Published explanation or conditions attached
10	Dec-10	Album Resources Private Ltd. /OZ Minerals Ltd.	Minmetals Resources Ltd.	SOEAustralian subsidiary of the Central SOE, Minmentals (SCIC). (See above)		Resources	Approval with conditions	Commercial objectives: Maintain the operation of the former OZ Minerals assets as a separate business with commercial objectives, including the maximisation of product prices;Location and nationality requirements: Operate the mines using companies incorporated, headquartered, and managed in Australia under a predominantly Australian management team. Market-based pricing: for all minerals produced on arms-length terms by a sales team headquartered in Australia;Production and employment: Maintain or increase production and employment in certain mines; Maintain and increase levels of Indigenous employment; reopen and develop certain areas (subject to project feasibility and economic conditions);Legality: Comply with Australian industrial relations laws and honour employee commitments.

11	Mar-12	Gloucester Coal Ltd. / Felix Resources Ltd.	Yancoal Australia Ltd., the subsidiary of Yanzhou Coal Mining Company Ltd.	SOESubsidiary of the provincial SOE, Shandong Energy (SCIC). (See above)	Merger	Resources (coal and iron ores)	Approval with conditions	Listing requirement: List Yancoal Australia on the ASX by the end of 2012Reduce ownership: Yanzhou reduces ownership in Yancoal Australia to less than 70% by the end of 2013; ownership in the Syntech Resources and Premier Coal mines to 70% by the end of 2014 and manage these mines through the listed Yancoal in the interim;Market-based pricing: for coal produced at their Australian mines;Location: Yancoal remains incorporated, headquartered, and managed in Australia;Nationality and residential requirements: Yancoal Australia uses a predominately Australian management and sales team; Yancoal Australia and its operating subsidiaries have at least two Australian resident directors, one of whom will be independent from the acquirer; Yancoal Australia's CEO and CFO are Australian residents;Board Meeting location: the majority of Yancoal Australia's board meetings holds in Australia.

(*continued*)

Table 7.1 (continued)

No	Date	Target	Investor	Investor type	Form of entry	Industry	Decision	Published explanation or conditions attached
12	Aug-12	Asset of Cubbie Station	Shandong RuYi Scientific & Technological Group Co. Ltd. and Lempriere Pty Ltd. (Australia)	POE with State linkages:municipal SOE (Jining Chengtou) acquired a 25.99% stake in 2019 but divested;has CCP committee established in 2003.	Acquisition through consortium (80% owned by Shandong Ruyi)	Agriculture	Approval with conditions	RuYi undertakes to:Reduce ownership: reduce ownership in the Cubbie Group from 80% to 51% to an independent third party (or parties) within three years and seek to list Cubbie Group to achieve this sell down.Restrict board position: board positions decline proportionally with the sell down.The Consortium undertakes to:Operating rights: Cubbie Group is managed and operated by a subsidiary of Lempriere;Resident and Board composition requirement: establish and maintain a Board that consists of six members and includes two Australian-resident independent directors with relevant experience and one director appointed by Lempriere;Employment: maintain all existing employees and the existing arrangements;Legality: comply with all relevant State and Commonwealth rules and regulations;Water entitlement: investigate ways to improve the efficiency of water usage across Cubbie Group's properties, and sell any surplus water allocations through the water market.

2013								
1	Dec-13	Gloucester Coal Ltd./Felix Resources Ltd.	Yanzhou Coal Mining Company	SOESubsidiary of provincial SOE, Shandong Energy (SCIC). See above,		Resources (coal and iron ores)	Change of conditions	Considering the significant challenges for the Australian coal industry, including slowing demand, declining coal prices and a number of mine closures, the Treasurer decided toremove conditions placed on Yanzhou Coal Mining Company that restricted its ownership of Yancoal Australia Limited. So long as Yanzhou continues to own at least 51 per cent of the shares of Yancoal, Yanzhou will ensure Yancoal continues to operate so that it remains solvent. In addition, Yanzhou will extend its existing loans to Yancoal if required, and will support Yancoal's plans to expand the Moolarben open cut mine.

(*continued*)

Table 7.1 (continued)

2013								
2	Dec-13	SP AusNet and SPI (Australia) Assets Pty Ltd. and SPI (Australia) Trust	State Grid Corporation of China	SOECentral SOECategorised as Special Commercial SOE.	Acquisition (19.9% of SP AusNet and 60% of SPI Assets and SPI Trust)	Infrastructure	Approval with conditions	Nationality requirement on Boards: At least 50% of the members to be appointed by State Grid to the Boards of SP AusNet and Jemena must be Australian ordinarily resident in Australia.
3	Apr-15	John Holland Group	China Communications Construction Company	SOECentral SOEDesignated as a pilot SCIC in 2014.	Full acquisition	Infrastructure	Approval without conditions	CCCC is the fourth-largest construction company in the world by revenue, with a presence in over 80 countries.
4	Nov-15	S. Kidman and Co Ltd.	Genius Link Group and Shanghai Pengxin	POE with State linkage:close cooperative relations with major SOEs.participated in flow-out MOR with respect to its subsidiaries in 2022.	Acquisition (80%)	Agriculture	Rejection	National security grounds: Given the size and significance of the total portfolio of Kidman along with the national security issues around access to the WPA, an acquisition by foreign investors only would be contrary to the national interest.

5	Nov-15	99-year lease of TransGrid	Bidders included State Grid and China Southern Grid(the winner is NSW Electricity Networks Consortium)	SOEState Grid: Central SOE, Special, categorised as Special Commercial SOE. Southern Grid became Central SOE in 2022, categorised as Special Commercial SOE.		Infrastructure	Rejection	Indirect disclosure:TransGrid is a critical piece of national infrastructure that underpins the NSW economy. Therefore, the operation and control of its transmission system and telecommunications business must be undertaken solely from within Australia; Electricity supply data and personal information must be accessible and held solely within Australia.
6	Feb-16	The land and assets of the Tasmanian Land Company, including the Van Diemen's Land Company (VDL)	Moon Lake Investments	POE(Investment vehicle solely owned by a Chinese businessman)		Agriculture	Approved with conditions	Standard taxation conditions.Employment: maintain all existing employees on terms no less favourable than the existing arrangements. Further investment undertakings: to undertake a number of investment projects in the VDL farms, which will provide additional economic activity and jobs in Tasmania.Supply impacts: no impact on milk and milk products supplies in Australia.

(continued)

Table 7.1 (continued)

2013								
7	Aug-16	the 99-year lease of Ausgrid	State Grid Corp of China and Hong Kong's Cheung Kong Infrastructure Holdings	SOECentral SOE, Special Commercial Soe (see above).	Acquisition (50.4%)	Infrastructure	Rejection	Indirect disclosure:The Australian government will work closely with NSW to ensure that national security requirements are met under any future transaction process.
8	Apr-16	S. Kidman and Co Limited	Dakang Australia Holdings Pty Ltd and Australian Rural Capital Ltd	POE with State Linkage:Australian subsidiary of Shanghai Pengxin Group, a POE with State linkages, (see above).	Acquisition through consortium (80%)	Agriculture	Preliminary rejection	Same asabove: The size and significance of the Kidman portfolio.

9	Dec-16	S. Kidman and Co Limited	Australian Outback Beef Pty Ltd (67% owned by Hancock Beef Pty Ltd and 33% held by Shanghai CRED Real Estate Stock Co. Ltd	POE (purely privately-owned)*Principal business in real estate	Full acquisition (except the Anna Creek and its outstation)	Agriculture	Approval with conditions	Operating rights: Australian-owned Hancock will control the Board and day-to-day operation of the business. Location and nationality: Kidman will remain majority Australian owned and remain an Australian incorporated company headquartered in Australia.*Previous security concerns resulting in earlier rejections were mitigated by excision of Anna Creek, part of which is located in the WPA, from the sale, to be acquired by Williams Family (Australia).

(*continued*)

Table 7.1 (continued)

2013								
10	Nov-19	Bellamy's Australia Ltd	China Mengniu Dairy Company Ltd.	SOEPrimary shareholder is central SOE, China National Oils, Foodstuffs and Cereals Co. (COFCO) in 2009. COFCO was designated as a pilot SCIC in 2014. Directors with COFCO backgrounds dominated the board of Mengniu from 2021.	Full acquisition	Agriculture	Approval with conditions	Resident and Nationality requirements: a predominantly Australian resident citizen Board in Bellamy's;Location: Bellamy's remains headquartered in Australia for at least ten years;Future investment undertaking: an investment of at least $12 million in establishing or improving infant milk formula processing facilities in Victoria.
11	Aug-20	Northern Minerals Ltd	Baogang Group Investment (Australia) Pty Ltd.	SOEAustralian subsidiary of Central SOE, Baowu Group (see above).	Acquisition (11.1%)	Resources (rare earth)	Rejection	Undisclosed (not in the national interest)
12	Aug-20	AVZ Minerals	Yibin Tianyi Lithium Industry	POE with State linkage:Established by POEs, Canmax Technologies Co. Ltd. (75%) and Contemporary Amperex Technology Co. Ltd. (CATL) (25%), in 2018.CATL has close strategic relations with SOEs and participated in flow-out MOR in 2022.	Acquisition (11.77%)	Resources (critical minerals)	Rejection	Undisclosed (not in the national interest)

13	Aug-20	Lion-Dairy and Drinks Pty Ltd	China Mengniu Dairy Company Ltd.	SOESubsidiary of Central SOE, COFCO (SCIC) (see above).	Full acquisition	Agriculture	Preliminary Rejection	Undisclosed (not in the national interest)The treasury stated that the rejection is not country specific. It's about the individual facts around a particular case.
14	Jan-21	ProBuild	China State Construction Engineering Corporation (CCEC)	SOECentral SOECategorised as General Commercial SOEWith wide strategic cooperative relations with provincial governments and major SOEs.Executives with political connection	Full acquisition	Infrastructure	Rejection	UndisclosedNational security concerns that the deal could give foreignintelligence services access to information about critical infrastructure, including Victoria's police headquarters' design and vaccine laboratories.

of conditions attached. However, they are included in the discussion below as significant factual evidence.

It can be assumed that the Treasury's published decisions indicate high-level concerns from the Australian government with regard to certain types of foreign investment. A quick count of decisions listed in Table 7.1 suggests that in terms of the type of investors, 19 out of 26 decisions responded to applications from Chinese SOEs. The 19 SOE decisions included 12 conditional approvals, 6 (preliminary) rejections and 1 decision on condition changes. There are two possible explanations for the high proportion of decisions concerning SOEs. First, all investment proposals from Chinese SOEs (which fall under the definition of FGI) are subject to review under the Australian foreign investment framework, whereas only POE investments that satisfy the review triggering events are subject to review. Secondly, the Australian government is concerned more about Chinese SOE investors and the types of investment proposals made by them than about Chinese POE investors.

Before 2013, 11 out of 12 published decisions were in the resources sector. This is a reflection of the fact that Chinese investments in Australia were heavily resource-intensive at the time.[70] After 2013, however, the sectors in which published decisions on Chinese investment proposals were made have diversified and include 6 in agriculture (3 in relation to a proposed acquisition of the same target, Kidman Station), 5 in infrastructure and only 3 in resources. This indicates the increasing sectoral diversity of Chinese investment in Australia and a broadening of Australia's concerns regarding Chinese investments in various industries. The China Global Investment Tracker, the only publicly accessible dataset launched by the American Enterprise Institute and the Heritage Foundation that compiles Chinese outbound investment valued at over USD 100 million (mega investment) from 2005, confirms the increasing diversity of Chinese investment in Australia.[71] According to the dataset, China investors made a total of 45 mega (investment valued more than USD 100 million) investments in Australia across five sectors between 2008 and 2012, with the energy sector accounting for 44 percent and the metals sector for 38 percent.[72] From 2013 to 2022, however, Australia received 122 mega investments from Chinese investors across 11 sectors, with 28 percent in the real estate sector, 24 percent in the energy sector, 14 percent in the metals sector and 11 percent in the health sector.[73]

As explained above, under the Australian foreign investment framework, FGIs are subject to mandatory pre-notification requirements and review pursuant to the national interest test for acquisition and green-field investments. However, all the published decisions were made on acquisitions (except Yancoal Australia's acquisition of Gloucester Coal in 2012), suggesting that the Australian government is more

[70] KPMG and USYD (2024), p. 5.

[71] The American Enterprise Institute and the Heritage Foundation (2025) China Global Investment Tracker. https://www.aei.org/china-global-investment-tracker/. Accessed 25 Aug 2025.

[72] Ibid. The five sectors include metals, energy, real estate, transport, agriculture and finance.

[73] Ibid. The 11 sectors include metals, energy, real estate, finance, logistics, agriculture, tourism, health, utilities, entertainment and transport.

concerned about acquisition as a means of entry for Chinese investments than with green-field investment, which is more welcomed because it brings in new capital and jobs to the local community.

In terms of decision types, most of the published decisions (16 of 26) are approvals containing conditions. The conditions imposed by the Treasurer on the investors were designed to ensure that the specific investment could provide the claimed economic benefits to regional Australia and the broader community. The conditions typically include commitments to maintain or increase employment, ensure the targets' continuous presence in Australia and limitations on foreign control (through imposing conditions in relation to foreign ownership, location, listing status, legal compliance, operating rights, the composition of the Board, management team and sales team, etc.); ensure investors' future development or investment projects, and mitigate the potential conflict of interests when the acquirer is also the target's major customer, as is typical for Chinese investments in resources (through imposing conditions in relation to the commercial basis of sales, market pricing requirement, information barriers and a Code of Conduct).

Despite their wide discretion to reject foreign investment without the need to explain, successive Treasurers have only rarely rejected investment proposals.[74] According to the FIRB Annual Reports, from 2013 to 2021, only 15 investment proposals were rejected in total.[75] Therefore, it can be safely assumed that the rejection of a proposal is a sign of high-level concern from the Australian government. Table 7.1 reveals that 8 of the 15 rejection decisions were made in respect of proposed Chinese investments. Four of these were made in 2020, indicating that the Australian government's concerns regarding Chinese investments have significantly risen.

In terms of the implications of China's latest round of SOE reforms, as shown in Table 7.1, virtually all the SOE investors listed or their parent companies have been significantly affected and subjected to tighter political control by the Chinese government or the CCP. These changes have happened mainly in three ways (a) inter-SOE mergers (Sinosteel merged into Baowu Group; Yankuang merged into Shandong Energy; Chinalco, Anshan Iron and Steel Group have merged (now Ansteel Group); China Minmetals, State Grid and China Southern Grid themselves are national champions that have absorbed smaller SOE peers in the same or related industries); (b) SOEs have been designated as SCICs to function as a professional operator of State-owned capital and to undertake the policy mission of serving national strategies when making investments. (Baowu Group; Chinalco; China Minmetals; Hunan Valin Iron and Steel Group (Hunan Valin);[76] Shandong Energy;

[74] Bath (2012), pp. 5–34.

[75] FIRB (2018) Foreign Investment Review Board Annual Report 2016-17. Report; FIRB (2022) Foreign Investment Review Board Annual Report 2020-21. Report.

[76] 《国务院关于推进国有资本投资、运营公司改革试点的实施意见》 [Opinions of The State Council on the Implementation of the Pilot Reform of State-Owned Capital Investment and Operation Companies]. (People's Republic of China) The State Council. 30 July 2018 ('*Opinions on SCIOs*').

China Communications Construction Company (CCCC); China National Oils, Foodstuffs and Cereals Corporation (COFCO)); (c) SOEs have been classified in the MOR as 'Special Commercial SOEs' with policy tasks to serve national policy goals, such as safeguarding national security in operations (State Grid and China Southern Grid).

China's latest round of SOE reforms also affect POEs. 4 out of 7 POE investors listed in Table 7.1 have built up political connections in the reforms through: (a) participating in flow-in or flow-out MOR (Shanghai Pengxin, Dakang Australia and Yibin Tianyi Lithium); (b) concluding strategic partnership agreements with major SOEs or governments at various levels (Shanghai Pengxin); and (c) establishing a CCP committee within its governance structure (Shandong RuYi). Among the other 3 POE investors, Shanghai CRED Real Estate and Taifeng Yuanchuang are in the real estate sector. Chinese SOEs have been required to withdraw from real estate in the State economy restructuring programs promoted in the latest round of SOE reforms, which may explain why they are not affected by the reforms.

Notably, almost all of the changes to Chinese investors due to the SOE reforms happened after the FIRB's decision on the relevant investments, demonstrating how significantly the ongoing SOE reforms have impacted established Chinese investments in Australia, let alone future investments.

Although the 2021 comprehensive legislative reforms to Australia's foreign investment framework highlighted the prominence of national security concerns regarding foreign investment, it seems that the Australian government has always been reluctant to disclose specific national security grounds unless the reasons are rather obvious, such as being directly related to defence and military issues. As shown in Table 7.1, only 4 published decisions (1 before 2013 and 3 after 2013) explicitly cited national security explanations, and they were all related to access to the Woomera Prohibited Area (WPA), Australia's mass weapons range. The persistent secrecy on national security grounds for investment decisions is unsurprising, as it is standard practice in the world to keep national security-related information confidential.[77]

As noted above, most of the Treasurer's published decisions on Chinese investments were in the resources sector (14 decisions in total), suggesting the prominence of concerns from the various Australian governments regarding growing Chinese influence over Australia's resources. Australia's resources sector is persistently a desirable investment target for Chinese SOEs. China Global Investment Tracker indicates that between 2008 and 2022, SOEs were responsible for 89 of the 95 mega investments from China in Australia's metals sector and 92 of the 98 mega investments in the energy sector.[78] According to the KPMG and the USYD's 2024 Report on Chinese Investment in Australia, mining and renewable energy accounted for 98 percent of the total Chinese investment in Australia for 2023.[79] The largest

[77] Knight and Voon (2020), pp. 104–139.

[78] The American Enterprise Institute and the Heritage Foundation (n 71).

[79] KPMG and USYD (2024), pp. 4, 5.

Chinese investment was made by Chinese SOE Baowu Group to form a joint venture with Rio Tinto for the development of the Western Range iron ore project in Western Australia.[80]

In addition, as shown in Table 7.1, the published five decisions in infrastructure sector were all on bids from SOEs and given after 2013, with two conditional approvals and three rejections. This reflects Australian government's rising concerns over Chinese SOEs' involvement in Australian infrastructure assets Apparently, Australia is not alone in this regard, as the escalating Sino-Western tensions have led to a rise in the controversy surrounding Chinese SOE infrastructure investments in developed countries due to potential security risks. In 2021, Canada ordered Chinese telecom SOE China Mobile to divest its stake in a Canadian subsidiary over national security concerns pursuant to the *Investment Canada Act*.[81] In 2022, the UK ordered Chinese SOE CGN to relinquish its stake in Sizewell C power station to regain the government control over the nuclear power infrastructure.[82]

Given Chinese SOEs' persistent interest in Australian resource sector and Australia's growing concerns over Chinese SOE involvement in infrastructure, the following sub-sections provide in-depth analyses of how Australia's foreign investment framework has been applied to Chinese SOE investments in critical minerals and energy resources sectors and the infrastructure sector, as well as the implications of the latest round of SOE reforms on the investments in these sectors.

7.2.2 Chinese SOE Investments in Australia's Resources Sector

Historically, Chinese investments in Australia (and elsewhere) were focused on resources due both to Australia's abundant natural resources and to China's massive demand for resources to fuel its rapid industrialization. Similar to the infrastructure sector, the resources sector in China falls under government-defined critical industries dominated by a handful of State-owned mining giants. Thus, most Chinese investors in Australian resources are central SOEs, large local SOEs (which refer to SOEs owned by the Chinese local governments), or their core subsidiaries. Among the 11 resources investors listed in Table 7.1, only Taifeng Yuanchuang (which invested in IMX Resources and Outback Iron in 2010) and

---

[80] Ibid.

[81] China Mobile applied for a judicial review of the divestment order before the Federal Court of Canada but failed in the court battle. Jim Bronskill (2021) Chinese Telecom Firm Loses Court Battle Against Order to Divest Canadian Subsidiary. National Post. https://nationalpost.com/news/canada/chinese-controlled-firm-loses-court-bid-to-pause-ottawas-divestment-order. Accessed 25 Aug 2025.

[82] Shapps and Hunt (2022).

Yibin Tianyi Lithium Industry (Yibin Tianyi) (which proposed to invest in AVZ Minerals in 2020) are POEs. Hunan Valin, Yanzhou Coal Mining and its subsidiary Yancoal Australia are under provincial SOEs, while the remaining 6 are under central SOEs.

The boom in Chinese investment in the mining industry in Australia in 2008 and 2009 sparked heated debates in Australia regarding the growing Chinese influence in the country's resources sector.[83] In 2009, the Australian Senate Economics References Committee released a report on foreign SOE investments, summarising the major concerns regarding major Chinese SOE investments in resources.[84] The concerns centred on the impact on competition and the potentially divided loyalties of directors nominated by Chinese SOE investors serving on the boards of Australian targets.[85] Even though Australia experienced a boom of investments from the US and Japan in the resources sector in the mid-1960s and 1970s, which also sparked economic nationalism and sentiment,[86] intensive investments by SOEs from a non-allied country were especially sensitive.

Chinese investments in the Australian resources sector can be roughly divided into those seeking traditional mining resources and those seeking 'critical minerals', a generic term now widely used by countries to refer to metallic and non-metallic minerals that are indispensable for their technological advances and economic growth, such as lithium, nickel and rare earths.[87]

Chinese investments in traditional mineral resources appear to cause the Australian government fewer concerns than investments in critical minerals. In addition to the investments in coal and iron ores approved prior to 2013 listed in Table 7.1, the FIRB has approved a series of acquisition proposals from Chinese SOEs in traditional minerals over the past few years, such as Yancoal's acquisition of Rio Tinto's coal assets (Coal & Allied) in 2017,[88] and Sinosteel Corporation's acquisition of Australian Crosslands Resources' Oakajee mine, port and rail project in Western Australia in 2019.[89] This stance may be largely attributable to the widely recognised benefits of foreign investment in assisting the development of Australia's mineral reserves, which typically entails enormous up-front costs.[90] As a result of this stance, more than 90 percent of Australian mining projects at the time had some

[83] Mendelsohn and Fels (2014), p. 61; KPMG and USYD (2024), p. 8.

[84] Economic References Committee (n 9).

[85] Ibid.

[86] Ibid. p. 64; Thirlwell (2008).

[87] See, e.g., Department of Industry, Science and Resources (2023) Australia's Critical Minerals List. https://www.industry.gov.au/publications/australias-critical-minerals-list. Accessed 25 Aug 2025.

[88] Rio Tinto (2017) Rio Tinto Completes Divestment of Coal & Allied Industries Limited for $2.69 Billion. https://www.riotinto.com/en/news/releases/2017/coal-and-allied-divestment-completed. Accessed 25 Aug 2025.

[89] Scarr (2019).

[90] Economic References Committee (n 9), p. 67; 'Discussion Paper on Foreign Investment and State- owned Enterprises: Managing the Risks to Maximise the Benefits' (n 41), p. 7.

level of foreign ownership, according to a 2016 Treasury paper on foreign investment in Australia.[91]

Despite a relative openness to Chinese SOE investments in traditional minerals, the conditions attached to approvals in Table 7.1 indicate that the Australian government is now attempting to prevent further loss of control over its strategic minerals to Chinese interests. Successive Treasurers have imposed conditions such as restricting ownership to a minority or non-controlling level (for the acquisitions of Rio Tinto,[92] Murchison Metals,[93] Fortescue Metals,[94] Gindalbie Metals,[95] IMX Resources and Outback Iron[96]), requiring the future reduction of Chinese ownership (for Yancoal Australia in its investments in Gloucester Coal Limited/Felix Resources),[97] and requiring the target mines to be operated by the investor's Australian subsidiary listed on the ASX (for Yanzhou Coal Mining's acquisition of Felix Resources).[98]

Another major concern that Chinese resource investments raise in Australia is the possibility of anti-competitive pricing and vertical integration. This could occur when the Chinese mining SOE is a major customer of the Australian mineral supplier it is acquiring, as the investor, after the acquisition, has the incentive to manipulate prices to secure the target's supplies for its own gain. This is neither a hypothetical presumption nor an unusual case. China is a significant market for Australian mineral exports, accounting for more than 80 percent of iron ore exports and a third of liquefied natural gas exports in 2018.[99] For example, in the investment proposals listed in Table 7.1, China's Hunan Valin was a major customer of its Australian target, Fortescue Metals.[100] In this case, special conditions may be imposed to mitigate the conflict of interests, such as regulating the behaviour of directors appointed by the investors (in relation to Hunan Valin's acquisition of Fortescue Metals),[101] requiring the targets to be operated for commercial objectives and requiring market-based pricing for minerals produced by the targets by Australian sale teams (for Minmetals' acquisition of Album Resources/OZ Minerals and Yanzhou Coal Mining's investment in Gloucester Coal/Felix Resources).[102]

Chinese investments in Australia's critical minerals, however, are of higher sensitivity. The Australian government has identified 26 critical minerals based on

[91] Foreign Investment and Trade Policy Division (2016) Foreign Investment into Australia. Treasury. Working Paper, p. 6.

[92] Swan (2008a).

[93] Swan (2008b).

[94] Swan (2009a).

[95] Swan (2009b).

[96] Swan (2010).

[97] Swan (2012).

[98] Sherry (2009).

[99] Gaetjens (2018) Chinese Investment and Australia Forum. Speech.

[100] Swan (2009a).

[101] Ibid.

[102] Sherry (2009); Swan (2010).

assessing Australia's geographic endowment, potential with global needs, and supply risks.[103] Due to the scarcity of these minerals and their strategic importance for Australia's sustainable development, securing the supply of these minerals has become a matter of national interests and security. Though critical minerals are not explicitly linked to the national security test under Australia's foreign investment framework, the FIRB's Guidance Note indicates foreign investment in critical minerals may raise national security risks due to the fact that critical minerals are vulnerable to supply chain manipulation and disruption that could jeopardise Australia's national security.[104]

Chinese acquisitions of Australia's critical minerals mines are certain to cause concerns in Canberra because China is already the world's primary geographic source for many critical minerals owing to its natural abundance, processing capacity and, more importantly, its global acquisitions in the past decades. As of August 2023, China controls the production and supply of 98 percent of global dysprosium, and more than 85 percent of the 17 rare earths as a group.[105] The operations of the foreign investment framework has reflected the FIRB's primary concern about Chinese investments in critical minerals and the continued loss of control over strategic natural resources to China. In 2009, the FIRB intervened in Chinese central SOE China Nonferrous Metal Mining Group's proposed acquisition of Australian rare-earths mining company Lynas, suggesting that it would require that the investor reduce its stake and proportion of board seats to less than 50 percent of each. The requirement led to the collapse of the deal.[106] In contrast, in 2017, the then-Treasurer approved two acquisition proposals from Chinese SOEs of minority stakes in Australian critical mineral producers: Sinomine Resource Group's acquisition of an 11.4 percent stake in Prospect Resources and Great Wall Motor Company's acquisition of a 3.5 percent stake in Pilbara Minerals.[107]

However, as Table 7.1 shows, in August 2020, the Treasurer rejected Chinese Baogang Group's bid for an 11.1 percent of stake in Northern Minerals, a producer of heavy rare earth element dysprosium and Yibin Tianyi's bids to acquire an 11.77 percent of stake in AVZ Minerals, the majority owner of the Manono Lithium and Tin Project in Congo. (The project is to mine one of the world's largest and highest-grade hard rock lithium resources deposits). These rejections send a signal that Australia is committed to protecting its critical mineral deposits from further loss to China. The decisions were published without explanation, but the rationale is clear: China already dominates the global supplies of the minerals produced by the targets

[103] Geoscience Australia (2025) Critical Minerals at Geoscience Australia. https://www.ga.gov.au/scientific-topics/minerals/critical-minerals. Accessed 25 Aug 2025.

[104] *Guidance 8* (n 57), p. 12.

[105] China Power Team (2021) Does China Pose a Threat to Global Rare Earth Supply Chains? https://chinapower.csis.org/china-rare-earths/. Accessed 25 Aug 2025.

[106] Taylor (2009) China Again Fails in Bid for Australian Resources. Reuters. https://www.reuters.com/article/us-australia-china-idUKTRE58N1HK20090924. Accessed 25 Aug 2025.

[107] Both deals allowed Chinese investors to secure offtake agreements for fixed amounts of mineral concentrate from the respective mine projects.

(ie dysprosium and lithium),[108] and approving the deals would, therefore, potentially escalate Australia's dependency on China and the consequent exposure to deliberate supply disruptions by the Chinese government.

However, due to the fact that the majority of Chinese investors are from central or major local SOEs which have undergone inter-SOE consolidation in the latest round of SOE reforms, the Australian government's efforts to mitigate the concerns about losing strategic resources to China through imposing various conditions to limit the extension of Chinese influence over Australian targets may be largely ineffective.

The investors in Table 7.1 are typical examples: Sinosteel, the acquirer of Australian iron ore producers Midwest and Murchison Metals, was a central SOE at the time the acquisitions were approved, but it merged into Baowu Group in 2020 under the direction of the Chinese government. In 2020, Baowu Group's Australian subsidiary, Baogang Group Investment, proposed to acquire a minority stake in another Australian mining company, Northern Minerals (rejected). If the transaction had been approved, three Australian mines would have fallen under the influence of a single Chinese mining behemoth owned directly by Beijing. More importantly, in 2018, Baowu Group was designated as a SCIC, signifying that it no longer primarily serves commercial objectives but instead national policy objectives.

In addition, inter-SOE consolidation can also be achieved through contract-based strategic cooperative partnerships that have been widely established between major SOEs in the latest round of SOE reforms. Taking investors listed in Table 7.1 as examples: Ansteel Group (previously Anshan Iron and Steel Group, which holds a minority stake in Australia's Gindalbie Metals) signed strategic Cooperation Agreements with Chinalco (the subsidiary of which Aluminium Corporation of China, invested in Rio Tinto) and Minmetals (which acquired Album Resources Private Ltd/OZ Minerals) in 2016 and 2017 respectively.[109] Chinalco and Baowu Group are establishing a joint venture to mine Simandou, the world's largest untapped high-grade iron ore deposit in Guinea. In addition, the strengthened personnel rotation mechanisms among major SOEs in the latest round of SOE reforms further enhance the inter-SOE connections. For example, the former CEO of Chinalco, Lin Yao, was the CEO of Ansteel before 2019.[110]

With the advance of China's ongoing SOE reforms, Chinese State-owned mining giants have become increasingly interconnected and entangled in a

[108] China Power Team (n 105).

[109] The Central SASAC (2015) 《鞍钢集团与中国五矿全面深化战略合作》 [Anshan Iron & Steel Group and China Minmetals Deepen Strategic Co-operation in a Comprehensive Manner]. http://www.sasac.gov.cn/n2588025/n2588124/c3812939/content.html. Accessed 25 Aug 2025; Chinamining (2017) 《鞍钢与中铝公司加强交流合作》 [Anshan Iron & Steel and Chinalco Intensify Their Partnership]. https://zlzb.chinalco.com.cn/xwzx/gsyw/202103/t20210301_76761.html. Accessed 25 Aug 2025.

[110] Reuters (2019) China's Chinalco Names Ansteel Boss as its New Chairman. Nasdaq. https://www.nasdaq.com/articles/chinas-chinalco-names-ansteel-boss-as-its-new-chairman-2019-10-24. Accessed 25 Aug 2025.

government-controlled net, thus collectively pursuing the same policy goals at the government's direction. These strengthened political inter-connections, however, could substantially undermine the effectiveness of the Treasurer's restrictions on individual Chinese resources investment in limiting Chinese influence over Australian mining operations.

7.2.3 *Chinese SOE Investments in Australia's Infrastructure Sector*

Before 2015, Chinese SOE investors had relatively unfettered access to Australian infrastructure. For example, before the Treasurer blocked China's State-owned power giant State Grid from acquiring a majority stake in Australia's largest electricity distributor, Ausgrid, in 2016, the enterprise had acquired controlling stakes in infrastructure assets across Australia, including 60 percent of Jemena, an energy company that owns and operates vast electricity, gas and water transportation assets across the east coast, 50 percent of ACTEW AGL, the electricity and gas provider for Canberra and 46.56 percent of ElectraNet, an electricity transmission company in South Australia.[111]

Australia's previously welcoming stance towards Chinese SOE infrastructure investments was shaped by the period of relative optimism in Australian-China relations signalled by the 2015 conclusion of the current ChAFTA, reflecting the close economic and trade relationship between the two countries. However, the government's stance has since shifted. Since 2015, the Treasurer of the time has rejected three acquisition proposals made by Chinese SOEs in the infrastructure sector, as shown in Table 7.1. These include the bids from State Grid and China Southern Grid for a 99-year lease of TransGrid, the New South Wales (NSW) electricity transmission network,[112] in 2015; State Grid's bid for the 99-year lease of Ausgrid, the NSW electricity distribution network, in 2016,[113] and China State Construction Engineering Corporation (CSCEC) 's bid to acquire ProBuild, one of Australia's largest construction companies, in 2021.[114]

Despite its refusal to disclose specific security reasons for the rejection decisions, the Australian government's concerns about Chinese infrastructure investments centre primarily on potential national security risks. In the Treasury's published decision approving NSW Electricity Networks Consortium to acquire TransGrid, the Treasurer explained that TransGrid was such a critical national

[111] Coorey (2016) Scott Morrison Says Ausgrid Sale to Chinese 'Contrary to the National Interest'. Financial Review. https://www.afr.com/politics/scott-morrison-says-ausgrid-sale-to-chinese-contrary-to-the-national-interest-20160811-gqptc1. Accessed 25 Aug 2025.

[112] Morrison (2015).

[113] Morrison (2016).

[114] Frydenberg (2021).

infrastructure that operation, control and access to its data must be held solely within Australia.[115] In the Ausgrid decision, the Treasurer stated that State Grid's investment proposal did not meet national security requirements.[116]

China's latest round of SOE reforms warrants Australia's increased vigilance against Chinese infrastructure investments. The infrastructure sector in China itself falls within the category of 'critical industries' that have been monopolised by a small number of central SOEs (which refer to SOEs directly owned and supervised by the Chinese central government) as a result of the ongoing State economy restructuring programs. As a result, most Chinese investors interested in Australian infrastructure are central SOEs or their core subsidiaries. This is corroborated by the fact that Chinese central SOEs, including State Grid, China Southern Grid, CCCC and CSCEC, initiated all infrastructure investments listed in Table 7.1.

In the latest round of SOE reforms, Chinese central SOEs in critical industries are being transformed to be subject to tightened political control. Taking the investors listed in Table 7.1 as examples, China's duopoly State power grids, State Grid and China Southern Grid have been classified as 'Special Commercial' in the MOR. This means that they are required by the Chinese government to primarily serve policy missions such as implementing national strategies, protecting national security and supporting the national economy rather than seeking profits.[117] In 2015, as noted above, the FIRB granted China's CCCC unconditional approval to acquire Australia's leading infrastructure and construction company, John Holland.[118] In 2014, the Chinese central government designated CCCC as a SCIC despite its status as the world's leading infrastructure construction company. As a SCIC, CCCC is tasked with making investments in support of major national policies, such as the *Belt and Road Initiative* and *Made in China 2025 Development Initiative*, and with acting at the direction of the government to achieve specific goals, such as promoting technological development or ensuring national security.[119]

In addition, in the latest round of SOE reforms, State-owned infrastructure monopolies are forming expansive strategic alliances with each other, local governments and State-affiliated entities (including military-related entities). For example, CCCC's strategic cooperative partners include State Grid, China South Grid and China Electronics Technology Group, which is a central SOE founded with the aim of leveraging civilian electronics for the benefit of the People's Liberation Army;[120]

---

115 Morrison (2015).

116 Morrison (2016).

117 《关于国有企业功能界定与分类的指导意见》 [Guiding Opinions on the Definition and Classification of Functions of State-Owned Enterprises]. (People's Republic of China) SASAC, MOF and NDRC. 7 December 2015. For detailed discussion regarding the SOE classification in China's mixed ownership reform, see Chap. 3 Sect. 3.1.

118 Hockey (2015).

119 *Opinions on SCIOs* (n 76).

120 Xinhua Net (2021) 《国家电网公司与中建集团举行合资公司成立云揭牌仪式》 [State Grid Corporation and China Construction Group Hold Online Opening Ceremony for Establishment of Joint Venture Company]', http://www.xinhuanet.com/energy/2021-01/15/c_1126986863.htm.

China South Grid's supply chain partners include the Ministry of Industry and Information Technology (MIIT), China General Nuclear Power Group, which is a Chinese State-owned energy corporation with military linkages, and Huawei.[121] Even though it is not classified as a 'Special Commercial SOE' nor designated as an SCIC in the ongoing SOE reforms, CSCEC has established a vast network of partnerships in recent years with local governments, including the governments of Nanjing, Chongqing and Xi'an.[122] The increasingly dense connections between Chinese infrastructure SOEs and sensitive State-affiliated entities could significantly amplify the national security risks associated with their investments in Australian infrastructure.

The Australian government has recognised the significance of infrastructure in relation to the protection of national security. Although the national security test newly introduced in the foreign investment framework has no additional effect on FGI investments in the pre-establishment phase (due to its integration into the national interest test), the creation of a separate test in cases where the national interest review is not applicable is intended in part to address rising security concerns regarding foreign investment in infrastructure. According to the amended FATA, the triggering events for pre-establishment national security review include a proposed foreign acquisition of a direct interest in or establishment of 'critical infrastructure' defined by the SOCI Act.[123] In the 2021 amendment to the SOCI Act, the coverage of critical infrastructure under the law was significantly expanded from four to eleven sectors and twenty-two asset classes, including communications, data storage or processing, defence, energy, financial services and markets, food and grocery, health care and medical, higher education and research, space technology, transportation, water and sewerage.[124] The scope of the FIRB national security review has been correspondingly enlarged. The Australian government also established the Cyber and Infrastructure Security Centre in 2021 to assist in managing the complex and evolving national security risks to Australia's critical infrastructure, including advising on national security risk assessments on critical infrastructure investments in the FIRB review.[125]

Accessed 25 Aug 2025; China State Construction (2022) 《中建集团与南方电网签署战略合作协议》 [China Construction Group and Southern Power Grid Sign Strategic Co-operation Agreement]. https://www.cscec.com/xwzx_new/gsyw_new/202201/3472396.html. Accessed 25 Aug 2025.

[121] 李语, 杨彬 [Li Yu and Yang Bin] (2022) 《南方电网公司第二届供应链合作伙伴大会在广州举行》 [The Southern Power Grid Corporation's Second Supply Chain Partner Conference was Held in Guangzhou]. People. http://gd.people.com.cn/n2/2022/0729/c123932-40059740.html. Accessed 25 Aug 2025.

[122] See, e.g., The People's Government of Nanjing (2023) 《市政府与中国交建签署战略合作协议》 [Municipal Government and CCCC Sign a Strategic Cooperation Agreement]. https://www.nanjing.gov.cn/njxx/202303/t20230310_3858944.html. Accessed 25 Aug 2025.

[123] *2025 Policy* (n 14), p. 3.

[124] *Security Legislation Amendment (Critical Infrastructure) Bill 2021* (Cth).

[125] Australian Government Department of Home Affairs (2025) Cyber and Infrastructure Security Centre. https://www.cisc.gov.au/. Accessed 25 Aug 2025.

Due to Australia's increased focus on security concerns regarding critical infrastructure and enhanced legislative protections, obtaining approval to invest in Australia's critical infrastructure has become more difficult for Chinese SOE investors. In addition, the amended SOCI Act also allows the Federal Government to intervene in any transactions involving infrastructure that pose threats to national security. The retrospective national security review mechanisms under the amended SOCI Act and the FATA provide additional protection for Australian critical infrastructure. In 2021, the National Security Committee of the Cabinet commissioned a Department of Defence review under the FATA to reassess the potential national security risks of China's Landbridge's lease of the Port of Darwin.[126] In 2022, Prime Minister Anthony Albanese launched the second security review of the 99-year lease of the Port of Darwin under the SOCI Act (as well as other legislations such as the Defence Act 1903) as committed in the 2022 election.[127] Though Landbridge is a POE, and both the retrospective reviews concluded that there was no national security justification for unravelling the deal, the reviews highlights the possibility that the Australian government could strip Chinese SOE investors of approved infrastructure-related contracts on national security grounds under the SOCI Act or FATA, which increases uncertainty surrounding Chinese SOEs' infrastructure investments in Australia.

7.3 How Can We Better Address Chinese SOEs in Investment Screening?

With the development of society, technologies and the global geopolitical landscape for more than a decade and the progress of the China's SOE reforms, the range and severity of concerns that Chinese SOE investments trigger in Australia have increased dramatically. The above analyses demonstrate that in the context of China's most recent round of SOE reforms, Australia's strengthened foreign investment framework and practical applications are insufficient to address the threats posed by investments from Chinese SOEs or their affiliated investors to Australia's national interest or security. To better address investments from Chinese SOEs or their affiliates that are undergoing changes due to the latest round of SOE reforms, it is recommended that the FIRB and the Treasurer consider the following additional factors when evaluating investments proposed or made by Chinese investors.

---

[126] Zu (2022), pp. 467–483.

[127] Department of the Prime Minister and Cabinet (2023) Review – Port of Darwin lease.

7.3.1 Ownership Structure of Chinese POE Investors

As noted in Sect. 7.1, the FATR defines FGI in a way that includes all foreign government agencies, SOEs, SWFs and other entities with substantial ownership ties to a foreign government (with an interest of at least 20 percent) or governments (an aggregate interest of at least 40 percent).[128] This FGI definition is solely based on ownership and is not particularly broad. For instance, it is narrower than the scope of 'government-controlled enterprises' under the UNCTAD World Investment Report, which sets the threshold for control of an enterprise as 10 percent or more of the voting power, so any enterprise in which a government holds no less than a 10 percent stake is considered as government controlled.[129]

The FATR's FGI definition may pose challenges when applied to capture Chinese government-related investments due to its solely ownership-based threshold. The implementation of flow-in MOR in the ongoing SOE reforms rarely results in a significant SOE reducing its State ownership to less than 20 percent, with the exception of those that are on the verge of insolvency or suffer from severe overcapacity.[130]

However, the participation of POEs in flow-in MOR necessitates a closer examination of the political ties of Chinese POE investors. As noted above, the MOR is carried out at the direction of the government. Each participant in the POE is selected by the SOE or its respective government owners with the objective of establishing a business partnership between the parties.[131] Using Yibin Tianyi as an example, the Chinese POE proposed acquiring Australian mining company AVZ Minerals in 2020 (rejected). As shown in Table 7.1, Yibin Tianyi is owned by two Chinese POEs: 75 percent by Canmax Technologies and 25 percent by Contemporary Amperex Technology (CATL). In 2022, CATL participated in flow-in MOR by acquiring a 26 percent of stake in China's largest molybdenum producer, CMOC Group, a municipal SOE.[132] Despite its significant shareholding, CATL has pledged not to seek control of CMOC Group, which is a typical practice in the implementation of flow-in MOR.[133] This ownership connection has strengthened CATL and CMOC Group's existing cooperative relationship, as the two companies collaborate in international mining operations, such as the Kisanfu copper-cobalt mine in Congo. In addition, CATL's political connections are reflected in its strategic partnerships with the Shanghai municipal government and major SOEs such as BAIC

[128] FATR (n 13) s. 17.

[129] UNCTAD (2022) Methodology Note-World Investment Report 2022. Report, p. 3.

[130] For detailed discussion regarding the MOR, see Chap. 3.

[131] For detailed discussion regarding the SOE-POE business partnership, see Chap. 3 Sect. 3.2.2.

[132] CMOC Group Limited (2021) 《洛阳钼业与宁德时代达成战略合作》 [CMOC Group and CATL Reach Strategic Co-operation]. https://www.cmoc.com/html/2021/News_0411/92.html. Accessed 25 Aug 2025.

[133] For detailed discussion regarding flow-in MOR, see Chap. 3 Sect. 3.2.1.

Motor Corporation.[134] CATL's strong political ties inevitably raise the possibility that Yibin Tianyi is also subject to political influence as a result of CATL's substantial minority shareholding. The FGI definition does not, however, encompass Chinese POE participants in flow-in MOR.

Flow-out MOR also poses a challenge to the FIRB's ability to accurately identify Chinese investors with political ties in investment screening. As the primary means of implementing flow-out MOR, Chinese governments at different levels typically invest in major POEs via their investment funds, while Chinese SOEs invest in POEs either directly or indirectly via their subsidiaries or industrial investment funds (usually in the case where the SOE is a SCIC). For example, Shandong Ruyi and Shanghai Pengxin both received investments from investment funds controlled by local governments in China (from Jining City Urban Construction Investment Fund, which is owned by the municipal government of Jining, in 2019 and Kunming Industrial Development Equity Investment Fund, which is owned by the provincial government of Kunming, in 2022, respectively).[135] The resulting State ownership, however, signifies not only State support for the invested firms, but also the formation of a cooperative partnership between the POEs and their SOE or government shareholders.

With the advance of the MOR in the latest round of SOE reform, an increasing number of Chinese POEs are being embedded into a State-controlled equity network consisting of governments, SOEs, public entities and related companies. These interconnections facilitate the sharing of information, technologies and other strategic assets between the entities with the objective to enhance the overall strength of the Chinese State economy. Given the fixed shareholding threshold of 20 percent, however, the FGI definition under the FATR is unable to capture these POEs with minority State ownership. Consequently, the investments proposed by these politically related investors Australia are only subject to mandatory notification requirements if they are 'reviewable actions' or 'reviewable national security actions'. Otherwise, the FIRB can only review their investments retroactively under the Treasurer's call-in or last-resort powers when they raise national security or interest concerns.

Therefore, the author suggests that, when evaluating investment proposals directly or indirectly from China, the FIRB should pay particular attention to examining the ownership of the investors and beneficial owners of investment interests to ascertain whether Chinese SOEs or State-owned industrial investment funds hold a

[134] CATL (2021) 《宁德时代与上海市政府签订战略合作框架协议》 [CATL and Shanghai Municipal Government Sign Strategic Co-operation Framework Agreement]. https://www.catl.com/news/1028.html. Accessed 25 Aug 2025; CATL (2023) 《宁德时代与北汽集团签署战略合作协议》 [CATL and BAIC Group Sign Strategic Cooperation Agreement]. https://www.catl.com/news/7100.html. Accessed 25 Aug 2025.

[135] Nikhil Kurian Nainan (2019) China's Ruyi Says Jining City Urban Construction Invests $495 Mln to Become No.2 Shareholder. Reuters. https://www.reuters.com/article/ruyi-shareholders-idUSL3N27D0ED. Accessed 25 Aug 2025; Pengdu (2025) 《鹏都农牧投资者关系》 [Investor Relations]. http://www.pengdunongmu.com/ir.html. Accessed 25 Aug 2025.

minority interest. This tracing should not be contingent on a 20 percent or so threshold. In the case where the Chinese investor is wholly privately-owned, it is also necessary to investigate whether the POE holds shares in SOEs, regardless of the size of the shareholding and whether there are any strategic partnerships between the POE and SOEs or governments. In light of China's distinctive political economy, a non-substantial minority shareholding is sufficient to permit a substantial SOE-POE linkage, and a strategic cooperation agreement between POE and State-related entities could be the externalisation of such a linkage.

It should be noted that the approach suggested here is not an implicit expansion of the FGI definition specifically for Chinese investments. It is suggested that it would be desirable to add to the existing 'character of investor' factor of the national interest test special consideration of: first, the ownership structure of foreign entities in which foreign governments hold, directly or indirectly, the ability to influence the entity's decisions; and second, foreign entities that hold interests in FGIs, in light of the possibility of political connections being formed or strengthened in the context of China's SOE reforms.

7.3.2 The CCP Control Within Chinese SOE Governance System

As a part of the ongoing SOE reforms, the Chinese government requires State-invested companies to implement a corporate governance structure distinct from more internationally recognised governance structures, known as the 'Modern Chinese SOE Governance System with Chinese Characteristics'.[136] The modern SOE governance system was developed to place SOE governance under the CCP's overall oversight, primarily through the CCP's ultimate authority in deciding major corporate matters and the mandatory cross-officeholding between the Party Committee and regular governance organs.[137]

China's modern SOE governance system requires the establishment of a CCP cell known as the 'Party Committee' as a distinct decision-making organ in addition to the board of directors.[138] According to the *Trial Regulation on the Work at Primary-level Party Organizations of State-owned Enterprises* (the *Trial Regulation)* issued by the CCP Central Committee in 2019, almost all major corporate issues, like organisational changes or foreign investment, must be discussed by the Party Committee before any decisions is made by the board of directors (which is, how-

---

136 《国务院办公厅关于进一步完善国有企业法人治理结构的指导意见》[Guiding Opinions on Further Improving the Corporate Governance Structure of State-Owned Enterprises]. (People's Republic of China) The General Office of the State Council. 24 April 2017 ('*Guiding Opinions on SOE Governance*').

137 For detailed discussion regarding China's SOE governance system reform, see Chap. 4.

138 《中国共产党章程》 [Constitution of the Communist Party of China]. Adopted at the 20th CCP National Congress. 22 October 2022, art. 33.

ever, typically predominated by 'outside' directors) or management teams.[139] In addition, the *Trial Regulation* requires that SOEs clarify the duties of the Party Committee in their Articles of Association, particularly their precedence in deciding on the specified major issues.[140] Accordingly, a Chinese company's Articles of Association could provide the FIRB with insight into the CCP cell's precise role in the particular company's governance practices. For instance, Minmetals, the Chinese SOE investor that acquired the Australian mining firm Album Resources Private Ltd/OZ Minerals, specifies the mechanism ensuring the CCP control over the group in its Articles of Association, which are published on its website (Chinese website only).[141]

In addition, the modern SOE governance system promoted in the latest round of SOE reforms mandates cross-officeholding between the Party Committee and regular governance organs, thereby consolidating the CCP control over SOE governance.[142] Therefore, to determine the extent to which an investor is subject to political control, the FIRB can also investigate the backgrounds of the investor's top executives, who are typically dispatched from the SOE's headquarters in China. For example, the CEO of Yancoal Australia, Caibao Zhang, also serves as the deputy secretary of the Party Committee of the Shandong Energy Group.[143] The non-executive director of Minmetals Resources, Shuqiang Zhang, was a member of the Party Committee of Minmetals Non-ferrous Metals (the acquirer of Album Resources and OZ Minerals, as shown in Table 7.1).[144]

7.3.3 Special Designation and Classification of Chinese SOE Investors

As a basis for implementing the MOR, the Chinese government is classifying SOEs according to their roles in national economic and social development into 'Public Welfare', 'Special Commercial' and 'General Commercial'.[145] Based on this categorisation, the government can adopt targeted reform policies and development strategies, including the assignment of differentiated operation objectives. In addition, in the State-owned capital administration reform, the Chinese government has also designated many major SOEs as SCICs or SCOCs (collectively referred to as

---

139 *Trial Regulation* (n 62) art. 15.

140 Ibid. art. 13; see also *Guiding Opinions on SOE Governance* (n 136).

141 Minmetals (2025) 《工作体系》 [Working System]. http://www.minmetals.com.cn/ddjj/gztx/. Accessed 25 Aug 2025.

142 *Trial Regulation* (n 62) art. 14.

143 Shandong Eenergy Group (2025) 《集团概况》 [Group Profile]. http://www.shandong-energy.com/page/jituan/company-leaders.html. Accessed 25 Aug 2025.

144 MMG (2025) Board of Directors. https://www.mmg.com/who-we-are/board-of-directors/. Accessed 25 Aug 2025.

145 For detailed discussion regarding MOR, see Chap. 3.

SCIOs) and entrusted them with the tasks of implementing national policies and development strategies, increasing the returns on State-owned capital and the authority to operate State-owned capital and exercise shareholder rights in other SOEs.[146] In general, for Chinese SOEs categorised as 'Public Welfare' or 'Special Commercial' or designated as SCIOs, how they carry out policy tasks is given greater weight than profitability in their annual performance evaluation, with the results having a direct bearing on the careers of SOE leaders and the funding available to the SOE the following year.

As has been discussed above, many Chinese SOE investors active in Australia have been classified as 'Special Commercial' or designated as SCIOs in the ongoing reforms. As a general summary, 12 of the 18 SOE investments listed in Table 7.1 were proposed by investors that were later designated as SCICs (or their parent companies were so designated), while 3 of the remaining 6 SOE investments were proposed by SOEs classified as 'Special Commercial'. For example, Chinalco, the Chinese central SOE, acquired a substantial stake in Rio Tinto through its subsidiary in 2008 and was subsequently designated as an SCIC in 2018.[147] Douglas Ritchie, a former senior executive at Rio Tinto, supported a follow-up acquisition by Chinalco in 2009, stating 'not only do I find [Chinese SOEs] commercial in their approach, but I find that their standards… are as good as those of equivalent corporations elsewhere'.[148] However, after a decade, Chinalco's new identity as a SCIC raises questions about the commercial nature test for FGI investment under Australia's foreign investment framework, as it indicates that the SOE is pursuing broader strategic objectives. This necessitates a careful examination of whether the non-commercial objectives are contrary to Australia's national interests.

Hence, the author suggests that the FIRB should consider how a Chinese SOE investor is categorised or designated in Chinese domestic regulations as a *prima facie* indication of the investor's political background and, potentially, any policy motivations for the transaction under review. The Treasurer's decision to exercise call-in or last-resort powers to conduct a unilateral review of an admitted investment by a Chinese SOE should also take this into account. As stated in the 2023 Policy, investments by FGIs that do not operate solely for commercial purposes do not necessarily result in the transaction being rejected.[149] Chinese SOE investments motivated primarily by the pursuit of high yields on State-owned capital may be less likely to compromise Australia's national interests.

---

[146] For detailed discussion regarding SCIOs, see Chap. 4 Sect. 4.1.2.2.

[147] Aluminium Corporation of China (2025) 《资质荣誉》 [Qualifications and Honours]. https://www.chinalco.com.cn/gywm/gywm_zzry/. Accessed 25 Aug 2025.

[148] Economic References Committee (n 9), p. 56.

[149] *2025 Policy* (n 14), p. 10.

7.3.4 Inter-SOE Consolidations and Tactic Alliance

As part of the latest round of SOE reforms, the Chinese government is promoting inter-SOE consolidations to strengthen SOE dominance in industries it considers critical. The consolidation is primarily carried out through government-orchestrated mergers and contractually based strategic cooperative relationships between SOEs in the same or complementary industries.

As Table 7.1 shows, all the Chinese SOE investors listed have been affected by consolidations. In addition to consolidation in the same sectors, Chinese SOEs are consolidating across industries along the industrial chain, which can be reasonably assumed to be a result of the *Made in China 2025 Development Initiative*. The investors in Table 7.1 provides a typical example: In 2017, COFCO, State Grid and Baowu Group signed a cooperation framework agreement in Beijing to establish a central enterprises supply chain alliance formally.[150] The consolidations along the industrial chain between these Chinese industrial giants highlight the likelihood that Chinese SOE partners will acquire Australian businesses separately along industrial chains in preparation for domestic consolidations under government direction. This could allow China to achieve dominance over certain sectors of the Australian economy without raising red flags in FIRB reviews of individual SOE investments.

Early in 2009, the then-Liberal Party leader Malcolm Turnbull opposed Chinalco's proposed follow-up investment in Rio Tinto, raising concerns that Chinalco might transfer its interests in the Australian iron ore mines involved to another Chinese SOE.[151] This indicates that the Australian government was cognizant of the risk of strategic alliances between Chinese SOE investors at the time. However, the ongoing SOE reforms have made this possibility more plausible than ever.

In light of this, the author suggests that the FIRB and other advisory agencies should monitor consolidations among Chinese SOE investors in Australia, both those proposing new investments and those with existing investments. The FIRB, when assessing a Chinese SOE investment, should investigate whether the investor has shareholding ties or strategic partnerships with other Chinese SOE investors in Australia. If necessary, the investigation could be expanded to include investments by Chinese POEs with equity ties to SOEs. If inter-SOE consolidation is discovered, the Australian regulators should evaluate whether the consolidation would lead to excessive Chinese influence over Australian strategic sectors or assets and whether the consolidation would raise concerns of competitive distortion, supply manipulation or national security risks. If so, the Treasurer can restrict the admission of newly proposed investments or unilaterally subject existing investments to retrospective reviews.

---

[150] 公秀华 [Gong Xiuhua] (2017) 《央企供应链金融联盟在京成立》 [China's Central Enterprises Supply Chain Finance Alliance was Formed in Beijing]. CNR. http://finance.cnr.cn/jjgd/20170927/t20170927_523968005.shtml. Accessed 25 Aug 2025.

[151] Economic References Committee (n 9), p. 53.

7.4 Concluding Remarks

Despite the rising Sino-Western geopolitical tensions, Australia continues to attract substantial investments from Chinese SOEs and companies likely affiliated with SOEs in the context of China's latest round of SOE reforms. Therefore, understanding Chinese SOEs and the latest round of SOE reforms that are reshaping them is a crucial step for Australia in figuring out how to constrain the potential detriments associated with Chinese SOE investments while maximising the benefits to the local economy and public welfare. This chapter maps the screening landscape under Australia's recently tightened investment framework for Chinese SOE investments, and sheds light on the operations of the framework in relation to Chinese investment since 2008, with a particular emphasis on the implications of China's latest round of SOE reforms on the operations and Chinese investment in Australia's infrastructure and resources sectors. China's ongoing SOE reforms, which have resulted in tighter political control over Chinese SOEs and the growing political ties of Chinese POEs, presents serious challenges to Australia's foreign investment framework in terms of identifying the non-commercial objectives of Chinese investments and ensuring Australia's national interests. Therefore, the chapter suggests specific factors that the FIRB should consider when evaluating investments from Chinese investors, including the ownership structure of Chinese non-SOE investors, the CCP's leadership within Chinese SOE investors' governance system, the special classification or designation of Chinese SOEs in the SOE reforms and the possibility of tactical alliance among different Chinese SOE investors. By taking these factors into consideration, the Australian government can more effectively address Chinese investment in the context of the latest round of SOE reforms with a goal to safeguard vital national interests.

References

Administrative Decisions (Judicial Review) Act 1977 (Cth) sch. 1(h)
Air Navigation Act 1920 (Cth) s. 11A and Qantas Sale Act 1992 (Cth) s. 7
Airport Act 1996 (Cth) pt. 3, div. 3
Aluminium Corporation of China (2025) 《资质荣誉》 [Qualifications and Honours]. https://www.chinalco.com.cn/gywm/gywm_zzry/. Accessed 25 Aug 2025
Australian Government Department of Home Affairs (2025) Cyber and Infrastructure Security Centre. https://www.cisc.gov.au/. Accessed 25 Aug 2025
Banking Act 1959 (Cth)
Bath V (2012) Foreign investment, the national interest and national security: foreign direct investment in Australia and China. Sydney Law Rev 34(1):17
BCA (2014) Discussion Paper on Foreign Investment and State-Owned Enterprises: Managing the Risks to Maximise the Benefits. p 9 https://www.bca.com.au/discussion_paper_on_foreign_investment_and_state_owned_enterprises_new. Accessed 25 Aug 2025
Broadcasting Service Act 1993 (Cth) s. 121 FD (3), (4)

Bronskill J (2021) Chinese telecom firm loses court battle against order to divest Canadian subsidiary. National Post. https://nationalpost.com/news/canada/chinese-controlled-firm-loses-court-bid-to-pause-ottawas-divestment-order. Accessed 25 Aug 2025
Canwest Global Communications Corporation and Others v Treasurer of the Commonwealth of Australia [1997] FCA 730
Cathy Pacific Airways Limited v Assistant Treasurer and Minister for Competition Policy and Consumer Affairs (2010) 186 FCR 168
CATL (2021) 《宁德时代与上海市政府签订战略合作框架协议》 [CATL and Shanghai Municipal Government Sign Strategic Co-operation Framework Agreement]. https://www.catl.com/news/1028.html. Accessed 25 Aug 2025
CATL (2023) 《宁德时代与北汽集团签署战略合作协议》 [CATL and BAIC Group Sign Strategic Cooperation Agreement]. https://www.catl.com/news/7100.html. Accessed 25 Aug 2025
China Power Team (2021) Does China Pose a Threat to Global Rare Earth Supply Chains? https://chinapower.csis.org/china-rare-earths/. Accessed 25 Aug 2025
China State Construction (2022) 《中建集团与南方电网签署战略合作协议》 [China Construction Group and Southern Power Grid Sign Strategic Co-operation Agreement]. https://www.cscec.com/xwzx_new/gsyw_new/202201/3472396.html. Accessed 25 Aug 2025
Chinamining (2017) 《鞍钢与中铝公司加强交流合作》 [Anshan Iron & Steel and Chinalco Intensify Their Partnership]. https://zlzb.chinalco.com.cn/xwzx/gsyw/202103/t20210301_76761.html. Accessed 25 Aug 2025
CMOC Group Limited (2021) 《洛阳钼业与宁德时代达成战略合作》 [CMOC Group and CATL Reach Strategic Co-operation]. https://www.cmoc.com/html/2021/News_0411/92.html. Accessed 25 Aug 2025
Coorey P (2016) Scott Morrison Says Ausgrid Sale to Chinese 'Contrary to the National Interest'. Financial Review. https://www.afr.com/politics/scott-morrison-says-ausgrid-sale-to-chinese-contrary-to-the-national-interest-20160811-gqptc1. Accessed 25 Aug 2025
Department of Industry, Science and Resources (2023) Australia's Critical Minerals List. https://www.industry.gov.au/publications/australias-critical-minerals-list. Accessed 25 Aug 2025
Department of the Prime Minister and Cabinet (2023) Review – Port of Darwin lease. Media Release
DFAT (2018) Factsheet: Investment and Investor-State Dispute Settlement (ISDS). https://www.dfat.gov.au/sites/default/files/chafta-fact-sheet-investor-state-dispute-settlement.pdf. Accessed 25 Aug 2025
DFAT (2022) Statistics on who invests in Australia. https://www.dfat.gov.au/trade/trade-and-investment-data-information-and-publications/foreign-investment-statistics/statistics-on-who-invests-in-australia. Accessed 25 Aug 2025
Drysdale P (2011) A new look at Chinese FDI in Australia. China World Econ 19(4):61
Economic References Committee (2009) Foreign investment by state-owned entities. Report, p 47
Economic References Committee (2021) Greenfields, Cash Cows and the Regulation of Foreign Investment in Australia. Report
Esplugues C (2018) Australia: The 'National Interest' Test. In: Esplugues C (ed) Foreign investment, strategic assets and national security. Intersentia, p 355
Financial Sector (Shareholding) Act 1988 (Cth)
FIRB (2010) Australia's Foreign Investment Policy
FIRB (2018) Foreign Investment Review Board Annual Report 2016-17. Report
FIRB (2020) Guidance 8: National Security Test. https://foreigninvestment.gov.au/sites/firb.gov.au/files/guidance-notes/GN8-NationalSecurity-210303.pdf. Accessed 25 Aug 2025
FIRB (2022) Foreign Investment Review Board Annual Report 2020-21. Report
FIRB (2025) Australia's Foreign Investment Framework. https://foreigninvestment.gov.au/investing-in-australia/foreign-investment-framework. Accessed 25 Aug 2025
Foreign Acquisitions and Takeovers Act 1975 (Cth)
Foreign Acquisitions and Takeovers Regulation 2015 (Cth)

Foreign Investment and Trade Policy Division (2016) Foreign Investment into Australia. Treasury. Working Paper, p 6

Foreign Investment Reform (Protecting Australia's National Security) Act 2020 (Cth)

Free Trade Agreement between the Government of Australia and the Government of the People's Republic of China, signed 17 June 2015, [2015] ATS 15 (entered into force 20 December 2015)

Frydenberg J (2020) Major reforms to Australia's foreign investment framework pass the parliament. Treasury Portfolio

Frydenberg J (2021) Interview with Chris Smith, 2GB Radio. Ministers Treasury Portfolio

Gaetjens P (2018) Chinese Investment and Australia Forum. Speech

Geoscience Australia (2023) Critical Minerals at Geoscience Australia. https://www.ga.gov.au/scientific-topics/minerals/critical-minerals. Accessed 25 Aug 2025

Hockey J (2013) Foreign Investment Decision. Ministers Treasury Portfolio

Hockey J (2015) Foreign investment decision: acquisition of John Holland Group by China Communications Construction Company. Ministers Treasury Portfolio

Jiang H (2018) Beam light on Australia's national interest test: an empirical study of Chinese investments under it. Asia Pac Law Rev 26(1):14–35

Knight L, Voon T (2020) The evolution of national security at the interface between domestic and international investment law and policy: the role of China. J World Invest Trade 2020(1):111–114

KPMG and USYD (2024) Demystifying Chinese investment in Australia 2024. Report, p 4

Leisure and Entertainment Pty Ltd v The Honourable Ralph Wills, Federal Treasurer of the Commonwealth of Australia (1996) 64 FCR 205

Lin Y (2020) 'Made in China 2025' and China's cross-border strategic M&As in OECD countries. J Chin Econ Bus Stud 18(2):91–114

Luo Y, Xue Q, Han B (2010) How emerging market governments promote outward FDI: experience from China. J World Bus 45(1):68–79

Marie Madeline Wight v The Honourable Chris Pearce, MP, Parliamentary Secretary to the Treasurer (2007) 157 FCR 485

Mendelsohn R, Fels A (2014) Australia's Foreign Investment Review Board and the Regulation of Chinese Investment. China Econ J 7(1):59–83

Minmetals (2025) 《工作体系》 [Working System]. http://www.minmetals.com.cn/ddjj/gztx/. Accessed 25 Aug 2025

MMG (2025) Board of Directors. https://www.mmg.com/who-we-are/board-of-directors/. Accessed 25 Aug 2025

MOFCOM, NBS and SAFE (2022) 2021 Statistical Bulletin of China's Outward Foreign Direct Investment. China Commerce and Trade Press, p 30

Morrison S (2015) Foreign investment approval - 99 year lease of TransGrid. Ministers Treasury Portfolio

Morrison S (2016) Statement on decision to prohibit the 99-year lease of 50.4 per cent of Ausgrid under current proposed structure. Ministers Treasury Portfolio

Nikhil Kurian Nainan (2019) China's Ruyi Says Jining City Urban Construction Invests $495 Mln to Become No.2 Shareholder. Reuters. https://www.reuters.com/article/ruyi-shareholders-idUSL3N27D0ED. Accessed 25 Aug 2025

OECD (2009) Recommendation of the Council on Guidelines for Recipient Country Investment Policies Relating to National Security. https://legalinstruments.oecd.org/public/doc/227/227.en.pdf. Accessed 25 Aug 2025

OECD (2016) G20 Guiding Principles for Global Investment Policymaking. https://www.oecd.org/daf/inv/investment-policy/G20-Guiding-Principles-for-Global-Investment-Policymaking.pdf. Accessed 25 Aug 2025

Parliament of Australia (2008) Treasurer's 2008 guidelines for assessing proposals by SOEs. https://www.aph.gov.au/Parliamentary_Business/Committees/Senate/Economics/Completed_inquiries/2008-10/firb_09/report/e03. Accessed 25 Aug 2025

Pengdu (2025) 《鹏都农牧投资者关系》 [Investor Relations]. http://www.pengdunongmu.com/ir.html. Accessed 25 Aug 2025
Productivity Commission (2020) Foreign Investment in Australia. Research Paper, p 16
Reuters (2019) China's Chinalco Names Ansteel Boss as its New Chairman. Nasdaq. https://www.nasdaq.com/articles/chinas-chinalco-names-ansteel-boss-as-its-new-chairman-2019-10-24. Accessed 25 Aug 2025
Rio Tinto (2017) Rio Tinto Completes Divestment of Coal & Allied Industries Limited for $2.69 Billion. https://www.riotinto.com/en/news/releases/2017/coal-and-allied-divestment-completed. Accessed 25 Aug 2025
Scarr L (2019) Treasurer Josh Frydenberg Ticks off Chinese Government Stake in Oakajee Port and Rail project. The West Australian. https://thewest.com.au/business/infrastructure/treasurer-josh-frydenberg-ticks-off-chinese-government-stake-in-oakajee-port-and-rail-project-ng-b881371522z. Accessed 25 Aug 2025
Security Legislation Amendment (Critical Infrastructure Protection) Bill 2022 (Cth)
Security Legislation Amendment (Critical Infrastructure) Bill 2021 (Cth)
Security of Critical Infrastructure Act 2018 (Cth) s. 5, as amended by Security Legislation Amendment (Critical Infrastructure Protection) Act 2022 (Cth)
Shandong Eenergy Group (2025) 《集团概况》 [Group Profile]. http://www.shandong-energy.com/page/jituan/company-leaders.html. Accessed 25 Aug 2025
Shapps G, Hunt J (2022) UK government takes major steps forward to secure Britain's energy independence. Department for Business, Energy & Industrial Strategy and Great British Nuclear. Press Release
Sherry N (2009) Foreign investment decision – Felix Resources. Ministers Treasury Portfolio
Swan W (2008a) Chinalco's acquisition of shares in Rio Tinto. Ministers Treasury Portfolio
Swan W (2008b) Foreign investment approval: Sinosteel's interests in Murchison Metals Ltd. Ministers Treasury Portfolio
Swan W (2008c) Interview with David Speers, Sky News. Ministers Treasury Portfolio. Transcripts
Swan W (March 2009a) Foreign Investment Decision. Ministers Treasury Portfolio
Swan W (May 2009b) Foreign Investment Decision. Ministers Treasury Portfolio
Swan W (2010) Foreign Investment Decision. Ministers Treasury Portfolio
Swan W (2012) Foreign Investment Decision. Ministers Treasury Portfolio
Taylor R (2009) China Again Fails in Bid for Australian Resources. Reuters. https://www.reuters.com/article/us-australia-china-idUKTRE58N1HK20090924. Accessed 25 Aug 2025
Telstra Corporation Act 1991 (Cth) pt. 2A, div. 4, ss. 8BG-8BJ
The American Enterprise Institute and the Heritage Foundation (2023) China Global Investment Tracker. https://www.aei.org/china-global-investment-tracker/. Accessed 25 Aug 2025
The Central SASAC (2015) 《鞍钢集团与中国五矿全面深化战略合作》 [Anshan Iron & Steel Group and China Minmetals Deepen Strategic Co-operation in a Comprehensive Manner]. http://www.sasac.gov.cn/n2588025/n2588124/c3812939/content.html. Accessed 25 Aug 2025
The People's Government of Nanjing (2023) 《市政府与中国交建签署战略合作协议》 [Municipal Government and CCCC Sign a Strategic Cooperation Agreement]. https://www.nanjing.gov.cn/njxx/202303/t20230310_3858944.html. Accessed 25 Aug 2025
The Treasury (2025) Australia's Foreign Investment Policy. https://foreigninvestment.gov.au/sites/foreigninvestment.gov.au/files/2025-03/australias-foreign-investment-policy-v2.pdf. Accessed 25 Aug 2025
Thirlwell M (2008) Is the Foreign Investment Review Board acting fairly? Lowy Institute. https://www.lowyinstitute.org/sites/default/files/pubfiles/Thirlwell%2C_Is_the_Foreign_Investment_Review_1.pdf. Accessed 25 Aug 2025
UNCTAD (2022) Methodology Note-World Investment Report 2022. Report, p 3
UNCTAD (2023) World Investment Report 2023. UNCTAD/WIR/2023. Annual Report
Xinhua Net (2021) 《国家电网公司与中建集团举行合资公司成立云揭牌仪式》 [State Grid Corporation and China Construction Group Hold Online Opening Ceremony for Establishment

of Joint Venture Company]', http://www.xinhuanet.com/energy/2021-01/15/c_1126986863.htm. Accessed 25 Aug 2025
Zhou W, Crochet V, Wang H (2025) Demystifying China's critical minerals strategies: rethinking 'de-risking' supply chains. World Trade Rev 24(2):257–281
Zu H (2022) A new perspective on motivations behind Chinese Overseas Investment: a case study on the Darwin Port Deal. Aust J Polit Hist 68(3):467–483

Additional Sources

《中国共产党国有企业基层组织工作条例(试行)》 [Trial Regulation on the Work at Primary-level Party Organizations of State-Owned Enterprises]. (People's Republic of China) The CCP Central Committee. 30 December 2019
《中国共产党章程》 [Constitution of the Communist Party of China]. Adopted at the 20th CCP National Congress. 22 October 2022, art. 33
《关于国有企业功能界定与分类的指导意见》 [Guiding Opinions on the Definition and Classification of Functions of State-Owned Enterprises]. (People's Republic of China) SASAC, MOF and NDRC. 7 December 2015
《关于深化国有企业改革的指导意见》 [The Guiding Opinions on Deepening the Reform of State-Owned Enterprises]. (People's Republic of China) The CCP Central Committee and the State Council. 24 August 2015
《国务院关于推进国有资本投资、运营公司改革试点的实施意见》 [Opinions of The State Council on the Implementation of the Pilot Reform of State-Owned Capital Investment and Operation Companies]. (People's Republic of China) The State Council. 30 July 2018
《国务院办公厅关于进一步完善国有企业法人治理结构的指导意见》[Guiding Opinions on Further Improving the Corporate Governance Structure of State-Owned Enterprises]. (People's Republic of China) The General Office of the State Council. 24 April 2017
公秀华 [Gong Xiuhua] (2017) 《央企供应链金融联盟在京成立》 [China's Central Enterprises Supply Chain Finance Alliance was Formed in Beijing]. CNR. http://finance.cnr.cn/jjgd/20170927/t20170927_523968005.shtml. Accessed 25 Aug 2025
李语, 杨彬 [Li Yu and Yang Bin] (2022) 《南方电网公司第二届供应链合作伙伴大会在广州举行》 [The Southern Power Grid Corporation's Second Supply Chain Partner Conference was Held in Guangzhou]. People. http://gd.people.com.cn/n2/2022/0729/c123932-40059740.html. Accessed 25 Aug 2025

Chapter 8
Chinese SOE Investments Under the Australia-China International Investment Agreements: Wild Grass with Hidden Thorns

Abstract This chapter examines the regulatory challenges posed by Chinese SOE investments under the Australia-China International Investment Agreements (IIAs). Despite the extensive IIA framework between Australia and China, which includes agreements such as the Australia-China Bilateral Investment Treaty and the China-Australia Free Trade Agreement (ChAFTA), Chinese SOE investments present significant risks to Australia's national interests, particularly following China's latest round of SOE reforms. These reforms have enhanced the political influence of SOEs, increasing concerns over non-competitive investment practices. The chapter investigates the potential for Chinese SOEs to bring Investor-State Dispute Settlement (ISDS) claims against Australia, especially in the context of Australia's tightened foreign investment framework. The analysis identifies specific risks under the current IIAs, focusing on possible breaches of expropriation and National Treatment obligations. The findings highlight that the existing IIAs may not provide sufficient safeguards for Australia to regulate Chinese SOE investments effectively. In response, the chapter recommends that future treaty negotiations, particularly the renegotiation of ChAFTA, incorporate stronger policy space protections. It suggests introducing SOE-specific rules to address non-competitive practices in future agreements (renegotiated ChAFTA), ensuring that Australia can protect its strategic interests while maintaining a fair investment environment.

Australia and China are significant players in the international investment arena, and both actively contribute to the growth of international investment law. As of December 2023, China has signed 160 International Investment Agreements (IIAs), including 145 Bilateral Investment Treaties (BITs) and 25 Free Trade Agreements (FTAs) with investment chapters.[1] Australia has concluded 29 IIAs, including 24 BITs and 25 FTAs.[2]

[1] UNCTAD (2025b) International Investment Agreements Navigator - China. https://investmentpolicy.unctad.org/international-investment-agreements/countries/42/china. Accessed 3 Sep 2025.

[2] UNCTAD (2025a) International Investment Agreements Navigator - Australia. https://investmentpolicy.unctad.org/international-investment-agreements/countries/11/australia. Accessed 3 Sep 2025.

T. Gu, *Chinese SOE Reforms and Global FDI*, Contemporary Chinese Civil and Commercial Law, https://doi.org/10.1007/978-981-92-3181-2_8

Over the past few decades, Australia and China have developed a robust bilateral investment relationship, leading to the conclusion of multiple IIAs, including the *Australia-China Bilateral Investment Treaty* (CABIT),[3] the *China-Australia Free Trade Agreement* (ChAFTA),[4] and the *Regional Comprehensive Economic Partnership* (RCEP).[5] Additionally, in 1993, Australia and Hong Kong signed a BIT,[6] which was replaced by the *Australia-Hong Kong Investment Agreement* (AHKIA) as part of the *Australia-Hong Kong Free Trade Agreement* concluded in 2019.[7] The four IIAs are concurrently in force, constituting an IIA framework governing Australia and China's cross-border investment activities.

As demonstrated in Chap. 7, Chinese investment has raised prominent concerns from the Australian government regarding the potential negative impacts on Australia's national interests. Australia has significantly enhanced the legislative framework for foreign investment screening in 2021. This highlights the risk of conflict between Australia's domestic foreign investment policy and its obligations under the Australia-China IIA framework, which could lead to increased international investment arbitration claims filed by Chinese SOE investors against Australia based on the treaties. In addition, despite the continuing significance of Chinese SOE investments in Australia, none of the Australia-China IIAs contain rules specifically for SOEs, suggesting that Australia can only rely on its domestic laws to regulate Chinese SOE investments, albeit at the risk of treaty breaches.

This chapter seeks to explore how effective the current IIAs between Australia and China are in balancing Australia's interests with those of Chinese SOE investors, focusing on the potential risks that the treaties pose to Australia regarding Chinese SOE investments in the context of China's latest round of SOE reforms. This chapter is structured into four sections:

Section 8.1 identifies the potential grounds for Chinese SOE or SOE-affiliated investors to bring a claim against Australia under the current IIAs between the two countries. Section 8.2 examines how effective the CPTPP-modelled SOE rules in Australia's recent IIAs with other countries may be in assisting Australia to regulate Chinese SOE investments if incorporated in a future IIA with China (particularly the renegotiated ChAFTA investment chapter). Section 8.3 examines the role of Chinese SOEs in Chinese investor-State dispute settlement (ISDS) practice and

[3] *Agreement between the Government of Australia and the Government of the People's Republic of China on the Reciprocal Encouragement and Protection of Investments*. [1988] ATS 14 (signed and entered into force 11 July 1988) ('CABIT').

[4] *Free Trade Agreement between the Government of Australia and the Government of the People's Republic of China*. Signed 17 June 2015. [2015] ATS 15 (entered into force 20 December 2015) ('ChAFTA').

[5] *Regional Comprehensive Economic Partnership Agreement*. Signed 15 November 2020. [2020] ATS 1 (entered into force 1 January 2022) ('RCEP').

[6] *Agreement between the Government of Hong Kong and the Government of Australia for the Promotion and Protection of Investments*. Signed 15 September 1993. [1993] ATS 30 (entered into force 15 October 1993).

[7] *Free Trade Agreement between Australia and Hong Kong, China and associated side letters*. Signed 26 March 2019. [2020] ATS 4 (entered into force 17 January 2020) ('AHKIA').

Table 8.1 The Key Provisions in Co-existing IIAs between Australia and China

IIAs	MFN	NT	FET	Expropriation	General exceptions	Security exceptions	ISDS
CABIT	√ -Post-establishment.	×	√	√	×	×	√ -only for disputes concerning the amount of compensation for expropriation
ChAFTA (Subject to future work programme)	√ -Pre-establishment. -Excluding ISDS.	√ -pre-establishment (nonreciprocal)	×	×	√ -not applicable to the Investment Chapter	√	√ -only for disputes over NT breach -public welfare carve-out
RCEP (Subject to future work programme)	√ -Excluding ISDS.	√	√	√ -public welfare carve-out	√	√ -a reference to critical infrastructure	× -Future work programme
AHKIA	√ -Extends to expansion but subject to law. -Excludes ISDS.	√ -extends to expansion but is subject to law.	√	√ -public welfare carve-out	√	√ -a reference to critical infrastructure	√ -excluding foreign investment decisions on approval

highlights the expected rise in ISDS claims filed by Chinese SOE investors as a result of the Chinese government's policy stance. Section 8.4 provides Australia with recommendations for potential improvements to the renegotiated ChAFTA investment chapter with the goal of preserving more policy space under the treaty while more comprehensively addressing Chinese SOE investments. Section 8.5 concludes.

8.1 Risks of ISDS Claims for Australia Regarding Chinese SOE Investments

As of December 2023, four IIAs, including CABIT, ChAFTA, RCEP and AHKIA, are in effect simultaneously between Australia and China. Different protections are provided by the treaties for covered investments, including an ISDS clause, granting investors protected by the treaties the ability to institute ISDS arbitration to compel the host State to fulfil (some of) its commitments under the treaties.[8] These treaty protections therefore may provide Chinese SOE (-affiliated) investors with potential bases to pursue ISDS proceedings against Australia.

8.1.1 Brief Overview of Australia-China IIAs

The signing of the four IIAs between Australia and China spans over three decades. Table 8.1 below compares the key provisions of the four IIAs to illustrate the substantial variation in their contents, resulting from the evolving treaty-making practices of the two countries over time.

The 1988 CABIT was Australia's first BIT. This decades-old BIT typically affords limited substantive protections, including, among other things, fair and equitable treatment (FET), most-favoured-nation treatment (MFN, which refers to the Parties' commitment to treatment no less favourable than that accorded to investments of nationals of any third country), non-impairment protection and expropriation protection.[9] In common with other Chinese BITs signed during the same period,[10] CABIT limits ISDS arbitrability to disputes relating to the amount of compensation for expropriation.[11]

ChAFTA was signed in 2015 amid the relative optimism in relations between Australia and China. Its investment chapter is a work-in-progress IIA that defers most of the substantive protections to subsequent negotiations on a comprehensive

[8] Dolzer et al. (2022), p. 9.

[9] CABIT (n 3) art. III (a)-(c), VIII.

[10] Levine (2019), p. 207.

[11] CABIT (n 3) art. XII.2.

Investment Chapter,[12] with the exception of MFN, national treatment (NT, which refers to the Parties' commitment to treatment no less favourable than that accorded to investments of their investors) and the ISDS clause. CABIT remains in force until the conclusion of the amended investment chapter.[13] Notably, the NT provision in ChAFTA is non-reciprocal, with Australia's commitment extending to the pre-establishment stage (i. e. establishment and acquisition) while China's commitment is limited to the post-establishment stage.[14] This nonreciprocal NT commitment reflected China's approach towards market access for foreign investment, as well as a hope for future relaxation.[15] Indeed, China has committed to shifting to pre-establishment NT supported by a negative list in the work programme although the work programme has not resulted in the promised drafting of a comprehensive investment chapter.[16]

ChAFTA does, however, provide a remarkably comprehensive ISDS clause. It currently limits arbitrable disputes to those concerning NT violations and exempts from ISDS non-discriminatory measures for public welfare objectives.[17] ChAFTA also empowers the Parties to issue joint interpretations on treaty provisions and annexes binding on the ISDS tribunal[18] and includes innovations in ISDS procedures and disciplines.[19]

AHKIA and RCEP were negotiated amidst growing international apprehension regarding the potential encroachment of IIAs upon the regulatory sovereignty of host States.[20] Therefore, despite offering extensive investment protections, both treaties include explicit safeguards for regulatory space. For example, they contain a security exception clause and a general exception clause modelled on WTO clauses,[21] which allow the host States autonomy to adopt measures necessary for protecting their essential security interests,[22] and non-discriminatory measures that serve specific public welfare objectives, respectively.[23]

---

[12] ChAFTA (n 4) art. 9.9.

[13] Bath (2017a), p. 195; Voon and Sheargold (2017), pp. 227–233.

[14] ChAFTA (n 4) art. 9.3.

[15] Matteo Vaccaro-Incisa (2021), p. 282; Bath (2017b), p. 68.

[16] ChAFTA (n 4) art. 9.9.

[17] Ibid. art. 19.12, 9.11.4.

[18] Ibid. art. 9.18.2, 9.19.

[19] Wang (2017), pp. 29–30.

[20] Thompson et al. (2019), pp. 859–880; Voon et al. (2014b), pp. 451–473; UNCTAD (2015) IIA Issues Note: Recent Trends in IIAs and ISDS. Report, p. 2.

[21] The WTO security exception clauses include Article XXI of GATT and Article XIV bis of GATS. WTO general exception clauses refer to Article XX of the GATT and/or Article XIV of the GATS. Notably, ChAFTA also contains a WTO-modelled security exception clause. ChAFTA (n 4) art. 16.3.

[22] RCEP (n 5) art. 17.13 (b) (iii); AHKIA (n 7) art. 19.

[23] RCEP (n 5) art. 17.12; AHKIA (n 7) art. 18.

AHKIA includes a broad ISDS clause that applies to disputes concerning violations of any substantive obligations in the treaty,[24] excluding foreign investment decisions on approval.[25] RCEP does not, however, include an ISDS clause; instead, it provides a work programme for subsequent ISDS negotiations.[26] Given that many RCEP Parties, including Australia, New Zealand, Indonesia and Malaysia, have officially announced that they will not consent to ISDS in future IIAs,[27] it is less likely that an ISDS clause will be introduced, as such amendment will require approval by all Parties. Due to the absence of the ISDS mechanism in RCEP, the following subsections do not address potential violations of RCEP.

AHKIA could be an additional basis for Chinese SOEs investing through Hong Kong. In practice, Chinese SOEs invest abroad frequently via their Hong Kong subsidiaries.[28] A myriad of factors drive this onward-journeying investment practice, such as Hong Kong's advanced business services and superior access to foreign financing markets, as well as the Chinese government's policy since the early 1990s that encourages SOEs to establish subsidiaries in Hong Kong to list on the Stock Exchange of Hong Kong.[29] In contrast to shell companies in tax havens, Chinese BGs generally establish Hong Kong subsidiaries to play a substantial role within the groups. For instance, China Mobile Group established China Mobile Limited as an offshore holding company to hold all overseas subsidiaries from Hong Kong.[30] As a result, contesting the jurisdiction of an AHKIA-based arbitration based on the treaty's denial of justice clause or alleging an abuse of rights in the ISDS process would be difficult for Australia.[31]

Current IIAs between Australia and China define 'covered investment' as established in or lawfully admitted by the host Party,[32] limiting protections to the post-establishment stage (subject to the pre-establishment extension of NT and MFN obligations in ChAFTA). By including government-owned or controlled entities in the definitions of 'company' or 'enterprise', the treaties all make it clear that investments made by SOEs of Parties are entitled to treaty protections.[33] As demonstrated in Chap. 7, Australia has significantly strengthened its foreign investment review mechanism under the FATA or the *Security of Critical Infrastructure Act 2018* (the

[24] AHKIA (n 7) art. 24.1.

[25] Ibid. annex III.

[26] The negotiations shall commence no later than January 1, 2024. RCEP (n 5) art. 10.8.1.

[27] Gao (2022) The Investment Chapter in the Regional Comprehensive Economic Partnership: Enhanced Rules Without Enforcement Mechanism. No 446, ERIA. Discussion Paper, p. 16; Kawharu and Nottage (2018), pp. 32–70; Crockett (2018), pp. 159–179.

[28] Sutherland et al. (2019), pp. 337–359.

[29] 肖立晟, 徐子桐, 范小云 [Xiao Lishen, Xu Zitong and Fan Xiaoyun] (2022) 《估算中国的IFDI和OFDI—来自避税天堂与返程投资的证据》 [Estimating China's IFDI and OFDI—Evidence from Tax Havens and Round-Tripping Investment]. 金融研究 [Financial Studies] 500(2): 40–60.

[30] China Mobile Limited (2021) Blue Ocean: Digital Economy—Annual Report 2020. Report.

[31] AHKIA (n 7) art. 14.

[32] Ibid. art. 1; CABIT (n 3) art. I.1. (b); ChAFTA (n 4) art. 9.1 (a); RCEP (n 5) art. 10.1 (a).

[33] CABIT (n 3) art. I.1. (a); AHKIA (n 7) art. 1; ChAFTA (n 4) art. 9.1 (b).

SOCI Act) over the past three years, making Chinese SOE investments more susceptible to retrospective review based on national security concerns. The definitions pave the way for Chinese SOEs to challenge Australia's regulatory measures through ISDS proceedings under the IIAs. Existing legal scholarship has examined the potential conflicts between Australia's reformed foreign investment framework and international investment law.[34] The subsequent subsections identify the specific claims a Chinese SOE investor could potentially bring against Australia under the existing Australia-China IIAs.

8.1.2 Violation of Expropriation Provisions Under CABIT and AHKIA

As discussed in Chap. 7, Chinese SOEs already hold substantial stakes in Australia's strategic assets, such as critical minerals and infrastructure assets. Such significant holdings may raise red flags with the Australian government, potentially leading to the initiation of retrospective reviews under the FATA (through the call-in or last-resort powers) or SOCI Act (exclusively for investments involving 'critical infrastructure' governed by the law) out of concern for national security. For example, the Australian government has launched two security reviews to reassess the potential national security risks of the Chinese-owned road freight company Landbridge's 99-year lease of the Port of Darwin under the FATA in 2021 and the SOCI Act (as well as other legislation such as the *Defence Act 1903*) in 2022.[35] Though the investor at issue is not a Chinese SOE and both the retrospective reviews concluded that there was no national security justification for unravelling the deal, the reviews suggest an even greater likelihood that the Australian government could strip Chinese SOE investors of approved infrastructure-related contracts on national security grounds under the relevant laws.

If national security concerns are determined to exist, the results of such a retrospective security review could result in the imposition or modification of conditions on the investment, the requirement of divestment or the reversal of the investment. The measures would significantly affect the investment at issue and may lead the investor to claim violation of the expropriation provision in CABIT or AHKIA, which prohibits host States from taking measures of similar effects of expropriation 'unless the measures are in the public interest, non discriminatory, in accordance with the law of the Contracting Party which has admitted the investment and against reasonable compensation'.[36] AHKIA specifies the economic impact, the degree of

---

[34] See, e.g., Voon and Merriman (2022b), pp. 62–113; Voon and Merriman (2022a), pp. 75–114.

[35] Zu (2022), pp. 467–483; Department of the Prime Minister and Cabinet (2023) Review – Port of Darwin lease. Media Release.

[36] CABIT (n 3) art. VIII; The expropriation clause of AHKIA is worded similarly. AHKIA (n 7) art. 10.

interference with reasonable expectations and the character of the government action as factors in determining indirect expropriation.[37] When determining whether an indirect expropriation has occurred, modern ISDS practices generally require interference with the investment's property rights,[38] such as the substantial deprivation of at least one of the essential components of the property rights.[39] Earlier tribunals tended to a less stringent approach, requiring a significant removal of 'the use or reasonable-to-be-expected economic benefits' of the investment.[40] In light of the criteria outlined in AHKIA and established in the ISDS practices, an order of divestment, reversal or imposition of conditions that result from a retrospective national security review could readily satisfy the criteria, regardless of the approach taken.

In addition, in the case of a national security-based retrospective review, investors affected would not be entitled to compensation according to the FATA or SOCI Act. In this case, the investor may claim an illegal expropriation due to a lack of reasonable compensation. In practice, when the investment at issue is related to public infrastructure and the host State government mandates divestment, the investor may be compensated by having their investment stake purchased by the government. For example, while the Australian government has made no such order as of December 2023, the government of the UK in 2022 ordered Chinese SOE CGN to sell its stake in the Sizewell C power station and bought the entire stake to regain control over the power infrastructure.[41] In such case, whether the amount of compensation can be deemed 'reasonable' would then become an additional contentious issue in arbitration when determining whether an illegal expropriation has occurred.[42]

When confronted with the expropriation claim, Australia might invoke specific explicit safeguards for policy space in CABIT and AHKIA as defences in arbitration. However, that the successful invocation of the defences is contingent on the specific circumstances of the disputes.

---

[37] AHKIA (n 7) annex II art. 3 (a).

[38] For detailed discussion in this regard, see, e.g., Ortino (2020), pp. 80–82.

[39] *El Paso Energy International Company v Argentina (Award)* (ICSID Arbitral Tribunal, Case No ARB/03/15, 31 October 2011) p. 245; *Pope & Talbot Inc v Canada (Interim Award)* (ad hoc Tribunal, UNCITRAL, 26 June 2000) p. 102.

[40] *Metalclad Corporation v The United Mexican States (Award)* (ICSID Arbitral Tribunal, Case No ARB(AF)/97/1) [103]. This was quoted in *CME Czech Republic B V The Czech Republic (Partial Award)* (1993) 9 ICSID Rep 121, [606].

[41] Department for Business, Energy & Industrial Strategy et al (2022) UK Government Takes Major Steps Forward to Secure Britain's Energy Independence. Press Release.

[42] Both CABIT and AHKIA outline the methodology to calculate reasonable compensation. CABIT (n 3) art. VIII.2; AHKIA (n 7) art. 11.2.

8.1.2.1 Potential Defences for Australia Under CABIT

As noted earlier, CABIT only allows ISDS for disputes that relate to the amount of compensation for expropriation.[43] As a result, a Chinese SOE investor may file an ISDS claim alleging that Australia's retrospective security review and subsequent actions violate CABIT's expropriation clause. However, previous ISDS tribunals have reached divergent conclusions on whether ISDS clauses similar to the provisions in CABIT limit arbitrability to the determination of the quantum of compensation for expropriation or extend to determining questions concerning the existence and illegality of expropriation.[44] Australia may immediately defend itself by raising a jurisdictional challenge centred around the interpretation of the ISDS clause in CABIT. If the tribunal adopts the narrow interpretation, then it may deny its jurisdiction over the claim.

In addition, as noted earlier, CABIT exempts non-discriminatory measures 'in the public interest' from expropriation.[45] Given that the purpose of Australia's national security review mechanism is to protect national security, which is considered a legitimate public interest, this broad public objective carve-out may serve as a viable defence for Australia in defeating an expropriation claim filed by a Chinese SOE investor.

However, a Chinese SOE investor may assert factual discrimination in the review mechanism's implementation to avoid the public objective carve-out, which has been a frequent charge made by the Chinese government when criticising other countries' exclusion of Chinese SOEs from major projects.[46] In practice, however, the onerous evidentiary burden might hinder such an assertion from being established. As demonstrated in Chap. 7, in the implementation of the Australian foreign investment framework, the Treasurer rarely provides explicit justifications for his or her decisions on foreign investment. As a result, a Chinese SOE investor could only rely on circumstantial evidence, such as official statements from the Australian government affirming that the investor's State-owned status influenced the government's decision, to prove Australia has a policy of intentionally discriminating against Chinese SOE investments in legal applications.

---

[43] CABIT (n 3) art. XII.2.

[44] For the expansive interpretation approach, see, e.g., *Government of the Lao People's Democratic Republic v Sanum Investments Ltd* [2015] SGHC 15; and *Sanum Investment Ltd v Government of the Lao People's Democratic Republic* [2016] SGCA 157; For the narrow interpretation approach, see, e.g., *AsiaPhos Limited and Norwest Chemicals Pte Ltd v People's Republic of China* (ICSID Arbitral Tribunal, Case No ADM/21/1, 16 February 2023) [84]-[89].

[45] CABIT (n 3) art. VIII.1.

[46] See, e.g., Embassy of the PRC in the UK (2021) 《驻英国使馆发言人就中英核电合作答记者问》 [Spokesman of the Embassy in the UK Answered Reporters' Questions on Sino-British Nuclear Power Co-operation]. http://gb.china-embassy.gov.cn/lcbt/sgryr/202107/t20210727_8969161.htm. Accessed 3 Sep 2025.

8.1.2.2 Potential Defences for Australia Under AHKIA

AHKIA allows ISDS for disputes concerning any substantive obligations,[47] but excludes from ISDS Australia's decision under its foreign investment framework 'on whether or not to approve a foreign investment proposal'.[48] Because Australia's initiation of retrospective security review is not an admission decision on newly proposed investments, a Chinese SOE could potentially bring such expropriation claim under AHKIA if its investment was made through a Hong Kong subsidiary.

AHKIA, like CABIT, exempts non-discriminatory measures 'for a public purpose' from expropriation,[49] affording Australia a potential defence against an expropriation claim filed by a Chinese SOE contesting its retrospective security review and subsequent actions. In addition, AHKIA contains a WTO-modeled general exception clause (Article 18) and a security exception clause (Article 19). To the extent that the exceptions are relevant to this chapter: Article 18 excepts from treaty protection unarbitrary and justifiable measures that are *necessary* for protecting public morals or public order, securing compliance with laws relating to personal data protection or conserving exhaustible natural resources;[50] Article 19 covers measures to protect essential security interests (about radioactive materials, military equipment and establishment and national emergency), especially adding on the measures relating to critical infrastructure are covered.[51]

As discussed in Chap. 7, Australia's reformed foreign investment framework emphasises sensitive data, critical minerals (mostly exhaustive resources),[52] and critical infrastructure. The SOCI Act is exclusively for infrastructure protection. Therefore, Articles 18 and 19 of AHKIA could shield measures adopted based on the SOCI Act or FATA for protecting personal data, critical minerals and critical infrastructure. However, at least the following conditions must be met for Australia to be able to invoke the exception clauses successfully:

To invoke Article 18 of AHKIA, Australia must establish the nexus between the contested measures and the specified objectives.[53] Notably, AHKIA clarifies that the public moral or public order exception can only be invoked when a 'genuine and sufficiently serious threat is posed to one of the fundamental interests of the society'.[54] This makes it hard for Australia to demonstrate that the continued presence of the Chinese SOE investments on current conditions (if any) poses a threat of such magnitude. If Australia seeks to justify the contested measure for personal data

---

[47] AHKIA (n 7) art. 24.1.

[48] Ibid. annex III.

[49] AHKIA (n 7) art. 10.1, annex II art. 3 (b).

[50] Ibid. art. 18.1.

[51] Ibid. art. 19 footnote 10.

[52] Australia currently designates 31 critical minerals, which can be accessed at https://www.ga.gov.au/scientific-topics/minerals/critical-minerals. Accessed 3 Sep 2025.

[53] For discussion about the application of the WTO general exception clause in ISDS, see generally Mitchell et al. (2018), pp. 323–331.

[54] AHKIA (n 7) n 9.

protection, it must demonstrate that it is *necessary* for the objectives.[55] ISDS tribunals may follow the WTO case law to apply a rigorous necessary test, holistically weighing the relative importance of the interest pursued by the measure.[56] In this case, Australia must prove that no other measure contributes as much to the objective with less 'restrictive impact on international commerce' as the contested measure does to Chinese investment.[57]

If seeking to invoke a critical infrastructure exception under Article 19, Australia must ensure that the investment involves 'critical infrastructure' defined in AHKIA, which includes communications, power, transportation and water infrastructure.[58] The definition of critical infrastructure under the SOCI Act is significantly broader than in AHKIA, covering 11 sectors, including defence, space technology, data storage and processing, etcetera.[59] Australia's foreign investment policy directly incorporates critical infrastructure governed by the SOCI Act into national security businesses that could trigger a national security test for foreign investment.[60] Therefore, only measures adopted under the SOCI Act or FATA against Chinese SOE investments in the communications, power, transportation or water sectors might be shielded by Article 19 of AHKIA.

In conclusion, CABIT and AHKIA may expose Australia to the risk of Chinese SOE investors filing ISDS claims challenging its retrospective security review on the grounds that the review and subsequent actions violate the expropriation clauses of the treaties. Although Australia could potentially use treaty exceptions or exemptions as a defence against such claims, the efficacy of such defences is dependent on the specific circumstances of the dispute, such as the claimant's ability to prove factual discrimination in the review and subsequent actions, the objectives of the contested measures, whether the investment in question involves specified infrastructure and the tribunal's interpretation approach concerning CABIT's ISDS clause.

---

55 See generally Bahmaei and Sabzevari (2023), pp. 97–123.

56 Appellate Body Report (1996) United States – Standards for Reformulated and Conventional Gasoline. WTO Doc WT/DS2/AB/R 17–19.

57 Appellate Body Report (2005) United States – Measures Affecting the Cross-Border Supply of Gambling and Betting Services. WTO Doc WT/DS285/AB/R [306]; Appellate Body Report (2007) Brazil – Measures Affecting Imports of Retreaded Tyres. WTO Doc WT/DS332/AB/R [143], [156].

58 AHKIA (n 7) n 10.

59 *Security of Critical Infrastructure Act* 2018 (Cth) s. 5, as amended by *Security Legislation Amendment (Critical Infrastructure Protection) Act 2022* (Cth), act. 8D.

60 For detailed discussion regarding Australia's foreign investment framework, see Chap. 7 Sect. 7.1.

8.1.3 Breach of National Treatment Under ChAFTA

Prior to later negotiations on incorporating more substantive protections and a broader ISDS clause in the future comprehensive investment chapter, the current ChAFTA only commits Australia to providing pre-establishment NT and MFN protections for covered Chinese investment,[61] and ISDS is only permitted for disputes relating to NT obligation breach.[62] Since Australia's *ex-ante* screening and *ex-post* monitoring of foreign investment under its foreign investment framework do not apply to domestic investors, a Chinese SOE investor may still file an ISDS claim against Australia under the current ChAFTA, alleging that Australia's foreign investment decision on admission or retrospective review and the subsequent actions constitute an NT breach of the treaty. When confronted with such an NT claim, Australia may use three explicit safeguards for policy space in ChAFTA as defences.

The first potential defence is the non-conforming measures (NCMs) that Australia lists in Annex III as being exempt from treaty obligations, which explicitly include measures adopted under Australia's foreign investment policy.[63] Accordingly, Australia may argue that its measure adopted under the FATA or FATR are shielded as an NCM and thus do not constitute a breach of ChAFTA. Nonetheless, this defence is associated with uncertainty: ChAFTA Annex III only covers existing NCMs and their amendment or modification to the extent that 'the amendment or modification does not decrease the conformity of the measure, as it existed immediately before the amendment'.[64] As discussed in Chap. 7, in response to national security concerns, Australia initiated a comprehensive set of reforms to its foreign investment policy that went into effect in January 2021.[65] The reforms significantly tightened the Australian foreign investment framework by, for example, introducing a new national security test and enhancing the Treasurer's compliance and retrospective review powers (call-in and last resort powers).[66] Voon and Merriman, in their comprehensive analysis of the risk of conflicts between Australia's reformed foreign investment screening mechanism and its obligations under international investment law, point out that Australia's 2021 foreign investment framework arguably reduces compliance with the NT obligation under IIAs.[67] This is because the reformed framework subjects foreign investors in Australia to additional pre-establishment and retrospective reviews and powers, whereas domestic investors in like circumstances are not.[68] As a result, if Australia's FATA or FATR-based measures for Chinese SOE investments are adopted based on powers introduced or

[61] ChAFTA (n 4) art. 9.3.

[62] Ibid. art. 19.12, 9.11.4.

[63] Ibid. art. 9.3, 9.4, 9.5, annex III pt. 1 s A art. 1.

[64] Ibid. art. 9.5.1 (c).

[65] *Foreign Investment Reform (Protecting Australia's National Security) Act 2020* (Cth).

[66] For detailed discussion regarding Australia's foreign investment reforms, see Chap. 7 Sect. 7.1.

[67] Voon and Merriman (2022b), pp. 13–15.

[68] Ibid.

enhanced in the 2021 reforms, such as retrospective security review based on the Treasurer's last resort power, they may not qualify for protection as an NCM under ChAFTA Annex III.

Notably, ChAFTA empowers the Parties to issue legally binding joint interpretations on the Schedule of NCMs.[69] This term may allow Australia to argue that Annex III covers measures adopted under the amended FATA or FATR when a Chinese SOE claimant challenges the scope of NCMs in arbitration. In such a case, the tribunal shall request the Parties' interpretation of the scope of NCM.[70] Accordingly, the success of Australia's use of the defence depends on two factors: first, the extent to which it can reach a consensus with China concerning the interpretation of the no further conformity reduction requirement, and second, whether the specific tribunal recognises the advanced agreed binding effect of the joint interpretation, which has become contentious in ISDS practice due to concerns that the Parties may abuse their interpretative power and thwart investors' reasonable expectations.[71] If Australia and China fail to reach a consensus on the scope of Annex III within 90 days, the tribunal will decide the issue.[72]

The second possible defence for Australia in ChAFTA is the public welfare carve-out for ISDS. ChAFTA exempts from ISDS measures 'that are non-discriminatory and for the legitimate public welfare objectives of public health, safety, the environment, public morals or public order'.[73] This ISDS carve-out may give Australia a foothold to argue its measures adopted under the FATA or SOCI Act that adversely affect Chinese SOE investments are for protection of national interest, which arguably falls under the 'public order' as a legitimate public welfare objective.[74] However, this defence may be weakened by two factors: First, comparable to the public welfare carve-out for expropriation in CABIT and AHKIA, a Chinese investor may assert that Australia's contested measure is implemented in a discriminatory manner to avoid the public objective carve-out. However, as discussed above, such a claim is subject to the investor's onerous evidentiary burden in establishing factual discrimination in legal applications. Secondly, to invoke the carve-out, Australia must issue a 'public welfare notice' to initiate a consultation with China on the applicability of the exclusion to the contested measure, which would trigger a 90-day suspension period of the ISDS procedure.[75] A joint decision reached by the two countries is binding on the tribunal, and if no such decision is reached, the tribunal will decide the issue.[76] Therefore, the defence's success is

---

[69] ChAFTA (n 4) art. 9.18.2, 9.19.

[70] Ibid. art. 9.19.1.

[71] Roberts (2010), pp. 179–225.

[72] ChAFTA (n 4) art. 9.19.2.

[73] Ibid. art. 9.11.4.

[74] Prodromou (2020), p. 196.

[75] ChAFTA (n 4) art. 9.11.5, 9.11.6.

[76] Ibid. art. 9.18.3, 9.11.8.

contingent on the result of the consultation, which introduces unpredictability amidst the ongoing geopolitical tensions between the Parties.

The preceding analysis demonstrates that Australia could be vulnerable to ISDS claims under the current IIA framework when it regulates a Chinese SOE investment. It should be noted that the potential claims outlined above are not exhaustive. Depending on the specifics of the circumstances, a Chinese SOE investor may bring other claims against Australia under the applicable treaties, such as a FET violation claim. However, in the 2020 decided case *Global Telecom v Canada*, the Egyptian claimant alleged that that Canada's national security review under the *Investment Canada Act* (which resulted in the claimant being barred from acquiring a controlling stake in the joint venture at issue) violates the FET obligation under the *Canada-Egypt Foreign Investment Promotion and Protection Agreement*.[77] The tribunal took the view that a host State's foreign investment decision is less likely to constitute a FET violation if the State can demonstrate the decision was based on genuine national interest or security concerns and the investor was given adequate opportunity to make its case in relation to the reviews.[78] This stance may imply that it will be difficult for a Chinese SOE investor to bring a FET violation claim to challenge Australia's national security review.

8.2 Australia's SOE Rules in IIAs: An Effective Way of Addressing Non-competitive Issues in Chinese SOE Investments?

Over the last two decades, Australia has incorporated SOE disciplines into a number of IIAs, with a particular emphasis on the competitive neutrality of Parties' SOEs in international business activities. The escalating political influence over Chinese SOEs as a result of the latest round of SOE reforms heightens concerns regarding the proliferation of their investments in Australia,[79] especially with respect to non-competitive issues. At present, none of the extant IIAs between Australia and China have incorporated SOE rules. This section investigates whether introducing SOE rules in an IIA with China would provide Australia with an efficient way of coping with the non-competitive issues associated with Chinese SOE investments.

[77] *Global Telecom Holding SAE v Canada (Award)* (ICSID Arbitral Tribunal, Case No ARB/16/16, 27 March 2020) [573]-[582].

[78] Ibid. [601]-[618]; see generally Paine (2021), pp. 533–547.

[79] For detailed discussion regarding the escalating political control, see Chap. 5.

8.2.1 Overview of Australia's SOE Rules in IIAs

Since signing the *Singapore-Australia Free Trade Agreement* (SAFTA) in 2003,[80] Australia has signed 17 FTAs, 10 of which include rules dealing specifically with SOEs applicable to the investment chapter.[81] Table 8.2 lists all of Australia's IIAs with special SOE rules, including the location and description of the rules. However, no IIA between Australia and China has contained special SOE disciplines. This may be attributed to the Chinese government's resistance, given the large number of SOEs in China that could pose significant compliance difficulties. This is supported by the fact that most of Australia's FTAs with countries with extensive SOEs do not include SOE rules, such as Thailand, Indonesia and other ASEAN member countries.[82]

Table 8.2 demonstrates a development in Australia's IIAs concerning SOE regulations: Before 2018, Australia signed 6 IIAs that include SOE rules. These SOE rules are all a handful of provisions in the competition chapter of the treaties, primarily focusing on the competitive neutrality of SOE in international trade and investment activities. Typically, they prohibit the Parties from granting SOEs competitive advantages simply because they are State-owned,[83] or require the Parties to adopt measures to address the anti-competitive conduct of SOEs.[84]

In 2018, the *Comprehensive and Progressive Agreement for Trans-Pacific Partnership* (CPTPP), a multilateral FTA to which Australia is one of the 12 Parties, was signed and entered into force, following a protracted negotiating process and evolution from the Trans-Pacific Partnership.[85] The treaty contains an SOE chapter, establishing a new practice for advanced and comprehensive SOE regulations in

[80] *Singapore-Australia Free Trade Agreement*. Signed 17 February 2003. [2003] ATS 16 (entered into force 28 July 2003), as amended by *Singapore–Australia Free Trade Agreement Amendments*. Signed 21 April 2005. [2006] ATS 9 (entered into force 24 February 2006) ('SAFTA').

[81] For example, SAFTA Investment Chapter defines 'enterprise' as including governmentally owned or controlled entities. Ibid. ch. 8 art. 1.

[82] For example, Thailand-Australia FTA, ASEAN-Australia-New Zealand FTA and Australia-Indonesia FTA do not have SOE rules.

[83] Notably, the prohibition on competitive advantage in the *Australia-US FTA* is applicable only to Australia. SAFTA (n 80) ch.12 art. 4; *Australia–US Free Trade Agreement*. Signed 18 May 2004. [2005] ATS 1 (entered into force 1 January 2005) art. 14.4.3 ('AUSFTA'); *Australia–Chile Free Trade Agreement*. Signed 30 July 2008. 2694 UNTS 3 (entered into force 6 March 2009) art. 14.5.4; *Free Trade Agreement between the Government of Australia and the Government of the Republic of Korea*. Signed 8 April 2014. [2014] ATS 43 (entered into force 12 December 2014) art. 14.4; *Agreement Between Australia and Japan for an Economic Partnership*. Signed 8 July 2014. [2015] ATS 2 (entered into force 15 January 2015) art. 15.4.

[84] *Malaysia–Australia Free Trade Agreement*. Signed 22 May 2012. [2013] ATS 4 (entered into force 1 January 2013) art. 14.4.3 ('MAFTA'); AUSFTA (n 83) art. 14.4.2.

[85] *Comprehensive and Progressive Agreement for Trans-Pacific Partnership*. Signed 8 March 2018. [2018] ATS 23 (entered into force 30 December 2018) ('CPTPP'), incorporating *Trans-Pacific Partnership Agreement*. Signed 4 February 2016. [2016] ATNIF 2 (not in force).

Table 8.2 The SOE Rules in Australia's IIAs

Name	Date	Location	SOE rules
Singapore-Australia FTA	2003	Chapter 12 Competition Policy	Competitive advantage prohibition (Article 4)
Australia-US FTA	2004	Chapter 14 Competition-related Matters	1. Consistent with treaty obligations (Article 14.4.1) 2. Sub-federal SOEs within the reach of anti-trust laws (only for the US) (Article 14.4.2) 3. Competitive advantage prohibition (only for Australia) (Article 14.4.3) 4. Transparency (Article 14.8)
Australia-Chile FTA	2008	Chapter 14 Competition Policy	1. Consistent with treaty obligations (Article 14.5.2) 2. Competitive advantage prohibition (Article 14.5.4) 3. Transparency (Article14.8)
Malaysia-Australia FTA	2012	Chapter 14 Competition Policy	Obligation to address SOEs' anti-competitive conduct (Article 14.4.3)
Korea-Australia FTA	2014	Chapter 14 Competition Policy	Competitive advantage prohibition (Article 14.4)
Japan-Australia Economic Partnership Agreement	2014	Chapter 15 Competition and Consumer Protection	Competitive advantage prohibition (Article 15.4)
CPTPP	2018	Chapter 17 State-owned Enterprises and Designated Monopolies	1. Commercial Considerations (Article 17.4) 2. Non-commercial Assistance (Article 17.6) 3. Transparency (Article 17.10)
Peru-Australia FTA	2018	Chapter 16 State-owned Enterprises and Designated Monopolies	1. Commercial Considerations (Article 16.4) 2. Non-commercial Assistance (Article 16.6) 3. Transparency
Australia- UK FTA	2021	Chapter 18 State-owned Enterprises and Designated Monopolies	1. Commercial Considerations (Article 18.4) 2. Non-commercial Assistance (Article 18.6) 3. Transparency

international trade and investment agreements.[86] The CPTPP SOE rules, as shown in Table 8.2, continue to emphasise the competitive neutrality of SOE commercial activities, with more specialised obligations imposed on the Parties. Many developed economies have modelled the SOE regulations of their FTAs after the CPTPP

[86] Zhou (2021), pp. 572–590.

SOE chapter.[87] Australia's subsequent FTAs with Peru (PAFTA) and the UK (A-UKFTA) also incorporate a CPTPP-modelled SOE chapter.[88]

In September 2021, China officially applied to join the CPTPP.[89] During Australian Prime Minister Anthony Albanese's visit to China, Chinese Premier Li Qiang called for Australia's support in joining the CPTPP, making this more of a real issue.[90] China's potential accession to the CPTPP indicates the country's preliminary readiness to accept, at least in part, the SOE disciplines thereof This may also lay the groundwork for the introduction of SOE rules to be on the table in upcoming negotiations between Australia and China on a comprehensive investment chapter of ChAFTA, though SOE rules are not mentioned explicitly in the future work programme.

As discussed in Chap. 7, the proliferation of Chinese SOE investments triggered concerns from the Australian government regarding the competitive distortion impact of Chinese SOE investments on the local market, due to Chinese SOEs' inherent closeness to the government owner and general operational opacity. As a result, a pressing question arises: if the CPTPP SOE rules are incorporated into IIAs with China, will Australia be able to effectively address the non-competitive issue in Chinese SOE investments?

8.2.2 *CPTPP SOE Disciplines and the China Challenge*

The CPTPP SOE Chapter (Chapter 17) comprises 15 provisions and 7 annexes. The chapter applies to the activities of the Parties' SOEs that have an impact on trade or investment between the Parties.[91] As noted earlier, the CPTPP SOE rules maintain an emphasis on the competitive neutrality of SOEs' international trade and investment activities. Under the CPTPP Chapter 17, the Parties are obligated to ensure that SOEs operate under commercial considerations (Article 17.4), prohibit non-commercial assistance (NCA) (Article 17.6) and adhere to a transparency require-

[87] For example, *North American Free Trade Agreement*. Canada-Mexico-United States of America. Signed 17 December 1992. [1994] CTS 2 (entered into force 1 January 1994).

[88] Free Trade Agreement between Australia and the Republic of Peru. Signed 12 February 2018. [2020] ATS 6 (entered into force 11 February 2020) ch. 16 ('PAFTA'); Free Trade Agreement between Australia and the United Kingdom of Great Britain and Northern Ireland. Signed 17 December 2021. [2022] ATNIF 3 (entered into force on 31 May 2023) ch. 18 ('A–UKFTA').

[89] Ministry of Foreign Affairs (2023) 《中国有意愿有能力加入CPTPP》 [China Willing, Capable of Joining CPTPP]. https://www.mfa.gov.cn/web/wjdt_674879/zwbd_674895/202308/t20230821_11129519.shtml. Accessed 13 Aug 2025.

[90] Mo and Fang (2023) 《澳洲总理访华特别报道:阿尔巴尼斯总理与中国国家主席习近平举行会晤》 [Special Report on Australian Prime Minister's Visit to China: Australian Prime Minister Albanese Meets with Chinese President Xi Jinping]. ABC. https://www.abc.net.au/chinese/2023-11-06/australian-pm-albanese-arrives-in-beijing-to-meet-xi-jinping/103067960. Accessed 13 Aug 2025.

[91] CPTPP (n 85) art. 17.2.1.

ment (Article 17.10). The provisions in Chapter 17 are subject to the State-State dispute settlement mechanism provided in the Chapter 28 of the CPTPP, potentially strengthening the enforceability of the SOE rules.[92] Chapter 17 of the CPTPP is largely imitated in the SOE chapters of Australia's subsequent IIAs with Peru (Chapter 16) and the UK (Chapter 18).

8.2.2.1 Regulating Policy-Driven Chinese SOE Investment: Limits of the CPTPP Model

The CPTPP SOE Chapter was shaped by US influence and reflects its early concerns about the global expansion of Chinese SOEs before the US withdrawal from the TPP in 2017.[93] Given the distinctive governance framework of Chinese SOEs and the trajectory of the latest round of reforms, neither the CPTPP SOE Chapter nor the SOE chapters in Australia's CPTPP-modelled agreements, such as PAFTA and A-UKFTA, is likely to address effectively the most challenging aspect of Chinese SOE investment, namely non-commercial drivers or political investment motivations.

A central limitation lies in the narrow definition of an SOE. Under the CPTPP, PAFTA and A-UKFTA, an SOE is defined as an enterprise 'principally engaged in commercial activities' in which a Party either (a) directly owns more than 50 per cent of share capital, (b) controls more than 50 per cent of voting rights, or (c) has the power to appoint a majority of the board or equivalent management body.[94]

In the context of China's current reforms, these ownership and control thresholds are not, on their face, difficult to meet. As shown in Chap. 3, the MOR aims to diversify SOE ownership but in practice State equity rarely falls below majority control except in sectors with overcapacity or in financially distressed enterprises. In the SOE governance system reform, Chinese SOEs are implementing a distinctive SOE governance system. This system emphasises the CCP's supremacy in SOE governance practices, particularly by ensuring the Party Committee's supreme position in corporate decision-making and enhancing political personnel connections.[95] Under the revised *Constitution of the CCP*, many Chinese SOEs have changed their Articles of Association (AAs) to establish the CCP's leadership over formal governance practices.[96] For example, COFCO Capital Holding, a wholly owned subsidiary of COFCO, has a standalone chapter in its AA outlining the Party Committee's

---

[92] Ibid. art. 28.3.

[93] Fleury and Marcoux (2016), pp. 445–465.

[94] CPTPP (n 85) art. 17.1; PAFTA (n 88) art. 16.1; A–UKFTA (n 88) art. 18.1.

[95] For detailed discussion regarding the unique governance system of Chinese SOEs, see Chap. 4 Sect. 4.2.

[96] 《中国共产党章程》 [Constitution of the Communist Party of China]. Adopted at the 20th CCP National Congress. 22 October 2022, art. 33.

leading role and specific functions in corporate governance.[97] Hence, the AAs of Chinese SOEs can provide concrete evidence of continued State dominance over board appointments and voting rights.

The definitional difficulty arises from the requirement that an SOE be 'principally engaged in commercial activities'. As noted earlier, in the MOR, Chinese SOEs are categorised by their contributions to national economic and social development. SOEs operating in critical industries are generally classified as 'Special Commercial', while those providing public utilities are typically classified as 'Public Welfare'. The two categories of SOEs are tasked with various policy missions, such as serving society and the national standard of living and ensuring national security.[98] In addition, SOEs designated as SCIOs in the State-owned assets management system reform are authorised to perform a portion of the SASACs' responsibilities, advancing national strategies and increasing the returns on State-owned capital.[99] Due to the assigned policy tasks, it is difficult to ascertain if China's 'Public Welfare' and 'Special Commercial' SOEs and SCIOs are *principally* involved in commercial activities, and so fall under the CPTPP's definition of SOE. This is problematic because many well-known Chinese global investors are 'Public Welfare' and 'Special Commercial' SOEs or SCIOs. For instance, China Minmetals, the acquirer of Australian company OZ Minerals, is categorised as 'Special Commercial', and Chinalco, which invested in Australian mining company Rio Tinto, is designated as a SCIO.[100] Although the CPTPP allows State-State consultation panels to assess an SOE's activities based on operational evidence rather than domestic categorisation alone, official designations may still serve as prima facie indicators of non-commercial objectives.

In addition, CPTPP Article 17.4 requires Parties to ensure that SOEs act in accordance with commercial considerations, yet this obligation applies only to the purchase or sale of goods and services. It does not extend to investment activities.[101] This omission leaves policy-driven outbound investment beyond the scope of direct treaty discipline, even though it is a key concern for many host states. The absence of an explicit prohibition on policy-driven investment may reflect a deliberate choice to preserve host State discretion in foreign investment facilitation. As discussed in Chap. 7, Australia applies a realistic approach to foreign government investors through its FIRB process, permitting policy-driven investments where they align with the national interest.[102] In China's socialist economy, SOE investment

---

[97] COFCO Capital (2021) Articles of Association of COFCO Capital Holding Company. http://newimg.cofco-capital.com/Uploads/Zlzbgb/File/2021/10/25/u617603267bc0b.pdf. Accessed 13 Aug 2025.

[98] For more detailed discussion regarding SOE classification, see Chap. 3 Sect. 3.1.

[99] For more detailed discussion regarding SCIOs, see Chap. 4 Sect. 4.1.2.2.

[100] The State Council (2022) 《5家中央企业正式转为国有资本投资公司》 [Five Central Enterprises Formally Transformed into State-Owned Capital Investment Companies]. https://www.gov.cn/xinwen/2022-06/21/content_5696886.htm. Accessed 13 Aug 2025.

[101] PAFTA (n 88) art. 16.4; A–UKFTA (n 88) art. 18.4.

[102] For more details regarding the realistic approach, see Chap. 7 Sect. 7.1.2.1.

inevitably aligns with national strategies such as the Go Global policy and the Belt and Road Initiative. The existence of policy objectives does not necessarily mean a conflict with host State's interests. A blanket prohibition would risk signalling economic protectionism and disregarding political-economic diversity, particularly where such investment can be reconciled with national interest considerations.

The CPTPP's limited capacity to regulate SOE policy-driven investment highlights a broader point. Treaty disciplines can promote competitive neutrality in certain market transactions, but they are neither designed nor necessarily suited to eliminate all State influence over cross-border capital flows. The more pressing governance challenge is to ensure that SOE policy-driven investment is managed with transparency and evaluated case by case against legitimate public interest criteria rather than subjected to categorical exclusion.

8.2.2.2 Compliance Hurdles for China Under CPTPP SOE Rules

Despite its predicted ineffectiveness in curbing SOEs' politically motivated investments, the CPTPP nonetheless presents significant challenges for China in meeting the SOE-specific rules in Chapter 17 if the country were to join the treaty or if such provisions were incorporated into Australia–China IIAs.

To address competitive distortions arising from government aid to SOEs, CPTPP Article 17.6 prohibits Parties from providing their SOEs with NCA that causes 'adverse effects on the interests of another Party' or 'injury to a domestic industry of another Party'.[103] This represents an evolution from Australia's pre-CPTPP SOE rule, which imposed a more general prohibition on conferring competitive advantages on SOEs. As discussed in Chap. 5, despite China's shift away from a command economy, SOEs continue to receive both explicit and implicit fiscal or financial support from the government in pursuit of State policy objectives. For example, policy-aligned investment projects by SOEs may receive funding from the Special Fund for Foreign Trade and Economic Development administered by MOF and MOFCOM, or below-market-rate policy loans from State-owned banks.[104] Such measures could potentially constitute a violation of the NCA prohibition under the CPTPP.

Importantly, CPTPP Article 17.1 limits the scope of NCA to government assistance provided to an SOE by virtue of that SOE's government ownership or control. China might contend that outbound investment subsidies are granted based on the declared alignment of projects with national policy rather than the ownership status of the investor.[105] However, empirical evidence indicates a substantial preference for SOEs in the allocation of financial aid. For example, data released by the Guangdong

---

[103] PAFTA (n 88) art 16.6; A–UKFTA (n 88) art. 18.6.

[104] For detailed discussion in this regard, see Chap. 5 Sect. 5.1.3.

[105] See, e.g., 《外经贸发展专项资金管理办法》 [Measures for the Management of Special Project Fund for Foreign Trade and Economic Development] (People's Republic of China). MOF and MOFCOM. 9 April 2014, art. 10.

provincial government in 2023 shows that 100 of the 148 FDI projects receiving MOF–MOFCOM funding were proposed by SOEs.[106] The stated policy-based rationale, combined with the opacity of approval processes, is unlikely to be sufficient to negate a causal link between State ownership and the provision of assistance.

In addition, the transparency requirements in CPTPP Chapter 17 present a further challenge for China. Article 17.10 obliges each Party to publish, on an official website accessible to the other Parties, a list of its SOEs.[107] Upon request from another Party, the responding Party must also disclose detailed information on a given SOE, including the percentage of shares or voting rights it holds, the official titles of any government officials serving as officers or directors, the SOE's annual revenue and total assets over the most recent three-year period, any exemptions or immunities the SOE enjoys under domestic law,[108] and any policy or programme providing NCA, provided that the request includes an explanation of how such measures affect or could affect trade or investment between the Parties.[109]

This breadth of transparency obligations creates compliance difficulties for China beyond the NCA context, as they extend to institutional, financial, and governance information that goes to the heart of the Party-SOE relationship. Many Chinese SOEs operate within complex corporate structures involving cross-shareholdings, multiple layers of subsidiaries, and mixed-ownership vehicles. In practice, the formal shareholder registers may not fully capture the extent of Party-State control exercised through CCP committees embedded within the enterprise, or through indirect equity and contractual arrangements. Disclosing the titles of government officials on SOE boards may also expose politically sensitive appointments that China has historically treated as confidential under State secrecy rules.

China's track record under the WTO further underscores these challenges. When China acceded in 2001, it undertook comparable transparency commitments for trade-related measures, yet compliance has often been partial or delayed.[110] In the NCA context, the opacity of SOE funding channels, which may combine overt budgetary transfers with covert policy lending or preferential regulatory treatment, would make it difficult for CPTPP consultation panels to verify whether China's disclosures are comprehensive. For the non-NCA elements, similar obstacles arise. Incomplete publication of SOE lists, selective disclosure of financial data, and reluctance to reveal exemptions or immunities could frustrate the operation of the transparency mechanism. These gaps would not only impede enforcement but also

---

106 Department of Commerce of Guangdong Province (2023) 《关于中央财政2023年度外经贸发展专项资金(促进对外投资合作事项)分配方案的公示》 [Announcement on the 2023 Distribution Plan of the Special Funds for the Development of Foreign Trade and Economic Cooperation (Matters of Promoting Foreign Investment and Cooperation) of the Central Government]. http://com.gd.gov.cn/attachment/0/523/523779/4204348.pdf. Accessed 13 Aug 2025.

107 CPTPP (n 85) art. 17.10.1.

108 Ibid. art. 17.10.3.

109 Ibid. art. 17.10.4.

110 Chen (2012), pp. 25–50.

weaken the CPTPP's objective of ensuring a level playing field in markets where SOEs compete with private and foreign enterprises.

Overall, the CPTPP SOE Chapter faces two fundamental limitations in its application to Chinese SOEs. First, its definitional scope and transaction-based disciplines leave policy-driven outbound investment, central to the CCP's MOR and SCIO framework, largely beyond direct treaty control. Second, its substantive obligations on NCA and transparency create compliance demands that strike at the core of the Party-SOE relationship, confronting the opacity and political embedding that define China's SOE governance.

These constraints operate together to produce a significant gap between the CPTPP's competitive neutrality objectives and the realities of Chinese SOE reform and practice. While Chinese SOEs remain key instruments of China's socialist economic development, their distinctive governance structures and State-embedded functions make it inherently difficult to design IIA provisions that effectively address their non-commercial conduct. Australia's CPTPP-modelled SOE rules represent an important step forward in the international regulatory agenda, offering innovation and breadth in tackling SOE-related distortions. Yet the preceding analysis shows that even full acceptance of the CPTPP SOE Chapter by China, without reservations, would be unlikely to resolve the competitive concerns surrounding Chinese SOE investments. Addressing these issues would require SOE disciplines that are not only comprehensive in scope but also progressive in confronting the political and institutional specificities of China's Party-State economy.

8.3 Chinese SOEs in ISDS Arbitrations: Will There Be More?

The earlier discussion demonstrates that, in theory, Australia is vulnerable to ISDS claims under the current Australia-China IIAs regarding its regulatory measures affecting Chinese SOE investments. This section investigates the actual involvement of Chinese SOEs in ISDS. Although Chinese SOE investors have not yet instituted a direct challenge against Australia in international investment arbitration, the analysis in this section can provide Australia with insight into the growing likelihood that Chinese SOEs will file IIA-based ISDS claims against Australia in the context of the latest round of SOE reforms. Given the extensive discussion of China's experience in ISDS arbitration in legal scholarship (as both a respondent and the home State of the claimant),[111] this section will not examine the merits of the cases but instead will focus on the potential change of Chinese SOEs' role in Chinese ISDS practices.

[111] See, e.g., Chaisse and Olaoye (2020), pp. 134–193; Zhang (2017), pp. 241–243.

8.3.1 *The Role of Chinese SOEs as Claimant in ISDS Arbitration*

Although most of China's existing IIAs include an ISDS clause,[112] China has limited involvement in ISDS arbitration as a respondent or home State of the claimants. Since the first Chinese IIA-based claim was submitted in 2007 by Tza Yap Shum, a Hong Kong individual investor,[113] Chinese investors have only filed 19 ISDS claims (as of December 2023) including one brought by a Macau investor and 6 by Hong Kong investors. Table 8.3 compiles all publicly known Chinese IIA-based ISDS claims filed by Chinese investors as of November 2023, sourced from UNCTAD's International Investment Dispute Settlement Navigator (ISDS Navigator) database.[114] The table includes essential information such as the time, claimant types, treaty basis, alleged breaches, case status and the implications of the latest round of SOE reforms for the claimants.

Table 8.3 reveals that Chinese SOEs have been particularly inactive in instituting ISDS arbitrations. As of December 2023, Chinese SOEs have only filed 4 ISDS claims, including 2 claims submitted by the subsidiaries of Chinese central BGs (PowerChina, China Railway and China National Building Material) and 2 claims submitted by municipal SOEs (Beijing Urban Construction Group (BUCG) and Beijing Shougang). Considering the significant part SOEs play in total Chinese FDI,[115] the low number of SOE ISDS claims is surprising.

Many studies have looked into possible explanations for Chinese investors' general lack of engagement with ISDS, such as the fact that China's IIAs signed prior to 2000 only provide highly limited ISDS access.[116] Chinese investors' general reluctance in seeking redress under international investment law,[117] and the cultural resistance common in Asia towards engaging in formal legal disputes.[118] In addition to these common factors, there may be other reasons why Chinese SOEs have not been particularly active in initiating ISDS arbitration.

To begin with, Chinese SOEs typically are industry-dominant players with government backing, making them highly wealthy and thus less sensitive to financial

---

[112] Matteo Vaccaro-Incisa (2021), p. 24.

[113] Tza Yap Shum filed the ISDS claim under the *China - Peru BIT (*1994*)*. He claimed that the measures taken by Peru's tax authority amounted to an indirect expropriation of its investment in TSG del Peru SAC and, as such, violated the treaty. The investor prevailed the arbitration. *Señor Tza Yap Shum v The Republic of Peru (Award)*. ICSID Arbitral Tribunal. Case No ARB/07/6. 7 July 2011.

[114] UNCTAD (2025c) ISDS Navigator - China. https://investmentpolicy.unctad.org/investment-dispute-settlement/country/42/china. Accessed 13 Aug 2025.

[115] By the end of 2021, SOEs had accounted for 51.6 percent of China's stock of non-financial FDI. MOFCOM, NBS and SAFE (2022) 2021 Statistical Bulletin of China's Outward Foreign Direct Investment. China Commerce and Trade Press, p. 30.

[116] Bath (2017b), p. 70.

[117] Li (2021), pp. 375–427.

[118] Nottage and Romesh Weeramantry (2012), pp. 19–62; Wang (2011), pp. 204–233.

Table 8.3 The IIA-based ISDS Arbitrations Filed by Chinese Investors

No	Year	Case Name	Investor type	Treaty	Status	The claimant's involvement in China's SOE reforms?
1	2022	Huawei v Sweden	POE	China-Sweden BIT 1982 (amended in 2004)	Pending	N/A
2	2022	Junefield v Ecuador	POE (Hong Kong)	China - Ecuador BIT (1994) (terminated in 2018)	Pending	Yes
3	2022	PCCW v Saudi Arabia	POE (Hong Kong)	China - Saudi Arabia BIT (1996)	Pending	Yes
4	2022	PowerChina Huadong Engineering Corporation and China Railway 18th Bureau Group Company v Viet Nam	SOEs	ASEAN - China Investment Agreement (2009)	Pending	Yes
5	2021	Alpene v Malta	POE (Hong Kong)	China - Malta BIT (2009)	Pending	The investor had an Iranian background with no substantial connection with China.
6	2021	Beijing Everyway Traffic and Lighting Tech v Ghana	POE	China - Ghana BIT (1989)	Lack of jurisdiction	N/A
7	2021	Qiong Ye and Jianping Yang v Cambodia	Individual investors	ASEAN - China Investment Agreement (2009)	Pending	Yes
8	2021	Wang Jiazhu v Finland	Individual investor	China - Finland BIT (2004)	Jurisdiction upheld	N/A
9	2021	Fengzhen Min v Korea	Individual investor	China – Korea BIT (2007)	Pending	N/A
10	2020	Shift Energy v Japan	POE (Hong Kong)	Hong Kong - Japan BIT (1997)	Pending	N/A

(continued)

Table 8.3 (continued)

No	Year	Case Name	Investor type	Treaty	Status	The claimant's involvement in China's SOE reforms?
11	2020	Wang Jing, Li Fengju, Ren Jinglin and others v Ukraine	Individual investors	China - Ukraine BIT (1992)	Pending	Yes
12	2019	Jetion Solar Co. Ltd and Wuxi T-Hertz Co. Ltd. v Greece	SOE	China - Greece BIT (1992)	Claim withdrawn	Yes
13	2018	Zhongshan Fucheng Industrial Investment Co. Ltd. v Nigeria	POE	China - Nigeria BIT (2001)	The investor prevails	N/A
14	2017	Sanum Investments Ltd. v Laos	POE (Macau)	China – Laos BIT (1993)	Host State prevails	The investor is a subsidiary of a Dutch holding company owned by Americans, with no connection with China.
15	2014	Beijing Urban Construction Group v Yemen	SOE	China - Yemen BIT (1998)	Jurisdiction upheld	N/A
16	2012	Ping An v Belgium	POE	Belgium-Luxembourg Economic Union (BLUE)- China BIT (1984),	Lack of jurisdiction	Yes
17	2011	Philip Morris v Australia	POE (Hong Kong)	Australia - Hong Kong BIT (1993) (terminated)		N/A
18	2010	Beijing Shougang and Others v Mongolia	SOE	China - Mongolia BIT (1991)	Lack of jurisdiction	N/A
19	2007	Tza Yap Shum v Peru	Individual investors (Hong Kong)	China - Peru BIT (1994)	The investor prevails	The investor had no connection with Mainland China.

loss than Chinese POEs and individual investors.[119] Therefore, a Chinese SOE investor might consider ISDS proceedings unnecessary in pursuing redress due to the protracted duration and potentially challenging enforcement of decisions.[120] This is corroborated by Table 8.3, which indicates that only 6 of the 17 ISDS cases have resulted in final awards, including 3 that were decided on the basis of lack of jurisdiction. Among the decided cases, Chinese POE Zhongshan Fucheng won its case against Nigeria in 2021, but it allegedly still has not received full payment from Nigeria for expropriation and damages.[121]

Secondly, politics often plays a role in Chinese SOEs' investment decisions, and in this instance, political considerations could affect how Chinese SOEs resolve investment disputes. While political considerations are typically hidden behind the scenes, there are instances of high-profile SOE investments that had apparent political backing: During President Xi Jinping's official visit to the UK in 2015, the Chinese State-owned energy corporation China General Nuclear Power Corporation (CGN) signed an investment agreement with the French energy company EDF Energy for the joint development of three nuclear-generating stations in the UK.[122] As demonstrated in Chap. 6, the Xi Jinping administration continues the 'Go Global' policy, encouraging Chinese SOEs to pursue global expansion with policy objectives.[123] In this light, Chinese SOEs that have made overseas investments with overt or covert government backing may hesitate to engage in ISDS arbitration with the host States. The hesitation may stem from concerns regarding the potential damage to China's diplomatic ties with the host States and the consequent loss of lucrative business prospects in the countries. In addition, Chinese SOEs may prefer that the government mediate their disputes with the host States, which may lead to a more favourable settlement of the disputes. Nonetheless, the ongoing Sino-Western geopolitical tensions make the State-State dialogue difficult, which may lead to an increase in future ISDS claims initiated by Chinese SOE investors.

Other factors may also contribute to the inactivity of Chinese SOEs in ISDS, such as the leaders' lack of English proficiency and SOE executives' fear of being exposed for misconduct in overseas operations in ISDS proceedings,[124] which could be detrimental to their careers. The latter factor has become highly significant since

[119] Yu and Zhou (2013) 《国有垄断企业问题研究:文献回顾及政策建议》 [Research on State-Owned Monopolies: Literature Review and Policy Recommendations]. Brookings. https://www.brookings.edu/wp-content/uploads/2016/06/Chinese-State-Owned-Enterprises.pdf. Accessed 13 Aug 2025.

[120] Voon et al. (2014a), pp. 41–68.

[121] Zhongshan Fucheng then has applied to a UK court and a US court for the recognition and enforcement of the award. *Zhongshan Fucheng Industrial Investment Co Ltd v Federal Republic of Nigeria* [2023] EWCA 867.

[122] Nakano and Melton (2015).

[123] For detailed discussion on China's foreign investment policy, see Chap. 6 Sect. 6.1.

[124] Shining et al. (2018).

the SASAC enhanced the accountability system for losing State-owned assets in 2018 during the latest round of SOE reforms.[125]

In 2021, China's central SASAC issued the *Opinions on Further Deepening the Construction of Central Enterprises under the Rule of Law*, which mandates that the central SOEs increase their understanding of the regulations governing international dispute settlement and the legal frameworks of the host States where they operate significant projects to enhance their capacity to safeguard their interests during global expansion.[126] Consistent with this central document, local SASACs have issued these exact requirements to their respective local SOEs.[127] These government mandates may result in a rise in future ISDS cases initiated by Chinese SOE investors. This can be extrapolated from the rise in China's WTO dispute complaints over the past decade. As of December 2023, China has filed 23 WTO disputes, of which 13 were initiated after 2012, with 8 initiated within the past five years (including 7 against the US and 1 against Australia).[128] This exemplifies China's growing inclination and competence in utilising international dispute settlement mechanisms.

The current Chinese administration's encouragement of SOEs to resort to ISDS is substantively driven by the growing prevalence of restrictive or prohibitive measures targeting Chinese SOE investment in many Western countries, such as Australia, as discussed in Chap. 7. Although such restrictions are publicly justified on grounds of national security or interest, it is hard to disentangle them from the broader context of intensifying geopolitical tensions. Against this backdrop, it is reasonable to view the Chinese government as having a strong imperative to encourage its SOEs to challenge such measures under IIAs. What Chinese SOEs might once resisted, pursuing claims through ISDS, has now become a strategic tool not only to safeguard their overseas commercial interests and State-owned assets but affirm the government's stance within the international investment law order, rather than merely denouncing such measures in press conferences of the Ministry of Foreign Affairs.[129] In turn, however, the increasing resort of Chinese SOEs to ISDS can be expected to intensify the already strong backlash against ISDS provisions in host States, particularly in IIAs concluded with China.[130] ISDS was created as a procedural safeguard enabling foreign investors to directly challenge regulatory

---

125 For detailed discussion regarding the system, see Chap. 5 Sect. 5.2.1.

126 《关于进一步深化法治央企建设的意见》 [Opinions on Further Deepening the Construction of Central Enterprises under the Rule of Law]. (People's Republic of China) The Central SASAC. 17 October 2021.

127 See, e.g., 《关于进一步深化上海法治国企建设的意见》 [Opinions on Further Deepening the Construction of SOEs under the Rule of Law in Shanghai]. (People's Republic of China) The Shanghai SASAC. 9 May 2023.

128 WTO (2025) Disputes by Member. https://www.wto.org/english/tratop_e/dispu_e/dispu_by_country_e.htm. Accessed 13 Aug 2025.

129 See, for example, GMW (2022) 《加拿大以"国家安全"为由要求3家中企撤资，中国外交部回应》 [Canada orders three Chinese companies to divest on grounds of "national security"; Chinese Ministry of Foreign Affairs responds]. https://m.gmw.cn/baijia/2022-11/04/1303185787.html. Accessed 13 Aug 2025.

130 For the backlash against ISDS, see generally Farrington and Jevremović (2025), pp. 1–17.

measures adopted by host States, yet it has been criticised by States for constraining regulatory sovereignty.[131] The increasing use of ISDS by Chinese SOEs is likely to intensify these concerns and prompt (non-ally) countries to further retreat from ISDS, in order to preserve greater regulatory autonomy over Chinese investment within their territories. This trend makes it increasingly unlikely that agreements such as ChAFTA or RCEP will incorporate ISDS mechanisms in any future renegotiations, should such negotiations occur. In addition, China's potential accession to the CPTPP, which includes an ISDS mechanism,[132] could encounter heightened resistance from existing parties concerned about the prospect of ISDS claims initiated by Chinese investors.[133]

8.3.2 Implications of SOE Reforms on ISDS Claims Filed by Chinese POEs

Chinese SOEs' inactivity in bringing ISDS claims does not necessarily imply that they are altogether detached from international investment arbitration, as Chinese POEs and individual claimants are becoming increasingly entangled in a relation network with SOEs as part of the ongoing latest round of SOE reforms.

As shown in Table 8.3, claimants in 3 of 8 ISDS claims filed by Chinese POE investors have significant connections to SOEs due to the latest round of SOE reforms. In the recent cases filed in 2022, *Junefield v Ecuador* and *PCCW v Saudi Arabia*, the claimants are Hong Kong POEs.[134] As a result of the ongoing SOE reforms, both companies have become entangled in an equity network with Chinese SOEs. Specifically, Junefield, the claimant in *Junefield v Ecuador*, is a Hong Kong-based mining company that is 66.75 percent owned by Macrolink Group, a mainland POE. Macrolink Group and China International Capital Corporation (CICC), a Chinese State-owned investment bank, reached an agreement in 2020 whereby CICC would facilitate the introduction of SOEs as strategic investors in Macrolink.[135]

---

[131] Ibid. pp. 1, 2

[132] CPTPP (n 85) ch. 9 s. B.

[133] As of September 2025, CPTPP members have not reached unanimous agreement on China's accession. While countries such as Japan, Canada, and Australia have expressed caution, citing concerns over China's economic policies and coercive practices, others, including Malaysia and Singapore, have taken a more supportive stance. Ken Heydon (2024) Australia can encourage China's credibility in the CPTPP. East Asia Forum. https://eastasiaforum.org/2024/09/23/australia-can-encourage-chinas-credibility-in-the-cptpp/#:~:text=In%20Brief,Australia%20about%20China's%20economic%20coercion. Accessed 13 Aug 2025.

[134] *Junefield Gold Investments Limited v Republic of Ecuador*. PCA Case No. 2023-35. 4 October 2022; *PCCW Cascade (Middle East) Ltd v Kingdom of Saudi Arabia*. ICSID Arbitral Tribunal. Case No ARB/22/20. 26 July 2022.

[135] China Beijing Equity Exchange (2020)《中央企业混合所有制改革暨中央企业民营企业协同发展项目推介会成功举办》 [Conference on Promoting Projects of the Mixed Ownership Reform for Central Enterprises and Synergistic Development between Central Enterprises and

PCCW, the claimant in *PCCW v Saudi Arabia*, is the leading telecommunications provider in Hong Kong. China Unicom, the second-largest wireless telecom in China, has held the position of its second-largest shareholder since 2005. This ownership connection has allowed PCCW to collaborate extensively with mainland SOEs during the latest round of SOE reforms. For example, PCCW and Lenovo, a Chinese State-owned technology company, formed the joint venture PCCW Lenovo Technology Solutions Limited in 2022 to provide services to the Asia-Pacific region.[136]

Chinese mainland insurance firm Ping An filed the case *Ping An v Belgium* in 2012, challenging Belgium's forced nationalisation of its business.[137] Founded initially as an SOE, Ping An sold its majority stake to an overseas investor in 1994. However, in 2016, Shenzhen Investment Holdings, the investment vehicle owned by Shenzhen provincial government, acquired a 5.27 percent stake in Ping An and became the second largest shareholder.[138] Though Ping An's shareholding structure is still rather dispersed and it thus cannot be considered an SOE, its governance practice has reflected an enhancement in political connections following Shenzhen Investment Holdings' investment: For example, Ping An's board of directors now includes two former officials of the Shenzhen government who are now executives at Shenzhen Investment Holdings, and its deputy general manager is a former official of the State Council.[139] Ping An also collaborated closely with the Shenzhen government by signing a strategic cooperative agreement in 2020 to aid in the city's public housing construction.[140]

In 2 of the 5 claims filed by Chinese individual investors, claimants were entangled in relation networks with SOEs during the ongoing reforms. The first case is *Qiong Ye and Jianping Yang v Cambodia*. The claimants in this case are the board members of Emaxx Telecom, a Cambodian telecom operator in which Mainland China-based POE Jilin Asia Link owns a controlling 65% stake. The majority stake in Jilin Asia Link was acquired in 2021 by the CEO of the Chinese SOE Dalian Liang Yun Group. After that, Jilin Asia Link and the SOE have maintained a substantial association, as exemplified by Dalian Liang Yun's 2022 free transfer of a

---

Private Enterprises was Successfully Held]. https://www.cbex.com.cn/zl_244/gqhgfwzq/gzdt/202010/t20201016_65093.html. Accessed 13 Aug 2025.

[136] LPS (2025) Lenovo PCCW Solutions Company Overview. https://www.pccwsolutions.com/site/en/about-us/company-overview. Accessed 13 Aug 2025.

[137] *Ping An Life Insurance Company, Limited and Ping An Insurance (Group) Company, Ltd v The Government of Belgium*. ICSID Arbitral Tribunal. Case No ARB/12/29. 30 April 2015.

[138] Ping An (2025a) Major Shareholders. https://group.pingan.com/investor_relations/major_shareholders.html. Accessed 13 Aug 2025.

[139] Ping An (2025b) Our Leadership. https://group.pingan.com/about_us/our_leadership.html. Accessed 13 Aug 2025.

[140] People (2020) 《中国平安集团与深圳市政府签署战略合作协议》 [Ping An and Shenzhen Government Sign Strategic Cooperation Agreement]. http://sn.people.com.cn/n2/2020/0609/c380804-34074674.html. Accessed 13 Aug 2025.

subsidiary to Jilin Asia Link, which aimed to utilise the POE as a shell for a subsequent back-door listing.[141]

The claimants in the second case, *Wang Jing, Li Fengju, Ren Jinglin and others v Ukraine*, are beneficial owners of corporations that were in the process of acquiring a 75 percent stake in Motor Sich, a Ukrainian aerospace company. Wang is the owner of the Chinese aerospace company Beijing Skyrizon Aviation Industry Investment Company (Skyrizon Aviation) and the CEO of Beijing Xinwei Technology Group, a Chinese State-owned manufacturer of telecommunications equipment. The other claimants are beneficial owners of offshore corporations that are also acquirers. Additionally, they held directorships or were shareholders of Chinese firms connected to Skyrizon Aviation. In 2021, the US Department of Commerce added Skyrizon Aviation to the 'Military End User' list, subjecting them to export restrictions on designated items based on the findings that the company has significant ties to the People's Liberation Army.[142] It was also discovered that all the acquirers had obtained financial support from China Development Bank, China's State-owned policy bank that finances investment projects per national economic development policies.[143] These facts suggest that the several acquirers were acting as proxies on behalf of a true 'commander', who was most likely the SOE or the government, possibly to circumvent any anti-monopoly investigation or national security-based review at the time of entry.

The analysis above reveals that the latest round of SOE reforms has substantial implications for Chinese investors who have resorted to ISDS arbitrations, irrespective of ownership types. Many Chinese non-SOE investors may not have had any political connections at the time of investment, but the subsequently formed ownership ties or cooperative relations with SOEs may contribute to incentivising them to pursue remedies under international investment law.

As noted earlier, the Chinese government encourages SOEs to increase their comprehension of and participation in international dispute settlement. In addition, China has adopted an encouraging attitude towards international arbitration in the recent few years.[144] In 2022, the Chinese central government launched an 'international arbitration talent training programme' with a stated purpose of training 3000 judicial professionals specializing in international arbitration by 2025.[145] These

141 Asia Link Technology (2022) 《关于受赠股权资产暨关联交易的公告》 [Announcement on Equity Asset Donation and Associated Transaction]. https://www.asialink.com/Public/Uploads/file/2022-12-13/KuBqMKBttoFDA.pdf. Accessed 13 Aug 2025.

142 US Department of Commerce (2021) Commerce Adds China National Offshore Oil Corporation to the Entity List and Skyrizon to the Military End-User List. Press Releases.

143 Stack (2021) 'Predatory' Chinese Takeover of Ukraine Defense Firm Was Facilitated by a U.S. Law Firm. OCCRP. https://www.occrp.org/en/the-pandora-papers/predatory-chinese-takeover-of-ukraine-defense-firm-was-facilitated-by-a-us-law-firm. Accessed 13 Aug 2025.

144 See, e.g., China Trade News (2021) 《国际仲裁是解决跨境纠纷的首选方法》 [International Arbitration is the Preferred Method of Resolving Cross-Border Disputes]. https://www.chinatradenews.com.cn/epaper/content/2021-11/30/content_75721.htm. Accessed 13 Aug 2025.

145 Ministry of Justice (2022) 《司法部, 教育部, 科学技术部, 国务院国有资产监督管理委员会, 中华全国工商业联合会, 中国国际贸易促进委员会关于做好涉外仲裁人才培养项目实施

policies reflect China's pursuit to make its voice to be heard on a broader forum, particularly amid the fraught geopolitical tensions. In practice, there has been a rise in ISDS claims brought by Chinese investors in the past few years. Notably, in October 2022, China's telecom giant Huawei filed a notice of dispute challenging the UK government's exclusion of Huawei from the 5G rollout under the 1986 China-UK BIT.[146] This came shortly after Huawei filed an ISDS claim against Sweden in January 2022 regarding a similar exclusion.[147] This notice foreshadows Huawei's subsequent ISDS claim. During the same time frame, 9 ISDS claims have been filed against China. While there is currently no conclusive evidence linking Huawei to the Chinese government or military,[148] the company's recent frequent use of ISDS may be influenced, at least in part, by the Chinese government's encouraging stance on international dispute settlement.

Given the consistent sensitivity of Chinese SOEs to political dynamics and State policy, the latest round of SOE reforms involving the expansion of SOE equity connections in private sectors may lead to an increase in ISDS claims initiated by Chinese POE investors affiliated with SOEs in the future.

8.4 Suggestions for the Future of IIAs: How Should We Move Forward?

The growing likelihood that Chinese SOE investors may initiate ISDS claims against Australia under the current IIA framework, coupled with the limited effectiveness of Australia's CPTPP-modelled SOE disciplines in regulating Chinese SOEs, underscores the need for Australia and other host States to develop more robust strategies for managing Chinese SOE and affiliated POE investments.

As noted earlier, the investment chapter of ChAFTA remains a work-in-progress, with most substantive provisions, including those on expropriation, transfer, and ISDS, left for future negotiations.[149] These negotiations were intended to commence within three years of the agreement's entry into force.[150] As of August 2025, however, there is no evidence to suggest that Australia and China have engaged in

工作的通知》 [Circular of Ministry of Justice, Ministry of Education, Ministry of Science and Technology, the SASAC of the State Council, All-China Federation of Industry and Commerce, China Council for the Promotion of International Trade on the Implementation of Foreign Arbitration Talent Training Programme]. http://www.moj.gov.cn/pub/sfbgw/zwxxgk/fdzdgknr/fdzdgknrtzwj/202204/t20220411_452524.html. Accessed 13 Aug 2025.

[146] Bohmer (2023) Uncovered: Huawei Puts the United Kingdom on Notice of Treaty Dispute. IAReporter. https://www.iareporter.com/articles/uncovered-huawei-puts-the-united-kingdom-on-notice-of-treaty-dispute/. Accessed 13 Aug 2025.

[147] Du (2023), pp. 1–54.

[148] Ibid. 36.

[149] ChAFTA (n 4) art. 9.9.3.

[150] Ibid. art. 9.9.1.

substantive interactions on the negotiations, which may be attributed to the ongoing geopolitical tensions between the two countries.

Notwithstanding, the future work programme of ChAFTA still presents Australia with a tangible opportunity to develop and implement specific strategies to address Chinese SOE investments in the upcoming comprehensive investment chapter. When Australia's domestic foreign investment framework focuses on mitigating threats that Chinese SOE investments may pose to Australia's national interests, the problem that Australia should expect to solve is to ensure that its IIA with China can preserve sufficient policy space for it to regulate Chinese investments from SOEs or SOE-affiliated investors without the risk of IIA violation, thereby striking a better balance between Australia's interests and those of Chinese SOE investors.

This section sets out targeted recommendations for strengthening the renegotiated ChAFTA to address Chinese SOE investments under the latest round of SOE reforms. These recommendations are equally relevant to other host States seeking to refine their IIAs with China to manage the intersection of investment openness, national security concerns, and the distinctive features of Chinese SOE governance.

First of all, Australia, along with other host States, should incorporate targeted measures in future IIA negotiations with China to preserve sufficient regulatory autonomy when addressing risks posed by Chinese SOE investments. As demonstrated in Sect. 8.1, the current Australia–China IIA framework exposes Australia to potential ISDS claims by Chinese SOE investors alleging that regulatory measures against their proposed or established investments breach the expropriation provisions in CABIT and AHKIA (in cases where investments are channelled through Hong Kong subsidiaries) or the national treatment obligation in ChAFTA.

The existing policy space safeguards in these treaties do not adequately shield Australia from such claims. This deficiency creates a structural vulnerability in circumstances where regulatory measures, particularly those linked to national security, strategic industries, or sensitive infrastructure, intersect with the commercial interests of Chinese SOEs. To address this, Australia and other host States should prioritise strengthening regulatory space provisions in future IIAs with China through the following approaches.

8.4.1 Limiting Access to ISDS

The most straightforward approach for Australia and other host States to mitigate the risk of ISDS claims is to limit access to the ISDS mechanism in future IIAs with China, including any forthcoming investment chapters. It is a viable option for these States to seek the removal of ISDS clauses altogether during future negotiations, following the approach of the Australian Labour government, which stated in its 2021 National Platform that it will not consent to any agreements with ISDS provisions and will work with trading partners to remove such provisions from existing agreements.[151] Australia's Trade Minister Dan Farrell reiterated this position in November 2022.[152]

Such a proposal, however, may face resistance from China in future negotiations. This is partly because the current exceptionally narrow ISDS clause in ChAFTA already departs from China's 2010 Model BIT Draft (which allows arbitrability for breaches of substantive treaty provisions) and from its prevailing IIA practice.[153]

If China objects to removing the ISDS clause, Australia and other host States should avoid broadening the current scope of arbitrable disputes beyond breaches of the treaty's national treatment obligation. This is especially pressing in the case of ChAFTA, since Article 9.9 commits the parties to incorporate additional substantive provisions in the forthcoming investment chapter.

In addition to keeping the ISDS mechanism as narrowly applicable as possible, host States should seek to explicitly exclude measures taken under their foreign investment review frameworks from ISDS, adopting an ISDS carve-out comparable to that found in the Canada–China BIT. This provision reads:

> A decision by Canada following a review under the Investment Canada Act…with respect to whether or not to: (a) initially approve an investment that is subject to review; or (b) permit an investment that is subject to national security review; shall not be subject to the dispute settlement provisions…under this Agreement.[154]

Unlike the narrower ISDS carve-out in AHKIA, which only protects Australia's admission decisions on newly proposed investments (as discussed in Sect. 8.1), this broader model shields not only decisions on new Chinese SOE investments but also retrospective national security reviews of established investments. Since China has already accepted such a carve-out in its IIA with Canada, it is reasonable to expect that similar provisions could be negotiated into ChAFTA or other IIAs with China, thereby strengthening host States' ability to regulate SOE-related investments without heightened ISDS exposure.

---

[151] Nottage (2022) Australia's (Dis)Engagement with Investor-State Arbitration: A Sequel. USYD https://japaneselaw.sydney.edu.au/2022/11/australias-disengagement-with-investor-state-arbitration-a-sequel/#:~:text=On%2014%20November%20Australia%27s%20current,their%20impact%20in%20existing%20agreements. Accessed 13 Aug 2025.

[152] Labor (2021) Labor's 2021 National Platform. https://alp.org.au/media/2594/2021-alp-national-platform-final-endorsed-platform.pdf. Accessed 13 Aug 2025; Farrell (2022); Ibid.

[153] Zhang (2017), pp. 244–246.

[154] *Agreement Between the Government of Canada and the Government of the People's Republic of China for the Promotion and Reciprocal Protection of Investments*. Signed 9 September 2012 (entered into force 1 October 2014) annex D 34 ('*Canada-China BIT*').

8.4.2 Expanding the Scope of NCMs

As discussed in Sect. 8.1, while the NCMs listed in ChAFTA Annex III explicitly protect measures adopted under Australia's foreign investment policy from treaty breaches, it remains uncertain whether Australia's reformed FATA and FATR still fall within Annex III. This uncertainty stems from the ratchet qualification, under which the scope of NCMs only extends to amendments or modifications of existing NCMs to the extent that such changes do not decrease the measure's conformity with the treaty.[155]

For Australia, this means that unless Annex III is updated, the significant 2021 reforms to its foreign investment framework may not be fully shielded from NT or MFN challenges. Accordingly, Australia should seek to update its NCM schedule in any future ChAFTA renegotiations to explicitly reflect its reformed foreign investment regime. In parallel, it should also seek to remove the ratchet qualification entirely, thereby preserving full policy space to amend or adapt its foreign investment screening mechanisms in response to evolving economic, security, or geopolitical conditions.

This recommendation is equally relevant for other host States negotiating or revising IIAs with China, particularly given that since 2020 many jurisdictions, including the US, EU, Canada, Japan, and South Korea, have tightened their foreign investment screening regimes.[156] By ensuring that their NCM schedules are up to date and free from restrictive ratchet clauses, host States can maintain the necessary regulatory flexibility to address the complex and potentially shifting risks posed by foreign SOE participation in strategic sectors. In particular, this approach enables host States to respond to emerging threats without risking claims of treaty breach, including measures that tighten screening criteria, expand the scope of review, or introduce retrospective assessments of established investments.

Notably, the removal of the ratchet qualification is not only in host States' interest but can also align with China's regulatory trajectory. China itself has tightened its inbound investment framework, most notably by formalising a national security review mechanism under the *Foreign Investment Law 2019* and by maintaining a negative list for foreign investment in key sectors.[157] Since China has already committed to transitioning to a negative-list based pre-establishment NT obligation in the future ChAFTA investment chapter,[158] it has a parallel interest in safeguarding its own ability to adjust foreign investment controls without triggering treaty disputes. This shared regulatory interest can be leveraged in negotiations to secure mutually acceptable amendments to the scope and operation of NCMs.

---

[155] ChAFTA (n 4) art. 9.5.1 (c).

[156] See, generally, Voon and Merriman (2022a), pp. 75–114.

[157] For detailed discussion regarding the national security review system, see Chap. 6 Sect. 6.2.2.1.

[158] Ibid. art. 9.9.3 (c).

By updating NCM schedules, removing ratchet constraints, and aligning these reforms with China's own regulatory posture, host States can create a more robust and future-proof treaty framework—one that balances openness to investment with the capacity to manage the unique policy challenges associated with SOE investments.

8.4.3 Enhancing the Exceptions to Treaty Protections

The comparison of the four concurrent IIAs between Australia and China in Sect. 8.1 reveals that ChAFTA lacks a number of explicit policy space safeguards found in CABIT, RCEP and AHKIA, which raises the risk that Australia will be challenged by Chinese SOE investors through ISDS under ChAFTA. Therefore, it is proposed that Australia should seek to add the following safeguards to the future ChAFTA investment chapter.

The first safeguard is related to the non-discriminatory protections. All Australia-China IIAs commit the Parties to providing MFN and NT protections to covered investments in 'like circumstances,' with AHKIA and RCEP clarifying that whether a differential treatment is accorded in 'like circumstances' is determined by the totality of circumstances, including whether the differing treatment is based on legitimate public welfare objectives.[159] However, such clarification is not found in ChAFTA. In the absence of such clarification, some ISDS tribunals still considered the legitimate public objective when determining 'like circumstances'.[160] Nonetheless, it is still recommended that in future ChAFTA negotiations, Australia push for an explicit 'legitimate public welfare objective' clarification to be added to the 'like circumstance' qualification for non-discriminatory obligations. Such clarification can provide Australia more certainty in protecting its measures under the foreign investment framework from NT or MFN violations, as they can be justified by the legitimate objective of protecting national security or national interests.

The second policy space safeguard is related to the general and security exception clauses. The current ChAFTA's general exception clause (Article 16.2) does not apply to the investment chapter, and its security exception clause (Article 16.3), while applicable to the investment chapter, does not include a reference to critical infrastructure. As discussed in Sect. 8.1, AHKIA's general exception clause may protect Australia's measures under the FATA or SOCI Act from treaty breaches,[161] because the measures are readily considered as necessary to protect public order, ensure compliance with personal data protection laws or conserve exhaustible natural resources (if the investment at issue involves personal data or exhaustible critical

[159] AHKIA (n 7) footnote. 3; RCEP (n 5) ch. 10 footnote. 17.

[160] See, e.g., *Pope & Talbot Inc v Canada (Award)*. (2001) 7 ICSID Rep 102, [78]; *United Parcel Service of America Inc v Canada (Award on Jurisdiction)*. (2002) 7 ICSID Rep 285, [175]–[177].

[161] AHKIA (n 7) art. 18.

minerals). In addition, the security exception clauses in AHKIA and RCEP that explicitly refer to critical infrastructure afford Australia more policy leeway in regulating Chinese SOE investments in Australian infrastructure assets.[162] It is therefore recommended that Australia, in future negotiations, seek to expand the application scope of Article 16.2 to include the investment chapter and add a reference to critical infrastructure to Article 16.3. This recommendation, however, is conditional on future investment chapter negotiations involving amendments to provisions outside of the chapter.

8.4.4 Incorporating SOE Rules Specially for Chinese SOEs

Although ChAFTA's future work programme does not explicitly reference the inclusion of SOE rules in the future treaty, the proliferation of Chinese SOE investments in Australia and the ineffectiveness of the CPTPP-modelled SOE rules, as demonstrated in Sect. 8.2, highlight the necessity of considering how to tailor a set of SOE rules (modelled on the CPTPP SOE rules) specifically for Chinese SOEs. In addition, China's application to join the CPTPP suggests a possible willingness to negotiate SOE rules with Australia. If future ChAFTA does not include SOE rules, the following recommendations on Chinese SOE-specific rules can provide inspiration for Australia in considering China's application to join the CPTPP and other countries in negotiating IIAs with China.

As discussed in Sect. 8.2, the ineffectiveness of the CPTPP SOE rules in regulating Chinese SOEs stems in part from the CPTPP's narrow definition of SOE, which includes a problematic criterion requiring that SOEs be 'principally engaged in commercial activities'. This criterion does not correspond to the reality of Chinese SOEs in the context of ongoing SOE reforms, as SOEs classified as 'Public Welfare' and 'Special Commercial' and designated as SCIOs would fail such criterion due to the explicit policy tasks assigned to them. As a result, it is recommended that, if both Parties consent to introducing CPTPP-modelled SOE rules in ChAFTA, Australia seek to remove the criterion from the SOE definition, which is essential to the effectiveness of the substantive SOE rules.

In addition, as demonstrated in Sect. 8.2, the existing substantive rules in the CPTPP SOE Chapter, namely the prohibition on NCA, commercial consideration requirement and transparency obligation, are unlikely to address the non-competitive issues associated with Chinese SOEs. The ineffectiveness is primarily due to Chinese SOEs' intricate linkage with the government which has been significantly enhanced in the latest round of SOE reforms. In fact, Chinese SOEs' non-competitive issues are rooted in the unique circumstances of the Chinese State economy. As demonstrated in Chap. 2, in the latest round of SOE reforms, the Chinese

[162] Ibid. art. 19; RCEP (n 5) art. 17.13.

government continues to uphold the policy stance since 1978 of fostering SOE dominance over critical industries. The government is even promoting inter-SOE consolidations to intentionally create monopolies in critical industries with the publicly stated purpose of eliminating 'unreasonable competition' in critical industries.[163] In the MOR, foreign investors, along with Chinese POEs, have been excluded from participating in flow-in MOR of SOEs in critical industries, which dashes the expectation that the MOR would enable foreign investors to gain access to China's critical industries through acquiring a stake in the SOEs therein.[164]

Given that the Chinese government is enhancing SOE dominance in a significant portion of the national economy and that it is unrealistic to expect the government to change its reform goal, it is critical for countries like Australia to compel China to address anti-competitive practices of its SOEs, imposing an additional general obligation on China under international investment law to subject its SOEs to antitrust law.

As discussed in Chap. 3, the applicability of the *Anti-Monopoly Law* (AML) to SOEs has been has long been debated in China.[165] The contentions are primarily rooted in Article 7 of the law, which can be interpreted as containing a carve-out for SOEs in critical industries,[166] and the fact that the administrative enforcement of AML in practice is selective, aligning with government policy and interests.[167] Given this context, it is recommended that Australia attempt to incorporate an SOE rule in renegotiated ChAFTA that is modelled on that in the *Australia-Malaysia FTA*, which states' the Parties shall apply competition measures to address anti-competitive conduct to the business activities of government-owned and non-government-owned businesses'.[168] A similar provision is also found in the *Australia-US FTA* which obliges the US to 'ensure that anti-competitive activities by sub-federal state enterprises are not excluded from the reach of its national antitrust laws solely by reason of their status as sub-federal state enterprises'.[169] Incorporating such rules could help level the playing field for Australian investors competing against Chinese SOEs in the Chinese market and provide them with an alternative means of redress under international law due to the *de facto* inapplicability of China's AML against SOEs. In addition, it is recommended that Australia ensure that the SOE rules fall within the applicable scope of a treaty-based

[163] For detailed discussion regarding the inter-SOE consolidations, see Chap. 2 Sect 2.3.1.1.

[164] For detailed discussion regarding MOR, see Chap. 3.

[165] For detailed discussion regarding the applicability of the AML to SOEs, see Chap. 3 Sect. 3.2.2.1.

[166] Ng et al. (2020), pp. 297–311.

[167] Ibid. 297–311; Kovacic (2017), pp. 693–711.

[168] MAFTA (n 84) art. 14.4.3.

[169] AUSFTA (n 83) art. 14.4.2.

State-State dispute settlement mechanism, as the CPTPP does,[170] so as to ensure the enforceability of the rules.[171]

8.5 Concluding Remarks

This chapter examines how well the current Australia-China IIA framework balances the interests of Chinese SOE investors with Australia's policy space for protecting national interests. This chapter demonstrates that Australia is vulnerable to ISDS claims brought by Chinese SOEs under the IIAs between Australia and China by outlining potential treaty obligations that Australis' regulatory measures adopted under the amended FATA, FATR or SOCI Act may cause. In addition, in the context of China's latest round of SOE reforms, even if the CPTPP-modelled SOE rules are incorporated into the future ChAFTA or China successfully joins the CPTPP, the innovative rules are less likely to help Australia in effectively addressing the non-competitive issues associated with Chinese SOE investments.

Given the Xi Jinping administration's recent supportive stance towards international dispute settlement and the rising frequency of ISDS claims filed by Chinese investors, it is reasonable to expect an increase in ISDS claims brought by Chinese SOE investors. Given the circumstances, this chapter offers Australia recommendations for possible improvements to the renegotiated investment chapter of ChAFTA, with the goal of preserving more policy space under the treaty while more comprehensively addressing Chinese SOE investments. The recommendations include potential revisions of the existing ChAFTA in response to the potential ISDS claims identified in Sect. 8.1 and modifications to the CPTPP SOE rules tailored to Chinese SOEs.

As China's 'Go Global' policy and SOE reforms gain momentum, Chinese SOE investments will keep expanding around the world. Meanwhile, global geopolitical tensions are likely to keep pushing countries to tighten their foreign investment policy. As a result, not only Australia, but every country that has received or seeks to receive investments from Chinese SOEs faces the challenge of striking a balance between their national interests and the interests of Chinese SOE investors, which is essential for maintaining mutually beneficial international investment relationships with China under international investment law.

---

170 CPTPP (n 85) art. 28.3.

171 Australia's SOE rules in IIAs prior to the CPTPP are not subject to dispute settlement mechanism provided in the treaties, as a result of the entire competition chapter being excluded from the application of the dispute settlement clause. See, e.g., SAFTA (n 80) ch. 12 art. 8; AUSFTA (n 83) art. 14.11; MAFTA (n 84) art. 20.3.

References

Agreement Between Australia and Japan for an Economic Partnership. Signed 8 July 2014. [2015] ATS 2 (entered into force 15 January 2015) art. 15.4

Agreement between the Government of Australia and the Government of the People's Republic of China on the Reciprocal Encouragement and Protection of Investments. [1988] ATS 14 (signed and entered into force 11 July 1988)

Agreement Between the Government of Canada and the Government of the People's Republic of China for the Promotion and Reciprocal Protection of Investments. Signed 9 September 2012 (entered into force 1 October 2014) annex D 34

Agreement between the Government of Hong Kong and the Government of Australia for the Promotion and Protection of Investments. Signed 15 September 1993. [1993] ATS 30 (entered into force 15 October 1993)

Appellate Body Report (1996) United States – Standards for Reformulated and Conventional Gasoline. WTO Doc WT/DS2/AB/R 17-19

Appellate Body Report (2005) United States — Measures Affecting the Cross-Border Supply of Gambling and Betting Services. WTO Doc WT/DS285/AB/R [306]

Appellate Body Report (2007) Brazil - Measures Affecting Imports of Retreaded Tyres. WTO Doc WT/DS332/AB/R [143], [156]

Asia Link Technology (2022) 《关于受赠股权资产暨关联交易的公告》 [Announcement on Equity Asset Donation and Associated Transaction]. https://www.asialink.com/Public/Uploads/file/2022-12-13/KuBqMKBttoFDA.pdf. Accessed 13 Aug 2025

AsiaPhos Limited and Norwest Chemicals Pte Ltd v People's Republic of China (ICSID Arbitral Tribunal, Case No ADM/21/1, 16 February 2023) [84]-[89]

Australia–Chile Free Trade Agreement. Signed 30 July 2008. 2694 UNTS 3 (entered into force 6 March 2009) art. 14.5.4

Australia–US Free Trade Agreement. Signed 18 May 2004. [2005] ATS 1 (entered into force 1 January 2005) art. 14.4.3

Bahmaei M-A, Sabzevari H (2023) Self-judging security exception clause as a kind of Carte Blanche in investment treaties: nature, effect and proper standard of review. Asian J Int Law 13(1):97–123

Bath V (2017a) Substantive provisions in ChAFTA's investment chapter. In: Picker CB, Wang H, Zhou W (eds) The China-Australia Free Trade Agreement: a 21st-century model. Hart Publishing, p 195

Bath V (2017b) The south and alternative models of trade and investment regulation: Chinese investment and approaches to international investment agreements. In: Morosini F, Badin MRS (eds) Reconceptualizing international investment law from the global south. Cambridge University Press, p 68

Bohmer L (2023) Uncovered: Huawei Puts the United Kingdom on Notice of Treaty Dispute. IAReporter. https://www.iareporter.com/articles/uncovered-huawei-puts-the-united-kingdom-on-notice-of-treaty-dispute/. Accessed 13 Aug 2025

Chaisse J, Olaoye KF (2020) The Tired Dragon casting doubts on China's investment treaty practice. Berkeley Bus Law J 17(1):181–190

Chen S (2012) China's compliance with WTO transparency requirement: institution-related impediments. Amsterdam Law Forum 4(4):25–50

China Beijing Equity Exchange (2020)《中央企业混合所有制改革暨中央企业民营企业协同发展项目推介会成功举办》 [Conference on Promoting Projects of the Mixed Ownership Reform for Central Enterprises and Synergistic Development between Central Enterprises and Private Enterprises was Successfully Held]. https://www.cbex.com.cn/zl_244/gqhgfwzq/gzdt/202010/t20201016_65093.html. Accessed 13 Aug 2025

China Mobile Limited (2021) Blue Ocean: Digital Economy—Annual Report 2020. Report

China Trade News (2021) 《国际仲裁是解决跨境纠纷的首选方法》 [International Arbitration is the Preferred Method of Resolving Cross-Border Disputes]. https://www.chinatradenews.com.cn/epaper/content/2021-11/30/content_75721.htm. Accessed 13 Aug 2025

CME Czech Republic B v The Czech Republic (Partial Award) (1993) 9 ICSID Rep 121, [606]

COFCO Capital (2021) Articles of Association of COFCO Capital Holding Company. http://newimg.cofco-capital.com/Uploads/Zlzbgb/File/2021/10/25/u617603267bc0b.pdf. Accessed 13 Aug 2025

Comprehensive and Progressive Agreement for Trans-Pacific Partnership. Signed 8 March 2018. [2018] ATS 23 (entered into force 30 December 2018) ('CPTPP'), incorporating Trans-Pacific Partnership Agreement. Signed 4 February 2016. [2016] ATNIF 2 (not in force)

Crockett A (2018) The termination of Indonesia's BITs: changing the bathwater, but keeping the baby? In: Chaisse J, Nottage L (eds) International investment treaties and arbitration across Asia. Brill, pp 159–179

Department for Business, Energy & Industrial Strategy et al (2022) UK Government Takes Major Steps Forward to Secure Britain's Energy Independence. Press Release

Department of Commerce of Guangdong Province (2023) 《关于中央财政2023年度外经贸发展专项资金(促进对外投资合作事项)分配方案的公示》 [Announcement on the 2023 Distribution Plan of the Special Funds for the Development of Foreign Trade and Economic Cooperation (Matters of Promoting Foreign Investment and Cooperation) of the Central Government]. http://com.gd.gov.cn/attachment/0/523/523779/4204348.pdf. Accessed 13 Aug 2025

Department of the Prime Minister and Cabinet (2023) Review – Port of Darwin lease. Media Release

Dolzer R, Kriebaum U, Schreuer C (2022) Principles of international investment law. Oxford University Press, p 9

Du M (2023) Huawei strikes back: challenging national security decisions before investment arbitral tribunals. Emory Int Law Rev 37(1):4

El Paso Energy International Company v Argentina (Award) (ICSID Arbitral Tribunal, Case No ARB/03/15, 31 October 2011) p 245

Embassy of the PRC in the UK (2021) 《驻英国使馆发言人就中英核电合作答记者问》 [Spokesman of the Embassy in the UK Answered Reporters' Questions on Sino-British Nuclear Power Co-operation]. http://gb.china-embassy.gov.cn/lcbt/sgryr/202107/t20210727_8969161.htm. Accessed 3 Sep 2025

Farrell D (2022) Trading our way to greater prosperity and security. Speech. The Australian APEC Study Centre

Farrington F, Jevremović N (2025) Between a rock and a hard place: the impact of replacing or abolishing ISDS on investment-affected parties. J Int Dispute Settlement 16(3):1–17

FIRB (2023) Australia's Foreign Investment Policy. https://foreigninvestment.gov.au/sites/foreigninvestment.gov.au/files/2023-06/AUSTRALIAS_FOREIGN_INVESTMENT_POLICY.pdf. Accessed 13 Aug 2025

Fleury JS, Marcoux J-M (2016) The US shaping of state-owned enterprise disciplines in the trans-pacific partnership. J Int Econ Law 19(2):445–465

Foreign Investment Reform (Protecting Australia's National Security) Act 2020 (Cth)

Free Trade Agreement between Australia and Hong Kong, China and associated side letters. Signed 26 March 2019. [2020] ATS 4 (entered into force 17 January 2020)

Free Trade Agreement between Australia and the Republic of Peru. Signed 12 February 2018. [2020] ATS 6 (entered into force 11 February 2020) ch. 16

Free Trade Agreement between Australia and the United Kingdom of Great Britain and Northern Ireland. Signed 17 December 2021. [2022] ATNIF 3 (entered into force on 31 May 2023) ch. 18

Free Trade Agreement between the Government of Australia and the Government of the People's Republic of China. Signed 17 June 2015. [2015] ATS 15 (entered into force 20 December 2015)

Free Trade Agreement between the Government of Australia and the Government of the Republic of Korea. Signed 8 April 2014. [2014] ATS 43 (entered into force 12 December 2014) art. 14.4

Henry S Gao (2022) The Investment Chapter in the Regional Comprehensive Economic Partnership: Enhanced Rules Without Enforcement Mechanism. No 446, ERIA
Global Telecom Holding SAE v Canada (Award) (ICSID Arbitral Tribunal, Case No ARB/16/16, 27 March 2020) [573]-[582]
GMW (2022) 《加拿大以"国家安全"为由要求3家中企撤资，中国外交部回应》 [Canada orders three Chinese companies to divest on grounds of "national security"; Chinese Ministry of Foreign Affairs responds]. https://m.gmw.cn/baijia/2022-11/04/1303185787.html. Accessed 13 Aug 2025
Government of the Lao People's Democratic Republic v Sanum Investments Ltd [2015] SGHC 15
Heydon K (2024) Australia can encourage China's credibility in the CPTPP. East Asia Forum. https://eastasiaforum.org/2024/09/23/australia-can-encourage-chinas-credibility-in-the-cptpp/#:~:text=In%20Brief,Australia%20about%20China's%20economic%20coercion. Accessed 13 Aug 2025
Junefield Gold Investments Limited v Republic of Ecuador. PCA Case No. 2023-35. 4 October 2022
Kawharu A, Nottage L (2018) The curious case of ISDS arbitration involving Australia and New Zealand. Univ West Aust Law Rev 44(2):32–70. https://www.ga.gov.au/scientific-topics/minerals/critical-minerals. Accessed 3 Sep 2025
Kovacic WE (2017) Competition policy and state-owned enterprises in China. World Trade Rev 16(4):696–697
Labor (2021) Labor's 2021 National Platform. https://alp.org.au/media/2594/2021-alp-national-platform-final-endorsed-platform.pdf. Accessed 13 Aug 2025
Levine M (2019) Towards a fourth generation of Chinese treaty practice. In: Chaisse J (ed) China's international investment strategy. Oxford University Press, p 207
Li J (2021) In pursuit of fairness: how Chinese multinational companies react to U.S. government bias. Harv Int Law J 62(2):399–400
LPS (2025) Lenovo PCCW Solutions Company Overview. https://www.pccwsolutions.com/site/en/about-us/company-overview. Accessed 13 Aug 2025
Malaysia–Australia Free Trade Agreement. Signed 22 May 2012. [2013] ATS 4 (entered into force 1 January 2013) art. 14.4.3
Matteo Vaccaro-Incisa G (2021) China's treaty policy and practice in international investment law and arbitration: a comparative and analytical study. Brill
Metalclad Corporation v The United Mexican States (Award) (ICSID Arbitral Tribunal, Case No ARB(AF)/97/1) [103]
Ministry of Foreign Affairs (2025) 《中国有意愿有能力加入CPTPP》 [China Willing, Capable of Joining CPTPP]. https://www.mfa.gov.cn/web/wjdt_674879/zwbd_674895/202308/t20230821_11129519.shtml. Accessed 13 Aug 2025
Ministry of Justice (2022) 《司法部, 教育部, 科学技术部, 国务院国有资产监督管理委员会, 中华全国工商业联合会, 中国国际贸易促进委员会关于做好涉外仲裁人才培养项目实施工作的通知》 [Circular of Ministry of Justice, Ministry of Education, Ministry of Science and Technology, the SASAC of the State Council, All-China Federation of Industry and Commerce, China Council for the Promotion of International Trade on the Implementation of Foreign Arbitration Talent Training Programme]. http://www.moj.gov.cn/pub/sfbgw/zwxxgk/fdzdgknr/fdzdgknrtzwj/202204/t20220411_452524.html. Accessed 13 Aug 2025
Mitchell AD, Munro J, Voon T (2018) Importing WTO general exceptions into international investment agreements: proportionality, myths and risks. In: Sachs L, Johnson L, Coleman J (eds) Yearbook on International Investment Law & Policy 2017. Oxford University Press, pp 323–331
Mo X, Fang J (2023) 《澳洲总理访华特别报道:阿尔巴尼斯总理与中国国家主席习近平举行会晤》 [Special Report on Australian Prime Minister's Visit to China: Australian Prime Minister Albanese Meets with Chinese President Xi Jinping]. ABC. https://www.abc.net.au/chinese/2023-11-06/australian-pm-albanese-arrives-in-beijing-to-meet-xi-jinping/103067960. Accessed 13 Aug 2025

MOFCOM, NBS and SAFE (2022) 2021 Statistical Bulletin of China's Outward Foreign Direct Investment. China Commerce and Trade Press, p 30

Nakano J, Melton M (2015) The UK-China Civilian Nuclear Agreement. CSIS. https://www.csis.org/analysis/uk-china-civilian-nuclear-agreement. Accessed 13 Aug 2025

Ng W et al (2020) State interest and the state-centered approach to competition law in China. Antitrust Bull 65(2):297–311

North American Free Trade Agreement. Canada-Mexico-United States of America. Signed 17 December 1992. [1994] CTS 2 (entered into force 1 January 1994)

Nottage L (2022) Australia's (Dis)Engagement with Investor-State Arbitration: A Sequel. USYD https://japaneselaw.sydney.edu.au/2022/11/australias-disengagement-with-investor-state-arbitration-a-sequel/#:~:text=On%2014%20November%20Australia%27s%20current,their%20impact%20in%20existing%20agreements. Accessed 13 Aug 2025

Nottage L, Romesh Weeramantry J (2012) Investment arbitration in Asia: five perspectives on law and practice. Arbitr Int 28(1):31

Ortino F (2020) The origin and evolution of investment treaty standards: stability, value, and reasonableness. Oxford University Press, pp 80–82

Paine J (2021) Global Telecom Holding v Canada: interpreting and applying reservations and carve-outs in investment treaties. J Int Arbitr 38(4):612, 616

PCCW Cascade (Middle East) Ltd v Kingdom of Saudi Arabia. ICSID Arbitral Tribunal. Case No ARB/22/20. 26 July 2022

People (2020) 《中国平安集团与深圳市政府签署战略合作协议》 [Ping An and Shenzhen Government Sign Strategic Cooperation Agreement]. http://sn.people.com.cn/n2/2020/0609/c380804-34074674.html. Accessed 13 Aug 2025

Ping An (2025a) Major Shareholders. https://group.pingan.com/investor_relations/major_shareholders.html. Accessed 13 Aug 2025

Ping An (2025b) Our Leadership. https://group.pingan.com/about_us/our_leadership.html. Accessed 13 Aug 2025

Ping An Life Insurance Company, Limited and Ping An Insurance (Group) Company, Ltd v The Government of Belgium. ICSID Arbitral Tribunal. Case No ARB/12/29. 30 April 2015

Pope & Talbot Inc v Canada (Award). (2001) 7 ICSID Rep 102, [78]

Pope & Talbot Inc v Canada (Interim Award) (ad hoc Tribunal, UNCITRAL, 26 June 2000) p 102

Prodromou Z (2020) The public order exception in international trade, investment, human rights and commercial disputes. Kluwer Law International, p 196

Regional Comprehensive Economic Partnership Agreement. Signed 15 November 2020. [2020] ATS 1 (entered into force 1 January 2022)

Roberts A (2010) Power and persuasion in investment treaty interpretation: the dual role of states. Am J Int Law 104(2):200–211

Sanum Investment Ltd v Government of the Lao People's Democratic Republic [2016] SGCA 157

Security of Critical Infrastructure Act 2018 (Cth) s. 5, as amended by Security Legislation Amendment (Critical Infrastructure Protection) Act 2022 (Cth), act. 8D

Shining G, Kwan E, Lao J (2018) The rise of Chinese investors as claimants: what are the likely impacts on international arbitration? King & Wood Mallesons. https://www.kwm.com/global/en/insights/latest-thinking/rise-of-chinese-investors-as-claimants-likely-impacts-on-international-arbitration.html. Accessed 13 Aug 2025

Singapore-Australia Free Trade Agreement. Signed 17 February 2003. [2003] ATS 16 (entered into force 28 July 2003), as amended by Singapore–Australia Free Trade Agreement Amendments. Signed 21 April 2005. [2006] ATS 9 (entered into force 24 February 2006)

Stack G (2021) 'Predatory' Chinese takeover of Ukraine defense firm was facilitated by a U.S. law firm. OCCRP. https://www.occrp.org/en/the-pandora-papers/predatory-chinese-takeover-of-ukraine-defense-firm-was-facilitated-by-a-us-law-firm. Accessed 13 Aug 2025

Sutherland, Hennart J-F, Anderson JR (2019) How does the routing of FDI to and via tax havens confound our understanding of Chinese MNE identity? A critical review of the empirical literature on Chinese MNEs. Asian Bus Manag 18(5):341–342

The State Council (2022) 《5家中央企业正式转为国有资本投资公司》 [Five Central Enterprises Formally Transformed into State-Owned Capital Investment Companies]. https // www.gov.cn/xinwen/2022-06/21/content_5696886.htm. Accessed 13 Aug 2025
Thompson A, Broude T, Haftel YZ (2019) Once Bitten, Twice Shy? Investment disputes, state sovereignty, and change in treaty design. Int Organ 73(4):859–880
Tza Yap Shum filed the ISDS claim under the China - Peru BIT (1994) Señor Tza Yap Shum v The Republic of Peru (Award). ICSID Arbitral Tribunal. Case No ARB/07/6. 7 July 2011
UNCTAD (2015) IIA Issues Note: Recent Trends in IIAs and ISDS. Report, p 2
UNCTAD (2025a) International Investment Agreements Navigator - Australia. https://investmentpolicy.unctad.org/international-investment-agreements/countries/11/australia. Accessed 3 Sep 2025
UNCTAD (2025b) International Investment Agreements Navigator - China. https://investmentpolicy.unctad.org/international-investment-agreements/countries/42/china. Accessed 3 Sep 2025
UNCTAD (2025c) ISDS Navigator - China. https://investmentpolicy.unctad.org/investment-dispute-settlement/country/42/china. Accessed 13 Aug 2025
United Parcel Service of America Inc v Canada (Award on Jurisdiction) (2002) 7 ICSID Rep 285, [175]–[177]
US Department of Commerce (2021) Commerce Adds China National Offshore Oil Corporation to the Entity List and Skyrizon to the Military End-User List. Press Releases
Voon T, Merriman D (2022a) Incoming: how international investment law constrains foreign investment screening. J World Invest Trade 24(1):75–114
Voon T, Merriman D (2022b) Is Australia's foreign investment screening policy consistent with international investment law? Melbourne J Int Law 23(1):62–113
Voon T, Sheargold E (2017) Australia, China, and the co-existence of successive international investment agreements. In: Picker C, Wang H, Zhou W (eds) The China Australia Free Trade Agreement: a 21st century model. Hart Publishing, pp 227–233
Voon T, Mitchell AD, Munro J (2014a) Legal responses to corporate manoeuvring in international investment arbitration. J Int Dispute Settlement 5(1):41–68
Voon T, Mitchell AD, Munro J (2014b) Parting ways: the impact of mutual termination of investment treaties on investor rights. ICSID Rev 29(2):451–473
Wang G (2011) Chinese mechanisms for resolving investor-state disputes. Jindal J Int Aff 1(1):222–223
Wang H (2017) An analytical introduction to ChAFTA: features and challenges. In: Picker CB, Wang H, Zhou W (eds) The China-Australia Free Trade Agreement: a 21st-century model. Hart Publishing, pp 29–30
WTO (2025) Disputes by Member. https://www.wto.org/english/tratop_e/dispu_e/dispu_by_country_e.htm. Accessed 13 Aug 2025
Yu H, Zhou Y (2013) 《国有垄断企业问题研究:文献回顾及政策建议》 [Research on state-owned monopolies: literature review and policy recommendations]. Brookings https://www.brookings.edu/wp-content/uploads/2016/06/Chinese-State-Owned-Enterprises.pdf. Accessed 13 Aug 2025
Zhang S (2017) A comparative review of the investor-state arbitration clause in ChAFTA from China's perspective: moving forwards or sideways? In: Picker C, Wang H, Zhou W (eds) The China-Australia Free Trade Agreement: a 21st-century model. Hart Publishing, pp 241–243
Zhongshan Fucheng Industrial Investment Co Ltd v Federal Republic of Nigeria [2023] EWCA
Zhou W (2021) Rethinking the (CP)TPP as a model for regulation of Chinese state-owned enterprises. J Int Econ Law 24(3):572–590
Zu H (2022) A new perspective on motivations behind Chinese overseas investment: a case study on the Darwin Port Deal. Aust J Polit Hist 68(3):467–483

Additional Sources

《中国共产党章程》 [Constitution of the Communist Party of China]. Adopted at the 20th CCP National Congress. 22 October 2022, art. 33

《关于进一步深化上海法治国企建设的意见》 [Opinions on Further Deepening the Construction of SOEs under the Rule of Law in Shanghai]. (People' s Republic of China) The Shanghai SASAC. 9 May 2023

《外经贸发展专项资金管理办法》 [Measures for the Management of Special Project Fund for Foreign Trade and Economic Development] (People' s Republic of China). MOF and MOFCOM. 9 April 2014, art. 10

op《关于进一步深化法治央企建设的意见》 [Opinions on Further Deepening the Construction of Central Enterprises under the Rule of Law]. (People's Republic of China) The Central SASAC. 17 October 2021

肖立晟, 徐子桐, 范小云 [Xiao Lishen, Xu Zitong and Fan Xiaoyun] (2022) 《估算中国的IFDI 和OFDI—来自避税天堂与返程投资的证据》 [Estimating China' s IFDI and OFDI—Evidence from Tax Havens and Round-Tripping Investment]. 金融研究 [Financial Studies] 500(2):44

Chapter 9
Conclusion

Abstract This chapter draws together the central findings of this study and highlights their broader theoretical and legal significance. Its core contribution lies in reconceptualising contemporary Chinese State capitalism through the institutional transformation of SOE reforms under Xi Jinping. The chapter demonstrates that the latest round of the reforms has not merely intensified State influence over the economy. It has reconstituted the organisational logic through which Chinese SOEs are structured, governed, and deployed. This transformation has two defining features: the strengthening of State-owned capital through concentration, selective marketisation, and ownership restructuring, and the deeper embedding of political control within corporate governance and delegated shareholder structures. The chapter further shows that this institutional logic extends beyond China's domestic political economy through SOE outbound FDI, which is increasingly politically structured, strategically directed, and organised through coordinated State-owned capital networks. On that basis, it highlights that Chinese SOE investment is better understood not as ordinary commercial activity by firms that happen to be State-owned, but as a transnational extension of domestic State-owned capital governance. The chapter concludes by drawing out the implications of this reconceptualisation for host-State foreign investment screening and the design of international investment agreements.

Since 1978, SOE reforms have remained one of the central projects of China's economic transformation. The Xi Jinping administration's assumption of power in 2012 marked the beginning of a fourth round of SOE reforms distinguished by its exceptional scale, institutional complexity, and political continuity. Encompassing the restructuring of the State economy, MOR, reform of SOE governance, and reform of the State-owned assets management system, this latest round of reform has reshaped not only the organisation of China's SOEs but also the broader institutional logic through which the Chinese Party-State governs capital.

This study has examined the design and implementation of these reforms to explain how contemporary Chinese SOEs have been reorganised, politically re-embedded, and projected outward. Its central finding is that the latest round of SOE reforms has not merely strengthened the connections between SOEs, the State, and

T. Gu, *Chinese SOE Reforms and Global FDI*, Contemporary Chinese Civil and Commercial Law, https://doi.org/10.1007/978-981-92-3181-2_9

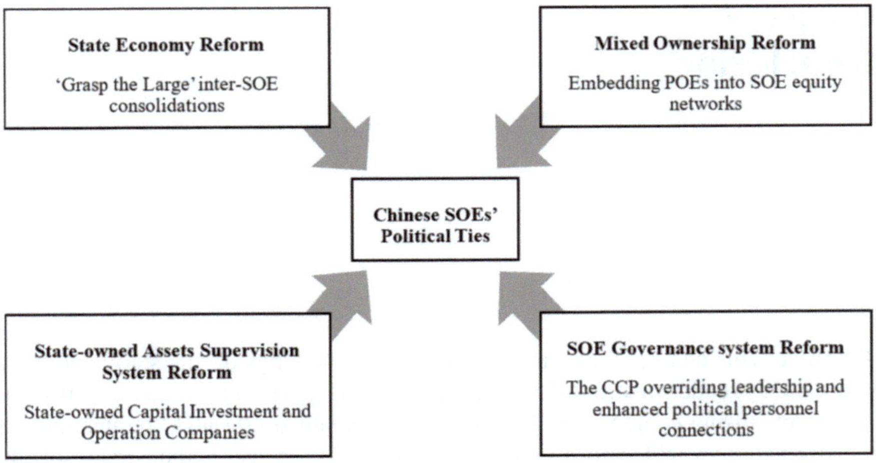

Fig. 9.1 How China's Latest Round of SOE Reforms Strengthens SOEs' Political and Party Connections

the CCP in a general sense. It has reconstituted the institutional form through which those connections are organised and exercised. That transformation is visible in four closely related developments: group-level SOE restructuring and inter-SOE consolidation, the incorporation of POEs into SOE-centred equity networks, the deeper entrenchment of Party organisation within SOE governance, and the growing role of State-owned capital investment and operation platforms with policy-bearing functions. These developments are summarised in Fig. 9.1 above.

More fundamentally, these developments reveal a transformation in the institutional logic through which Chinese SOEs are organised, governed, and deployed. The latest round of SOE reforms has not merely intensified State influence over the economy in a general sense. It has reshaped the organisation of State-owned capital, reconfigured the exercise of political control, and extended both beyond China's borders through outbound FDI. The analysis that follows draws out the broader theoretical and legal significance of this transformation.

9.1 Reconceptualising Contemporary Chinese State Capitalism

Chinese State capitalism under Xi Jinping has become a major focus of scholarly and policy attention.[1] The growing prominence of the State and the CCP in the economy is widely recognised,[2] but the institutional mechanisms through which this

[1] See, e.g., Du (2023), pp. 125–150; Pearson et al. (2021), pp. 207–213; Milhaupt and Zheng (2015), pp. 665–722; Lin and Milhaupt (2023), pp. 835–853; Liebman and Milhaupt (2016).

[2] Ozery (2022), pp. 43–94; Pearson et al. (2021), p. 207.

prominence is reproduced, consolidated, and redirected have often been described in broad and undifferentiated terms. By tracing the design and implementation of the latest round of SOE reforms, this study offers a more exact account of the organisational logic of contemporary Chinese State capitalism.

Its central theoretical contribution lies in reconceptualising the organisational logic of contemporary Chinese State capitalism through two defining features. The first is the strengthening of State-owned capital through concentration and ownership restructuring. The second is the embedding of political control through corporate governance and delegated shareholder functions. Together, these features show that Xi-era Chinese State capitalism is characterised not simply by a stronger State presence in the economy, but by a more systematically organised form of State-owned capital and a more deeply institutionalised mode of political control.

9.1.1 Strengthening State-owned Capital Through Concentration and Ownership Restructuring

The Chinese Party-State's active role in the economy has long been understood as operating through multiple capacities, including market regulation, control over the institutions that enforce market order, and ownership of a vast number of SOEs, commercial banks, and policy banks.[3] This study adds a further theoretical dimension to this understanding. It shows that, under Xi Jinping, the Party-State has placed increasing emphasis on organising macro-level industrial development through the operation of State-owned capital. More specifically, contemporary Party-State intervention increasingly works through the strategic allocation, concentration, and reorganisation of State-owned capital in ways designed to sustain growth and restructure industrial capacity under the so-called 'new normal'.[4]

This mode of intervention is exercised through three closely related techniques: sectoral concentration, selective marketisation, and ownership restructuring. The ongoing restructuring of the State economy builds on the earlier reform logic of 'Grasp the Large and Release the Small', first advanced during the second round of SOE reforms. That reform emerged from the severe weakness of the State economy in the 1990s. Its core logic was to preserve State dominance in strategic sectors closely tied to national interests while permitting greater competition and privatisation in non-strategic sectors. In practical terms, 'Grasp the Large' preserved dominant positions for central SOEs in critical industries, while 'Release the Small' facilitated the withdrawal or privatisation of local SOEs that had lost

[3] Ozery (2022), p. 11.

[4] In 2014, President Xi Jinping introduced the concept of the 'new normal', signalling China's shift from high-speed growth to a medium-to-high growth model driven by structural upgrading and innovation. Xinhua News Agency (2014) 《习近平首次系统阐述"新常态"》 [Xi Jinping Systematically Elaborates the "New Normal" for the First Time]. People. http://politics.people.com.cn/n/2014/1109/c1001-26000293.html. Accessed 10 April 2026.

competitiveness outside the strategic core. This differentiated structure has remained a durable feature of China's State economy. Successive leaderships maintained State-backed SOE dominance in critical industries and restricted entry by foreign enterprises and POEs through administrative and regulatory barriers.

The latest round of reform under Xi does not depart from this logic. It deepens it. Inter-BG mergers serve the function of 'Grasp the Large' by concentrating State-owned capital in critical industries and consolidating national champions into larger business groups capable of exerting dominance at both the domestic and global levels. At the same time, a series of slim-down programmes advances the logic of 'Release the Small' by improving the efficiency and strategic focus of central SOE groups. Measures directed at disposing of zombie enterprises, reducing leverage, resolving overcapacity, narrowing principal business lines, and compressing low-profit subsidiaries all pursue the same objective: removing peripheral and inefficient assets so that State-owned capital can be concentrated more tightly in sectors regarded as strategically significant.

The same logic extends into high-technology sectors, but here it operates less through direct monopoly preservation than through selective marketisation and ownership restructuring. In the latest round of SOE reforms, MOR has become the principal mechanism through which the Party-State extends the reach of State-owned capital into innovation-intensive sectors. Formally, MOR is framed as an effort to integrate State and non-State ownership by restructuring the shareholding and capital structures of SOEs. In practice, however, this study demonstrates that it operates through two distinct channels: flow-in MOR, under which SOEs diversify their shareholding structures through share issuance, sale of registered capital, or stock market listing; and flow-out MOR, under which SOEs acquire equity stakes in POEs.

Flow-in MOR is implemented on the basis of the official classification of SOEs into 'Public Welfare', 'Special Commercial', and 'General Commercial' categories according to their roles in national economic and social development. Only 'General Commercial' SOEs, including some operating in forward-looking strategic sectors, are permitted to reduce State ownership to a minority stake and are expected to operate primarily according to commercial logic. Yet even here the reform does not indicate a retreat of the State. Flow-in MOR is designed to allow selected SOEs to bring in carefully chosen non-State shareholders able to provide capital, technology, research and development capacity, and managerial expertise. Selective marketisation therefore functions not as a pathway towards privatisation, but as a mechanism through which State-owned capital absorbs and organises external strategic resources for its own development.

Flow-out MOR extends this logic further. It is best understood as a partial nationalisation programme directed particularly at POEs in high-technology sectors. Through equity acquisitions, central SOEs establish durable relationships with technologically competitive private firms, thereby extending the reach of State-owned capital into sectors regarded as essential to industrial upgrading and technological self-strengthening. The purpose is not simply to acquire profitable firms, but to incorporate innovative private-sector capacity into a broader State-led industrial framework. Ownership restructuring thus becomes a mechanism for extending the organisational reach of State-owned capital beyond the formal boundaries of the traditional State sector.

This process is reinforced by the rise of SCICs, which serve as professional platforms for the operation of State-owned capital. SCICs are tasked with investing in support of national development strategies, either through direct investment in sectors related to their principal businesses or through specialised industrial investment funds. They therefore provide an institutional vehicle through which flow-out MOR and related forms of strategic investment can be pursued on a larger and more coordinated scale. These developments demonstrate that selective marketisation and ownership restructuring are not alternatives to State control. They are mechanisms through which State-owned capital extends its coordinating capacity into sectors, firms, and technologies beyond the traditional core of the State economy.

From this perspective, MOR is not merely a reform of SOE ownership. It is an equity-based mechanism for reorganising the boundaries of the State sector. Flow-in MOR allows SOEs to draw strategic resources from non-State actors into State-led corporate structures, while flow-out MOR enables State-owned capital to move outward into selected private firms and high-technology sectors. The broader result is the construction of a State-centred network of capital relations in which selected POEs become linked, and in some instances subordinated, to the strategic objectives of the Party-State. The case studies examined in Chap. 3 further demonstrate that MOR can facilitate resource transfer, business coordination, and durable strategic alignment between SOEs and POEs even where the connecting stake is not formally controlling.

This logic is now being articulated more clearly in legal form through the draft *State-owned Assets Management Law* (SAML), released for public consultation on 27 December 2025 after review by the Standing Committee of the 14th National People's Congress.[5] Comprising nine chapters and 76 articles, the draft SAML seeks to establish a unified legal framework for the supervision and management of State-owned assets. More importantly for present purposes, it redefines SASACs' functions primarily in terms of macro-level State-owned capital management.[6] Under the draft law, SASACs are tasked not merely with supervising SOEs as investors, but with optimising the structure of the State economy, including by concentrating enterprise State-owned assets in critical industries and forward-looking strategic sectors.[7] The draft SAML therefore reinforces this study's broader claim that contemporary Chinese State capitalism operates through an industrially differentiated logic of State-owned capital allocation, combining intensified concentration in strategic sectors with selective marketisation and ownership restructuring elsewhere.

---

[5] 《中华人民共和国国有资产法(草案)》 [State-owned Assets Management Law (Draft)]. (People's Republic of China). 27 December 2025.

[6] Ibid arts 13, 17.

[7] Ibid art 24.

9.1.2 Embedding Political Control in Chinese State Capitalism: Corporate Governance and Delegated Shareholder Functions

A second defining feature of Chinese State capitalism under Xi lies in the way political control is exercised over SOEs. Although the Party-State continues to rely on SOEs to promote growth, generate wealth within the State sector, and advance national strategic objectives,[8] political control in the latest round of SOE reforms is no longer primarily characterised by external administrative intervention. Instead, it has been increasingly internalised within the delegated structure of State shareholder functions and the corporate governance of SOEs themselves.

China's contemporary SOE governance framework comprises two interrelated dimensions: an external governance structure through which State shareholder powers are exercised, and an internal corporate governance structure through which enterprise decision-making is organised. These dimensions operate together to sustain political oversight and strategic control over SOEs. In the latest round of SOE reforms, both have been significantly reconfigured in ways that make political control more institutionalised, integrated, and durable.

Externally, the reform has reduced reliance on direct SASAC-centred supervision and shifted towards a more differentiated system of delegated State shareholder governance. The centralised SOE and State-owned assets supervision framework established in 2003 during the third round of reform was built on a dual-layer delegation of State ownership functions: the State delegated shareholder rights to governments at various levels, which in turn delegated them to subordinate SASACs. In practice, however, this framework encountered persistent difficulties. Most notably, SASACs were overburdened by their dual roles as State shareholders and supervisory authorities, and the overlap between these functions weakened the effectiveness of both. The problem was not merely administrative inefficiency. It exposed the limits of a supervision model in which political control depended too heavily on centralised bureaucratic oversight while the State's ownership role remained comparatively passive.

It was against this background that the Xi Jinping administration introduced the System of Authorised Operation of State-owned Capital. This system adds an additional layer to the delegation of State shareholder functions by authorising the core companies of business groups to exercise shareholder powers over lower-tier group members, while encouraging further internal delegation down the group hierarchy. The significance of this reform lies not simply in administrative decentralisation. It reorganises political control through an ownership-mediated chain of authority. Political oversight is thereby increasingly exercised through delegated shareholder functions within group structures, rather than through direct and centralised

[8] Pearson et al. (2021), p. 207.

bureaucratic supervision alone. The result is not a retreat of political control, but its reconstitution in a more mediated, more internal, and potentially more durable form.

Internally, the Xi-era response has not been to remove politics from the enterprise, but to embed it more explicitly within the enterprise's formal governance architecture. The latest round of SOE governance reforms has advanced what is officially termed the Modern SOE Governance System with Chinese Characteristics. This system comprises two closely related developments. The first is the functional differentiation of the external governance structure, particularly through the delegation of State shareholder functions to core group companies and the rise of State-owned capital investment and operation companies as specialised vehicles for managing State-owned capital. The second is the codification and institutionalisation of CCP leadership within SOE corporate governance, most clearly through the structurally subordinate and procedurally dependent position of boards of directors *vis-à-vis* Party Committees. In practical terms, this has been pursued by incorporating Party leadership into the Articles of Association, assigning the Party Committee a superior role in major decision-making, and requiring personnel cross-office holding between the Party Committee and conventional governance organs.

These developments demonstrate that contemporary Chinese State capitalism operates not through episodic administrative interruption of enterprise autonomy, but through the institutional embedding of political authority into both shareholder governance and internal corporate decision-making.

This transformation also explains a further feature of Xi-era SOE governance: the attempt to combine greater corporate autonomy with intensified political control. At first sight, the System of Authorised Operation of State-owned Capital and the Modern SOE Governance System may appear to pull in opposite directions, the former promoting managerial and group-level autonomy, and the latter intensifying CCP control within the firm. Yet the two reforms are not contradictory. Their compatibility depends precisely on the internalisation of political control within SOE governance. Once Party leadership is structurally embedded in the corporate decision-making process, greater operational autonomy does not necessarily create space for political divergence. On the contrary, enterprise autonomy can expand while remaining institutionally aligned with Party directives.

This point carries a broader theoretical implication. A defining feature of Xi Jinping's approach to SOE governance is not the replacement of commercial logic by political command, but the construction of a framework in which commercial operation and political control are expected to coexist in an integrated manner. This marks an important departure from the conventional dichotomy under which Chinese SOEs are often understood either as market-oriented firms or as mere instruments of State policy. Under the current reform model, SOEs are expected to remain commercially active and globally competitive, while their autonomy is exercised within a governance structure that keeps their strategic direction politically aligned.

The viability of this model is reinforced by an important policy reality. For most SOEs, excluding those with explicitly non-commercial mandates such as certain SCOCs, the strategic objectives promoted under Xi broadly coincide with commercial imperatives of growth, expansion, and industrial upgrading. The State Council's repeated commitment to making SOEs 'stronger, better, and larger' and transforming them into 'world-class enterprises' illustrates that political expectations are increasingly framed through the language of competitiveness and market power.[9] Likewise, initiatives such as *Made in China 2025* assign SOEs a leading role in moving up and dominating global value chains in advanced manufacturing sectors.[10] These objectives differ from older policy burdens traditionally associated with SOEs, such as broad social welfare provision or generalised maintenance of social stability, which now apply more selectively. In practice, this convergence between State strategy and commercial expansion has facilitated the emergence of Chinese SOEs as national and global industrial champions. Accordingly, the strengthening of CCP leadership should not be understood as negating the commercial character of SOEs. It is better understood as reorganising that commercial character within a politically embedded governance framework.

Taken together, this study demonstrates that contemporary Chinese State capitalism rests on a dual transformation. On the one hand, State-owned capital is strengthened through concentration, selective marketisation, and ownership restructuring. On the other hand, political control is embedded more deeply within the governance and ownership structures through which that capital is organised. This dual transformation helps explain why Xi-era Chinese SOEs remain commercially expansive, increasingly sophisticated, and deeply political at the same time. It also provides a more precise conceptual foundation for understanding the external implications of China's SOE reforms, including the political and legal significance of SOEs' growing role in outbound investment.

9.2 The Outward Projection of Chinese State Capitalism

The preceding section shows that Xi-era reform strengthens Chinese State capitalism through the strategic allocation, concentration, and reorganisation of State-owned capital, while embedding political control more deeply within corporate governance and delegated shareholder structures. These changes do not remain confined to the Chinese political economy. They also shape how Chinese SOEs invest abroad, the purposes those investments are expected to serve, and the organisational forms through which they are carried out. SOE outbound FDI should therefore not be understood as a separable sphere of market activity undertaken by firms that happen to be State-owned. It is better understood as a transnational extension of the domestic organisation of State-owned capital.

---

[9] 《关于推动中央企业结构调整与重组的指导意见》 [Guiding Opinions on Promoting Structural Adjustment and Reorganization of Central Enterprises]. (People's Republic of China) The General Office of the State Council. 26 July 2016.

[10] 《中国制造2025》 [Made in China 2025]. (People's Republic of China) The State Council. 19 May 2015.

9.2.1 *Politically Structured Outbound Investment*

Chinese SOE outbound FDI is not merely politically consequential. It is politically structured from the outset. The significance of the latest round of SOE reforms lies not only in the fact that Chinese SOEs remain subject to State influence when investing abroad, but in the way outbound FDI is now organised through a denser framework of governance arrangements, approval systems, financial mechanisms, and post-investment supervision. Outbound FDI is therefore not simply exposed to political review after a commercial decision has been made. The investment decision itself is formed within an institutional environment designed to secure alignment with Party-State priorities.

As this study demonstrates, one source of this political structuring lies in the internal governance of SOEs. Once the Party Committee occupies a central position in SOE major decision-making, and once senior executives remain institutionally bound within Party-State governance arrangements, outbound FDI decisions cannot be treated as autonomous managerial acts in any straightforward sense. Decisions concerning outbound FDI are taken within a structure in which political authority is already embedded. The outward movement of capital is therefore shaped from within the enterprise rather than merely constrained from outside by subsequent State review.

A further source of discipline lies in the differentiated policy roles assigned to particular categories of SOEs. SOEs designated as policy-bearing or strategically significant entities are not expected to behave as ordinary commercial investors detached from national priorities. Their policy responsibilities are carried into the investment process itself. Where an SOE is tasked with serving broader State objectives, its FDI choices become part of a larger political-economic mission rather than an isolated commercial undertaking. The implication is significant. The domestic classification and functional differentiation of SOEs do not remain internal administrative arrangements. They become mechanisms through which Chinese State capitalism shapes investment behaviour beyond the national economy.

This politically structured character of SOE outbound FDI is reinforced by the approval architecture governing outbound investment. As this study systematically reveals, Chinese SOEs must proceed not only through the general approval and recordation systems applicable to Chinese firms, but also through additional SOE-specific approval channels tied to State-owned capital governance. These arrangements create a differentiated framework in which outbound FDI by SOEs remains more tightly linked to State supervision than investment by POEs. What matters here is not simply that approval exists, but that the architecture of approval reflects and reproduces the distinct governance status of SOEs within Chinese State capitalism. State-owned capital does not move abroad on the same institutional terms as private capital.

The same logic extends to the financial conditions under which outbound FDI is pursued. Government-backed project funds and policy loans are not neutral market instruments. They function as selective channels through which the Party-State supports overseas investment that conforms to preferred strategic directions. Financial support therefore does not merely facilitate investment that would otherwise occur. It also shapes the kinds of investment likely to be undertaken. The terms on which capital is made available become part of the governance of outward expansion.

Nor does political structuring end once capital has crossed the border. China's latest round of SOE reforms has strengthened Party-State oversight over overseas subsidiaries and operations through a multi-layered framework of supervision extending to offshore assets, subsidiary finance, disciplinary oversight, and in-process control. Crucially, this supervision does not rely solely on direct bureaucratic command from the centre. It also depends on the core companies of BGs to maintain oversight over lower-tier entities abroad. The delegated structure of domestic State-owned capital governance is thus reproduced in transnational form. What appears abroad is not a break from domestic institutional logic, but its continuation.

The broader implication is that Chinese SOE outbound FDI is politically structured not only because it is important to the State, but because it is organised through the same governance architecture that defines Chinese State capitalism at home. The outward movement of SOE capital is therefore better understood as a transnational deployment of politically governed capital than as ordinary commercial expansion subject to incidental State oversight.

9.2.2 Strategic Direction Through National Security and Industrial Policy

The outward reach of Chinese State capitalism is also visible in the substantive purposes that SOE outbound FDI is increasingly expected to serve. The significance of overseas investment lies not only in how it is governed, but also in what it is directed to achieve. Under the Xi Jinping administration, outbound FDI by Chinese SOEs has become more closely aligned with broad national security priorities and long-term industrial strategy. This development is theoretically important because it shows that Chinese State capitalism projects itself abroad not merely by extending the ownership of Chinese SOEs into foreign markets, but by directing State-owned capital outward in pursuit of strategic national objectives.

At the centre of this shift is the enlarged conception of national security that has emerged under Xi. National security is no longer confined to conventional questions of territorial integrity or military protection. It now encompasses a far wider range of economic, technological, and resource-related interests regarded as indispensable to national prosperity and resilience. Once this broader conception is incorporated into foreign investment policy, outbound FDI becomes more than an instrument of international commercial engagement. It becomes one of the channels through which the Party-State seeks to secure strategic resources, acquire technological capabilities, and strengthen control over critical supply chains.

This logic is reinforced by the integration of outbound investment policy with industrial strategy. Initiatives such as *Made in China 2025* and the *Modern Industrial Chain Length Action Plan* show that overseas investment is not treated as a generic means of external expansion. It is increasingly directed towards sectors and assets regarded as essential to China's future position in global production and technological competition. In this respect, SOE outbound FDI becomes one of the external instruments through which domestic industrial upgrading is pursued. Capital is deployed abroad not only to generate returns, but to secure the external inputs necessary for restructuring China's internal economic capacity.

What this reveals is that Chinese State capitalism operates across borders through strategically directed capital allocation. Domestic reform strengthens the organisational capacity of State-owned capital and embeds political control more deeply within SOEs. Foreign investment policy, in turn, supplies the substantive objectives that this reorganised capital is expected to pursue abroad. The relationship between SOE reforms and outbound FDI is therefore not incidental. Domestic reform creates the institutional means through which strategic FDI abroad becomes more feasible, more coordinated, and more politically directed.

The investment patterns examined in this study strongly support this interpretation. Chinese SOE acquisitions in developed countries have been concentrated in sectors such as energy, critical minerals, and advanced technology. These are not random sites of commercial opportunity. They correspond closely to the strategic priorities articulated in Chinese State policy. The concentration of investment in critical minerals is particularly revealing. Once specific minerals were identified as essential to national resource security, Chinese SOEs intensified their acquisition activity in precisely those areas. Such behaviour is difficult to explain adequately through ordinary firm-level profit-seeking alone. It is better understood as evidence that outbound FDI has been substantively integrated into the strategic logic of Chinese State capitalism.

This outward strategic direction of capital also clarifies why Chinese SOE investment often generates heightened concern in developed host States. The issue is not simply that the investor is State-owned, nor merely that the investment may produce competitive or security-sensitive effects. The deeper issue is that such investment may form part of a broader system in which State-owned capital is directed abroad to advance strategic national objectives. This is precisely why the study's analysis of SOE reforms matters beyond domestic Chinese political economy. It provides the conceptual basis for understanding why Chinese SOE investment has a distinct legal and political salience in host-State regulatory regimes.

9.2.3 Networked State Capital Beyond the Border

Chinese State capitalism projects itself abroad not only through politically supervised and strategically directed investment, but also through increasingly coordinated and networked forms of State-owned capital deployment. The latest round of SOE reforms has intensified the interconnections among Chinese SOEs through group restructuring, inter-SOE consolidation, equity participation, and contractual collaboration. These changes have implications that extend well beyond the domestic economy. They shape the organisational form through which Chinese State-owned capital moves abroad. Outbound FDI can no longer be analysed adequately as a series of discrete firm-level transactions. It increasingly needs to be understood as part of a wider network of coordinated State-owned capital relations.

This networked character is visible in the strategic alliance structures adopted by Chinese SOEs when investing in developed countries. As domestic reform has deepened the organisational ties among SOEs, Chinese SOEs have become better positioned to expand abroad through collaborative rather than purely separate corporate action. That collaboration may take different forms. It may involve distinct SOEs acquiring foreign assets separately and subsequently being consolidated through domestic restructuring. It may also involve multiple SOEs clustering and coordinating on overseas projects while retaining formal separateness. In either case, the strategic significance of the investment cannot be captured fully by examining the conduct of a single firm in isolation.

The importance of this development lies in what it reveals about the organisational character of Chinese State capitalism. State-owned capital is not projected internationally only through individual enterprises acting as autonomous units. It is also projected through coordinated relationships among SOEs that have been strengthened by domestic reform. The cross-border movement of capital is therefore shaped not only by the status of the investing firm, but by the wider network of State-owned capital relations in which that firm is embedded. This extends the argument developed in the preceding sections of this chapter. If State-owned capital is being reorganised domestically through concentration and ownership restructuring, and if political control is being embedded more deeply within governance and delegated shareholder functions, then the outward projection of that system should likewise be expected to occur through coordinated and relational forms rather than atomised transactions alone.

The overseas acquisition–domestic consolidation pattern illustrates this clearly. Separate acquisitions abroad may appear, at the point of transaction, to involve distinct actors and discrete commercial decisions. However, their strategic significance often becomes more visible only once those assets are subsequently integrated through domestic restructuring in China. The investment thus forms part of a broader State-owned capital strategy that exceeds the boundaries of any single transaction as it initially appears to host-State regulators. A similar point applies to overseas strategic collaboration, where multiple Chinese SOEs cooperate on foreign projects. Such cooperation does not merely reflect ordinary business convenience. It reflects the outward deployment of domestically organised State-owned capital networks in pursuit of broader strategic purposes.

The theoretical importance of this networked outward deployment is considerable. It shows that the transnational extension of Chinese State capitalism cannot be reduced to the ownership profile of individual investing firms. Nor can it be understood solely through the binary question whether a particular SOE acts commercially or politically. What matters is also the relational organisation of State-owned capital across enterprises, sectors, and projects. This helps explain why formal minority shareholding, apparent corporate separateness, or transaction-level fragmentation may not necessarily diminish the strategic significance of Chinese SOE investment abroad. State-owned capital may still operate as a coordinated force even where its organisational unity is not immediately visible at the level of the single investor.

What emerges from these developments is a form of Chinese State capitalism with a genuinely outward-facing organisational logic. SOE outbound FDI is politically structured through governance, approval, finance, and post-investment supervision. It is substantively directed towards the advancement of national security and industrial policy. It is increasingly organised through networked forms of State-owned capital coordination strengthened by domestic reform. Outbound investment is therefore not a market sphere analytically separate from the domestic transformation of the State sector. It is one of the principal means through which that transformation acquires a transnational expression.

This conclusion is central to the study's theoretical contribution. It shows that Xi-era Chinese State capitalism is not confined to a domestic system of ownership, governance, and political control. It is also a form of State-owned capital organisation capable of projecting those arrangements across borders through SOE outbound FDI. The domestic strengthening of State-owned capital, the deeper embedding of political control, and the outward deployment of strategically directed and networked FDI together provide a fuller account of the institutional logic of contemporary Chinese State capitalism. They also provide the conceptual bridge to the legal analysis that follows. Once SOE outbound FDI is understood as a transnational projection of domestic State capitalism, the challenges it presents for developed host States and for international investment law can be analysed on a more accurate foundation.

9.3 Legal Responses to the Outward Projection of Chinese State Capitalism

This study has shown that modern Chinese SOEs are no longer adequately captured by conventional assumptions of enterprise autonomy, commercial separateness, or ownership transparency. Any legal response built on those assumptions will therefore be incomplete. What is required is not a general tightening of controls against all Chinese SOE outbound FDI, but a more precise legal response to the institutional structure of contemporary Chinese State capitalism. This has implications both for domestic foreign investment screening and for the design of IIAs. The Australian case is especially revealing in this respect, but the underlying challenge is not uniquely Australian. It concerns a broader mismatch between existing legal frameworks and the transformed organisation of Chinese State-owned capital identified in this study.

9.3.1 Recalibrating Domestic Screening for Politically Embedded and Organised State-owned Capital

Domestic foreign investment screening regimes in many jurisdictions are designed to identify risks associated with foreign State ownership, strategic sector exposure, or national security sensitivity. Those concerns remain important, but this study shows that they are no longer sufficient when applied to the contemporary structure of Chinese State capitalism. The problem is not that host States lack screening powers. It is that many inbound FDI screening frameworks still rely too heavily on formal ownership, direct control, or visible State affiliation, even though the most significant features of modern Chinese SOEs increasingly lie in governance-based political control, delegated shareholder structures, and coordinated State-owned capital networks. FDI screening regimes may therefore be institutionally well equipped in form while remaining only partially responsive in substance. Australia illustrates this problem with particular clarity.

Australia's foreign investment framework provides a particularly useful example because it has developed a relatively sophisticated set of screening tools and already recognises the special significance of foreign government investors. Yet, as this study shows, even this comparatively developed regime does not always map neatly onto the organisational realities of modern Chinese SOEs. The difficulty does not lie in the absence of legal authority to review or intervene. It lies in the fact that the framework was not designed to address a form of State-owned capital that is commercially active, politically embedded, and organised through layered patterns of ownership and coordination. In this respect, the Australian case reveals not the weakness of screening as such, but the limits of screening criteria built around an earlier and simpler understanding of State-linked investment.

This limitation appears most clearly in the treatment of foreign government investors. Australia's framework correctly recognises that foreign government investors cannot be treated as fully independent from their State owners and therefore subjects them to heightened scrutiny. That starting point remains sound. It is nevertheless insufficient. This study has shown that the political significance of Chinese SOE investment cannot be captured by formal State ownership or direct control alone. Under Xi-era reform, political control is increasingly embedded in governance structures, delegated shareholder functions, policy-bearing classifications, and coordinated State-owned capital networks. A screening framework that focuses too heavily on formal ownership or visible State affiliation therefore risks missing the deeper institutional channels through which political influence is now exercised.

The Australian case makes this difficulty especially clear in relation to factors that may appear to mitigate concern. Minority non-State shareholding, the presence of external investors, or the apparent separateness of the investing entity may reduce concern under a conventional ownership-based analysis. Yet the findings of this study show that such features do not necessarily reduce political alignment or strategic significance. Flow-in mixed ownership reform does not necessarily dilute State influence. It often enables State-owned capital to absorb external resources while preserving political control. Likewise, the apparent separateness of an investing firm may say little about whether it forms part of a wider pattern of coordinated State-owned capital deployment. In this respect, the formal indicia that have traditionally shaped screening analysis become less reliable when applied to modern Chinese SOEs.

This difficulty becomes even more significant once Chinese SOE investment is considered in its current sectoral and organisational context. In Australia, concern about Chinese SOE investment is no longer confined to a narrow set of conventional resource transactions. It has expanded across sectors such as strategic minerals, infrastructure, and other politically sensitive assets. At the same time, the investors themselves have been reshaped through inter-SOE consolidation, SCIC designation, policy classification, and the deepening of Party-State control. The legal significance of a proposed investment therefore cannot be assessed adequately by looking only at the formal ownership profile of the immediate investor. Review must also consider the governance structure of the investor, the role of Party leadership within enterprise decision-making, the enterprise's policy classification, its place within a wider SOE group, and its relationship to State-owned capital investment and operation platforms. These are not secondary details. In the contemporary Chinese context, they are among the principal institutional mechanisms through which State capitalism operates.

More specifically, recalibration requires at least four institutional adjustments. First, screening criteria should move beyond formal State ownership and direct control to require express consideration of governance-based political embeddedness, including Party leadership arrangements, delegated State shareholder structures, policy-bearing classifications, and the investor's strategic functions within the wider State sector. Second, review should extend beyond the immediate investing entity to the investor's wider group structure, affiliations with other SOEs, links to State-owned capital investment or operation platforms, and any broader pattern of coordinated State-owned capital deployment relevant to the transaction. Third, entry review should be complemented by stronger post-entry mechanisms, including notification duties and retrospective review where the investor's ownership, governance arrangements, policy status, or organisational position changes materially after approval. Fourth, host States should strengthen disclosure obligations so that review is not confined to formal shareholding data, but also captures governance arrangements, the role of Party leadership, group structure, affiliated investments, and material forms of State-backed financing or coordination.

The need for stronger post-entry control is particularly clear in the Chinese context. If Chinese State capitalism projects itself through delegated group structures and continuing oversight over overseas subsidiaries, the risk profile of an investment cannot always be assessed fully at the point of entry alone. Retrospective review mechanisms therefore take on particular significance. Their importance lies not only in enabling host States to respond to new facts, but in enabling them to respond to subsequent changes in the investor's political and organisational position. This is especially important where inter-SOE consolidation, SCIC designation, policy reclassification, or strengthened Party-State control occurs after an investment has already been approved. A screening framework responsive to contemporary Chinese State capitalism must therefore attend not only to who the investor is at the point of entry, but also to how that investor may later be reorganised within the wider State sector.

The Australian experience thus reveals a broader problem for host-State screening regimes. Many such regimes remain too closely tied to formal ownership categories, visible State control, or transaction-specific analysis. Yet the challenge presented by contemporary Chinese SOE investment increasingly lies in governance-based political embeddedness, delegated ownership structures, and coordinated State-owned capital networks. Australia brings this mismatch into particularly sharp relief, but the underlying issue is not uniquely Australian. It is more general. Host-State screening must be recalibrated if it is to respond effectively to the contemporary institutional logic of Chinese State capitalism. Without such recalibration, the law risks responding to an earlier model of State ownership rather than to the transformed organisation of State-owned capital identified in this study.

9.3.2 Preserving Treaty Space in IIAs to Regulate the Outward Projection of Chinese State Capitalism

The implications of this study extend equally to IIAs. If contemporary Chinese SOE investment can no longer be adequately understood as ordinary commercial investment undertaken by firms that happen to be State-owned, the assumptions built into many existing IIAs become less secure. The issue is not simply whether Chinese SOEs may invoke treaty protection. It is whether treaty protections framed around assumptions of ordinary investor conduct can be coherently applied to investments that may function as transnational extensions of domestic State-owned capital governance. Once Chinese SOE outbound FDI is understood as politically structured, strategically directed, and organised through coordinated State-owned capital networks, the legal balance between investor protection and host-State regulatory autonomy becomes more difficult to sustain on conventional terms.

In the Australian context, this tension arises within an IIA framework that includes CABIT, ChAFTA, AHKIA, and RCEP. These agreements regulate Australia–China cross-border investment from different doctrinal starting points and preserve overlapping forms of investor protection. Yet none of them was negotiated against the institutional background identified in this study: a model of Chinese State capitalism in which commercial activity, embedded political control, and strategically directed outbound FDI have become increasingly intertwined. The resulting problem is not merely one of doctrinal complexity. It is a deeper mismatch between inherited treaty assumptions and the transformed organisational logic of the investors that those treaties may now be asked to govern.

This difficulty becomes especially acute where host-State screening or post-entry intervention is used to address risks associated with Chinese SOE FDI. Once such measures are taken, they may themselves give rise to treaty-based claims. In the Australian setting, retrospective security review or subsequent intervention affecting an existing investment may expose the State to claims framed under the expropriation protections in CABIT and AHKIA. Measures affecting admission, conditions of operation, or differential treatment of investors may also generate arguments under the national treatment discipline in ChAFTA, depending on the structure of the measure and the way the claim is framed. The point is not that such claims would necessarily succeed. It is that the existing treaty framework may constrain precisely those forms of host-State regulation that become more important once Chinese SOE investment is understood as an outward projection of Chinese State capitalism.

It is not merely a doctrinal difficulty, but a conceptual mismatch between the investor presupposed by IIAs and the institutional form of the modern Chinese SOE. Much of contemporary IIAs still assumes a legally distinct and commercially oriented enterprise whose relationship to the home State can be identified primarily through ownership or formal control. This study shows that modern Chinese SOEs do not fit comfortably within that model. They remain commercially active, but their commercial activity is increasingly organised within governance structures that embed political authority, delegated shareholder functions, and wider networks of State-owned capital coordination. The legal significance of Chinese SOE investment therefore cannot be reduced to the conventional question whether the investor is public or private. It concerns the growing instability of that distinction itself.

This structural difficulty is compounded by the transaction-centred design of IIA law. Treaty analysis typically proceeds by focusing on a particular claimant, a particular investment, and a particular State measure. Yet the contemporary outward projection of Chinese State capitalism may derive much of its political and strategic significance from features that exceed the boundaries of any single transaction, including subsequent group restructuring, coordinated investment patterns, and evolving forms of State-owned capital organisation. In this respect, the friction between host-State regulation and treaty protection is not merely doctrinal. It reflects a deeper mismatch between the legal form through which IIAs organise investment disputes and the institutional form through which modern Chinese State-owned capital operates across borders.

For that reason, future IIA design should preserve clearer and more reliable policy space for the regulation of Chinese SOE and SOE-affiliated investment. This does not require abandoning investment protection as such. It requires a more carefully calibrated form of protection, one that remains attentive to the institutional transformation of the investor. More specifically, this study points to four adjustments in future IIA design. First, IIAs should preserve explicit treaty space for foreign investment screening, national security review, and post-entry intervention where the political or strategic significance of an investment materially changes after entry. Second, treaty definitions of SOEs should not rely too heavily on formal ownership or on whether the enterprise is principally engaged in commercial activities. Third, treaty language should be more attentive to affiliated and coordinated forms of investment, wider group structures, and delegated State-owned capital networks, rather than focusing exclusively on the immediate claimant. Fourth, IIAs should contain stronger exceptions, carve-outs, and non-conforming measures capable of protecting non-discriminatory regulation directed at politically embedded and strategically organised State-owned capital.

This study also shows the limits of relying on standard SOE disciplines of the kind found in modern trade and investment agreements. This is particularly clear in relation to the CPTPP SOE chapter, which has become a leading reference point for advanced SOE disciplines and is especially relevant given China's application to join the CPTPP and Australia's familiarity with that model. CPTPP-style rules on commercial considerations, non-commercial assistance, and transparency may be valuable in some settings, but they do not fully capture the institutional logic identified in this study. The challenge presented by Chinese SOEs under Xi does not lie only in overt subsidy or visible departure from commercial rationality. It also lies in the fact that political control is embedded within governance structures and delegated shareholder arrangements, while outbound FDI is coordinated through wider State-owned capital networks. Rules built around a narrower conception of SOE behaviour may therefore fail to address the features of contemporary Chinese State capitalism that are most significant in legal terms.

This point is particularly important in relation to how IIAs define the enterprise they seek to regulate. Future IIA design should not depend too heavily on whether the enterprise is principally engaged in commercial activities, because this study has shown that commercial operation and political alignment are no longer analytically opposed. Nor should treaty design assume that formal legal separateness, minority non-State shareholding, or the absence of direct majority ownership necessarily weakens State influence. If the analysis developed in this study is sound, IIA rules must become more sensitive to governance-based political control, delegated shareholder structures, and coordinated State-owned capital networks. Without that shift, treaty law will remain more responsive to an earlier model of State ownership than to the current organisation of Chinese SOEs.

The broader implication is therefore clear. International investment law can no longer rely comfortably on older distinctions between State and market, public and private, or commercial and political investor conduct. Those distinctions become unstable when confronted with a form of State capitalism in which political authority is embedded within commercially active firms and projected outward through strategically organised State-owned capital. The task for host States is not to reject IIA-based investment protection as such, but to ensure that treaty design remains responsive to the institutional transformation of the investors it is expected to govern.

The Australian case makes this problem especially visible. The legal challenge posed by Chinese SOE investment is not exhausted by questions of nationality, formal ownership, or competitive neutrality. It arises from the encounter between host-State legal regimes and a transformed model of Chinese State capitalism whose domestic organisation now has a distinct outward projection. The legal response developed in this study follows directly from that diagnosis. IIAs must preserve sufficient space to regulate politically embedded and strategically organised State-owned capital without destabilising the legal framework of investment protection.

For Australia, the future work programme of ChAFTA provides the most tangible treaty setting in which these adjustments could be pursued. If a more comprehensive investment chapter is negotiated in the future, it would offer a concrete opportunity to recalibrate the treaty balance between investor protection and regulatory autonomy in light of the institutional changes analysed in this study. More specifically, it would provide a setting in which Australia could seek clearer limits on ISDS in relation to screening and national security review, broader protection for non-discriminatory regulatory measures, and treaty language more responsive to SOE-affiliated and politically embedded investment. That opportunity matters not only bilaterally. It also illustrates a broader challenge for host States that maintain IIAs with China while seeking to preserve policy space in relation to strategically significant Chinese investment. The issue is structural: IIAs must remain capable of governing cross-border investment without assuming that all investors operate according to the same institutional logic.

9.4 Conclusion

China's latest round of SOE reforms has done far more than preserve the State sector as a central pillar of the Chinese economy. It has reconstituted the institutional form through which Chinese SOEs are organised, governed, and projected. State-owned capital has been concentrated, restructured, and extended. Political control has been embedded more deeply within the governance and ownership architecture of the State sector. These domestic transformations have not remained within China's borders. They have also travelled outward through politically structured, strategically directed, and increasingly coordinated outbound investment. The significance of the Xi-era reforms therefore lies not simply in a stronger State presence in the economy, but in the consolidation of a more systematic and outward-facing form of Chinese State capitalism.

This transformation changes not only how Chinese SOEs should be understood, but also how the legal and regulatory problems they present abroad should be framed. The central issue is no longer captured adequately by formal State ownership, competitive neutrality, or conventional assumptions of investor autonomy. It lies in the encounter between host-State legal regimes and a form of State capitalism whose political embeddedness, strategic direction, and coordinated organisation exceed the categories on which many existing screening regimes and IIAs still rely. If this study establishes one central point, it is that the legal significance of modern Chinese SOEs cannot be understood without first understanding the institutional transformation that has reshaped them. What is at stake, ultimately, is not only how to understand Chinese SOEs, but how to rethink the relationship between State power, capital organisation, and cross-border investment in an era in which the boundaries between the political and the commercial are being redrawn.

References

Du M (2023) Unpacking the Black Box of China's State capitalism. German Law J 24(1):125–150

Liebman BL, Milhaupt CJ (2016) Regulating the visible hand?: The institutional implications of Chinese State capitalism. Oxford University Press

Lin LY-H, Milhaupt CJ (2023) China's corporate social credit system: the dawn of surveillance state capitalism? China Q 256:835–853

Milhaupt CJ, Zheng W (2015) Beyond ownership: State capitalism and the Chinese firm. Georgetown Law J 103(3):665–722

Ozery TG (2022) The politicization of corporate governance: a viable alternative? Am J Comp Law 70(1):54

Pearson M, Rithmire M, Tsai KS (2021) Party-State capitalism in China. Curr Hist 120(827): 207–213

Xinhua News Agency (2014) '习近平首次系统阐述"新常态"' [Xi Jinping Systematically Elaborates the "New Normal" for the First Time], People, http://politics.people.com.cn/n/2014/1109/c1001-26000293.html. Accessed 10 Apr 2026

Additional Sources

《中华人民共和国国有资产法(草案)》 [State-owned Assets Management Law (Draft)] (People's Republic of China), 27 December 2025, arts 13, 17, 24.

《中国制造2025》 [Made in China 2025] (People's Republic of China) The State Council, 19 May 2015.

《关于推动中央企业结构调整与重组的指导意见》 [Guiding Opinions on Promoting Structural Adjustment and Reorganization of Central Enterprises] (People's Republic of China) The General Office of the State Council, 26 July 2016.

MIX
Papier aus verantwortungsvollen Quellen
Paper from responsible sources
FSC® C105338

If you have any concerns about our products,
you can contact us on
ProductSafety@springernature.com

In case Publisher is established outside the EU,
the EU authorized representative is:
Springer Nature Customer Service Center GmbH
Europaplatz 3, 69115 Heidelberg, Germany

Printed by Libri Plureos GmbH
in Hamburg, Germany